SOMETH

ABOUT T

AUThOR

ISSN 0276-816X

something ABOUT THE AUTHOR®

**Facts and Pictures about Authors
and Illustrators of Books for Young People**

VOLUME 115

GALE GROUP

Detroit
New York
San Francisco
London
Boston
Woodbridge, CT

Library of Congress Catalog Card Number 72-27107

ISBN 0-7876-4033-6
ISSN 0276-816X

Printed in the United States of America

10 9 8 7 6 5 4 3 2 1

Contents

Authors in Forthcoming Volumes

Below are some of the authors and illustrators that will be featured in upcoming volumes of *SATA*. These include new entries on the swiftly rising stars of the field, as well as completely revised and updated entries (indicated with *) on some of the most notable and best-loved creators of books for children.

*Douglas Adams: English author Adams is the creator of the popular "The Hitchhiker's Guide to the Galaxy" series. The concept, which began as an idea for a radio program, has spawned five novels, a stage play, a television series, and a computer game.

Ian Andrew: Originally trained as an illustrator, Andrew turned to the genre of animation while in college. In *Back to the Blue,* the English animator used a pencil-and-pastel technique to bring the pages to life.

*Matt Groening: Widely known for his wildly popular animated television series, *The Simpsons,* Groening is also the author of the "Life in Hell" comic strip. His recent efforts include two new editions to the Simpson library of books, *Bart Simpson's Treehouse of Horror: Heebie-Jeebie Hullabaloo* and *Homer's Guide to Being a Man.*

*William Joyce: Author, illustrator, and screenwriter Joyce is lauded for his wacky and colorful characters. *Rolie Polie Olie,* a picture book adapted from his Emmy Award-winning television show, is written in verse and tells the tale of a round robot living in a totally round world.

Joe R. Lansdale: Though Lansdale's preferred genre is fantasy, his works frequently contain elements of mystery, horror, western, and science fiction. His stories, which number over one hundred, often reveal a dark view of human nature and of everyday life.

Reeve Lindbergh: The author of over a dozen children's books, Lindbergh is the daughter of famed aviator Charles Lindbergh and writer Anne Morrow Lindbergh. Published in 1997, *North Country Spring* depicts the coming of spring in New England in rhyming couplets.

*Anne McCaffrey: Hailed as a trendsetter in the genre of science fiction, McCaffrey is the first female to win the Nebula and Hugo Awards and, more recently, the first sci-fi writer to receive the Margaret A. Edwards Award for lifetime achievement in young adult literature. The author has garnered much favorable critical attention for her works, most notably the "Dragonriders of Pern" series.

William R. Miller: Miller has written a number of books about the lives of African Americans, including Zora Neale Hurston, Frederick Douglass, and Richard Wright. Inspired by the experiences of civil rights hero Rosa Parks, *The Bus Ride* relates the story of a young girl who effects change through her brave actions.

Leone Peguero: Australian writer Peguero is the author of several picture books for younger readers that are especially suitable for reading aloud due to their combination of humor and simple language infused with piquant vocabulary.

Maria Rendon: Born in Mexico, illustrator Rendon utilizes a variety of materials, such as wood, metals, and glass, to communicate the meaning of the work to readers.

*Cynthia Voigt: Voigt has won a number of prestigious awards, including the Newbery Medal and the the Edgar Allan Poe Award. She has been recognized for her vivid descriptions, universal themes, and skillful handling of controversial subjects, such as racism and verbal abuse.

YongSheng Xuan: Versatile and talented, Xuan is a Chinese artist who is applauded for his work done in a wide variety of media, including watercolors, woodworking, and sculpture. In 1999, he published his first self-illustrated picture book, *The Dragon Lover and Other Chinese Proverbs.*

Introduction

Something about the Author (*SATA*) is an ongoing reference series that examines the lives and works of authors and illustrators of books for children. *SATA* includes not only well-known writers and artists but also less prominent individuals whose works are just coming to be recognized. This series is often the only readily available information source on emerging authors and illustrators. You'll find *SATA* informative and entertaining, whether you are a student, a librarian, an English teacher, a parent, or simply an adult who enjoys children's literature.

What's Inside SATA

SATA provides detailed information about authors and illustrators who span the full time range of children's literature, from early figures like John Newbery and L. Frank Baum to contemporary figures like Judy Blume and Richard Peck. Authors in the series represent primarily English-speaking countries, particularly the United States, Canada, and the United Kingdom. Also included, however, are authors from around the world whose works are available in English translation. The writings represented in *SATA* include those created intentionally for children and young adults as well as those written for a general audience and known to interest younger readers. These writings cover the entire spectrum of children's literature, including picture books, humor, folk and fairy tales, animal stories, mystery and adventure, science fiction and fantasy, historical fiction, poetry and nonsense verse, drama, biography, and nonfiction.

Obituaries are also included in *SATA* and are intended not only as death notices but also as concise overviews of people's lives and work. Additionally, each edition features newly revised and updated entries for a selection of *SATA* listees who remain of interest to today's readers and who have been active enough to require extensive revisions of their earlier biographies.

New Autobiography Feature

Beginning with Volume 103, *SATA* features three or more specially commissioned autobiographical essays in each volume. These unique essays, averaging about ten thousand words in length and illustrated with an abundance of personal photos, present an entertaining and informative first-person perspective on the lives and careers of prominent authors and illustrators profiled in *SATA*.

Two Convenient Indexes

In response to suggestions from librarians, *SATA* indexes no longer appear in every volume but are included in alternate (odd-numbered) volumes of the series, beginning with Volume 57.

SATA continues to include two indexes that cumulate with each alternate volume: the Illustrations Index, arranged by the name of the illustrator, gives the number of the volume and page where the illustrator's work appears in the current volume as well as all preceding volumes in the series; the Author Index gives the number of the volume in which a person's biographical sketch, autobiographical essay, or obituary appears in the current volume as well as all preceding volumes in the series.

These indexes also include references to authors and illustrators who appear in Gale's *Yesterday's Authors of Books for Children, Children's Literature Review,* and *Something about the Author Autobiography Series.*

Easy-to-Use Entry Format

Whether you're already familiar with the *SATA* series or just getting acquainted, you will want to be aware of the kind of information that an entry provides. In every *SATA* entry the editors attempt to give as complete a picture of the person's life and work as possible. A typical entry in *SATA* includes the following clearly labeled information sections:

• *PERSONAL:* date and place of birth and death, parents' names and occupations, name of spouse, date of marriage, names of children, educational institutions attended, degrees received, religious and political affiliations, hobbies and other interests.

• *ADDRESSES:* complete home, office, electronic mail, and agent addresses, whenever available.

• *CAREER:* name of employer, position, and dates for each career post; art exhibitions; military service; memberships and offices held in professional and civic organizations.

• *AWARDS, HONORS:* literary and professional awards received.

• *WRITINGS:* title-by-title chronological bibliography of books written and/or illustrated, listed by genre when known; lists of other notable publications, such as plays, screenplays, and periodical contributions.

• *ADAPTATIONS:* a list of films, television programs, plays, CD-ROMs, recordings, and other media presentations that have been adapted from the author's work.

• *WORK IN PROGRESS:* description of projects in progress.

• *SIDELIGHTS:* a biographical portrait of the author or illustrator's development, either directly from the biographee—and often written specifically for the *SATA* entry—or gathered from diaries, letters, interviews, or other published sources.

• *FOR MORE INFORMATION SEE:* references for further reading.

• *EXTENSIVE ILLUSTRATIONS:* photographs, movie stills, book illustrations, and other interesting visual materials supplement the text.

How a SATA Entry Is Compiled

A *SATA* entry progresses through a series of steps. If the biographee is living, the *SATA* editors try to secure information directly from him or her through a questionnaire. From the information that the biographee supplies, the editors prepare an entry, filling in any essential missing details with research and/or telephone interviews. If possible, the author or illustrator is sent a copy of the entry to check for accuracy and completeness.

If the biographee is deceased or cannot be reached by questionnaire, the *SATA* editors examine a wide variety of published sources to gather information for an entry. Biographical and bibliographic sources are consulted, as are book reviews, feature articles, published interviews, and material sometimes obtained from the biographee's family, publishers, agent, or other associates.

Entries that have not been verified by the biographees or their representatives are marked with an asterisk (*).

Contact the Editor

We encourage our readers to examine the entire *SATA* series. Please write and tell us if we can make *SATA* even more helpful to you. Give your comments and suggestions to the editor:

BY MAIL: Editor, *Something about the Author,* The Gale Group, 27500 Drake Rd., Farmington Hills, MI 48331-3535.

BY TELEPHONE: (800) 877-GALE

BY FAX: (248) 699-8054

Acknowledgments

Grateful acknowledgment is made to the following publishers, authors, and artists whose works appear in this volume.

APPEL, ALLEN. McGlynn, Katherine, photographer. From a cover of *From Father to Son: Wisdom for the Next Generation* by Allen Appel. St. Martin's Press, 1993. Reproduced by permission of St. Martin's Press, Incorporated.

ARNOLD, KATYA. Arnold, Katya, photograph. Reproduced by permission. / Arnold, Katya, illustrator. From an illustration in *The Adventures of Snowwoman* by Katya Arnold. Holiday House, 1998. Copyright (c) 1998 by Katya Arnold. All Rights Reserved. Reproduced by permission.

BARR, NEVADA. Barr, Nevada, photograph by Judy Lawne. Reproduced by permission.

BARRETT, TRACY. Barrett, Tracy, photograph by David Crenshaw. Reproduced by permission. / From a cover of *Anna of Byzantium* by Tracy Barrett. Delacorte Press, 1999. Jacket illustration (c) 1999 by David Bowers. Reproduced by permission of Dell Books, a division of Random House, Inc.

BRACKERS de HUGO, PIERRE. (Pierre de Hugo). de Hugo, Pierre, illustrator. From an illustration in *Hidden World: Under the Sea* by Claude Delafosse. Scholastic, Inc. 1999. Copyright (c) 1999 by Scholastic, Inc. Reproduced by permission of Editions Gallimard. In the U.S. by permission of Scholastic, Inc.

BURNARD, DAMON. Burnard, Damon, photograph. Reproduced by permission. / Burnard, Damon, illustrator. From a cover of *The Amazing Adventures of Soupy Boy* by Damon Burnard. Houghton Mifflin Company, 1998. Copyright (c) 1997 by Damon Burnard. Reproduced by permission.

CLARKE, ARTHUR C. Clarke, Arthur C., photograph. AP/Wide World Photos. Reproduced by permission. / Scene from the film *2001: A Space Odyssey* (space suit stepping into hallway), photograph. The Kobal Collection. Reproduced by permission. / Heffernan, Phil and David Stevenson, illustrators. From a cover of *Childhood's End* by Arthur C. Clarke. Ballantine Books, 1990. Copyright (c) 1953, 1990 by Arthur C. Clarke. Reproduced by permission of Random House, Inc. / From a cover of *3001: The Final Odyssey* by Arthur C. Clarke. Ballantine Books, 1997. Reproduced by permission of Random House, Inc.

DAKOS, KALLI. Karas, G. Brian, illustrator. From a cover of *Don't Read This Book, Whatever You Do!: More Poems about School* by Kalli Dakos. Aladdin Paperbacks, 1993. Cover illustration copyright (c) 1993 by G. Brian Karas. Reproduced by permission of Aladdin Paperbacks, an imprint of Simon & Schuster Macmillan. / Adinolfi, JoAnn, illustrator. From an illustration in *Mrs. Cole on an Onion Roll, and Other School Poems* by Kalli Dakos. Aladdin Paperbacks, 1995. Text copyright (c) 1995 by Kalli Dakos. Illustrations copyright (c) 1995 by JoAnn Adinolfi. Reproduced by permission of Aladdin Paperbacks, an imprint of Simon and Schuster Children's Publishing Division.

DAVIS, YVONNE. Davis, Yvonne, photograph. Reproduced by permission.

de LINT, CHARLES. Bergen, David, illustrator. From a cover of *Moonheart: A Romance* by Charles de Lint. Orb Books, Tom Doherty Associates, Inc., 1994. Reproduced by permission of St. Martin's Press, Incorporated. / Howe, John, illustrator. From a cover of *Trader* by Charles de Lint. Tor, 1997. Copyright (c) 1997 by Charles de Lint. Reproduced by permission of St. Martin's Press, Inc.

ERLBACH, ARLENE. Erlbach, Arlene, photograph. Reproduced by permission. / Holm, Sharon Lane, illustrator. From a cover of *Happy Birthday, Everywhere!* by Arlene Erlbach. Millbrook Press, 1997. Illustration copyright (c) 1997 by Sharon Lane Holm. Reproduced by permission.

GABER, SUSAN. Gaber, Susan, illustrator. From a cover of *Good Times on Grandfather Mountain* by Jacqueline Briggs Martin. Orchard Books, 1992. Reproduced by permission of the publisher, Orchard Books, New York. / Gaber, Susan, illustrator. From an illustration in *The Princess and the Lord of Night* by Emma Bull. Harcourt Brace & Company, 1994. Illustrations copyright (c) 1994 by Susan Gaber. Reproduced by permission. / Gaber, Susan, illustrator. From an illustration in *Raisel's Riddle* by Erica Silverman. Farrar, Straus & Giroux, 1999. Illustrations copyright (c) 1999 by Susan Gaber. Reproduced by permission of Farrar, Straus and Giroux, LLC.

GONZALEZ, MAYA CHRISTINA. Gonzalez, Maya Christina, photograph. Reproduced by permission.

GORDON, AMY. Vojnar, Kamil, illustrator. From a cover of *When JFK Was My Father* by Amy Gordon. Houghton Mifflin, 1999. Jacket art (c) 1999 by Kamil Vojnar. Reproduced by permission of Houghton Mifflin Company.

GREENWOOD, PAMELA D. Greenwood, Pamela D., photograph. Reproduced by permission. / Miller, Edward, illustrator. From an illustration in *Cross a Bridge* by "Ryan Ann Hunter" (Pamela D. Greenwood and Elizabeth G. Macalaster). Holiday House, 1998. Text copyright (c) 1998 by Pamela D. Greenwood and Elizabeth G. Macalaster. Illustration copyright (c) 1998 by Edward Miller III. All rights reserved. Reproduced by permission.

HAYASHI, LESLIE ANN. Hayashi, Leslie Ann, photograph. Reproduced by permission. / Bishop, Kathleen Wong, illustrator. From a cover of *Fables from the Garden* by Leslie Ann Hayashi. A Kolowalu Book, University of Hawaii Press, 1998. (c) 1998 University of Hawaii Press. Reproduced by permission.

HINTON, S. E. Hinton, S. E., photograph by Thomas Victor. Reproduced by permission of the Estate of Thomas Victor. / Estevez, Emilio with Matt Dillon and Meg Tilly, in the film *Tex,* 1982, photograph. The Kobal Collection. Reproduced by permission. / Dillon, Matt, Mickey Rourke and William Smith, in the film *Rumble Fish,* 1983, photograph. The Kobal Collection. Reproduced by permission. / Rogers, Jacqueline, illustrator. From a cover of *The Puppy Sister* by S.E. Hinton. Bantam Doubleday Dell Books for Young Readers, 1995. Illustration copyright (c) 1995 by Jacqueline Rogers. Reproduced by permission from Bantam Doubleday Dell Books for Young Readers a division of Bantam Doubleday Dell Publishing Group, Inc. / Daniel, Alan, illustrator. From a cover of *Big David, Little David* by S.E. Hinton. Bantam Doubleday Dell Books for Young Readers, 1995. Illustration copyright (c) 1995 by Alan Daniel. Reproduced by permission by Bantam Doubleday Dell Books for Young Readers a division of Bantam Doubleday Dell Publishing Group, Inc.

JACKSON, ELLEN B. Winfield, Alison, illustrator. From a cover of *The Impossible Riddle* by Ellen Jackson. Whispering Coyote Press, 1995. Jacket illustration (c) 1995 by Whispering Coyote Press. Reproduced by permission of Charlesbridge Publishing, Inc. / Hubbard, Woodleigh Marx, illustrator. From a cover of *The Precious Gift: A Navaho Creation Myth* by Ellen Jackson. Simon & Schuster Books for Young Readers, 1996. Copyright (c) 1996 by Woodleigh Marx Hubbard. Reproduced by permission of Simon & Schuster Books for Young Readers, an imprint of Simon & Schuster Macmillan. / Ellis, Jan Davey, illustrator. From a cover of *Turn of the Century* by Ellen Jackson. Charlesbridge Publishing, 1998. Jacket illustration copyright (c) by Jan Davey Ellis. Reproduced by permission.

JONES, MARCIA THORNTON. Gurney, John Steven, illustrator. From a cover of *The Adventures of the Bailey School Kids: Giants Don't Go Snowboarding* by Debbie Dadey and Marcia Thornton Jones. Scholastic Inc., 1998. Illustration copyright (c) 1998 by Scholastic, Inc. Reprinted by permission.

KETTEMAN, HELEN. Warhola, James, illustrator. From a cover of *The Christmas Blizzard* by Helen Ketteman. Scholastic, 1995. Illustrations copyright (c) 1995 by James Warhola. All rights reserved. Used by permission of Scholastic, Inc. / Warhola, James, illustrator. From an illustration in *Bubba, the Cowboy Prince: A Fractured Texas Tale* by Helen Ketteman. Scholastic Press, 1997. Text copyright (c) by Helen Ketteman, 1997. Illustrations copyright (c) 1997, by James Warhola. Reproduced by permission from Scholastic Press, a division of Scholastic, Inc. / Goto, Scott, illustrator. From a cover of *Heat Wave* by Helen Ketteman. Walker and Company, 1998. Illustration copyright (c) 1998 by Scott Goto. Reproduced by permission.

KLEIN, JIM. Klein, Jim, photograph. Reproduced by permission.

KNUTSON, KIMBERLEY. From an illustration in *Bed Bouncers* by Kimberly Knutson. Macmillan Books for Young Readers, 1995. Copyright (c) 1995 by Kimberly Knutson. Reproduced by permission of Simon & Schuster Macmillan. / From an illustration in *Beach Babble* by Kimberley Knutson. Marshall Cavendish, 1998. Text and illustrations copyright (c) by Kimberley Knutson, 1998. Reproduced by permission.

KOSS, AMY GOLDMAN. Koss, Amy Goldman, photograph. Reproduced by permission.

LaROCHELLE, DAVID. LaRochelle, David, photograph. Reproduced by permission.

LEE, HECTOR VIVEROS. From an illustration in *I Had a Hippopotamus* by Hector Viveros Lee. Lee & Low Books Inc., 1996. Text and Illustrations copyright (c) 1996 by Hector Viveros Lee. Reproduced by permission.

LEWIN, BETSY. All personal photographs reproduced with permission from the author.

LEWIN, TED. All personal photographs reproduced with permission from the author.

LORENZ, ALBERT. Lorenz, Albert, photograph. Reproduced by permission. / From a cover of *Metropolis: Ten Cities, Ten Centuries* by Albert Lorenz with Joy Schleh. Harry N. Abrams, 1996. Reproduced by permission.

MACALASTER, ELIZABETH G. Macalaster, Elizabeth G., photograph. Reproduced by permission.

MANSON, AINSLIE KERTLAND. Reczuch, Karen, illustrator. From a cover of *Just Like New* by Ainslie Manson. Groundwood, 1995. Illustrations copyright (c) 1995 by Karen Reczuch. Reproduced by permission of Groundwood Books/ Douglas & McIntyre.

MITTON, JACQUELINE. Hair, Jonathon, illustrator. From a cover of *Aliens* by Jacqueline Mitton. Candlewick, 1998. (c) 1998 Jacqueline Mitton. Reproduced by permission of Walker Books Ltd. Published in the U.S. by Candlewick Press, Inc., Cambridge, MA.

MURPHY, STUART J. Murphy, Stuart J., photograph. Reproduced by permission.

NARAHASHI, KEIKO. From an illustration in *I Have a Friend* by Keiko Narahashi. Aladdin Paperbacks, 1998. Copyright (c) 1987 by Keiko Narahashi. Reproduced by permission of Simon & Schuster Macmillan. / From an illustration in *Is That Josie?* by Keiko Narahashi. Margaret K. McElderry Books, 1994. Copyright (c) 1994 by Keiko Narahashi. Reproduced by permission of Margaret K. McElderry Books, an imprint of Simon & Schuster Macmillan. / Narahashi, Keiko, illustrator.

something ABOUT the AUTHOR

ALDEN, Isabella (Macdonald) 1841-1930
(Pansy)

Personal

Born November 3, 1841, in Rochester, NY; died of cancer, August 5, 1930; daughter of Isaac and Myra (Spofford) Macdonald; married Gustavus R. Alden (a Presbyterian minister), May, 1866; children: Raymond Macdonald. *Education:* Attended Seneca Collegiate Institute, Ovid, NY, and the Young Ladies Institute, at Auburn, NY. *Religion:* Presbyterian.

Career

Author, mainly of children's literature and religious books. Editor of the *Presbyterian Primary Quarterly* and her own Christian magazine for children, *Pansy*.

Awards, Honors

First prize in writing contest, American Reform Tract and Book Society, for story later published as *Helen Lester*.

Writings

UNDER PSEUDONYM PANSY

Helen Lester, American Reform Tract & Book Society (Cincinnati), 1865.
Jessie Wells; or, How to Save the Lost, American Reform Tract & Book Society, 1865.

Bernie's White Chicken, Western Tract & Book Society (Cincinnati), 1867.
Tip Lewis and His Lamp, Lothrop (Boston), 1867.
Ester Ried: Asleep and Awake, Western Tract & Book Society, 1870.
Docia's Journal; or, God Is Love, J. P. Skelly (Philadelphia), 1871.
Three People, Western Tract & Book Society, 1871.
Julia Ried: Listening and Led, Western Tract & Book Society, 1872.
The King's Daughter, Lothrop, 1873.
Wise and Otherwise, Western Tract & Book Society, 1873.
Household Puzzles, Lothrop, 1874.
(With Faye Huntington) *Modern Prophets and Other Sketches,* Lothrop, 1874.
A Christmas Time, Lothrop, 1875.
Cunning Workmen, Lothrop, 1875.
(With Faye Huntington) *Dr. Dean's Way,* Lothrop, 1875.
Grandpa's Darlings, Lothrop, 1875.
Four Girls at Chautauqua, Lothrop, 1876.
Little Minnie, and Other Stories, Lothrop, 1876.
Pansy's Picture Book, Lothrop, 1876.
Pansy's Picture Library, four volumes, Lothrop, 1876.
Pictures from Bobby's Life; and Other Stories, Lothrop, 1876.
The Randolphs, Lothrop, 1876.
The Chatauqua Girls at Home, Lothrop, 1877, published as *Obeying the Call,* Marr (Glasgow), 1878.
Getting Ahead, Lothrop, 1877.
The Lesson in Story, two volumes, Lothrop, 1877.
Little People in Picture and Story, Lothrop, 1877.
Two Boys, Lothrop, 1877.

(With Faye Huntington) *From Different Standpoints*, Lothrop, 1878.

Little Fishers: And Their Nets, Lothrop, 1878.

Little Hands, Lothrop, 1878.

Links in Rebecca's Life, Lothrop, 1878.

Pretty Soon, Lothrop, 1878.

Red Ribbon, Lothrop, 1878.

Sidney Martin's Christmas, Lothrop, 1878.

Six Little Girls, Lothrop, 1878.

Little By Little, Lothrop, 1879.

Miss Priscilla Hunter, and My Daughter Susan, Lothrop, 1879.

My Daughter Susan, Lothrop, 1879.

Ruth Erskine's Crosses, Lothrop, 1879.

(With Mrs. C. M. Livingston) *Divers Women*, Lothrop, 1880.

A New Graft on the Family Tree, Lothrop, 1880.

Next Things and Dorrie's Day, Lothrop, 1880.

The Teacher's Helper, Lothrop, 1880.

What She Said: And What She Meant, Lothrop, 1880.

The Hall in the Grove, Lothrop, 1881.

Mrs. Harry Harper's Awakening, Lothrop, 1881.

The Pocket Measure, Lothrop, 1881.

(With Faye Livingston, Theodosia Maria Foster, and others) *Mary Burton Abroad, and Other Stories*, Lothrop, 1882.

Mrs. Solomon Smith Looking On, Lothrop, 1882.

Some Young Heroines, Lothrop, 1882.

Ester Ried Yet Speaking, Lothrop, 1883.

The Man of the House, Lothrop, 1883.

Pansy's Home Story Book, Lothrop, 1883.

Pansy's Scrap Book, Lothrop, 1883.

Side By Side, Lothrop, 1883.

Christie's Christmas, Lothrop, 1884.

An Endless Chain, Lothrop, 1884.

A Hedge Fence, Lothrop, 1884.

An Hour with Miss Streator, Lothrop, 1884.

Interrupted, Lothrop, 1884.

New Year's Tangles and Other Stories, Lothrop, 1884.

Gertrude's Diary, Lothrop, 1885.

In the Woods and Out, and Other Stories, Lothrop, 1885.

One Commonplace Day, Lothrop, 1886.

The Browning Boys, Lothrop, 1886.

Spun from Fact, Lothrop, 1886.

Stories and Pictures from the Life of Jesus, Lothrop, c. 1886.

Eighty-Seven, Lothrop, 1887.

A Golden Thought, and Other Stories, Lothrop, 1887.

Mother's Boys and Girls, Lothrop, 1887.

Six O'clock in the Evening, Lothrop, 1887.

Sunday Chat, Lothrop, 1887.

A Dozen of Them, Lothrop, 1888.

Judge Burnham's Daughters, Lothrop, 1888.

Monteagle, Lothrop, 1888.

Pansies for Thoughts, compiled by Faye Livingston, Lothrop, 1888.

(With Faye Livingston) *Profiles*, Lothrop, 1888.

Chrissy's Endeavor, Lothrop, 1889.

A Sevenfold Trouble, Lothrop, 1889.

"We Twelve Girls," Lothrop, 1889.

(With Faye Livingston) *Aunt Hannah and Martha and John*, Lothrop, 1890.

The Prince of Peace, Lothrop, 1890.

An April Walk and Other Stories from The Pansy, Lothrop, 1890.

Her Associate Members, Lothrop, 1891.

Miss Dee Dunmore Bryant, Lothrop, 1891.

Glimpses of Girlhood, Lothrop, 1892.

(With Faye Livingston) *John Remington Martyr*, Lothrop, 1892.

Pansy's Stories of American History, Lothrop, 1893.

Stephen Mitchell's Journey, Lothrop, 1893.

Twenty Minutes Late, Lothrop, 1893.

Stories and Pictures from the New Testament, Lothrop, 1893.

Only Ten Cents, Lothrop, 1894.

"Wanted," Lothrop, 1894.

Pansy's Boys and Girls Picture Book, Lothrop, 1895.

What They Couldn't: A Home Story, Lothrop, 1895.

Making Fate, Lothrop, 1896.

Their Vacation and Other Stories of Striving and Doing, Lothrop, 1896.

Overruled, Lothrop, 1897.

Sunday Book, Lothrop, 1897.

Agatha's Unknown Way, Revell, 1898.

As in a Mirror, Lothrop, 1898.

Yesterday, Framed in To-day, Lothrop, 1898.

(With Faye Livingston) *By Way of the Wilderness*, Lothrop, 1899.

A Modern Sacrifice: The Story of Kissie Gordon's Experiment, Lothrop, 1899.

Three Times Three: A Story for Young People, and Others, Revell, 1899.

Her Mother's Bible, Lothrop, 1900.

Missent; or, The Story of a Letter, Lothrop, 1900.

Pauline, Lothrop, 1900.

Mag and Margaret: A Story for Girls, Lothrop, 1901.

Unto the End, Lothrop, 1902.

Mara, Lothrop, 1903.

Doris Ferrand's Vocation, Lothrop, 1904.

David Ransom's Watch, Lothrop, 1905.

Ester Ried's Namesake, Lothrop, Lee & Shepard (Boston), 1906.

Ruth Erskine's Son, Lothrop, Lee & Shepard, 1907.

The Browns at Mt. Hermon, Lothrop, Lee & Shepard, 1908.

Lost on the Trail, Lothrop, Lee & Shepard, 1911.

The Long Way Home, Lothrop, Lee & Shepard, 1912.

Four Mothers at Chatauqua, Lothrop, Lee & Shepard, 1913.

Tony Keating's Surprises, Donohue (Chicago), 1914.

The Fortunate Calamity, Lippincott (Philadelphia and London), 1927.

An Interrupted Night, Burt (New York), 1929.

Memories of Yesterday, edited by Grace Livingston Hill, Lippincott, 1931.

Also author of *Our Darlings*, 1878; *People Who Haven't Time*, 1880; (with Faye Huntington) *That Boy Bob*, 1880; *Five Friends*, 1882; *Pansy's Stories of Child Life*, six volumes, 1884-89; *At Home Stories*, 1887; *Young Folks Worth Knowing*, 1889; *Helen the Historian*, 1891; *Worth Having*, 1893; *The Older Brother*, 1897; and *Reuben's Hindrances*, 1898.

EDITOR; UNDER PSEUDONYM PANSY

Young Folks Stories of American History and Home Life, first series, Lothrop, 1884.

Young Folks Stories of Foreign Lands, first series, Lothrop, 1884.

Young Folks Stories of American History and Home Life, second series, Lothrop, 1887.

Young Folks Stories of Foreign Lands, second series, Lothrop, 1887.

Young Folks Stories of American History and Home Life, third series, Lothrop, 1889.

Sidelights

As "Pansy," Isabella (Macdonald) Alden wrote nearly 150 books, of which almost half were for children. Many have been translated into other languages, including Japanese, Swedish, Armenian, and Bulgarian. Around the year 1900, her books were selling at the brisk pace of about one hundred thousand copies per year. Deeply religious, she saw her books as a way to bring Christian values to a young audience. The youngest of six children, Alden received her nickname, "Pansy," from her father, Isaac Macdonald. Active in promoting social reforms, he conducted her earliest education and most of all, encouraged her to write: a journal, stories, and reports on sermons. It is not surprising that she published her first story at age ten, in a local Gloversville, New York, newspaper.

Alden attended school at Seneca Collegiate Institute at Ovid, New York, and then the Young Ladies Institute, at Auburn, also in New York. At the Young Ladies Institute she worked as a student teacher, and her interest in pedagogy continued throughout her life. There she also wrote her first book, in response to a contest held by the American Reform Tract and Book Society for the best book making clear the path of salvation to children of ten to fourteen. She hid the story in a trunk when she finished, considering it a failure, but her boarding school roommate secretly sent it in to the contest just days before the deadline. The book not only won the contest, but was later published as *Helen Lester* (1865). The American Reform Society encouraged her to write more stories, and went on to publish her second book for children, *Jessie Wells; or, How to Save the Lost* (1865).

Looking back, Alden recalled that after writing her first book in response to this contest, she decided to devote all her writing to expounding Christian principles. "My very first little story books were written with a single distinct purpose in view, given over to the desire and determination to win souls for Jesus Christ," she once said, according to *Dictionary of Literary Biography* contributor J. B. Dobkin. Dobkin later quoted Alden as adding, "I saw the trend away from Christ long ago. I recognized the downward trend not only in girls and boys, but in their mothers and teachers and pastors.... It was then [after *Helen Lester*] that I dedicated my pen to the direct and continuous effort to win others for Christ and help others to closer fellowship with Him." Her writing was a part of a religious mission more than a literary endeavor, which may help to explain the fact that it was ignored by critics of the time.

Unsurprisingly, she went on to marry a minister. In May of 1866 she wed the Reverend Gustavus R. Alden, a descendant of John Alden. A few years later they moved from Almond, New York, to Utica, and then to New Hartford. Their only son, Raymond Macdonald Alden, was born on March 30, 1873. Due to his ill health, they spent several years in Winter Park, Florida, from which they moved to Pennsylvania and then to Palo Alto, California. Between assisting her husband with parish work, teaching a Sunday school class of a hundred children, raising her son, and writing her 150 books, Alden did not have to worry about tempting the devil with idle hands. In addition, she composed primary school lessons for *Westminster Teacher,* edited the *Presbyterian Primary Quarterly,* and, from 1874 to 1896, she edited a weekly religious magazine for children called *Pansy.* Every winter she wrote a serial story for the *Herald and Presbyter.* Alden's long hours working for the church provided material for many of her stories, and comfort for herself. Fiction offered her a way to reshape unruly, often distressing experiences to provide catharsis, meaning, and divine justice.

Her most significant works for adults included two lives of Christ: *The Prince of Peace* (1890) and *Yesterday, Framed in To-day: A Story of the Christ, and How To-day Received Him* (1898). In the latter, Christ's life is understood in a modern context. Of all her books, the best-selling were those in the Ester Ried series. These included *Ester Ried: Asleep and Awake* (1870), *Ester Ried Yet Speaking* (1883), and *Ester Ried's Namesake* (1906). Alden drew upon personal experience for writing this series, which was embraced by a generation of girls, but did not wear well for their daughters. *Four Girls at Chautauqua* (1876) was another favorite. Of a later book in that series, *Four Mothers at Chautauqua* (1913), a *The Boston Transcript* contributor wrote that "Chautauquans especially will be interested in Mrs. Alden's latest story, in which her original 'four girls' appear as 'four mothers.' They revisit the scenes of long ago.... The most interesting turn of the plot is a Cinderella-like episode which figures a poor relation." In *All the Happy Endings,* Helen Papashvily recounted the trademark images that characterized Alden's work: "So frequently did the cliches of grief appear—the lock of hair, the shoe, the sun's last rays on the fading cheek, the plaintive voice asking, 'Will Papa come home?'— that some later readers found amusement in these bits of sentimentality."

Despite the fact that she actively published for over sixty years, Alden outlived her popularity. As quoted by Dobkin, in a 1927 letter to her niece Grace Livingston Hill (who had suggested that she update the Ester Ried books), she expressed her disinclination to "modernize" herself for contemporary readers: "I am not capable of writing a story suited to the tastes of *present day* young people. They would smoke a cigarette over the first chapter, and toss it aside as a back number. I haven't faith in them, nor in my ability to help them." Alden lost both her husband and her son in 1924, and published just a couple more books before her own death from cancer in August, 1930. During her immense popularity, critics paid her no attention. The day after running her obituary, *The New York Times,* according to Dobkin, speculated in an editorial that the time may have come to redress that neglect: "Her *Chatauqua* [sic], *Ester Ried,* and *Life of Christ* series were pored over by countless admirers . . . . Now that comic strips are studied seriously as 'folk art,' it is not too much to expect a book about 'Pansy' from one of the determined students of American culture." As Dobkin ruefully observed, "This book remains unwritten in the history of American literature." Given the phenomenon of Alden's huge appeal, it will be surprising if this critical neglect continues, especially since scholars such as Jane Tompkins have helped to make "the sentimental" a category of interest and discussion within American literature.

Works Cited

Dictionary of Literary Biography, Volume 42: *American Writers for Children Before 1900,* Gale, 1985.
Review of *Four Mothers at Chautauqua, Boston Transcript,* August 2, 1913, p. 5.
Papashvily, Helen, *All the Happy Endings,* Harper, 1956.*

*   *   *

APPEL, Allen (R.) 1945-

Personal

Surname is pronounced "apple"; born January 6, 1945, in Bethlehem, PA; son of Allen R., Jr. and Irene (a homemaker; maiden name, Trippett) Appel; married Sharon Conway (a publicist), 1980; children: Allen R., IV, Leah Helen, Charles David. *Education:* West Virginia University, B.A., 1967.

Addresses

E-mail—appelworks@email.msn.com.

Career

Photographer, illustrator, and writer. *Member:* Mystery Writers of America, Authors Guild.

Awards, Honors

Recognition as one of year's best novels from American Library Association (ALA), 1986, for *Time after Time;* nominations for ALA Best Book for *Twice upon a Time* and *Till the End of Time.*

Writings

FICTION

Time after Time, Carroll & Graf (New York City), 1985.
Twice upon a Time, Carroll & Graf, 1988.
Till the End of Time, Doubleday (New York City), 1990.
(With Craig Roberts) *Hellhound,* Avon, 1994.

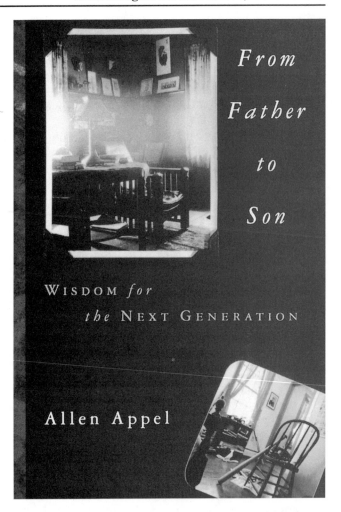

Allen Appel compiled this collection of advice from real-life fathers to their sons. (Cover photo by Katherine McGlynn.)

NONFICTION

From Father to Son: Wisdom for the Next Generation, St. Martin's Press (New York City), 1993.
Thanks, Dad, St. Martin's Press, 1994.

OTHER

(Illustrator) *Proust's Last Beer,* Viking, 1979.

Also the author of the screenplay, *The Ebony Streak.* Appel's works have been translated into Chinese and Korean.

Work in Progress

Two mystery novels; gift books for St. Martin's press on babies and dogs; screenplays.

Sidelights

Allen Appel takes his readers on fictional flights to Russia during the 1917 Revolution, to the Reconstruction Era America of Mark Twain, and to Japan during the 1945 bombing of Hiroshima. His time-traveling protagonist, Alex Balfour, at the center of his "Pastmaster" series, has won readers of all ages since publication of the first novel, *Time after Time.* Often classified as a science fiction writer, Appel is first of all a fiction writer. His professional historian-hero Balfour does not climb into an ornate time machine for his travels, nor does he take lessons in breaking the membrane of temporality. Instead, Alex Balfour steeps himself in a time period, falls asleep, and quite unwillingly wakes up in another world:

"The headache was gone. Alex Balfour was lying face down in a shallow trench. The ground was cold and hard and smelled of clay and mold. He had just enough time to lift his head up out of the dirt before the first shell slammed into the earth. A howling rush of air and then the explosion.... His ears rang with it. He flinched as a flare burst high in the air with a flat pop and drifted slowly down, hissing, emitting a cold magnesium light that drenched his limited landscape, coloring it a pale, monochromatic blue."

Such is the way that the reader and Balfour himself are introduced to his latent abilities in *Time after Time:* waking up *in medias res,* in the muddy hell of World War I trench warfare. "An editor friend of mine told me never to try and explain the unexplainable," Appel remarked to *Authors and Artists for Young Adults* in an interview. "So I don't bother with trying to tell how Balfour does his time-traveling. He just does it." And does it and does it. Balfour makes two encore appearances, in *Twice upon a Time* and *Till the End of Time,* shuttling back and forth between historical time zones like a frequent flyer. A writer for the *Washington Post Book World* summed up the appeal of the trilogy of books in reviewing the first of the series: "Part historical novel, part science fiction, part love story."

This "total adventure" is what Appel serves up in all the "Pastmaster" books, though it is also leavened with hard-hitting historical truths. As Gregory Benford noted in a *Washington Post Book World* review of *Till the End of Time,* the book is "a lively page-turner," but "not without moral purpose." Benford pointed out that "Appel is after larger game than the reader's attention span." It is this concern with historical accuracy and ethical questions that have helped to make Appel's books as popular in the classroom as at the beach. Appel explained that he "tried to put things into the novels that history teachers wouldn't tell students."

Born in Bethlehem, Pennsylvania, on January 6, 1945, Appel moved with his family to West Virginia when he was six. "I grew up and lived in West Virginia through college," Appel told *Authors and Artists for Young Adults.* One of three siblings, Appel formed an early love of reading. "My mom was always reading," Appel recalled in his interview. "And I just naturally picked up the habit too, as did my brother and sister. We had a rule in the family: fewer than three people at dinner and it was okay to read at the table. We spent a lot of silent meals together." At age eleven, laid up with a high fever, Appel was introduced to the Tarzan books by his mother who had an entire set of works by Edgar Rice Burroughs

in the attic. "I raced through them," Appel said. "And from there I went on to science fiction. And soon I was reading everything. My sister is two years older and I would read the books she brought home. I read everything two years too early."

Thoughts of actually becoming a writer himself didn't occur until later, however. After high school graduation, Appel attended West Virginia University, where he earned a B.A. in 1967. Thereafter he worked primarily as an illustrator and photographer. "I was self-taught in both," Appel said. "I can't draw to save my life, but I worked in collage illustration, often using my own photographs. I created something of a niche for myself, and worked as a freelancer for the *Washington Post* with their Sunday magazine sections." One day, however, sitting at his desk at the newspaper, Appel had a sudden epiphany: "I looked around and everybody I saw in the room was a writer. And I figured they weren't any smarter or imaginative than I was. Why couldn't I become a writer, too?"

It was a rhetorical question that led Appel on a several-year pursuit to learn how to write. By this time he had already earned a book credit with his 1979 work, *Proust's Last Beer,* which he illustrated and also conceived. A book describing how famous people died, this nonfiction debut gave him little in the way of education about how to construct fiction. Appel, who is self-taught, simply sat down and began a novel about the crossing of a chimp and a human. "When the dust settled I had a book told only with dialogue. Not even a 'he said' or 'she said.' So I went back in for a second draft and inserted that sort of stuff. The third draft I actually got around to adding descriptive passages." Though this first novel made the rounds of New York publishers, none were enthusiastic enough to buy it. Yet it served as an apprenticeship, or at least the beginnings of one.

Over the next several years, Appel tried his hand at westerns and romances, penning five more unpublished novels, but gaining confidence in his craft as he went along. Then a fortuitous meeting with Kent Carroll, an editor just setting out on his own in publishing, led to the "Pastmaster" series. Working with the germ of an idea about spending one's summer vacation not at the beach but in the Russia of 1917, Appel set to the task of crafting a hybrid novel—part sci-fi and part historical fiction. Like his protagonist, Alex Balfour, Appel immersed himself in the time period. "I'd never been to Russia, at that time the Soviet Union, and clearly had never been anywhere in 1917, so it was my job as a researcher to get the feel of the time and place right." He read histories, memoirs, and correspondence from the time. "I found out that Lenin had a lisp, something we don't really think about when you mention the name of that revolutionary. So in my book he sometimes sounds like Elmer Fudd." Photograph books of the time were also an aid in recreating the scene. "But they were all in black and white," Appel recalled. "I got the objects right, the look of the street and the things you might find in a drawing room, but I lost sleep over the colors. So I made a house yellow. What if houses weren't painted yellow then? What if some expert found out?"

However, concerns over such details faded in the urgency of plot; no experts on house paint stepped forward. Appel's fictional world came across whole and clear. Balfour, a history teacher at the New School and a gourmet cook, awakens from an incredibly realistic dream of being in the trenches of World War I. He puts it down to nightmare, overwork, too much drink taken. Except that his jeans are smeared with the same red clay he saw in his dream. Balfour continues to dream, going back to Russia during the first World War and the beginning of the Russian Revolution. Molly, his lover in the present, tells him that in fact at times he seems to disappear. Slowly Balfour begins to accept the fact that he is actually time-traveling.

In the course of such journeys in time and quite by accident, Balfour becomes an unwilling participant in the murder of the mad monk, Rasputin, after which he reappears in the present to confront Molly in the monk's sables. During further time travels he encounters Maxim Gorky speaking to workers and puts a word in the ear of the British consul about a spy named Mata Hari. But Balfour himself is arrested by the Czar's police as a suspected spy, and spends weeks imprisoned. More meetings with famous men occur: Pavlov busy walking three dogs, and Lenin, spluttering his words.

His guide through all these adventures is the young American, Maxwell Surrey, whom Balfour knows from the present as the old man who cared for him after he was orphaned as a teenager. And most surprising of all, Balfour meets another time traveler—his own father, who is leading a band of ruthless Cossacks and is intent on changing history. He tells his son, Alex, that he must prevent the assassination of the Czar and his family, but Alex Balfour has suddenly had too much of history, and goes back to the present. However, nagged by his own morality, he makes one final trip to the past, having learned "that we are responsible for things. For ourselves, other people, events. That inaction can be as destructive as out-and-out evil."

Upon publication of *Time after Time*, reviewers were generally positive if not enthusiastic about this first novel. Sybil Steinberg, writing in *Publishers Weekly*, felt that readers ready to withhold incredulity "will be rewarded by scenes of cliff-hanging and head-bashing, slaughter, torture and hairsbreadth escapes,... true romance and wholesome sex." Steinberg went on to conclude that *Time after Time* is an engrossing read. A reviewer for the *Washington Post Book World* dubbed the book a "compelling journey back in time" and an "absorbing first novel," while a contributor in *Booklist* called it "Riveting adventure, replete with romance and drama." Writing in the *New York Times Book Review*, Perry Glasser commented that Appel's novel was on one level "fine entertainment," but more than that in its entirety. Glasser praised *Time after Time*'s "vivid writing," and called the novel "something of a historical novel, something of a science fiction novel, partly the

story of a son's bitter relationship with his father, partly a romance." These features are "pleasingly balanced," concluded Glasser, "with grace and skill."

Sales of this initial title were encouraging enough for Appel to continue with the intended series. For his next title, *Twice upon a Time*, Appel chose an American setting. "And I wanted to talk about what I consider to be *the* issue of our time—race," Appel explained. "I wanted to write about black people and Native Americans, both then and now. The moral issues were very important for me in the writing." In this second novel, Alex Balfour has come to feel truly alive and free only when he is in the past, yet still he receives no warning when such journeys are beginning nor does he have any overt control over his destination. Molly, his partner and a reporter for the *New York Times*, sets things in motion when she takes on an assignment to cover a story about one John Raven, a Native American who claims to be a direct descendant of Crazy Horse, the "Architect, or rather strategist, of the Battle of the Little Bighorn," as Balfour tells her for background. Raven has shot two white men doing a land study on a South Dakota reservation, and Molly soon heads out to that state to interview him.

Studying up on the history of Native Americans and their struggles with the whites sets off a series of time travels for Balfour, journeys which at first seem to be unrelated to any one main event. Then Balfour finds himself taken back to the Philadelphia Exhibition of 1876 where he checks out the latest in technological advances and meets Mark Twain. Living with a group of emancipated slaves, Balfour conspires with one of them to release two captured Indians who are at the exhibit, and with Twain in tow, the five of them light out for the territories. Their trek westward includes a raft trip down the Mississippi. Meanwhile, back in the present, Molly is kidnapped by Raven just before the centenary of Custer's Last Stand, and Balfour, lost in time, arrives at the Little Big Horn in an attempt to stop the slaughter that he knows will soon happen.

Once again, critics praised Appel for his historical reconstruction. Andrea Caron Kempf noted in *Library Journal* that "Appel again demonstrates his unique blend of history and science fiction in a riveting novel that says much about freedom and slavery and the innate dignity of human beings." Kempf gave the book a "highly recommended" rating. Other reviewers applauded Appel's blend of entertainment and history. A *Kirkus Reviews* contributor dubbed the novel a "high-speed, deftly handled sequel" which blends "time-travel, authentic backgrounds, and speculative fancy." A critic writing for *Publishers Weekly* remarked that "Appel maintains a firm hold on the strands of his plot, keeping Alex's sensibility consistently modern without becoming patronizing or sentimental toward the times." "Suspense" and "period detail," this same reviewer concluded, "will keep readers turning these pages." High praise was given by Susan Jelcich in *Voice of Youth Advocates*, who commented that "Appel has created a perceptive, insightful, sometimes passionate blend of history, adventure, and moral responsibility." Jelcich concluded that "*Twice upon a Time* is entertaining, worthwhile reading that packs a punch as it amuses."

The third book in the series, *Till the End of Time,* finds Balfour transported back to World War II, attempting to stop the Japanese from developing their own atomic bomb. Appel again has Balfour making the acquaintance of the high and mighty from history: taking tea with Albert Einstein, meeting with Franklin Delano Roosevelt, having an affair with Betty Grable, and even lending a hand to a young lieutenant named John F. Kennedy as he saves the crew of his PT boat. The crux of the story deals with Balfour's attempt to stop the destructive use of the atomic bomb, a mission on which Einstein sends him to Roosevelt. But F. D. R. is too canny a politician to be limited in the use of this new weapon; he sends Balfour to the South Pacific on a fact-finding mission to get him out of the way. Meanwhile in the present, Molly is following a story about Japanese germ warfare that resonates with the historical tale which culminates at the bombing of Hiroshima, where Appel has set the Japanese atomic program (it actually was in Tokyo).

"This novel seems at first to be a simple action gambol," Benford noted in the *Washington Post Book World,* "but it raises issues seldom treated in our press." A *Publishers Weekly* reviewer found this third title in the "Pastmaster" series to be a "thoroughly absorbing and enjoyable adventure," concluding that "insights into the effects of time on human nature and on one man's actions attest to Appel's continuing ability to keep readers glued to the page." According to a *Kirkus Reviews* contributor, "Appel's generous dollops of history are as painlessly informative, and the tale he spins as rousing, as ever." Marcia R. Hoffman, writing in *Library Journal,* remarked that Appel "has assembled some believable and very human characters" in the bomb scene "which is exciting and well researched."

The popular series came to an abrupt end, however, when Appel delivered his fourth Balfour manuscript, tentatively titled *Sea of Time,* to Doubleday, only to have it rejected because the subject matter supposedly would not have wide enough appeal. "That limited subject matter just happened to be the sinking of the Titanic," Appel said in his interview. "I think maybe that editor was just a little bit wrong in light of the movie and the spin-offs that came a few years later. But at the time I was so angry that I just put the manuscript on the shelf and moved on to other projects. I still send it out to fans who write, asking about a sequel."

Since the last of the "Pastmaster" series, Appel has embarked on numerous projects. In 1994 he collaborated with Craig Roberts, a retired helicopter pilot, policeman, and Vietnam veteran, to write the thriller, *Hellhound,* about a conspiracy by Iraqi and Palestinian terrorists to kill former president Ronald Reagan and destroy southern California. A Russian colonel discovers the plot and teams up with a disgraced Los Angeles cop to ground the mission by outmaneuvering the deadly Hellhound

helicopter en route. A *Publishers Weekly* reviewer noted that Appel and Roberts "make a good team and deliver an imaginative novel of clear, direct military suspense" with a "rousing climax." Appel has also created a line of gift books, partly in collaboration with his wife, Sharon Conway Appel, in appreciation of parents. Additionally, he has largely left novel writing behind—at least for the time being—to work on screenplays. His first endeavor, *The Ebony Streak,* tells the story of Marshall "Major" Taylor, one of the greatest athletes of his day at the turn of the twentieth century and one of the first black world champions in any sport. A bicyclist in a time of worldwide passion for the sport, Marshall held the one-mile speed record. Though cheered in Europe, Marshall faced bigotry in his native America, dying penniless and unknown. As Appel put it, "Marshall is the most famous athlete that America ever forgot."

A full-time writer, Appel is brimming over with new plans and projects. But for many readers, it is still the "Pastmaster" series that makes his name known. "I receive fan letters all the time," Appel told *Authors and Artists for Young Adults.* "Lots of them are from young readers, too, ones who find truth in these books and write to me that they never knew history could actually be interesting. I think part of the draw of the books is that I never fudge. I never cheat. I don't let Alex Balfour get himself out of trouble by suddenly going back to the present. He is in the past and in trouble and he has to deal with it. He has to save himself. There is a level of engagement that young readers especially respond to. I have young kids myself, and find that so often in books intended for younger readers that the writer cheats at the end. 'It was all a dream.' The hero or heroine is saved by that device. With Alex Balfour the dream becomes reality. And reality can be deadly serious."

Works Cited

Appel, Allen, *Time after Time,* Carroll and Graf, 1985.

Appel, Allen, *Twice upon a Time,* Carroll and Graf, 1988.

Appel, Allen, interview with *Authors and Artists for Young Adults,* conducted July 20, 1999.

Benford, Gregory, "What Is and What Might Have Been," *Washington Post Book World,* August 15, 1990, p. 4.

Glasser, Perry, "The Professor Vanishes," *New York Times Book Review,* January 26, 1986, p. 12.

Review of *Hellhound, Publishers Weekly,* May 30, 1994.

Hoffman, Marcia R., review of *Till the End of Time, Library Journal,* September 1, 1990, p. 253.

Jelcich, Susan, review of *Twice upon a Time, Voice of Youth Advocates,* October, 1988. p. 190.

Kempf, Andrea Caron, review of *Twice upon a Time, Library Journal,* April 1, 1988, p. 56.

Steinberg, Sybil, review of *Time after Time, Publishers Weekly,* September 27, 1985, p. 83.

Review of *Till the End of Time, Publishers Weekly,* June 29, 1990, p. 85.

Review of *Till the End of Time, Kirkus Reviews,* July 1, 1990, p. 893.

Review of *Time after Time, Booklist,* October 1, 1985, pp. 189-90.

Review of *Time after Time, Washington Post Book World,* May 24, 1987, p. 12.

Review of *Twice upon a Time, Kirkus Reviews,* February 1, 1988, p. 139.

Review of *Twice upon a Time, Publishers Weekly,* February 19, 1988, pp. 72-73.

For More Information See

PERIODICALS

Booklist, September 1, 1990, p. 24; March 15, 1991, p. 1473.

Kliatt, spring, 1987, p. 19.

Locus, April, 1990, p. 35; September, 1990, p. 57.

New York Times Book Review, March 1, 1987, p. 34.

Washington Post, November 30, 1985; April 21, 1988.

ON-LINE

Allen Appel's Web site is located at http://www.appelworks.com.

—*Sketch by J. Sydney Jones*

* * *

ARMSTRONG, Martin Donisthorpe 1882-1974

Personal

Born October 2, 1882, near Newcastle-on-Tyne; son of Charles Armstrong (an architect) and Edith Lucy Donisthorpe Armstrong (second cousin of William Wordsworth); died February 24, 1974; married Jessie McDonald Aiken (ex-wife of Conrad Aiken), 1930; children: one. *Education:* Pembroke College, Cambridge University, B.A. (mechanical science). *Hobbies and other interests:* Music.

Career

Short-story writer, poet, novelist, children's literature writer, radio script writer, critic, editor, architect, and journalist. *Military service:* Private, Artists' Rifles, 1914; Eighth Middlesex Regiment, 1915; Ministry of Pensions.

Writings

Exodus, and Other Poems, Lynwood (London), 1912.

Thirty New Poems, Chapman & Hall (London), 1918.

The Buzzards, and Other Poems, Secker (London), 1921.

The Puppet Show (short stories), Golden Cockerel (Waltham St. Lawrence), 1922, Brentano's (New York), 1923.

(Compiler) *Jeremy Taylor: A Selection from His Works,* Golden Cockerel, 1923.

The Bazaar and Other Stories, Cape (London), 1924, Knopf (New York), 1924.

The Goat and Compasses (novel), Cape, 1925, published as *At the Sign of the Goat and Compasses,* Harper (New York), 1925.

Desert: A Legend (novel), Cape, 1926, Harper, 1926.

Lady Hester Stanhope (nonfiction), Howe (London), 1927, Viking (New York), 1928.

Saint Hercules, and Other Stories, Fleuron (London), 1927.

Sir Pompey and Madame Juno and Other Tales (short stories), Cape, 1927, Houghton Mifflin (Boston and New York), 1927.

The Stepson (novel), Cape, 1927, published as *The Water Is Wide,* Harper, 1927.

Laughing, Being One of a Series of Essays Edited by J. B. Priestley and Entitled: These Diversions, Jarrolds (London), 1928, Harper, 1928.

Saint Christopher's Day (novel), Gollancz (London), 1928, published as *All in a Day,* Harper, 1929.

Portrait of the Misses Harlowe, Mathews & Marrot (London), 1928.

(Translator) Don Pedro Antonio Alarcon, *The Three-Cornered Hat,* Howe (London), 1927; Simon & Schuster (New York), 1928.

The Bird-Catcher, and Other Poems, Secker (London), 1929.

The Sleeping Fury (novel), Gollancz, 1929, Harcourt Brace (New York), 1929.

The Fiery Dive and Other Stories, Gollancz, 1929, Harcourt Brace, 1930.

Adrian Glynde (novel), Gollancz, 1930, published as *Blind Man's Mark,* Harcourt Brace, 1931.

Collected Poems, Secker, 1931.

The Romantic Adventures of Mr. Darby and of Sarah His Wife (novel), Gollancz, 1931, Harcourt Brace, 1932.

The Paintbox (art criticism; for children), Black (London), 1931.

Lover's Leap: A Story in Three Voices (novel), Gollancz, 1932, Harcourt Brace, 1933.

The Foster-Mother (novel), Gollancz, 1933, Harcourt Brace, 1934.

54 Conceits: A Collection of Epigrams and Epitaphs Serious and Comic, Secker, 1933.

(Editor) *The Major Pleasures of Life,* Gollancz, 1934.

General Buntop's Miracle, and Other Stories (for children), Gollancz, 1934, Harcourt Brace, 1934.

Venus over Lannery (novel), Gollancz, 1936, Harcourt Brace, 1936.

A Case of Conscience and Other Tales, Gollancz, 1937.

Spanish Circus (history), Collins (London), 1937.

The Snake in the Grass (novel), Gollancz, 1938.

Victorian Peep-Show, Joseph (London), 1938.

Birds of Passage, Friends' Peace Committee (London), 1938.

(With Gerald Bullett, Havelock Ellis, John Hilton, Storm Jameson, Eric Linklater, J. B. Priestley, V. S. Pritchett, Bertrand Russell, and Hugh Walpole) *What Is Happiness?,* John Lane (London), 1938, Kinsey (New York), 1939.

Simplicity Jones and Other Stories, Collins (London), 1940.

The Butterfly (novel), Collins, 1941.

Chichester Concert (An Ode) (poems), Cambridge University Press (Cambridge), 1944.

Said the Cat to the Dog (short stories for children), Methuen (London), 1945.

Said the Dog to the Cat (short stories for children), Hodder & Stoughton (London), 1948.

(Editor) *The Essential Mary Webb,* Cape, 1949.

George Burrow (nonfiction), Barker (London), 1950, Swallow (Denver), 1950.
Selected Stories, Cape, 1951.

Sidelights

Martin Donisthorpe Armstrong is often remembered now as the friend who stole Conrad Aiken's wife away. He was also an amazingly prolific and facile writer, who composed in a crazy array of genres: poetry, biography, short story, novel, children's book, and radio play. He was also an able editor, selecting and introducing classic works. By all accounts, Armstrong was an agreeably charming man. But although he was a prolific writer, his books have not shown much staying power and are mostly forgotten today.

Armstrong was born to wealthy parents outside the town of Newcastle-on-Tyne. His father, Charles Armstrong, was an architect, and his mother, Edith Lucy Donisthorpe Armstrong, was a second cousin to William Wordsworth. As he recollects in his autobiographical account, *Victorian Peep-Show* (1938), his babyhood was idyllic. He was thoroughly educated, capping his studies with a B.A. at Cambridge University's Pembroke College. As quoted in *World Authors,* Armstrong said of his education: "[I] took a B.A. degree in mechanical science, a subject which [I] disliked intensely." He muddled through two years at an architectural firm, however, before giving it all up to live in Italy making "a close study, with no definite object but [my] own satisfaction, of ... Italian art." It was during this trip that he met Conrad Aiken, then a Harvard undergraduate; the two were to remain friends for twenty years, each editing and aiding the other's work.

Armstrong joined the army during World War I, managing to keep his head above water until Armistice Day. It was at this point that Armstrong's literary career began. He had published his first collection of poems, *Exodus, and Other Poems,* in 1912, but now he pursued writing as a career, practicing some freelance journalism and other work. Soon Armstrong began publishing poems in some of the better literary journals. He put out two more volumes of poetry: *Thirty New Poems* in 1918 and *The Buzzards* in 1921. The volumes were lukewarmly received, as were his early short stories. His 1923 collection of sketches, *Puppet Show,* was pronounced likable but unremarkable by a number of critics. "Deftly and neatly written," as one *New York Tribune* critic wrote, "[*Puppet Show* demonstrates] ... a particular knack of clear characterization. But that does not obviate the fact that the sketches are singularly colorless." Armstrong gradually moved away from poems and stories, however, choosing instead to focus on the big game of the modernist period: the novel.

His first venture into this new, larger arena was *The Goat and Compasses* (1925), a novel named for a pub in the seaside village of Crome. The book follows the silly and tragic affairs of three couples who frequent the pub. The novel was pronounced pleasing but nothing more by several reviewers. A critic for the *International Book Review* explained, "The originality of the book is largely in the excellence of its artistic method. There is comparatively little penetration in its manner of seeing life, though the several slight tales are soundly conceived and unexceptionable so far as they go."

Armstrong followed up his first novel with a book in a different vein: *Desert, A Legend* (1926). In this story set in ancient times, Armstrong attempts to tell the exotic tale of a man who follows a Christian hermit into a cell in the Egyptian desert, enduring wretched years of solitude and self-denial. But somehow Armstrong's style could not be hidden beneath the mystic sands; the book was pronounced, again, charming and no more. In a *Nation and Atheneum* review, Edwin Muir declared, "Mr. Armstrong has a theme with great possibilities, and he has not made enough of it. His very pleasant, somewhat too decorative, style tends to ... leave behind a conventionally unexceptionable picture." Armstrong's next effort, *The Water Is Wide* (1927), met with the same shrugs. As one commentator wrote in the *New Republic,* "It has the logic of a tragedy without the emotion."

As Armstrong was writing *Saint Christopher's Day* (1928), he became engaged to his old friend Conrad Aiken's ex-wife, Jessie MacDonald Aiken. Aiken was miffed, the more so when Armstrong's new book made the author a lot of money. Armstrong bought a house in the country, furnished it, and settled down with his new wife. But the ease and complacence that marked Armstrong's life so happily also marked his work less happily. His following novels were not as critically successful as *Saint Christopher's Day,* which was itself not a critical triumph. He turned more and more to writing "likable" and "charming" sketches. Particularly successful were his children's stories, which were entertaining and light. As Louis Kronenberger wrote in the *New York Times* of one of his more popular collections of children's stories, *General Buntop's Miracle, and Other Stories* (1934): "Mr. Armstrong's range may be predictable, but at least it is not narrow; and *General Buntop's Miracle* has the kind of variety of tone and subject matter that a book of light short stories ought to have. In his minor way, Mr. Armstrong fills a need: there are not too many writers like him who can be entertaining without insulting your intelligence, individual without being affected and unchanging without being dull. If such praise sounds a little condescending, it's not meant to be." Armstrong was branded throughout his career with the damnation of faint praise: his novels were written off as literary small talk.

Nevertheless, Armstrong published widely and was greatly enjoyed by many readers throughout his lifetime. In the last years of his life, he wrote a weekly column for the BBC journal *The Listener,* which ran for almost twenty years. He died on February 24, 1974, without eternal fame, perhaps, but having lived happily, well, and long.

Works Cited

Review of *The Goat and Compasses, International Book Review,* November, 1925.

Kronenberger, Louis, review of *General Buntop's Miracle, and Other Stories, New York Times,* September 9, 1934, p. 6.

Muir, Edwin, review of *Desert, A Legend, Nation and Atheneum,* July 10, 1926.

Review of *Puppet Show, New York Tribune,* June 24, 1923, p. 20.

Review of *The Water Is Wide, New Republic,* November 23, 1927.

World Authors, Wilson, 1996.

For More Information See

BOOKS

Dictionary of Literary Biography, Volume 197: *Late Victorian and Edwardian British Novelists, Second Series,* Gale, 1999.

Killorin, Joseph, editor, *Selected Letters of Conrad Aiken,* Yale University Press, 1978.

Rogers, Timothy, *Georgian Poetry, 1911-1922: The Critical Heritage,* Routledge & Kegan Paul, 1977.

PERIODICALS

Biography: An Interdisciplinary Quarterly, Volume 19, number 2, 1996.

Bookman, Number 76, 1929, pp. 286-88.

Library Chronicle of the University of Texas at Austin, Volume 23, number 1, 1993.*

*   *   *

ARNOLD, Katya 1947-

Personal

Born August 6, 1947, in Moscow, USSR (now Russia); daughter of Igor (a professor of mathematics) and Nina (an art historian) Arnold; married Alexander Melamid (an artist), 1970; children: Daniel Melamid, Andrey Arnold. *Education:* Received degree, 1965; Moscow Polygraph Institute, M.A., 1971. *Politics:* "Hate all." *Hobbies and other interests:* Mushrooms, reading, hiking, cooking, gardening.

Addresses

Home—56 West 11th St., No. 9RE, New York, NY 10011. *Agent*—Diane B. Foote, Holiday House, 425 Madison Ave., New York, NY 10017. *E-mail*—107754.3633@compuserve.com.

Career

Painter and illustrator. Painter, 1960—; illustrator for a children's magazine and for Moscow publishing houses, 1970—. Art teacher, 1965—. Makes frequent school visits. *Member:* Society of Children's Book Writers and Illustrators.

Katya Arnold

Awards, Honors

Aesop Accolade List, American Folklore Society, 1994, for *Baba Yaga.*

Writings

AUTHOR AND ILLUSTRATOR

(Reteller) *Baba Yaga: A Russian Folktale,* North-South, 1993.

(Reteller) *Baba Yaga and the Little Girl: A Russian Folktale,* North-South, 1994.

(Adapter) *Knock, Knock, Teremok!: A Traditional Russian Tale,* North-South Books, 1994.

(With Sam Swope) *Katya's Book of Mushrooms,* Holt, 1996.

(Reteller) Vladimir Grigorievich Suteev, *Duck, Duck, Goose?,* Holiday House, 1997.

(Reteller) Suteev, *Meow!,* Holiday House, 1998.

(Reteller) Suteev, *The Adventures of Snowwoman,* Holiday House, 1998.

(Reteller) Suteev, *Me Too!: Two Small Stories about Small Animals,* Holiday House, 2000.

That Apple's Mine!, Holiday House, in press.

Several of Arnold's books have been translated into French, Dutch, and Chinese.

ILLUSTRATOR

Eric A. Kimmel, reteller, *The Red Valiant Rooster: A Story from Hungary,* Holt, 1994.

Kimmel, reteller, *Onions & Garlic,* Holiday House, 1996.

Daniil Kharms, *It Happened like This: Stories and Poems,* translation by Ian Frazier, Farrar, Straus, 1998.

Also illustrator of *The Wise Man's Solution,* retold by Jean Casella, *Big Book* magazine.

Adaptations

Knock, Knock, Teremok! was adapted for television and performed on *Storytime,* PBS, 1995.

Work in Progress

Nose; "Hide & Seek" Nature Book; Give Me Back My Tail!

Sidelights

Russian-born author and illustrator Katya Arnold has written several children's books, among them *Baba Yaga and the Little Girl, Katya's Book of Mushrooms,* and *It Happened like This!.* She has also displayed her paintings around the world, and acted as an ambassador of Russian culture by retelling several popular Russian fables in English-language versions. In addition to her editions of *Baba Yaga* and *Baba Yaga and the Little Girl,* Arnold has contributed to the growing library of multicultural children's literature with her retellings of the stories of noted Slavic author Vladimir Grigorievich Suteev.

Born in Moscow in 1947, Arnold grew up in a house full of books because her father and mother were both well-educated academics. She was not allowed to explore the family library on her own, however, until she became a young reader. Instead, her mother would sit and read to her when she was ill and bedridden as a young child. She recalled in particular an illustrated copy of *Alice in Wonderland,* with its wonderful drawings by John Tenniel, that her mother painted with watercolors in shades of blue and red. "I watched the story come to life with her brush," the author once recalled in a publicity release for North-South Books. "Ever since that time, I have been stunned by the magic of color, the magic of creating a new world, and the different worlds, real and imagined, that people can live in."

Artistic talent was a tradition for the women in Arnold's family; her mother was an art historian, and her grandmother was a painter, sculptor, and writer. Her uncle wrote children's books. At the age of twelve, Arnold determined that she, too, would become an artist, and began to study painting. After receiving her undergraduate art degree in 1965, she attended the Moscow Polygraph Institute and graduated with a master's degree in 1971. While doing her graduate studies, she worked as an art teacher and provided illustrations to Russian-language children's magazines and Moscow-based book publishers. She continued to work as a teacher and painter while she, her artist husband, and their two children travelled around Europe. They lived for a time in Jerusalem and visited Italy, Scotland, France, Finland, and several other countries before settling in the United States.

Baba Yaga was Arnold's first book for young children to appear in the United States. Published in 1993, *Baba Yaga* retells an old Russian folktale originally collected by Aleksandr Afanas'ev in the nineteenth century. It begins with an elderly, childless couple bundling up a piece of wood like a baby, placing it in a cradle, and rocking it to sleep. Magically, the wood becomes a real boy, Tishka, and he is raised as the couple's own son. When the evil witch Baba Yaga kidnaps the little boy to eat for her dinner, Tishka tricks the witch's daughter into climbing in the oven, and Baba Yaga eats her own child. The furious witch discovers the frightened Tishka hiding in a tree and tries to gnaw her way through it, but a goose rescues him from the witch's wrath. According to Denise Anton Wright in *School Library Journal,* this book "presents a slice of Russian folklore in an authentic and masterful style." A reviewer for *Junior Bookshelf* appreciated the "splendidly colourful" illustrations in the "style of early woodcuts." Arnold's gouache illustrations are "a fitting match for this retelling," a *Publishers Weekly* critic concluded.

Arnold continued the adventures of the witch Baba Yaga in a sequel, *Baba Yaga and the Little Girl.* In this story,

"Don't worry," said Buddy. "I'll protect you!"
"Thank you," said Snowwoman. So off they went.

Based on a story by Russian animator Vladimir Suteev, **The Adventures of Snowwoman** *follows a snow creature as she brings joy to boys and girls on Christmas Eve. (Retold and illustrated by Arnold.)*

an evil stepmother attempts to rid herself of her troublesome stepdaughter by sending the unwitting girl to Baba Yaga to borrow a needle. Fortunately, the girl is coached by a loving aunt and avoids trouble. This story brings to life the menacing forests and clever heroes that characterize Russian folklore. Praising Arnold's artwork for accurately reflecting the theme of the story, *Booklist* reviewer Kay Weisman noted that "Arnold's thick black-line drawings resemble woodcuts; the vivid gouache colors give the artwork a fresh, modern look while remaining true to the story's classic roots."

Several of Arnold's books for young people retell the stories of Russian author Vladimir Suteev. Suteev, who was born in Russia in 1903, released his first animated film in 1931 and became known throughout his homeland. Equally popular as an author of picture books, Suteev based many of his stories on his films. One such story, *Duck, Duck, Goose?*, was transformed, under Arnold's pen, into "a quirky story imbued with the spirit of a folktale," according to a *Publishers Weekly* contributor. Cited by *School Library Journal* reviewer Christy Norris as "a pleasing tale about identity and acceptance," the picture book *Duck, Duck, Goose?* is about a vain goose taking over the best-looking parts of each of her animal friends in an attempt to improve her appearance. She ends up looking totally silly, with the beak of a pelican at one end and a peacock's tail at the other. In *Meow!*, a young puppy searches for the animal making the teasing yowl, suspecting a rooster, mouse, and even a bee before discovering a playful kitten. "Arnold's brash illustrations are great for this classic," noted a *Kirkus Reviews* contributor, adding that the pictures capture "the puppy's energetic bumblings and the cat's prickly-backed hiss perfectly."

In *The Adventures of Snowwoman*, again based on an animated film by Stueev, a group of children are preparing for Christmas, but worry because they have no Christmas tree. Deciding to ask Santa for one, they conjure up a Snowwoman, made from seven apples, a carrot, and an old stewpot, to be their messenger to the North Pole. Most of the story recounts Snowwoman's adventures on the way to the frigid North Pole. Praising both text and illustrations, *School Library Journal*

contributor Lisa S. Murphy commented that "Arnold's bold illustrations portray exuberant children, a big and beautiful Snowwoman, and the camaraderie of the forest animals with equal verve."

In addition to her career as a children's book author and illustrator, Arnold works as a teacher in Brooklyn, New York, where she shares her talents for painting and illustration with her students. She enjoys visiting schools to read her books, discuss Russian folklore, and explain how she creates her books.

Works Cited

Review of *Baba Yaga, Junior Bookshelf,* December, 1993, p. 224.

Review of *Baba Yaga, Publishers Weekly,* August 9, 1993, p. 478.

Review of *Duck, Duck, Goose?, Publishers Weekly,* May 5, 1997, p. 208.

Review of *Meow!, Kirkus Reviews,* April 1, 1998, p. 492.

Murphy, Lisa S., review of *The Adventures of Snowwoman, School Library Journal,* March, 1999, p. 162.

Norris, Christy, review of *Duck, Duck, Goose?, School Library Journal,* September, 1997, p. 172.

Publicity release, North-South Books, 1994.

Weisman, Kay, review of *Baba Yaga and the Little Girl, Booklist,* April 15, 1994, p. 1536.

Wright, Denise Anton, review of *Baba Yaga, School Library Journal,* January, 1994, p. 103.

For More Information See

PERIODICALS

Booklist, October 1, 1993, p. 347; April 1, 1994, p. 1563; April 15, 1998, p. 1449; December 1, 1998, p. 668.

Horn Book, September-October, 1997, p. 553.

Kirkus Reviews, November 1, 1998, p. 1596.

New York Times Book Review, March 13, 1994, p. 20; December 20, 1998, p. 24.

Publishers Weekly, April 13, 1998, p. 73; September 28, 1998, p. 57.

School Librarian, February, 1994, p. 15.

School Library Journal, August, 1994, p. 149; May, 1998, p. 106.

B

BARNARD, Bryn 1956-

Personal

Born February 2, 1956, in Los Angeles, CA; son of Ernest Raymond (an electrical engineer) and Elaine (an actress and playwright; maiden name, Elliott) Barnard; married Rebecca Parks, June 8, 1985; children: Wynn Adele, Parks Elliott. *Education:* University of California, Irvine, 1974-75; University Sains Malaysia, Penang, 1977; University of California, Berkeley, B.A. (Magna cum laude), 1979; Art Center College of Design, 1979-81.

Addresses

Home and office—417 Point Caution Drive, Friday Harbor, WA 98250-9222. *E-mail*—artists@rockisland. com.

Career

Children's book illustrator. University of Delaware, Newark, DE, assistant professor of art, 1991-95; University of the Arts, Philadelphia, PA, adjunct professor of illustration, 1994-96. Creative consultant for Matari Advertising, Jakarta; Citra: Lintas Advertising, Jakarta; SSC & B: Lintas Advertising, Kuala Lumpur; consulting associate, Universities Field Staff International. *Exhibitions:* Has had five solo shows and participated in more than fifty group exhibitions in the United States, Europe, and Asia; paintings are held in the permanent collections of the National Air and Space Museum in Washington, DC, Kennedy Space Center, Florida, Stennis Space Center, Mississippi, Jet Propulsion Laboratories, Pasadena, CA, and other private and corporate collections worldwide. *Member:* Society of Illustrators, Institute of Current World Affairs.

Awards, Honors

Crane-Rogers Foundation Fellowship, 1981-83; New Jersey State Arts Council Fellowship, 1992; Society of Illustrators, Los Angeles, Silver Medal, 1994; Fulbright Fellowship, 1999-2000.

Writings

ILLUSTRATOR

Harry Harrison, *Galactic Dreams* (short stories), Tor, 1994.

Victoria Crenson, *Bay Shore Park: The Death and Life of an Amusement Park,* W. H. Freeman (New York), 1995.

Mary Quattlebaum (reteller), *In the Beginning,* Time-Life for Children (Alexandria, VA), 1995.

Herman J. Viola, *North American Indians,* Crown (New York), 1996.

Lucille Recht Penner, *Westward Ho!: The Story of the Pioneers,* Random House, 1997.

Joyce Milton, *Gorillas: Gentle Giants of the Forest,* Random House (New York), 1997.

Melvin Berger, *Don't Believe It! Fibs and Facts about Animals,* Scholastic (New York), 1997.

Marjorie Cowley, *Anooka's Answer,* Clarion (New York), 1998.

Chris Eboch, *The Well of Sacrifice,* Clarion, 1999.

Lucille Recht Penner, *Big Birds,* Random House, 1999.

Monograph in *International Studio.*

Work in Progress

Illustrations for *Night of the Milky Way Railway,* by Miyazawa Kenji (Japanese fantasy classic); and author-illustrator of *The Driftwood Fence,* an ecological allegory.

Sidelights

Bryn Barnard told *SATA:* "Not many American illustrators start their art careers in Malaysia. Mine began there in 1973, when my polychrome dervish-as-spin-art act won the Johor Baru Mad Artist competition. Though I now live on an island in Puget Sound and have traded performance art antics for the illustrator's brush and mouse, my affection for Malaysia and the influence of that culture on my work remains undiminished. I have returned to the country again and again: in 1977-78 to study batik and perform with a shadow puppet theater troupe, in 1981-84 to investigate the art and ethos of intercultural advertising, and from November 1999 to February 2000, as a Fulbright fellow, to paint, draw, and lecture on illustration and design at the Universiti Sains Malaysia on the island of Penang.

"My mixed-media art incorporates acrylic, oil, transfer, and digital imagery and spans the range from magic realist landscapes, to scientific and historical tableaux, to children's book illustration. In my work for kids, my own children are my inspiration, models, and severest critics. If it passes muster with them, I know my work may have a chance in the wider world.

"Always based on observation, my style harkens to the work of the European academics. I worship at the shrines of the French painters Jean Leon Gerome and Alexandre Cabanel, the English neo-classicists Lawrence Alma-Tadema and J. W. Waterhouse, and the great Russian itinerants Vasily Vereshchagin, Ilya Repin, and Iwan Schischkin. One day, perhaps, I will be able to walk in their shadows."

Bryn Barnard has provided the illustrations for both fantasy-based children's novels and fact-based children's histories. In *Gorillas: Gentle Giants of the Forest,* author Joyce Milton provides information on where gorillas live, what they eat, how they care for their young, and profiles Dian Fossey, the most famous researcher and defender of these long-misunderstood animals. The result is a "fascinating introduction" to gorillas and their habitats, contended Hazel Rochman in *Booklist,* who dubbed Barnard's illustrations "dramatic and colorful." Barnard also contributed the illustrations to *Westward Ho!: The Story of the Pioneers,* a nonfiction treatment of the types of journeys made by early American settlers, written by Lucille Recht Penner. The author mixes generalized information with anecdotes about individual settlers, and "the plentiful illustrations lend an inviting air to the large pages," remarked Steven Engelfried in *School Library Journal.* For *Bay Shore Park: The Death and Life of an Amusement Park,* written by Victoria Crenson, Barnard's illustrations record the changes in the land over a period of nearly fifty years, when an amusement park in Maryland was first demolished by a steel company, which allowed no human visitors but left Mother Nature to run amok on the land, until it was purchased as public land and reclaimed for human use. *School Library Journal* reviewer Eva Elisabeth Von Ancken remarked, "Lush illustrations and text record the changes [to the land] over time," reminding readers of "the indomitable forces of nature."

Among Barnard's contributions to children's fiction may be included Marjorie Cowley's *Anooka's Answer,* a companion volume to the earlier, unillustrated *Dar and the Spear-Thrower.* These works are set in southern France during the Paleolithic era, some twelve thousand years ago; in *Anooka's Answer,* the author explores the quest for self-identity of twelve-year-old Anooka, whose mother left the clan years before to travel as a healer. "The addition of illustrations . . . will help youngsters understand a time period with which they have little familiarity," attested Jeanette Larson in *School Library Journal.* In Chris Eboch's *The Well of Sacrifice* Barnard contributed the illustrations to another highly regarded young adult novel featuring a coming-of-age crisis for a young girl on the verge of womanhood. In a story set among the ninth-century Mayans, Eveningstar Macaw saves the life of her hero-brother when the power-hungry high priest plans to send him and other contenders for the throne down into the Well of Sacrifice to either drown or be saved by the gods. This is "well-researched historical fiction and a good read," according to Cynthia M. Sturgis in *School Library Journal.* Barnard has also contributed the illustrations to *Galactic Dreams,* a collection of short stories by the popular humor writer for children Harry Harrison.

Works Cited

Engelfried, Steven, review of *Westward Ho!, School Library Journal,* March, 1998, p. 200.

Larson, Jeanette, review of *Anooka's Answer, School Library Journal,* December, 1998, p. 121.

Rochman, Hazel, review of *Gorillas, Booklist,* May 1, 1997, p. 1504.

Sturgis, Cynthia M., review of *The Well of Sacrifice, School Library Journal,* May, 1999, p. 122.

Von Ancken, Eva Elisabeth, review of *Bay Shore Park, School Library Journal,* August, 1995, p. 133.

For More Information See

PERIODICALS

Publishers Weekly, February 28, 1994, p. 76; March 29, 1999, p. 105.

* * *

BARR, Nevada 1952(?)-

Personal

Born c. 1952, in Nevada; daughter of a pilot and a pilot, mechanic, and carpenter; married (divorced). *Education:* California Politechnical University, B.A.; University of California, Irvine, M.A.

Addresses

Home—Mesa Verde National Park, CO, and Clinton, MS. *Agent*—c/o Putnam Publishing Group, 200 Madison Avenue, New York, NY 10016.

Career

Novelist and park ranger. Classic Stage Company, New York City, acted in off-Broadway shows; performed in television commercials and corporate and industrial films, Minneapolis, MN; United States National Park Service, law enforcement ranger in National Parks,

Tracy Barrett

Addresses

Home and office—2802 Acklen Ave., Nashville, TN 37212.

Career

Vanderbilt University, Nashville, TN, senior lecturer in Italian, 1984—. *Member:* Society of Children's Book Writers and Illustrators, The Authors Guild, Tennessee Writer's Alliance.

Writings

JUVENILE NONFICTION EXCEPT AS NOTED

Nat Turner and the Slave Revolt, Millbrook Press, 1993.
Harpers Ferry: The Story of John Brown's Raid, Millbrook Press, 1993.
Growing Up in Colonial America, Millbrook Press, 1995.
Virginia, Marshall Cavendish Corporation, 1997.
Tennessee, Marshall Cavendish Corporation, 1997.
Kidding around Nashville: What to Do, Where to Go, and How to Have Fun in Nashville, John Muir Publications, 1998.
Anna of Byzantium (fiction), Delacorte, 1999.
Kentucky, Benchmark Books, 1999.

OTHER

(Translator and author of introduction) *Cecco, as I Am and Was: The Poems of Cecco Angiolieri,* International Pocket Library, 1994.

Also author of five children's stories for the educational series "Reading Works," 1975. Editorial assistant, *Romance Philology,* 1978-79, and *Kidney International,* 1984.

Sidelights

Tracy Barrett told *SATA:* "I teach Italian language at a university and am the author of several scholarly articles on Italian literature as well as a forthcoming book of translations into English of a medieval Italian poet. I started writing for children in 1992 when I began feeling that my teaching was getting repetitious and I needed to branch out into different areas. As a child, I had always said I would be a writer when I grew up, but this ambition got lost in the shuffle of graduate school, marriage, and family. Perhaps because of my academic background, I am more drawn to nonfiction than to fiction when writing for children. I enjoy researching complicated and sometimes confusing events and organizing them into coherent and exciting narratives."

Barrett's efforts have resulted in two books about important events in American history. *Nat Turner and the Slave Revolt,* published as part of the "Gateway Civil Rights" series, tells the story of an African American slave and preacher who came to believe that God wanted him to free the slaves. Based on his visions, Turner led a group of slaves in a bloody revolt that took the lives of over 260 people. The book begins with Turner's court conviction in 1831, traces his upbringing and education, and concludes with the famous revolt. In a review for *Booklist,* Janice Del Negro praised Barrett's objectivity, stating that she "attempts to place the event in its historical context in a concise, noninflammatory text."

Barrett's next book was *Harpers Ferry: The Story of John Brown's Raid,* published as part of the "Spotlight on American History" series. The book profiles John Brown, an abolitionist who took weapons during a raid on the United States arsenal at Harpers Ferry, West Virginia, in 1859. Reviewing *Harpers Ferry* and several other books in the series for *School Library Journal,* George Gleason noted that they "cover their subjects well and occasionally include unusual tidbits of information."

Part of the "Celebrate the States" series from Benchmark Press, Barrett's *Virginia, Tennessee,* and *Kentucky* feature information on the geography, history, economy, and way of life in these states. Of special interest, according to Denise E. Agosto in *School Library Journal,* is a section called "state survey," in which famous people and popular tourist sites are discussed. The whole is "well-written," Agosto averred, and "will be useful for reports." In *Growing up in Colonial America,* Barrett covers aspects of the lives of the children of the European settlers in the American

ANNA of BYZANTIUM

TRACY BARRETT

Inspired by the story of the medieval princess, Barrett tells the gripping tale of Anna Comnena, who must wrestle control of the Byzantine kingdom from the hands of her younger brother and their conniving grandmother. (Cover illustration by David Bowers.)

colonies, carefully differentiating between her subject and the lives of Native American children and the children of slaves. In the first part of the book, the author details food, clothing, chores, education, and recreation among colonial children in Plymouth and in Chesapeake, two early settlements. In the second part, common childrearing practices of the day are recounted. Elaine Fort Weischedel in *School Library Journal* observed that similar books on children in the colonial era do not address the care of infants, as Barrett does. The section containing chapters on housing, attire, and recreation will be "of keenest interest to modern readers," according to Susan Dove Lempke in *Booklist*, but added that the whole "makes a good choice for reports or pleasure reading."

Barrett shared her thoughts on writing nonfiction for children with *SATA*: "When writing nonfiction, an author must pay scrupulous attention to accuracy and must present a balanced view. Children are interested in the truth and are willing to think about quite 'adult' issues if they are presented in a way accessible to them.

This does not mean talking down to children; it means keeping in mind their more limited exposure to ideas and helping them learn how to formulate their own ideas and opinions."

In 1999, Barrett tried her hand at fiction, publishing *Anna of Byzantium,* a historical novel centered on the real-life twelfth-century princess Anna Commena. In a first-person narrative, Barrett details the claustrophobic circumstances of seventeen-year-old Anna, who has been exiled to a convent for plotting to overthrow her brother. From there, Barrett uses flashbacks to detail Anna's earlier life as the chosen successor for her father the king, her education and upbringing, and her cruel fall from favor at the birth of a brother. "Barrett uses an effective first-person narrative to draw readers into Anna's story," remarked Ilene Cooper in *Booklist*. Cooper also praised Barrett's use of detail in making Anna's world real to the reader. The book traces Anna's transformation from beloved child to pawn in her grandmother's power schemes to outcast and eventually to scholar. Reviewers highlighted the fact that the crucial Byzantium empire is rarely treated in juvenile novels. And though Barrett's treatment of Anna's brother in particular contradicts the historical record, *Anna of Byzantium* succeeds as "a plausible character study of a brilliant and tempestuous young woman," according to Shirley Wilton in *School Library Journal.*

Works Cited

Agosto, Denise E., review of *Virginia, School Library Journal,* June, 1997, p. 130.

Review of *Anna of Byzantium, Publishers Weekly,* June 28, 1999, p. 80.

Cooper, Ilene, review of *Anna of Byzantium, Booklist,* April 1, 1999, p. 1425.

Del Negro, Janice, review of *Nat Turner and the Slave Revolt, Booklist,* August, 1993, pp. 2051-52.

Gleason, George, review of *Harpers Ferry: The Story of John Brown's Raid, School Library Journal,* January, 1994, p. 118.

Hearne, Betsy, review of *Nat Turner and the Slave Revolt, Bulletin of the Center for Children's Books,* April, 1993, p. 240.

Lempke, Susan Dove, review of *Growing up in Colonial America, Booklist,* December 15, 1995, p. 700.

Weischedel, Elaine Fort, review of *Growing up in Colonial America, School Library Journal,* December, 1995, p. 112.

Wilton, Shirley, review of *Anna of Byzantium, School Library Journal,* July, 1999, p. 92.

For More Information See

PERIODICALS

Horn Book Guide, spring 1994, pp. 156, 169.

BRACKERS de HUGO, Pierre 1960-
(Pierre de Hugo)

Personal

Born April 20, 1960, in Boulogne-Billancourt, France; son of Gerard and Marie-France (Loubiere) Brackers de Hugo; married, wife's name Louana, April 7, 1990; children: Ava, Astrelle, Adeea. *Education:* Attended a school of fine arts, Paris, 1980.

Addresses

Home—Le Moon Light, 17 blvd. Carnot, 06300 Nice, France. *Office*—c/o Gallimard Jeunesse, 5 Rue Sebastien Bottin, 75007 Paris, France. *E-mail*—pierre_de_hugo@wanadoo.fr.

Career

Illustrator.

Writings

AUTHOR AND ILLUSTRATOR, UNDER NAME PIERRE de HUGO

Les Bestioles de la Maison, Gallimard Jeunesse, 1996.
L'Ecureuil, Gallimard Jeunesse, 1998.
Le Kangourou, Gallimard Jeunesse, 1999.

It is also possible to stay under the sea in a research submarine, an underwater ship built for deep water.

Pierre Brackers de Hugo provided the illustrations for **Under the Sea,** *which helps young readers explore the wonders of the sea with the use of a paper flashlight. (Written by Claude Delafosse.)*

Le Lion, Gallimard Jeunesse, 1999, translation published as *Lions,* Scholastic Inc. (New York City), 2000.
Le Lapin, Gallimard Jeunesse, 2000.

ILLUSTRATOR, UNDER NAME PIERRE de HUGO

Les Felins, Larousse, 1986.
Quand les Animaux se degui sent, Gallimard, 1987.
(With Paul Bontemps) Diane Costa de Beauregard, *Des Animaux en Danger,* Gallimard, 1988, translation published as *Wildlife Alert!,* London Moonlight (London, England), 1989, published as *Animals in Jeopardy,* translated by Vicki Bogard, Young Discovery Library (Ossining, NY), 1991.
Elisabeth Cohat, *Le Bord de Mer,* Gallimard Jeunesse, 1990, translation published as *The Seashore,* London Moonlight, 1991, Scholastic Inc., 1995.
Vijay Singh, *The River Goddess,* London Moonlight, 1994, Creative Education (Mankato, MN), 1997.
Les Poissons, Gallimard Jeunesse, 1997.
Claude Delafosse, *Hidden World: Under the Sea,* Scholastic Inc., 1999.
Qui s'y Frotte, Gallimard Bayer, 1999.

Contributor of illustrations to children's dictionaries published in France. Books have been translated for publication in Taiwan, Italy, Malaysia, India, Spain, Japan, Greece, Croatia, the Netherlands, Germany, England, Turkey, and the United States.

Sidelights

Pierre Brackers de Hugo told *SATA:* "I have always been fascinated by the animal world, so drawing animals and nature scenes makes me feel like I am 'catching' for a moment their incredibly beautiful and so surprisingly various lights and colors. I like the precision in my work. I do a lot of research in the country, in museums, and I consult zoologists and scientists. Every new book is a fulfilling challenge, involving new research, new ideas, and a new way of keeping eyes and mind wide open.

"For a break, as a hobby I restore military objects, dating from the Napoleonic era, for collectors and museums, and I enjoy researching the ancient manufacturing techniques."

For More Information See

PERIODICALS

School Library Journal, September, 1995, p. 192.

* * *

BURNARD, Damon 1963-

Personal

Born May 31, 1963, in East Sussex, England. *Education:* Bath Academy of Art, B.F.A. (honors, in painting); attended graduate classes at Massachusetts College of Art, c. 2000.

Addresses

Office—c/o Houghton Mifflin Co., 215 Park Ave. S., New York, NY 10003. *E-mail*—damon.burnard@ gte.net.

Career

Writer and illustrator. Teacher in an after school program 1997-99; illustrator and cartoonist for newspapers and periodicals.

Writings

AUTHOR AND ILLUSTRATOR, EXCEPT AS NOTED

(Co-illustrator) Kenneth McLeish and Valerie McLeish, *Famous People*, Troll Associates, 1991.
Ernest the Heroic Lion-tamer, HarperCollins, 1993.
Revenge of the Killer Vegetables, Andersen Press, 1994.
Ivana the Inventor, HarperCollins, 1995.
Bullysaurus, Hodder & Stoughton, 1996.
Bullysaurus the Gladiator, Hodder & Stoughton, 1997.
The Amazing Adventures of Soupy Boy!, Houghton Mifflin, 1998.
Zebedee Zing, Taster to the King, HarperCollins, 1998.
Burger!, Houghton Mifflin, 1998.
Pork and Beef's Great Adventure, Houghton Mifflin, 1998.
Bullysaurus and the Alien, Hodder & Stoughton, 1999.
Bullysaurus under the Sea, Hodder & Stoughton, 2000.

Damon Burnard

Sidelights

Illustrator and cartoonist Damon Burnard has parlayed a job as a teacher at an after school program in his native England into a career as an author and illustrator of humorous, off-beat, graphic novels for the younger set. Critic Steve Rosson of *Books for Keeps* reviewed Burnard's second book, *Revenge of the Killer Vegetables,* with the warning "this is very, very silly indeed." Burnard has received similar reactions from other critics for titles such as *The Amazing Adventures of Soupy Boy!, Zebedee Zing, Taster to the King, Burger!,* and *Pork and Beef's Great Adventure.* He has also begun a multi-volume series about the adventures of Bullysaurus, whose extremely silly exploits are chronicled in *Bullysaurus, Bullysaurus the Gladiator, Bullysaurus and the Alien* and *Bullysaurus under the Sea.*

The Amazing Adventures of Soupy Boy! was Burnard's 1998 contribution to children's literature. In keeping with Burnard's preoccupation with comestibles, *Soupy Boy* focuses on a child named Ashley Fugg, whose childhood mishap—he fell into a vat of radioactive tomato juice—caused him to develop special powers that turn him into a large, crime-fighting soup can. In this wacky whodunit, an evildoer has kidnapped children's book author Kenneth Tepid, and Burnard weaves together elements that *Booklist* contributor John Peters characterized as "clues of varying quality, smart-aleck comments, and silly plot twists" to create a book designed to appeal to comic-book fans.

Burger! also has a comic-book format. In it a spaceman named Jeff lands on Earth with a mission. As chef for a powerful space alien master named Gluttor, Jeff must find a new recipe to please his master's demanding palate. Viewing Earth only as a planet of new (edible) animals, Jeff decides to fatten up a flock of humans by giving away free hamburgers, then boiling the plumpest human in oil for use as the main ingredient in a variation of "Forked Beast Burger." Fortunately, the efforts of an ardent vegetarian named Clementine Smith save mankind, and Jeff is convinced to concoct a vegetarian meal that pleases the finicky Gluttor. "With childlike humor, the comic-book format is right on target for beginning chapter-book and reluctant readers," commented Shawn Brommer in a *School Library Journal* appraisal of *Burger!* Praising Burnard for his sketchy inked cartoons, a *Publishers Weekly* reviewer felt compelled to warn readers to "expect kid-pleasing humor about extraterrestrial maggots, drooling gluttony and, yes, underwear."

Burnard's *Pork and Beef's Great Adventure* is also filled with action and whimsy, featuring illustrations that a *Publishers Weekly* contributor characterized as "bright as a crayon box." Pork is a pig, and Beef, of course, is a cow, and the two barnyard friends decide to go exploring. Setting their sights high, the duo decide to fly to the moon ... but how to go about it? Feathers and frosting figure prominently in their solution to the transportation dilemma, in a bit of fluff that *Booklist* reviewer Ilene Cooper characterized as "wonderfully silly" and "lots of fun ... for chapter-book readers."

Transformed by an accident at the Gloop Soup Factory, Ashley Fugg uses his new powers to become Soupy Boy, crime fighter extraordinaire. (Cover illustration by Burnard.)

While his stories may seem to go straight to readers' funny bones, Burnard views the craft of writing and illustrating children's books seriously. "My books are generally aimed at six- to ten-year olds," he explained to *SATA,* "and I aspire to entertain and to instill a joy of books and reading. I integrate words and pictures—not unlike a comic book—to lend pace, humor, and accessibility to my tales. However, the messages behind my stories are sophisticated and thoughtful, and are often concerned with problem-solving and conflict resolution. I am fascinated by the language and universality of fairy tales, and in stories that externalize internal processes of conflict and transformation."

Works Cited

Review of *The Amazing Adventures of Soupy Boy!; Burger!, Publishers Weekly,* October 19, 1998, p. 81.

Brommer, Shawn, review of *Burger!, School Library Journal,* December, 1998, p. 81.

Cooper, Ilene, review of *Pork and Beef's Great Adventure, Booklist,* March 1, 1998, p. 134.

Peters, John, review of *The Amazing Adventures of Soupy Boy!, Booklist,* January 1, 1999, p. 862.

Review of *Pork and Beef's Great Adventure, Publishers Weekly,* March 23, 1998, p. 99.

Rosson, Steve, review of *Revenge of the Vegetables, Books for Keeps,* March, 1995, p. 8.

For More Information See

PERIODICALS

Kirkus Reviews, October 1, 1998, p. 1455.
Magpies, July, 1996, p. 28.
School Librarian, May, 1995, p. 62.
School Library Journal, April, 1998, p. 91; January, 1999, p. 79.*

C

CAPUCILLI, Alyssa Satin 1957-

Personal

Born November 2, 1957, in Brooklyn, NY; married Bill Capucilli (a film set constructor); children: Peter, Laura. *Education:* Sarah Lawrence College, B.A.

Addresses

Home—29 Windsor Rd., Hastings-on-Hudson, NY 10706. *Agent*—Liza Voges, Kirchoff/Wohlberg, 866 U.N. Plaza, New York, NY 10017. *E-mail*— acapucilli@aol.com.

Career

Dancer, teacher, and author. Modern dancer, teacher, and performer, 1989—. Currently teaches creative movement for young children. *Member:* Society of Children's Book Writers & Illustrators.

Awards, Honors

American Booksellers Association Pick of the Lists designations: 1994, for *Good Morning, Pond;* 1996, for *Biscuit;* 1997, for *Bathtime for Biscuit.*

Writings

Peekaboo Bunny, illustrated by Mary Melcher, Scholastic, Inc. 1994.
Peekaboo Bunny Friends in the Snow, Scholastic, Inc., 1995.
Inside a Barn in the Country: A Rebus Read-along Story, illustrated by Tedd Arnold, Scholastic, Inc., 1995.
Good Morning, Pond, illustrated by Cynthia Jabar, Hyperion, 1994.
Wee Mouse Christmas, illustrated by Linda Birkinshaw, Random House, 1995.
Biscuit, illustrated by Pat Schories, HarperCollins, 1996.
Biscuit Finds a Friend, illustrated by Schories, HarperCollins, 1997.
Bathtime for Biscuit, illustrated by Schories, HarperCollins, 1997.
Hello, Biscuit!, illustrated by Schories, HarperCollins, 1998.
Biscuit's Picnic, illustrated by Schories, HarperCollins, 1998.
Happy Birthday, Biscuit!, illustrated by Schories, Harper-Collins, 1998.
Inside a House That Is Haunted: A Rebus Read-along Story, illustrated by Arnold, Scholastic, Inc., 1998.
(With Iris Hiskey Arno) *Wake up, Night,* Kidsbooks 1998.
Biscuit's New Trick, illustrated by Schories, HarperCollins, 2000.
Happy Easter, Biscuit!, illustrated by Schories, HarperCollins, 2000.
Happy Valentine's Day, Biscuit!, illustrated by Schories, HarperCollins, 2000.
Inside a Zoo in the City: A Rebus Read-along Story, illustrated by Arnold, Scholastic, Inc., 2000.
The Potty Book, illustrated by Dorothy Stott, Barron's Educational, 2000.
Mrs. McTats, illustrated by Joan Rankin, Margaret K. McElderry, 2000.

Capucilli's books have been translated into French, Hebrew, Afrikaans, Bulgarian, and Greek.

Sidelights

Alyssa Satin Capucilli is the imaginative author of books for both pre-schoolers and beginning readers. Her creations include lift-the-flap books for toddlers, featuring gentle, lovable characters and easily identifiable objects, and a series of beginning readers featuring Biscuit, the rambunctious golden-haired puppy.

Born in Brooklyn, New York, in 1957, Capucilli developed an early love of books, and looked forward to weekly trips to the library with her mother and sisters. "I could hardly wait to choose a special book from all of the books that lined the shelves," Capucilli recalled to *SATA.* "As a matter of fact, my sisters and I would often play library at home! We would take turns pretending to be the librarian, and we would recommend books to each other, check them out, and tell each other to 'SSSSHHH!'" Among Capucilli's favorite authors were Louisa May Alcott, author of *Little Women,* and Beverly Cleary, whose stories about Henry and his dog, Ribsy, she loved. "The funny thing was, although I loved to imagine myself as different characters in books," Capucilli added, "I never imagined that the authors who created them were real people!"

Although as a child she wrote many stories, poems, and puppet shows, Capucilli never took her writing seriously until many years later. In the meantime, she focused on her love of dance, a method, she explained, of "telling stories in another way." She became a professional dancer and soon was teaching as well as performing on stage. While reading to her own two children, her love-affair with children's books was rekindled,, and she began to split her time between work as a dance instructor and performer and work as a writer.

Capucilli's first published book was *Peekaboo Bunny,* a lift-the-flap book published in 1994. Illustrated by Mary Melcher, the book helps small children navigate in a garden, and it was popular enough to prompt a sequel, *Peekaboo Bunny Friends in the Snow.* The connection between objects and sounds has inspired several of Capucilli's books, including *Good Morning, Pond,* which uses repetition and rhythm to teach the names of pond-dwelling creatures, and books that tell stories using rebuses, pictures of items that, when sounded out in order, make words. One such, *Inside a Barn in the Country,* illustrated by Tedd Arnold, encourages young listeners to mimic barnyard noises and uses rebuses for the text. *Booklist* reviewer Stephanie Zvirin praised Capucilli's thoughtfully designed text as "part poetry, part puzzle game, and part tool for learning the sounds animals make." Noting that the text models itself after the familiar "This Is the House That Jack Built," a *Publishers Weekly* contributor said that "Capucilli and Arnold give their work plenty of extra bounce."

Capucilli introduced a new character to young readers in *Biscuit.* A small, soft-eared, lovable puppy the color of freshly baked, golden biscuits, Capucilli's Biscuit bounds into the life of a young girl, quickly becoming her best friend as she interprets his "Woof, Woof" to mean many things. From wanting a small snack before bedtime to being tucked in snugly under layers of blankets, the activities of Biscuit and his young owner are depicted in "oodles of contextual clues," easy-to-read sentences, and "repetitive words and phrases," according to *School Library Journal* reviewer Gale W. Sherman. Equally enthusiastic, *Booklist* contributor Ilene Cooper deemed Capucilli's story a "sweet entry to reading."

Novice readers have encountered Biscuit's "Woof, Woof" in several other books, among them *Biscuit Finds a Friend, Happy Birthday, Biscuit!,* and *Bathtime for Biscuit.* Illustrated by Pat Schories, the series has become so popular with readers that a stuffed toy puppy resembling the floppy-eared canine has become avail-able. In *Biscuit Finds a Friend,* the puppy noses a small duckling out from under the porch of his family's house, and the two become fast friends. Cooper deemed the story "just right" for beginning readers. In *Bathtime for Biscuit* the task of getting the pup into hot water is made easier through a variety of antics, and Capucilli tells her story in a way that "makes this a good choice for the youngest readers and listeners alike," in the opinion of *School Library Journal* contributor Sharon R. Pearce. Biscuit celebrates his first birthday with his many new friends in *Happy Birthday, Biscuit!,* offering equal appeal to "librarians who find it difficult to sustain a squirmy toddler's interest," according to Lauren Peterson's *Booklist* appraisal.

"I find that inspiration for stories and characters comes from so many places: our memories, our family, our friends, our pets, our own observations and our own wonderings," Capucilli explained. "I first got the idea to write about ... Biscuit after watching my daughter dog-sit a neighbor's huge golden retriever! But deep inside, I think that the *Biscuit* stories are really about that puppy I always imagined I would someday have, from when I was a young girl, reading and dreaming. And sometimes in stories, as in real life, dreams do come true! I finally got my puppy after all! He is a sweet and lovable chocolate Labrador retriever that my children named ... Huckleberry! Huck, as we like to call him, loves to dig in the mud, splash in the pond, play with friends *and* take bubble baths! But most of all, he likes to curl up next to me on our big pink couch when I am working, and that is just fine with me!"

Works Cited

Cooper, Ilene, review of *Biscuit, Booklist,* August, 1996, p. 1910.

Cooper, Ilene, review of *Biscuit Finds a Friend, Booklist,* May 1, 1997, p. 1503.

Review of *Inside a Barn in the Country, Publishers Weekly,* March 27, 1995, p. 84.

Pearce, Sharon R., review of *Bathtime for Biscuit, School Library Journal,* October, 1998, p. 87.

Peterson, Lauren, review of *Happy Birthday, Biscuit!, Booklist,* June 1, 1999, p. 1838.

Sherman, Gale W., review of *Biscuit, School Library Journal,* July, 1996, p. 57.

Zvirin, Stephanie, review of *Inside a Barn in the Country, Booklist,* January 15, 1995, p. 935.

For More Information See

PERIODICALS

Booklist, November 1, 1998, p. 506.
Publishers Weekly, January 3, 1994, p. 82.
School Library Journal, November, 1994, pp. 72-73; April, 1995, p. 98; June, 1997, p. 85; September, 1998, p. 165; June, 1999, p. 91.*

CASSON, Hugh Maxwell 1910-1999

OBITUARY NOTICE—See index for *SATA* sketch: Born May 23, 1910, in Hampstead, London, England; died August 15, 1999, in London, England. Architect, artist and journalist. Casson was an architect by trade but dabbled in other artistic endeavors, painting with watercolors and pen and wash techniques. As a result, he served as Prince Charles's painting mentor. In addition to his work as an architect and designer, Casson wrote and illustrated a number of books about architecture, and illustrated children's picture books as well. Casson was rather sickly as a child but made friends easily due to his clever wit. He attended boarding school near Canterbury and then Eastbourne College in Sussex before enrolling in Cambridge, from whose School of Architecture he graduated. He followed that with a Craven fellowship for a year of postgraduate study at the British School in Athens. Casson started an architecture firm with one of his former teachers, Christopher Nicholson, in 1937, and stayed there until 1940, when he became a camouflage officer with the Air Ministry during World War II. After the war Casson joined the Ministry of Town and Country Planning, but moved back to his private practice in 1948. That firm, Casson, Conder & Partners, designed several popular buildings including the Ismaili Centre across from the Victoria and Albert Museum, and buildings at Belfast and Birmingham universities. While maintaining a private practice Casson joined the staff of the Royal College of Art in 1953 and assumed leadership of the architecture department, changing its focus to interior design. Casson stayed at the college for more than twenty years. He actively participated in the Festival of Britain and took townscaping to a new level through his work there, serving as architectural adviser in both Bath and Brighton. He was knighted in 1952 and became a favorite designer of the royal family by 1953, when he designed the street decorations for Queen Elizabeth's coronation and refurbished several rooms at two of her homes. He had a number of important commissions during his career but also found time to write and illustrate many architecture books, including *Bombed Churches, An Introduction to Victorian Architecture,* and *Hugh Casson's London.* Casson also illustrated several children's books, including *The Pillow-Book Puzzles, Pushkin the Polar Bear,* and *Buttons.* In 1976 he was named president of the Royal Academy, whose fortunes improved greatly under Casson's strong fund-raising skills. He took up painting later in life and had several exhibitions of his artistic works in the 1980s. Prince Charles wrote the introduction for a collection of Casson's watercolors exhibited at Hampton Court Palace in 1998. In addition to the voluminous works he wrote, illustrated or edited, Casson also contributed articles to various architecture magazines and to *The Observer.*

OBITUARIES AND OTHER SOURCES:

BOOKS

Contemporary Designers, third edition, St. James Press, 1997.

PERIODICALS

Chicago Tribune, August 17, 1999, sec. 2, p. 9.
New York Times, August 19, 1999, p. B8.
Times (London; electronic), August 17, 1999.

* * *

CLARKE, Arthur C(harles) 1917-

Personal

Born December 16, 1917, in Minehead, Somersetshire, England; son of Charles Wright (a farmer) and Nora (Willis) Clarke; married Marilyn Mayfield, June 15, 1953 (divorced, 1964). *Education:* King's College, University of London, B.Sc. (first class honors), 1948. *Hobbies and other interests:* "Observing the equatorial skies with a fourteen-inch telescope," table-tennis, scuba diving, and "playing with his Rhodesian Ridgeback and his six computers."

Addresses

Agents—Scott Meredith Literary Agency, Inc., 845 Third Ave., New York, NY 10022; David Higham Associates, 5-8 Lower John St., Golden Square, London W1R 4HA, England.

Career

British Civil Service, His Majesty's Exchequer and Audit Department, London, England, auditor, 1936-41; Institution of Electrical Engineers, *Science Abstracts,* London, assistant editor, 1949-50; freelance writer, 1951—. Underwater explorer and photographer, in partnership with Mike Wilson, on Great Barrier Reef of Australia and coast of Sri Lanka, 1954-64. Has appeared on television and radio numerous times, including as commentator with Walter Cronkite on *Apollo* missions, CBS-TV, 1968-70, and as host of television series *Arthur C. Clarke's Mysterious World,* 1980, and *Arthur C. Clarke's World of Strange Powers,* 1984. Acted role of Leonard Woolf in Lester James Peries's film *Beddagama* (based on Woolf's *The Village in the Jungle*), 1979.

Director of Rocket Publishing Co., United Kingdom; founder, director, and owner, with Hector Ekanayake, of Underwater Safaris (a scuba-diving business), Sri Lanka; founder and patron, Arthur C. Clarke Centre for Modern Technologies, Sri Lanka, 1984—. Chancellor of University of Moratuwa, Sri Lanka, 1979—; Vikram Sarabhai Professor, Physical Research Laboratory, Ahmedabad, India, 1980; trustee, Institute of Integral Education, Sri Lanka. Fellow, Franklin Institute, 1971, King's College, 1977, and Institute of Robotics, Carnegie-Mellon University, 1981. Lecturer, touring United States and Britain, 1957-74. Board member of National Space Institute, United States, Space Generation Foundation, United States, International Astronomical Union (Search for ExtraTerrestrial Intelligence) Commission 51, International Space University, Institute of Fundamental

Arthur C. Clarke

Studies, Sri Lanka, and Planetary Society, United States. Chairperson, Second International Astronautics Congress, London, 1951; moderator, "Space Flight Report to the Nation," New York, 1961. *Military service:* Royal Air Force, radar instructor, 1941-46; became flight lieutenant. *Member:* International Academy of Astronautics (honorary fellow), International Science Writers Association, International Council for Integrative Studies, World Academy of Art and Science (academician), British Interplanetary Society (honorary fellow; chairperson, 1946-47, 1950-53), Royal Astronomical Society (fellow), British Astronomical Association, Association of British Science Writers (life member), British Science Fiction Association (patron), Royal Society of Arts (fellow), Society of Authors (council member), American Institute of Aeronautics and Astronautics (honorary fellow), American Astronautical Society (honorary fellow), American Association for the Advancement of Science, National Academy of Engineering (United States; foreign associate), Science Fiction Writers of America, Science Fiction Foundation, H. G. Wells Society (honorary vice president), Third World Academy of Sciences (associate fellow), Sri Lanka Astronomical Society (patron), Institute of Engineers (Sri Lanka; honorary fellow), Sri Lanka Animal Welfare Association (patron), British Sub-Aqua Club.

Awards, Honors

International Fantasy Award, 1952, for *The Exploration of Space;* Hugo Award, World Science Fiction Convention, 1956, for "The Star"; Kalinga Prize, UNESCO, 1961, for science writing; Junior Book Award, Boy's Club of America, 1961; Stuart Ballantine Gold Medal, Franklin Institute, 1963, for originating concept of communications satellites; Robert Ball Award, Aviation-Space Writers Association, 1965, for best aerospace reporting of the year in any medium; Westinghouse Science Writing Award, American Association for the Advancement of Science, 1969; Second International Film Festival special award, and Academy Award nomination for best screenplay with Stanley Kubrick, Academy of Motion Picture Arts and Sciences, both 1969, both for *2001: A Space Odyssey; Playboy* editorial award, 1971, 1982; D.Sc., Beaver College, 1971, and University of Moratuwa, 1979; Nebula Award, Science Fiction Writers of America, 1972, for "A Meeting with Medusa"; Nebula Award, 1973, Hugo Award, 1974, John W. Campbell Memorial Award, Science Fiction Research Association, 1974, and Jupiter Award, Instructors of Science Fiction in Higher Education, 1974, all for *Rendezvous with Rama;* Aerospace Communications Award, American Institute of Aeronautics and Astronautics, 1974; Bradford Washburn Award, Boston Museum of Science, 1977, for "contributions to the public understanding of science"; GALAXY Award, 1979; Nebula and Hugo Awards, both 1980, both for *The Fountains of Paradise;* special Emmy Award for engineering, National Academy of Television Arts and Sciences, 1981, for contributions to satellite broadcasting; "Lensman" Award, 1982; Marconi International Fellowship, 1982; Centennial Medal, Institute of Electrical and Electronics Engineers, 1984; E. M. Emme Astronautical Literature Award, American Astronautical Society, 1984; Grand Master Award, Science Fiction Writers of America, 1986; Vidya Jyoti Medal (Presidential Science Award), 1986; Charles A. Lindbergh Award, 1987; named to Society of Satellite Professionals Hall of Fame, 1987; named to Aerospace Hall of Fame, 1988; Special Achievement Award, Space Explorers Association, 1989; Lord Perry Award, 1992; Nobel peace prize nomination, 1994; Distinguished Public Service Medal, NASA, 1995; Space Achievement Medal and Trophy, BIS, 1995; Mohamed Sabeen Award for Science, 1996; Von Karman Award, IAA, 1996. D. Sc., Beaver College, 1971, and University of Moratuwa, 1979; D.Litt., University of Bath, 1988.

Writings

NONFICTION

Interplanetary Flight: An Introduction to Astronautics, Temple, 1950, Harper (New York City), 1951, 2nd edition, 1960.

The Exploration of Space (U.S. Book-of-the-Month Club selection), Harper, 1951, revised edition, Pocket Books, 1979.

The Young Traveller in Space, Phoenix, 1953, published as *Going into Space,* Harper, 1954, revised edition (with

Robert Silverberg) published as *Into Space: A Young Person's Guide to Space,* Harper, 1971.

The Exploration of the Moon, illustrated by R. A. Smith, Harper, 1954.

The Coast of Coral, Harper, 1956.

The Reefs of Taprobane: Underwater Adventures around Ceylon, Harper, 1957.

The Scottie Book of Space Travel, Transworld Publishers, 1957.

The Making of a Moon: The Story of the Earth Satellite Program, Harper, 1957, revised edition, 1958.

Voice across the Sea, Harper, 1958, revised edition, 1974.

(With Mike Wilson) *Boy beneath the Sea,* Harper, 1958.

The Challenge of the Spaceship: Previews of Tomorrow's World, Harper, 1959.

(With Wilson) *The First Five Fathoms: A Guide to Underwater Adventure,* Harper, 1960.

The Challenge of the Sea, Holt, 1960.

(With Wilson) *Indian Ocean Adventure,* Harper, 1961.

Profiles of the Future: An Inquiry into the Limits of the Possible, Harper, 1962, revised edition, Holt, 1984.

The Treasure of the Great Reef, Harper, 1964, new edition, Ballantine, 1974.

(With Wilson) *Indian Ocean Treasure,* Harper, 1964.

(With the editors of *Life*) *Man and Space,* Time-Life, 1964.

Voices from the Sky: Previews of the Coming Space Age, Harper, 1965.

(Editor) *The Coming of the Space Age: Famous Accounts of Man's Probing of the Universe,* Meredith, 1967.

The Promise of Space, Harper, 1968.

(With Neil Armstrong, Michael Collins, Edwin E. Aldrin, Jr., Gene Farmer, and Dora Jane Hamblin) *First on the Moon,* Little, Brown, 1970.

Report on Planet Three and Other Speculations, Harper, 1972.

(With Chesley Bonestell) *Beyond Jupiter,* Little, Brown, 1972.

The View from Serendip (autobiography), Random House, 1977.

Arthur C. Clarke's Mysterious World (also see below; television series), Yorkshire Television, 1980.

(With Simon Welfare and John Fairley) *Arthur C. Clarke's Mysterious World* (based on television series), A & W Publishers, 1980.

Ascent to Orbit, a Scientific Autobiography: The Technical Writings of Arthur C. Clarke, Wiley, 1984.

1984: Spring—A Choice of Futures, Del Rey, 1984.

(With Welfare and Fairley) *Arthur C. Clarke's World of Strange Powers* (also see below; based on television series of same title), Putnam, 1984.

(With Peter Hyams) *The Odyssey File,* Fawcett (New York City), 1985.

Arthur C. Clarke's July 20, 2019: Life in the 21st Century, Macmillan, 1986.

Arthur C. Clarke's Chronicles of the Strange and Mysterious, edited by Welfare and Fairley, Collins, 1987.

Astounding Days: A Science Fictional Autobiography, Bantam, 1989.

How the World Was One: Beyond the Global Village, Bantam, 1992.

By Space Possessed, Gollancz (London), 1993.

The Snows of Olympus: A Garden on Mars, Norton, 1995.

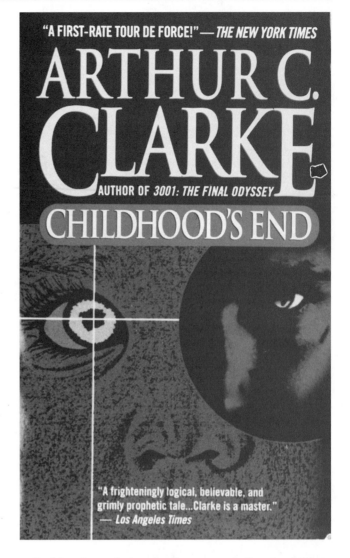

In this science-fiction classic, a race of alien Overlords brings about a golden age for mankind, but with terrible consequences. (Cover photo by Phil Heffernan.)

Front Line of Discovery, National Geographic Society, 1995.

Rogue Asteroids and Doomsday Comets, Wiley, 1997.

Arthur C. Clarke & Lord Dunsany: A Correspondence, Anamnesis Press, 1998.

(Co-editor with Ian MacAuley) *Greetings Carbon-Based Bipeds!,* St. Martin's Press, 1999.

Also author of introduction to *Inmarsat History.* Contributor to books, including *Mars and the Mind of Man,* Harper, 1973; *Frontline of Discovery: Science on the Brink of Tomorrow,* National Geographic Society, 1994; and *The Case for Mars,* Simon & Schuster, 1997.

FICTION

The Sands of Mars (also see below), Sidgwick & Jackson, 1951.

Prelude to Space (also see below), World Editions, 1951, published as *Master of Space,* Lancer Books, 1961, published as *The Space Dreamers,* Lancer Books, 1969.

Islands in the Sky, Winston, 1952, new edition, Penguin Books, 1972.

Childhood's End (also see below), Ballantine, 1953.

Against the Fall of Night (also see below), Gnome Press, 1953.

Expedition to Earth (also see below; short stories), Ballantine, 1953.

Earthlight (also see below), Ballantine, 1955.

Reach for Tomorrow (short stories), Ballantine, 1956.

The City and the Stars (also see below; based on novel *Against the Fall of Night*), Harcourt, 1956, new edition, Yestermorrow, 1999.

The Deep Range (also see below), Harcourt, 1957.

Tales from the White Hart, Ballantine, 1957.

The Other Side of the Sky (short stories), Harcourt, 1958.

Across the Sea of Stars (anthology; includes *Childhood's End* and *Earthlight*), Harcourt, 1959.

A Fall of Moondust (also see below), Harcourt, 1961, abridged edition, University of London Press, 1964.

From the Oceans, from the Stars (anthology; includes *The Deep Range* and *The City and the Stars*), Harcourt, 1962.

Tales of Ten Worlds (short stories), Harcourt, 1962.

Dolphin Island: A Story of the People of the Sea, Holt, 1963.

Glide Path, Harcourt, 1963.

Prelude to Mars (anthology; includes *Prelude to Space* and *The Sands of Mars*), Harcourt, 1965.

An Arthur C. Clarke Omnibus (contains *Childhood's End, Prelude to Space,* and *Expedition to Earth*), Sidgwick & Jackson, 1965.

(Editor) *Time Probe: The Science in Science Fiction,* Dial (New York City), 1966.

The Nine Billion Names of God (short stories), Harcourt, 1967.

A Second Arthur C. Clarke Omnibus (contains *A Fall of Moondust, Earthlight,* and *The Sands of Mars*), Sidgwick & Jackson, 1968.

(With Stanley Kubrick) *2001: A Space Odyssey* (screenplay; also see below), Metro-Goldwyn-Mayer, 1968.

2001: A Space Odyssey (novelization of screenplay), New American Library, 1968, published with a new introduction by Clarke, ROC (New York City), 1994.

The Lion of Comarre, Harcourt, 1968.

Against the Fall of Night, Harcourt, 1968.

The Lost Worlds of 2001, New American Library, 1972.

The Wind from the Sun (short stories), Harcourt, 1972.

(Editor) *Three for Tomorrow,* Sphere Books, 1972.

Of Time and Stars: The Worlds of Arthur C. Clarke (short stories), Gollancz, 1972.

Rendezvous with Rama (also see below), Harcourt, 1973, adapted edition, Oxford University Press, 1979.

The Best of Arthur C. Clarke, edited by Angus Wells, Sidgwick & Jackson, 1973, published as two volumes, Volume 1: *The Best of Arthur C. Clarke: 1937-1955,* Volume 2: *The Best of Arthur C. Clarke: 1956-1972,* 1977.

Imperial Earth: A Fantasy of Love and Discord, Gollancz, 1975, Harcourt, 1976.

Four Great Science Fiction Novels (contains *The City and the Stars, The Deep Range, A Fall of Moondust,* and *Rendezvous with Rama*), Gollancz, 1978.

The Fountains of Paradise, Harcourt, 1979.

(Editor with George Proctor) *The Science Fiction Hall of Fame,* Volume 3: *The Nebula Winners,* Avon, 1982.

2010: Odyssey Two, Del Rey, 1982.

The Sentinel: Masterworks of Science Fiction and Fantasy (short stories), Berkeley Publishing, 1983.

Selected Works, Heinemann, 1985.

The Songs of Distant Earth, Del Rey, 1986.

2061: Odyssey Three, Del Rey, 1988.

(With Gentry Lee) *Cradle,* Warner Books, 1988.

A Meeting with Medusa (bound with *Green Mars* by Kim Stanley Robinson), Tor Books, 1988.

(With Lee) *Rama II,* Bantam, 1989.

(With Gregory Benford) *Beyond the Fall of Night,* Putnam, 1990.

The Ghost from the Grand Banks, Bantam, 1990.

Tales from the Planet Earth, illustrated by Michael Whelan, Bantam, 1990.

(With Gentry Lee) *The Garden of Rama,* Bantam, 1991.

The Hammer of God, Bantam, 1993.

(With Lee) *Rama Revealed,* Bantam, 1994.

(With Mike McQuay) *Richter 10,* Bantam, 1996.

3001: The Final Odyssey, Ballantine, 1997.

Expedition to Earth, Ballantine, 1998.

Reach for Tomorrow, Ballantine, 1998.

Tales from the White Heart, Ballantine, 1998.

Arthur C. Clarke's Mysteries, Trans-Atlantic, 1998.

The Sands of Maris, Yestermorrow, 1999.

(With Paul Preuss) *Venus Prime,* Pocket Books, 2000.

OTHER

Opus 700, Gollancz, 1990.

Rama: The Official Strategy Guide, Prima Pub. (Rocklin, CA), 1996.

Also author of television series *Arthur C. Clarke's World of Strange Powers* and a movie treatment based on *Cradle.* Author of afterword to *Breaking Strain,* Avon, 1987, and *Maelstrom,* Avon, 1988, both by Paul Preuss. Contributor of more than 600 articles and short stories, occasionally under pseudonyms E. G. O'Brien and Charles Willis, to numerous magazines, including *Harper's, Playboy, New York Times Magazine, Vogue, Holiday,* and *Horizon.*

Clarke's works have been translated into Polish, Russian, French, German, Spanish, Serbo-Croatian, Greek, Hebrew, Dutch, and more than twenty other languages.

Adaptations

2010: Odyssey Two was filmed in 1984 by Metro-Goldwyn-Mayer (Clarke has a cameo in the film); the short story "The Star" was adapted for an episode of *The New Twilight Zone* by CBS-TV in 1985. The following works have been optioned for movies: *Childhood's End,* by Universal; *The Songs of Distant Earth,* by Michael Phillips; *The Fountains of Paradise,* by Robert Swarthe; and *Cradle,* by Peter Guber. Clarke has made the following sound recordings of his works for Caedmon: *Arthur C. Clarke Reads from his 2001: A Space Odyssey,* 1976; *Transit of Earth; The Nine Billion Names of God;* and *The Star,* 1978; *The Fountains of Paradise,* 1979; *Childhood's End,* 1979; and *2010:*

Odyssey Two. A full-length recording of *A Fall of Moondust* was made by Harcourt in 1976.

Sidelights

Arthur C. Clarke is renowned not only for his science fiction—which has earned him the title of Grand Master from the Science Fiction Writers of America and the unofficial "poet laureate of the space age," as David Brin writing in the *Los Angeles Times* dubbed him. Clarke also has a reputation for first-rate scientific and technical writing. His best known work in the latter field is "Extraterrestrial Relays," a 1945 article in which he first proposed the idea of communications satellites; Clarke has also published works on such diverse topics as underwater diving, space exploration, and scientific extrapolation. Nevertheless, it is Clarke's science fiction that has won him his reputation, with such novels as *Childhood's End* and *Rendezvous with Rama* being widely hailed as classics of the genre. In addition, his story "The Nine Billion Names of God" was named to the science fiction "Hall of Fame," while the movie *2001: A Space Odyssey,* co-written with director Stanley Kubrick, has been called the most important science fiction film ever made.

Clarke's fiction, which often deals with themes of exploration and discovery, almost always conveys to the reader a sense of wonder about the universe. Some critics, seeing the author's detailed descriptions of possible futures, have accused Clarke of ignoring the human element for the sake of science in his work. But while the development of scientific ideas and speculations plays a large role in Clarke's narratives, "what distinguishes Clarke's fictions from the usually more ephemeral examples of science fiction is his vision," Eric S. Rabkin asserted in his 1979 study *Arthur C. Clarke.* This vision, wrote Rabkin, is "a humane and open and fundamentally optimistic view of humankind and its potential in a universe which dwarfs us in physical size but which we may hope some day to match in spirit."

Born in 1917 in an English seaside town, Clarke discovered science fiction at the age of twelve, when he encountered the pulp magazine *Amazing Stories.* The encounter soon became an "addiction," as Clarke related in a 1983 article in the *New York Times Book Review:* "During my lunch hour away from school I used to haunt the local Woolworth's in search of my fix, which cost threepence a shot, roughly a quarter today." The young Clarke then began nurturing his love for the genre through the books of such English writers as H. G. Wells and Olaf Stapledon. He began writing his own stories for a school magazine while in his teens, but was unable to continue his schooling for lack of funds. He consequently secured a civil service job as an auditor, which left him plenty of free time to pursue his literary hobby. Alone in London, Clarke joined an association of several science fiction and space enthusiasts, and as he recalled in his 1977 autobiography *The View from Serendip,* "my life was dominated by the infant British Interplanetary Society [BIS], of which I was treasurer and general

propagandist." As part of his involvement with the BIS, Clarke wrote several scientific articles on the feasibility of space travel for the organization's journal; the BIS also gained him contacts with several science fiction editors and writers, which led to the publication of some of his short stories.

In 1941, although his auditor's position was still a reserved occupation, Clarke engaged in "what was probably the single most decisive act of my entire life," as he described it in *Ascent to Orbit, a Scientific Autobiography: The Technical Writings of Arthur C. Clarke;* he volunteered for the Royal Air Force. En route to becoming a radar instructor in a new system called Ground Controlled Approach, Clarke taught himself mathematical and electronics theory. After the war, Clarke entered college and obtained a degree in physics as well as pure and applied mathematics. Upon graduation, he spent two years as an assistant editor for a technical journal. But with publication of the novel *Childhood's End* (1953) and *The Exploration of Space,* which in 1952 was the first science book ever chosen as a Book-of-the-Month Club selection, Clarke began earning enough money to pursue writing full-time.

Besides allowing Clarke to leave his job, the success of *The Exploration of Space* also broke ground in explaining scientific ideas to a popular audience. What enabled the book to reach such a wide audience is a "charm and magnetism" that is due to "Clarke's ability to reduce complex subjects to simple language and his steadfast avoidance of fantasy as a substitute for factual narration," observed Roy Gibbons in the *Chicago Sunday Tribune.*

Clarke applied the same speculative techniques to other areas in the 1962 book *Profiles of the Future: An Inquiry into the Limits of the Possible.* The author "has a thorough grounding in science, and, in addition has a nimble and most receptive mind," Isaac Asimov stated in the *New York Times Book Review.* "Nothing reasonable frightens him simply because it seems fantastic, and—equally important—nothing foolish attracts him simply because it seems fantastic." Asimov went on to note that "this book offers all of us a chance to raise our eyes from the ground and to contemplate the scenery ahead. It is marvelous scenery indeed, and there could scarcely be a better guide to its landmarks than Arthur Clarke." Reviewer R.C. Cowen of the *Christian Science Monitor* expressed a similar opinion, praising *Profiles of the Future* as being "highly entertaining reading [that] also is informative, for the author is careful to adhere to the yardstick of natural laws that set the bounds of the possible." Cowen added that Clarke "helps a layman to learn the difference between rational speculation and . . . wholly baseless imaginings."

Although most speculative science texts are soon outdated, Clarke's work has withstood years of technical progress. In *The Promise of Space,* published in 1968 to "replace" *The Exploration of Space,* Clarke showed how many of his predictions have come true. Rather than simply cataloging recent discoveries, Clarke's work has

A scene from the motion picture **2001: A Space Odyssey,** *based on Clarke's novel of the same title and directed by Stanley Kubrick.*

incorporated them into new ideas: "All through the book Clarke not only recounts what has been done during the last two decades," wrote Willy Ley in the *New York Times Book Review,* "but has his eye on both the immediate results and the future." Similarly, *Science* contributor Eugene M. Emme asserted that the book contains "the best available summary of scientific and imaginative theory regarding space potentials.... Collectively they offer a most persuasive rationale." A 1984 revision of *Profiles of the Future* also withstands years of advancement: "Testing the limits of technological progress," observed David N. Samuelson in the *Los Angeles Times Book Review,* "it has remained remarkably current since its 1962 book publication." Gregory Benford, who hailed Clarke "a vindicated sage in his own time," theorized in the *Washington Post Book World* that while "books on futurology date notoriously, this one has not, principally because Clarke was unafraid of being adventurous." And *New York Times Book Review* writer Gerald Jonas offered this reason for Clarke's success: "What makes Clarke such an effective popularizer of science is that, without bobbling a decimal point or fudging a complex concept, he gives voice to the romantic side of scientific inquiry."

Although much of Clarke's early fiction reinforced the idea that space travel was an eventuality, *Childhood's End,* his first successful novel, is "Clarke's only work—fiction or nonfiction—in which 'The stars are not for Man,'" Thomas D. Clareson suggested in *Voices for the Future: Essays on Major Science Fiction Writers.* The

novel relates the appearance of the Overlords, a race of devil-shaped aliens who have come to guide Earth to peace and prosperity. After eliminating all individual governments and thus ending war, the Overlords use their superior technology to solve the problems of poverty, hunger, and oppression. The cost of this utopia is that most scientific research is set aside as unnecessary, and the exploration of space is forbidden. The motives of the Overlords become clear as the youngest generation of humans develops extrasensory powers; the children of Earth are to join the Overmind, a collective galactic "spirit" that transcends physical form. The need for science, technology, and space is eliminated with humanity's maturation, and the Earth itself is destroyed as her children join the Overmind.

Some critics have viewed *Childhood's End* as the first manifestation of the theme of spiritual evolution that appears throughout Clarke's fiction. Writing in the critical anthology *Arthur C. Clarke,* John Huntington described the novel as Clarke's solution to one of the problems posed by technological progress: how spiritual development can keep pace with scientific development when by making man comfortable, science often takes away man's curiosity and drive.

Childhood's End solves the problem with a stage of "transcendent evolution," and Huntington proposed that "it is its elegant solution to the problem of progress that has rightly earned *Childhood's End* that 'classic' status it now enjoys." However, Donald A. Wollheim considered this solution a negative one; writing in his 1971 book *The Universe Makers* he commented that *Childhood's End* "has always seemed to me to be a novel of despair. Others critics may see it as offering hope, but this tampering with humanity always struck me as being synthetic." Nonetheless, other critics have reaffirmed the novel as one of hope; *Childhood's End* "becomes a magnificently desperate attempt to continue to hope for a future for the race in the face of mounting evidence to the contrary," John Hollow wrote in *Against the Night, the Stars: The Science Fiction of Arthur C. Clarke.* Written in 1953 in the midst of the Cold War, "[the novel] becomes, in fact, a sometimes brilliant attempt to turn the contrary evidence to the positive," Hollow added. "It becomes nothing less than an effort to make positive the destruction of the race."

Clarke's best-known novel, *2001: A Space Odyssey,* was the result of four years of work on both the film version and the subsequent book. The collaboration between Clarke and director Stanley Kubrick began when the late filmmaker sought a suitable basis for making the "proverbial good science fiction movie," as Kubrick described it. The two finally settled upon Clarke's 1951 short story "The Sentinel," and developed it "not [into] a script, which in [Kubrick's] view does not contain enough of the visual and emotional information necessary for filming, but a prose version, rather like a novel," Michel Ciment related in *Focus on the Science Fiction Film.* The result "was of more help to him in creating the right atmosphere because it was more generous in its descriptions," Ciment wrote.

The film and the novel have the same basic premise: a large black monolith has been sent to Earth to encourage the development of man. First shown assisting in the "dawn of man" four million years ago, a monolith is next uncovered on the moon, and upon its unveiling sends a strong radio signal toward the outer planets. As a result the spaceship *Discovery,* operated by the intelligent computer HAL 9000, is sent in the direction of the signal to investigate. However, while the human crew is kept ignorant of the ship's true assignment, the HAL 9000 begins to eliminate what it sees as obstacles in the way of the mission—including the human crew. But first-captain Dave Bowman manages to survive and upon his arrival at a moon of Saturn (Jupiter in the film) encounters yet a third monolith, which precipitates a journey through the infinite. Bowman is transformed during this journey, and subsequently arrives at a higher evolutionary plane as the Star Child.

"Clarke's *2001: A Space Odyssey* was an extraordinary development in fiction, a novel written in collaboration with the director who was simultaneously filming it," observed Colin Greenland of the *Times Literary Supplement.* Clarke himself explained in the epilogue to the 1982 edition of *2001* that during the project he "often had the strange experience of revising the manuscript *after* viewing rushes based upon an earlier version of the story—a stimulating but rather expensive way of writing a novel." Because the book appeared three months after the movie's premiere, it was inevitable that critics would draw comparisons between the two. *New Statesman* contributor Brenda Maddox found the book lacking beside the movie; the novel "has all the faults of the film and none of its virtues." The critic elaborated: "The characters still have the subtlety of comic-strip men and, lacking the film's spectacular visual gimmickry ... the story must propel itself with little gusts of scientific explanation." In contrast, Eliot Fremont-Smith asserted in the *New York Times* that "the immense and moving fantasy-idea of *2001* ... is an idea that can be *dramatically* envisioned only in the free oscillations of the delicately cued and stretched mind." The critic added that the film "is too direct for this, its wonders too unsubtle and, for all their majesty, too confining." And where the movie may have been obscure, "all of it becomes clear and convincing in the novel. It is indeed an odyssey, this story, this exhilarating and rather chilling science fiction fantasy." Nevertheless, in comparing the visual genius of the film with the clarity of the book, Clarke himself admitted in *Focus on the Science Fiction Film* that both versions "did something that the other couldn't have done."

"Although it lacks some of the metaphysical fireworks and haunting visionary poetry of [his earlier work]," Clarke's *Rendezvous with Rama* is nevertheless "essentially an expression of wonder in the presence of Mystery," a *Virginia Quarterly Review* contributor commented. Written in 1973, the novel is the only work to win all four major awards in its genre; writing in the *Times Literary Supplement,* Thomas M. Disch hailed it as "probably [Clarke's] most considerable work of art." The book follows the appearance of an asteroid-like object which is hurtling directly towards the inner solar system—and which turns out to be a cylindrical, obviously unnatural artifact. An Earth ship is dispatched to the object, labelled "Rama," and a team led by commander Bill Norton enters to investigate. The exploration of the many mysterious aspects of Rama is interrupted by several distractions—including the emergence of what appears to be generated life forms and the arrival of a nuclear warhead sent by paranoid colonists from nearby Mercury. The study of Rama is concluded safely, however, although Norton's team has not gathered enough information to discern a purpose to the craft. Seemingly indifferent to a meeting with intelligent life, Rama then exits the solar system and continues its journey. "This is story-telling of the highest order," Theodore Sturgeon wrote in the *New York Times Book Review.* "There are perpetual surprise, constant evocation of the sense of wonder, and occasions of the most breathless suspense."

Although classic works such as *Childhood's End* and *Rendezvous with Rama* focus on the effects of extraterrestrial visitation, Clarke's next two works concentrate more on the achievements of humanity. *Imperial Earth: A Fantasy of Love and Discord* takes place in the quincentennial year of 2276. The novel includes demonstrations of outer planet mining operations, cloning, and spaceship propulsion systems, all woven into the story of Titan native Duncan Makenzie's visit to Earth. Duncan's trip serves many purposes; ostensibly it is to deliver an address at the quincenntenial celebration, but it is also to investigate political and scientific intrigues, as well as to procure, through cloning, an heir for the sterile Duncan. Through Duncan's eyes "Clarke not only supplies us with a fair number of technological wonders," observed Mark Rose in the *New Republic,* but the author also "makes much of such human matters as the political and psychological isolation of a distant colonial world such as Titan." Rose lauded the novel as "a literary performance conducted with genuine intelligence and grace." *National Review* contributor Steve Ownbey praised *Imperial Earth* as "a book nobody should miss. It's an utterly delightful tale, suspenseful and moving, full of unexpected chuckles and stunning surprises."

Clarke's 1979 Hugo- and Nebula-winning *The Fountains of Paradise* is even more technical in its basic premise: the construction of an orbital "space elevator" designed to make escaping the Earth's gravity a simple process. Based on actual scientific treatises, Clarke once again develops his idea "with sufficient technical detail to lend plausibility," said Gerald Jonas in the *New York Times Book Review,* "and the more plausible it sounds, the more stupendous it becomes." The novel also concerns Vannevar Morgan, the engineer obsessed with realizing the creation of his space elevator. Providing a "curious backdrop" to Morgan's enterprise is "a highly advanced galactic civilization [which] has already communicated with the human race through a robot probe," summarized Jonas. In addition, Morgan's story is paralleled by the account of Prince Kalidasa, who 2,000 years earlier challenged the gods by attempting to build a garden tower into heaven—on Taprobane, the same island that Morgan wants for his elevator. But while critics commended this parallel, they faulted Clarke for not sustaining it: "the direct interweaving of Kalidasa's story should have extended throughout the entire work rather than petering out," commented Paul Granahan in *Best Sellers.* Similarly, *New Republic* contributor Tim Myers criticized Clarke for ending the parallel: "The Indian king, the only character with nobility, is taken from us. We are left with Morgan, a pathetic egotist who is also hopelessly stereotyped."

Although Clarke (and others) insisted for several years that it was impossible to write a sequel to *2001,* in 1982 Clarke published *2010: Odyssey Two.* Incorporating elements of both the film and novel versions, as well as new information from the *Voyager* probes of Jupiter, in *2010* "Clarke sensibly steps back down to our level to tell the story of a combined Russian and American expedition to salvage Bowman's deserted ship, the *Discovery,*" related Colin Greenland in the *Times Literary Supplement.* Although the expedition finds the remains of the ship and repairs the HAL 9000, the purpose of the black monolith mystifies them. While some critics found this an adequate approach to a sequel, others chided Clarke for even attempting to follow up a "classic." *Science Fiction Review* writer Gene DeWeese argued that a key problem is that *2010* "is not so much a sequel to the original book, which was in many ways superior to the movie, but a sequel to and an explanation of the movie. Unfortunately, many of these explanations already existed [in the novel of *2001*]." *Washington Post Book World* contributor Michael Bishop noted a tendency on Clarke's part to over-explain: "Ponderous expository dialogue alternates with straightforward expository passages in which Heywood Floyd ... or the author himself lectures the reader." And Gerald Jonas of the *New York Times Book Review* complained that *2010* "violates the mystery [of the original] at every turn."

Despite the various criticisms, *2010* still "has its share of that same sense of wonder, which means that it is one of the dozen or so most enjoyable SF books of the year," said Gene DeWeese. "Clarke deftly blends discovery, philosophy, and a newly acquired sense of play," stated *Time* contributor Peter Stoler, creating a work that will "entertain" readers. Cary Neeper presented a similar assessment in the *Christian Science Monitor,* noting that "Clarke's story drives on to an exciting finish in which the mix of fantasy and fact leaves the reader well satisfied with a book masterfully written." And in contrast to the criticisms of the sequel's worthiness, Bud Foote claimed in the *Detroit News* that with "the book's penultimate triumph [of] a new, awesome and terrifying world transformation," Clarke has created "a fine book." The critic concluded that *2010* "is better than the original book, and it illuminates and completes the original movie. It is so good, in fact, that even Clarke couldn't write a sequel to it."

Despite this assertion, 1988 brought *2061: Odyssey Three,* the next chapter in the saga of the black monolith. The year 2061 will be the next appearance of Halley's comet; *Odyssey Three* follows Heywood Floyd on a survey of the object. While en route, his survey party is redirected to rescue a ship that has crashed on the Jovian moon of Europa—the one celestial object the monoliths have warned humans against visiting. Some critics have been skeptical of a second sequel, such as the *Time* reviewer who found that "the mix of imagination and anachronism is wearing as thin as the oxygen layer on Mars." Although Gerald Jonas of the *New York Times Book Review* also observed that "Mr. Clarke's heart is obviously not in the obligatory action scenes that advance the plot," he conceded that the author "remains a master at describing the wonders of the universe in sentences that combine a respect for scientific accuracy with an often startling lyricism." Clarke "is not to be measured by the same standards we apply to a mundane plot-smith," asserted David Brin in the *Los Angeles Times.* "He is, after all, the poet laureate of the Space Age. He is at his best making the reader feel, along with Heywood Floyd," continued Brin, "how fine it might be to stand upon an ancient comet, out under the stars, knowing that it is those dreams that finally come true that are the best dreams of all."

Between the publication of the two "Odyssey" sequels Clarke finished *The Songs of Distant Earth,* an elaborate revision and extension of a short story he first published in 1958. The novel takes place on the ocean world of Thalassa, where the few habitable islands there have been populated by descendants of an Earth "seedship," sent to perpetuate humanity even after the nova explosion of the Earth's sun. The Thalassan society is a type of utopia, for superstition, prejudice, and extreme violence no longer exist; the robots who raised the first generations eliminated all religion and art which might encourage these elements. The Thalassans are seemingly content with their world when the starship *Magellan* lands, bringing with it the last survivors (and witnesses) of the Earth's destruction. Although the ship is not permitted to colonize a world that has already been settled, the idyllic setting tempts the crew to a possible mutiny. Further complicating the situation is the emergence of a marine life form that appears to be intelligent, creating a possible conflict on two different fronts.

Although this dilemma "makes for an interesting novel," *Science Fiction Review* contributor Richard E. Geis faulted Clarke's plot as improbable, decrying the lack of individual conflict. Echoing previous criticisms, Geis commented that the "characters are uncomplicated, non-neurotic, with only minor problems to be solved.... Clarke has written a story of plausible high-tech future science and peopled it with implausible, idealized, 'nice' humans." In contrast, Dan K. Moran of the *West Coast Review of Books* maintained that "how Clarke deals with the mutiny is interesting; and his characters come alive throughout." Nevertheless, Moran noted that "the great flaw is the lack of sense-of-wonder. Nothing herein is really new, neither science nor Clarke's synthesis."

The "grand theme" that runs throughout Clarke's fiction "can be stated only in the form of a paradox," Gerald Jonas of the *New York Times Book Review* suggested. "Man is most himself when he strives greatly, when he challenges the very laws of the universe; yet man is small and the universe is large, and anything he creates must, in the long run, be dwarfed by the works of others." The science in Clarke's fiction provides a good backdrop for this theme; Gregory Benford wrote in the *Washington Post Book Review* that Clarke "prefers a pure, dispassionate statement of facts and relationships, yet the result is not cold. Instead, he achieves a rendering of the scientific esthetic, with its respect for the universal qualities of intelligence, its tenacity and curiosity. His fiction neglects conflict and the broad spectrum of emotion, which gives it a curiously refreshing honesty." Although Clarke's fiction "may appear to be about science, appear to be about numbers, appear to be about ideas," Eric Rabkin wrote in his 1979 book *Arthur C. Clarke,* "in fact at bottom whatever Clarke writes is about people and that means it is about the human spirit."

Published in 1997, Clarke's work revives Frank Poole, a member of the doomed spaceship Discovery, *who learns about the alarming last one-thousand years of the history of the human race.*

Clarke's faith in the human spirit is evident in his nonfiction book *The Snows of Olympus: A Garden on Mars.* Published in 1995, at a time when NASA struggled with massive budget cutbacks, this book optimistically looks toward a future when humans will visit and colonize the Red Planet. Clarke asserts that if money were no object, human beings could walk on Mars early in the twenty-first century. He outlines a three-part mission to Mars, beginning with robot probes, which would locate needed resources on the planet and choose suitable landing sites. Unmanned space freighters would follow with equipment and supplies, intended to support the third part of the mission: the landing of a human crew. Clarke predicts that once a human colony is established, work will begin to alter the environment of Mars to make it habitable by unprotected human beings. He even believes that it is possible to create oceans and large-scale agricultural projects there. *The Snows of Olympus* is illustrated with computer-generated art depicting the transformation of Mars. Clarke created the pictures himself, beginning with maps of the planet generated by NASA's *Voyager* probe. In addition to his speculations on the years to come, Clarke's book also takes a look at past conceptions of Mars, beginning with the late-nineteenth-century idea that the planet was populated by a race of intelligent beings who specialized in building canals.

Known as a futurist, Clarke turned to the past in *Astounding Days: A Science Fictional Autobiography.* Focusing on Clarke's youth and early days as a writer, the memoir is divided into three sections, each dedicated to one of the three editors who created the magazine *Astounding Science Fiction* (renamed *Analog* in the 1960s). Writing in *Wilson Library Bulletin,* Gene LaFaille described *Astounding Days* as a "rambling paean to the glory years of early science fiction." *Astounding Days* provides "a sweeping view of popular science and popular fiction," *Library Journal* reviewer Katherine Thorp stated.

As an octogenarian, Clarke turned once again toward the future, both immediate and distant. In *Richter 10,* written in collaboration with Mike McQuay, Clarke combines earthquakes, politics, and environmental disaster to produce a futuristic disaster novel. By the near-future year 2030, the Nation of Islam is orchestrating a civil war in California and demanding a state of its own, China is the dominant world power, southern Europe and the Middle East have been destroyed by Israel's nuclear weapons, and the ozone layer has vanished. The book's hero, Lewis Crane, is a leading authority on earth tremors and is able to predict earthquakes, but no one believes him when he predicts a giant earthquake that might wipe out the central United States. When the earthquake does not occur on time, the Nation of Islam attacks and the earth disintegrates into chaos. Crane, who has lost all credibility and support from his Chinese business sponsor, buys real estate on the moon and starts a space colony. A *Booklist* critic praised *Richter 10* as "a taut, well-written thriller that should satisfy both Clarke's fans and the many devotees of disaster novels."

In 1997 Clarke did what he had long said was impossible: he wrote the fourth installment of his Odyssey series, *3001: The Final Odyssey.* In *3001,* another manned space voyage finds the deep-frozen Frank Poole, long presumed dead, and revives him with fourth-millennium technology. Poole masters the use of the "braincap" and other gadgets, learns about Star City, and studies the thousand years of history he has slept through. During his long sleep, a monolith has exploded Jupiter, turning it and its moons into a secondary solar system. One moon, Europa, has been colonized by a monolith that monitors human behavior and influences the plant-like beings beneath the surface to grow. Poole is alarmed to learn that his old colleague, Dave Bowman, and HAL have both become absorbed by the monolith and that the black slab's superiors are intent on doing something unthinkable to the humans that they have enslaved. Writing in the *New York Times Book Review,* John Allen Paulos observed that while the plot hangs together "reasonably well," much of the enjoyment comes from Clarke's ruminations on high technology, Freudian therapy, computer security, terrorism, and religious mania. Ian Watson of the *Times Literary Supplement* suggested that what makes *3001* compelling reading is the way in which Clarke "retrofits" earlier episodes "so that they blend with the new future and the now ex-future." While he felt that there are not many surprises to be had in the novel, Watson still praised Clarke for having "the unnerving habit of proving that whatever it is, he imagined it first." Eric Korn of the *Economist* argued that the novel begs its most interesting question: What if the monolith's part in human evolution were a bad thing? Korn wrote, "In *2001,* the monoliths were doors of transcendent perception; in *3001,* they become banal and easily dealt-with alien threats." Korn found *3001* a "disappointing end" to the Odyssey series.

"Science fiction is often called escapism—always in a negative sense," Clarke told Alice K. Turner in a 1973 *Publishers Weekly* interview. "Of course it's not true. Science fiction is virtually the only kind of writing that's dealing with real problems and possibilities; it's a concerned fiction." Clarke added that "we know so much more now that we don't have to waste time on the petty things of the past. We can use the enormous technological advances in our work. Vision is wider now, and interest has never been deeper."

Although he has been involved with the SF genre for more than half a century, Clarke's writing style and the themes he writes about have not changed greatly over the years. "I guess I'm just an old conservative," the author told Charles Platt, the author of *Dream Makers: The Uncommon Men and Women Who Write Science Fiction.* "Although, really, if I have stayed true to the original form of my writing that's simply because I have a constant commitment to science." Clarke also commented to Platt that he is proud of retaining the "sense of wonder" in his writing: "I regard it as something of an achievement not to have become cynical.... I do remain an optimist, especially in my fiction, because I hope it may operate as a self-fulfilling prophecy."

Works Cited

Asimov, Isaac, review of *Profiles of the Future, New York Times Book Review,* April 14, 1963, pp. 22, 24.

Benford, Gregory, review of *Profiles of the Future* (revised edition), *Washington Post Book World,* March 25, 1984, p. 6.

Bishop, Michael, review of *2010, Washington Post Book World,* December 26, 1982, p. 6.

Brin, David, review of *2061, Los Angeles Times,* December 1, 1982.

Ciment, Michael, in *Focus on the Science Fiction Film,* edited by William Johnson, Prentice Hall, 1972.

Clareson, Thomas D., editor, *Voices for the Future: Essays on Major Science Fiction Writers,* Bowling Green University Press, 1976.

Clarke, Arthur C., *Ascent to Orbit, a Technical Autobiography: The Technical Writings of Arthur C. Clarke,* Wiley, 1984.

Clarke, Arthur C., *Astounding Days: A Science Fictional Autobiography,* Gollancz, 1989.

Clarke, Arthur C., *New York Times Book Review,* March 6, 1983.

Clarke, Arthur C., *2001: A Space Odyssey,* New American Library, 1968, published with new afterword, 1982.

Clarke, Arthur C., *The View from Serendip,* Random House, 1977.

Cowen, R. C., review of *Profiles of the Future, Christian Science Monitor,* February 26, 1963.

DeWeese, Gene, review of *2010, Science Fiction Review,* February, 1983.

Disch, Thomas M., review of *Rendezvous with Rama, Times Literary Supplement,* June 16, 1978, p. 662.

Emme, Eugene M., review of *Exploration of Space, Science,* August 30, 1968, pp. 874-875.

Foote, Bud, review of *2010, Detroit News,* November 28, 1982.

Fremont-Smith, Eliot, review of *2001, New York Times,* July 5, 1968.

Geis, Richard E., *Science Fiction Review,* summer, 1986.

Gibbons, Roy, *Chicago Sunday Tribune,* July 13, 1952.

Granahan, Paul, review of *Fountains of Paradise, Best Sellers,* May, 1979.

Greenland, Colin, review of *2010, Times Literary Supplement,* January 21, 1983.

Hollow, John, *Against the Night, the Stars: The Science Fiction of Arthur C. Clarke,* Harcourt, 1983, expanded edition, Ohio University Press, 1987.

Huntington, John, *Arthur C. Clarke,* Starmont House, 1979.

Jonas, Gerald, *New York Times Book Review,* October 30, 1977, p. 12.

Jonas, Gerald, review of *Fountains of Paradise, New York Times Book Review,* March 18, 1979, pp. 13, 25.

Jonas, Gerald, review of *2010, New York Times Book Review,* January 23, 1983, p. 24.

Jonas, Gerald, review of *2061, New York Times Book Review,* December 20, 1987, p. 18.

Korn, Eric, review of *3001, Economist,* April 12, 1997, p. 85.

LaFaille, Gene, review of *Astounding Days, Wilson Library Bulletin,* March, 1990.

Ley, Willy, review of *The Exploration of Space, New York Times Book Review,* August 25, 1968, p. 10.

Maddox, Brenda, review of *2001, New Statesman,* December 20, 1968.

Moran, Dan K., review of *Songs of the Distant Earth, West Coast Review of Books,* Number 1, 1986.

Myers, Tim, review of *Fountains of Paradise, New Republic,* March 24, 1979.

Neeper, Cary, review of *2010, Christian Science Monitor,* December 3, 1982, p. B3.

Olander, Joseph D., and Martin H. Greenburg, editors, *Arthur C. Clarke,* Taplinger, 1977.

Ownbey, Steve, review of *Imperial Earth, National Review,* May 14, 1976.

Paulos, John Allen, review of *3001, New York Times Book Review,* March 9, 1997.

Platt, Charles, *Dream Makers: The Uncommon Men and Women Who Write Science Fiction,* Volume II, Berkeley Publishing, 1983.

Rabkin, Eric S., *Arthur C. Clarke,* Starmont House, 1979.

Review of *Rendezvous with Rama, Virginia Quarterly,* winter 1974.

Review of *Richter 10, Booklist,* January 1-15, 1997, p. 778.

Rose, Mark, review of *Imperial Earth, New Republic,* March 20, 1976.

Samuelson, David N., review of *Profiles of the Future* (revised edition), *Los Angeles Times Book Review,* March 4, 1984.

Stoler, Peter, review of *2010, Time,* November 15, 1982.

Sturgeon, Theodore, review of *Rendezvous With Rama, New York Times Book Review,* September 23, 1973.

Thorp, Katherine, review of *Astounding Days, Library Journal,* March 1, 1990, p. 98.

Turner, Alice K., "Arthur C. Clarke," *Publishers Weekly,* September 10, 1973, pp. 24-25.

Review of *2061: Odyssey Three, Kirkus Reviews,* November 1, 1987.

Review of *2061: Odyssey Three, Time,* January 11, 1988.

Watson, Ian, review of *3001, Times Literary Supplement,* March 21, 1997.

Wollheim, Donald A., *The Universe Makers,* Harper, 1971.

For More Information See

BOOKS

Agel, Jerome, editor, *The Making of Kubrick's 2001,* New American Library, 1970.

Aldiss, Brian W., *Trillion Year Spree: The History of Science Fiction,* Atheneum (New York City), 1986.

Bleiler, E. F., editor, *Science Fiction Writers: Critical Studies of the Major Authors from the Early Nineteenth Century to the Present Day,* Scribners (New York City), 1982.

Contemporary Literary Criticism, Gale (Detroit), Volume 1, 1973, Volume 4, 1975, Volume 13, 1980, Volume 18, 1981, Volume 35, 1985.

Ketterer, David, *New Worlds for Old: The Apocalyptic Imagination, Science Fiction, and American Literature,* Indiana University Press, 1974.

Knight, Damon, *In Search of Wonder: Essays on Modern Science Fiction,* Advent, 1967, pp. 177-205.

Magill, Frank N., editor, *Survey of Science Fiction Literature,* Volumes 1-5, Salem Press, 1979.

Malik, Rex, editor, *Future Imperfect,* Pinter, 1980.

McAleer, Neil, *Arthur C. Clarke: The Authorized Biography,* Contemporary Books, 1992.

Moskowitz, Sam, *Seekers of Tomorrow: Masters of Science Fiction,* World Publishing, 1966.

Of Time and Stars: The Worlds of Arthur C. Clarke, Gollancz, 1972, pp. 7-10.

Reid, Robin Anne, *Arthur C. Clarke: A Critical Companion,* Greenwood Press, 1997.

Samuelson, David N., *Arthur C. Clarke: A Primary and Secondary Bibliography,* G. K. Hall, 1984.

Short Story Criticism, Volume 3, Gale, 1989.

Slusser, George Edgar, *The Space Odysseys of Arthur C. Clarke,* Borgo, 1978.

PERIODICALS

Algol, November, 1974.

Atlantic, April, 1963, p. 152; July, 1952.

Best Sellers, May, 1984, pp. 75-76; December 24, 1953, p. 13.

Book World, June 30, 1968, pp. 1, 3; December 19, 1971, p. 6.

Chicago Tribune, December 30, 1990, section 14, p. 6.

Christian Science Monitor, February 10, 1972, p. 10; August 8, 1973, p. 9; November 26, 1993, p. 15.

Commonweal, May 3, 1968.

Discover, May, 1997, pp. 68-69.

Extrapolation, winter, 1980, pp. 348-60; summer, 1987, pp. 105-29; spring, 1989, pp. 53-69.

Kirkus Reviews, November 1, 1987.

Library Journal, February 15, 1997, p. 164.

Locus, February, 1994, p. 75; November, 1993, p. 27.

Los Angeles Times, January 29, 1996.

Los Angeles Times Book Review, December 19, 1982; December 6, 1987; December 9, 1990, p. 10; February 3, 1991, p. 10; January 24, 1992, p. 1; August 8, 1993, p. 11; March 10, 1996.

Magazine of Fantasy and Science Fiction, September, 1979, pp. 25-26.

Nation, March 5, 1983.

National Review, November 20, 1962, pp. 403-4.

New Republic, May 4, 1968.

New Scientist, April 12, 1997, p. 44.

New Statesman, January 26, 1979.

Newsday, April 4, 1968; April 20, 1968.

Newsweek, October 30, 1961.

New Yorker, April 24, 1965; May 27, 1967; April 13, 1968; September 21, 1968; August 9, 1969, pp. 40-65; December 13, 1982; December 20, 1982.

New York Herald Tribune Book Review, July 13, 1952; August 10, 1952; August 23, 1953; March 2, 1958, p. 6.

New York Times, May 29, 1968; August 22, 1973, p. 35; December 4, 1984; February 26, 1985; April 7, 1993, p. C13, C19; November 28, 1994, p. A4; April 1, 1997; April 11, 1997.

New York Times Book Review, March 14, 1954; July 15, 1956, p. 20; January 18, 1976; May 11, 1986; May 6, 1990, p. 22; July 8, 1990, p. 22; February 3, 1991, p. 33; September 1, 1991, p. 13; June 13, 1993, p. 22; March 13, 1994, p. 30; January 28, 1996.

New York Times Magazine, March 6, 1966.

Omni, March, 1979.

People Weekly, December 20, 1982.

Playboy, July, 1986.
Publishers Weekly, June 14, 1976; January 6, 1984, p. 75; January 27, 1984, p. 72; January 22, 1996, p. 61.
Reader's Digest, April, 1969.
Saturday Review, July 5, 1952; April 20, 1968.
Science Fiction Review, March-April, 1979; August, 1981; May, 1984; fall, 1984, p. 26.
Science-Fiction Studies, July, 1979, pp. 230-31; November, 1997, pp. 441-58.
Time, July 19, 1968.
Times (London), November 25, 1982.
Times Literary Supplement, July 15, 1968; January 2, 1969; December 5, 1975; October 31, 1986.
Voice Literary Supplement, November, 1982, pp. 8-9.
Washington Post, February 16, 1982; November 16, 1982.
Washington Post Book World, November 25, 1990, p. 8; March 9, 1992, p. B1.
Western Folklore, Number 28, 1969, pp. 230-37.
World Press Review, April, 1985.*

* * *

CONE, Molly (Lamken) 1918-
(Caroline More, a joint pseudonym)

Personal

Born October 3, 1918, in Tacoma, WA; daughter of Arthur and Frances (Sussman) Lamken; married Gerald J. Cone, September 9, 1939; children: Susan, Gary, Ellen. *Education:* University of Washington, 1936-39.

Addresses

Home—P.O. Box 1005, Suquamish, WA 98392.

Career

Advertising copywriter and author of books for children.

Awards, Honors

Mishmash was named one of one hundred outstanding books for young readers, *New York Times;* Matrix Table honor award, Women in Communications, Inc., 1968; Literary Creativity citation, Music and Art Foundation (Seattle), 1968; Washington Press Women, first place awards, 1969, for *Annie, Annie,* 1970, for *Simon,* second place award, 1971, for *You Can't Make Me If I Don't Want To;* National Federation of Press Women first place award, 1970, for *Simon;* Centennial Award for Literary Contribution toward the Education of Jewish Children, 1970; Sugar Plum Award, Washington Press Women Field of Communications, 1972; Sidney Taylor Book Award, 1972; Shirley Kravitz Children's Book Award, Association of Jewish Libraries, 1973; Orbis Pictus honor, 1993, for *Come Back, Salmon.*

Writings

Only Jane, illustrated by Velma Ilsely, Thomas Nelson, 1960.
Too Many Girls, Thomas Nelson, 1960.
The Trouble with Toby, illustrated by Charles Geer, Houghton, 1961.
Mishmash, illustrated by Leonard Shortall, Houghton, 1962.
Reeney, illustrated by C. Geer, Houghton, 1963.
(With Margaret Pitcairn Strachan, under joint pseudonym Caroline More) *Batch of Trouble,* Dial, 1963.
Mishmash and the Substitute Teacher, illustrated by L. Shortall, Houghton, 1963.
Stories of Jewish Symbols, illustrated by Siegmund Forst, Bloch, 1963.
The Real Dream, illustrated by Bea Holmes, Houghton, 1964.
A Promise Is a Promise, illustrated by John Gretzer, Houghton, 1964.
Mishmash and the Sauerkraut Mystery, illustrated by Shortall, Houghton, 1965.
Who Knows Ten? Children's Tales of the Ten Commandments, illustrated by Uri Shulevitz, Commission of Jewish Education, 1965, revised, illustrated by Robin Brickman, UAHC Press, 1998.
The Jewish Sabbath, illustrated by Ellen Raskin, Crowell, 1966, selections republished as *The Story of Shabbat,* illustrated by Emily Lisker, HarperCollins, 2000.
Crazy Mary, illustrated by B. Holmes, Houghton, 1966.
Hurry, Henrietta (biography), Houghton, 1966.
The Jewish New Year, illustrated by Jerome Snyder, Crowell, 1966.
Purim, illustrated by Helen Borten, Crowell, 1967.
The Other Side of the Fence, illustrated by J. Gretzer, Houghton, 1967.
The House in the Tree: A Story of Israel, illustrated by Symeon Shimin, Crowell, 1968.
The Green, Green Sea: A Story of Greece, illustrated by Ric Estrada, Crowell, 1968.
Mishmash and Uncle Looey, illustrated by Shortall, Houghton, 1968.
Annie, Annie, illustrated by Marvin Friedman, Houghton, 1969.
Leonard Bernstein (biography), illustrated by Robert Galster, Crowell, 1970.
Simon, illustrated by Marvin Friedman, Houghton, 1970.
The Ringling Brothers (biography), illustrated by Ruth McCrea and James McCrea, Crowell, 1971.
You Can't Make Me If I Don't Want To, illustrated by M. Friedman, Houghton, 1971.
Number Four, Houghton, 1972.
Dance around the Fire, illustrated by M. Friedman, Houghton, 1974.
Mishmash and the Venus Flytrap, illustrated by Shortall, Houghton, 1976.
Call Me Moose, illustrated by Bernice Lowenstein, Houghton, 1978.
The Amazing Memory of Harvey Bean, illustrated by Robert MacLean, Houghton, 1980.
Mishmash and the Robot, illustrated by Shortall, Houghton, 1981.
Mishmash and the Big Fat Problem, illustrated by Shortall, Houghton, 1982.
Paul David Silverman Is a Father, photographs by Harold Roth, Elsevier-Dutton, 1982.
The Big Squeeze, Houghton, 1984.
The Mystery of Being Jewish, UAHC Press, 1989.

Come Back, Salmon: How a Group of Dedicated Kids Adopted Pigeon Creek and Brought It Back to Life, photographs by Sidnee Wheelwright, Sierra Club, 1992.

Listen to the Trees: Jews and the Earth, illustrated by Roy Doty, UAHC Press, 1995.

Squishy, Misty, Damp, and Musty: The In-between World of Wetlands, Sierra Club, 1996.

Hello, Hello, Are You There, God?, illustrated by Rosalind Charney Kaye, UAHC Press, 1999.

Author of play *Paul Bunyan and His Blue Ox,* in *Bold Journeys,* Macmillan, 1966.

"HEAR O ISRAEL" SERIES

First I Say the Shema, Commission on Jewish Education, 1972.

About Learning, illustrated by Iris Schweitzer, Commission on Jewish Education, 1972.

About Belonging, illustrated by Susan Perl, Commission on Jewish Education, 1972.

About God, illustrated by Claire R. Ross and John Ross, Commission on Jewish Education, 1973.

Adaptations

Selections from *Who Knows Ten?* were narrated by Peninnah Schram on *A Storyteller's Journey,* POM Records, 1978, and *A Storyteller's Journey II,* POM Records, 1981.

Sidelights

Inspired by both the events of her own life and her interest in Jewish culture, Molly Cone has written young adult novels, short story collections, and middle-grade nonfiction during a writing career that has spanned more than four decades. Commentators have acknowledged Cone for her many contributions to the body of juvenile literature. Notable among her fictional works are the novels *Too Many Girls, The Big Squeeze,* and the Mishmash series. Works on Jewish themes include *The Mystery of Being Jewish, Who Knows Ten?,* and books about Jewish holidays. Such nonfiction works as *Come Back, Salmon,* in which Cone describes the activities of young ecologists, and *Squishy, Misty, Damp, and Musty,* in which she explains the importance of wetlands, also caught reviewers' attention.

Born in Tacoma, Washington, in 1918, Cone grew up "in a square house on a quiet street in a family of five children and a live-in grandmother," as she once told *SATA.* "We were the largest family in the neighborhood and through necessity had the biggest car—my mother's seven-passenger Studebaker with a horn that blew 'Oooo-gah.'" Cone was the middle sister, but she gained a measure of self-confidence by keeping step with her brothers. "No other girl I knew climbed trees so expertly, pounded with hammer and nails so joyfully, or blushed as easily as I did," she later recalled. "I thought telling secrets inexcusable and felt with a passionate conviction that I could be anything I really wanted to be." And what she wanted to be was a writer. "In my mind, I always was," she revealed. "As far back as I can remember, I thought of myself only as a WRITER. And I hardly expected to wait until I grew up for other people to recognize it."

Although even as a youngster she was quite certain that she would be an author some day, Cone did not actually become a full-fledged, *published* writer until she had reached her late twenties, by which time she had attended classes at the University of Washington, married Gerald Cone, and begun a family. Her first book would not be started until she was in her late thirties and the mother of three: daughters Susan and Ellen and son Gary. Finally, Cone's *Only Jane* appeared in 1960, thus marking the beginning of her prolific career as a children's book author. The story of a fifteen-year-old girl who combats her feelings of shyness and blossoms at a summer dance, *Only Jane* won praise from several critics. The kudos Cone received for her first young adult novel convinced her to devote herself to writing for children.

Cone considers many of the novels she writes for young people "adventure stories—or a kind of adventure story with characters caught in the dilemma or sometimes trauma of growing up. A boy begins to forget things when his parents separate, a girl envies her best friend because this friend is always saying 'my mother won't let me,' a girl suddenly turns religious to the dismay and bafflement of her parents, a girl turns herself into a moose." In Cone's 1985 novel *The Big Squeeze,* a young-looking high school sophomore boy named Dudley finds that a role in a school play is the perfect vehicle for overcoming shyness. The "first-person narrative reveals an engaging character whose self-doubts are balanced by insight and whose intensity is leavened by humor," opined *Horn Book* reviewer Charlotte W. Draper. "Cone has done a great job of portraying the adolescent crush," added Kathryn M. Weisman in her *School Library Journal* appraisal of *The Big Squeeze,* "and she can write quite convincing dialogue."

Among Cone's most popular books have been her novels about a fun-loving, independent dog named Mishmash. In such titles as *Mishmash and the Venus Flytrap* and *Mishmash and the Big Fat Problem,* readers find the rambunctious puppy in predicament after predicament. For example, in *Mishmash and the Venus Flytrap,* Cone's tail-wagging hero suddenly goes missing after his owner, Miss Patch, brings home an insect-munching Venus' flytrap. And in *Mishmash and the Big Fat Problem,* the problem is Mishmash himself, for too much dog food and too many bone-shaped biscuits have ruined the puppy's slender figure.

Cone based the character Mishmash on a dog with whom she and her family once shared their home. "Our dog wasn't big and she wasn't black and her name wasn't Mishmash. It was Tiny," Cone told *SATA.* "She came to live with us full-grown—a small red-haired, very friendly cocker spaniel who insisted on helping the mailman deliver the mail, the milkman deliver the milk, and the paperboy deliver the paper and preferred eating what was on the table instead of the food in her dish on the floor. It was out of my contradictory feelings about Tiny that the first book called *Mishmash* evolved. And once I got into it, Mishmash-in-the-book became exactly like no other dog but himself."

Cone's nonfiction publications include works about Judaism and nature. In her 1992 book *Come Back, Salmon: How a Group of Dedicated Kids Adopted Pigeon Creek and Brought It Back to Life,* Cone focused on the work of students at the Jackson Elementary School in Everett, Washington. These earthsavers adopted a polluted waterway called Pigeon Creek and restored it to ecological health, creating a spawning ground for salmon. Critics found much to like about the work. Calling Cone's text "lively," *Booklist* contributor Kay Weisman praised Cone's use of interviews with both students and teachers and determined that the work could "inspire young readers." *Horn Book* reviewer Elizabeth S. Watson echoed that praise, calling *Come Back, Salmon* "a first-class book" and praising Cone's use of both background information on the effects of pollution and actual transcripts of conversations with students working on the project. "An inspiring story of young scientists in action," is how a *Kirkus* reviewer described the volume, while in *School Library Journal,* Tina Smith Entwistle noted that "it would be hard not to get caught up the excitement and anxiety of the students." Similar to *Come Back, Salmon,* Cone's 1996 *Squishy, Misty, Damp, and Muddy: The In-between World of Wetlands* answers many questions about the types of wetlands that exist in North America. This photo-essay illustrates the types of plants and animals that need a wetland environment in order to survive. Cone also reviewed the problems facing surviving wetlands and described efforts underway to save them from further destruction. Noting that the book has "a relatively broad focus," *Booklist* contributor Carolyn Phelan deemed *Squishy, Misty, Damp, and Muddy* "an attractive resource" for elementary school-aged students. Morever, reviewer Louise L. Sherman noted in *School Library Journal* that Cone both used "persuasive statistics ... to demonstrate the importance of this ecosystem" and presented the material in an "almost poetic introduction" to the topic.

Works Cited

Review of *The Big Squeeze, Kirkus Reviews,* November 1, 1984, pp. 102-103.

Review of *Come Back, Salmon, Kirkus Reviews,* March 15, 1992, p. 403.

Draper, Charlotte W., review of *The Big Squeeze, Horn Book,* March-April, 1985, p. 177.

Entwistle, Tina Smith, review of *Come Back, Salmon, School Library Journal,* April, 1992, p. 131.

Phelan, Carolyn, review of *Squishy, Misty, Damp, and Muddy, Booklist,* June 1, 1996, p. 1725.

Sherman, Louise L., review of *Squishy, Misty, Damp, and Muddy, School Library Journal,* August, 1996, pp. 133-34.

Watson, Elizabeth S., review of *Come Back, Salmon, Horn Book,* July-August, 1992, p. 465.

Weisman, Kathryn M., review of *The Big Squeeze, School Library Journal,* January 1985, p. 83.

Weisman, Kay, review of *Come Back, Salmon, Booklist,* May 1, 1992, p. 1596.

For More Information See

BOOKS

de Montreville, Doris, and Donna Hill, editors, *Third Book of Junior Authors,* H. W. Wilson, 1972.

PERIODICALS

Booklist, July 1, 1981, p. 1394; July, 1982, p. 1442.

Kirkus Reviews, April 15, 1981, p. 504; April 15, 1982, p. 488.

New York Times Book Review, August 30, 1992, p. 19.

Publishers Weekly, May 25, 1998, p. 83.

School Library Journal, August, 1981, p. 63; April, 1982, p. 67.*

D

DAKOS, Kalli 1950-

Personal

Born June 16, 1950, in Ottawa, Canada; daughter of John Peter (in the Air Force) and Betty (a secretary; maiden name, Athanas) Sperdakos; married John Kenton Desmarteau (a physician); children: Alicia Marie. *Education:* Queen's University, B.A., 1972, B.Ed., 1973; University of Nevada, Reno, M.A., 1979. *Hobbies and other interests:* Writing, teaching theater, consulting.

Addresses

Home—12004 Holly Crest Ct., Great Falls, VA 22066. *Agent*—Ann Tobias, 307 South Carolina Ave. S. E., Washington, DC 20003.

Career

Sir Alexander Mackenzie School, Inuvik, Northwest Territories, Canada, teacher, 1974-75; Storrington Public School, Kingston, Ontario, teacher, 1974-76; *Eagle Bulletin,* Syracuse, NY, reporter, 1984-86; Manlius Pebble Hill School, Syracuse, teacher, 1985-86; freelance writer, Great Falls, VA, 1986—; Braddock Elementary School, Annandale, VA, reading teacher, 1986-87; Edstar, Inc., Great Falls, president, 1990—. Has served as a lecturer and reading specialist at Northern Virginia Community College; has also worked as a language arts consultant. *Member:* International Reading Association, Society of Children's Book Writers and Illustrators, Virginia State Reading Association, Greater Washington Reading Council, Windstar Foundation.

Awards, Honors

Children's Choice Award, 1991, for *If You're Not Here, Please Raise Your Hand: Poems about School,* and 1994, for *Don't Read This Book, Whatever You Do!: More Poems about School.*

Writings

What's There to Write About?, Scholastic, 1989.
If You're Not Here, Please Raise Your Hand: Poems about School, illustrated by G. Brian Karas, Four Winds Press, 1990.
Don't Read This Book, Whatever You Do!: More Poems about School, illustrated by Karas, Four Winds Press, 1993.
Mrs. Cole on an Onion Roll, and Other School Poems, illustrated by JoAnn Adinolfi, Simon & Schuster, 1995.
The Goof Who Invented Homework and Other School Poems, illustrated by Denise Brunkus, Dial, 1996.
Get out of the Alphabet, Number 2!: Wacky Wednesday Puzzle Poems, illustrated by Jenny Graham, Simon & Schuster, 1997.
The Bug in Teacher's Coffee, illustrated by Mike Reed, HarperCollins, 1999.

Contributor to periodicals, including *Instructor, Young American, Child Life, Challenge, Chicadee, Jack and Jill, Children's Playmate,* and *Learning.*

Sidelights

Kalli Dakos told *SATA:* "I fell in love with writing when I was in the sixth grade. That year I enjoyed writing mysteries, and my teacher, Mr. Beecroft, always let me share them in front of the class. I loved the feeling of holding an audience entranced with my words, and knew that at some point in my life I would work as a writer. But I also wanted to be a teacher and spent years playing teacher with my younger sisters, neighbors, etc. I was a counselor in summer camps, and I loved running drop-in programs for students who were disadvantaged.

"When I was certified as an elementary school teacher, I accepted a position to teach grades five and six. This was followed by a year in the far north of Canada in a small town 120 miles above the Arctic Circle. I had one of the most fascinating years of my entire life teaching in Inuvik, Northwest Territories. I taught remedial reading in a large elementary school, and worked with

DON'T READ THIS BOOK, WHATEVER YOU DO!

MORE POEMS ABOUT SCHOOL

KALLI DAKOS

ILLUSTRATED BY G. BRIAN KARAS

Kalli Dakos used her own experiences as an elementary-school teacher as inspiration for this collection of thirty-seven poems about humorous happenings in the classroom. (Cover illustration by G. Brian Karas.)

children who had such severe reading problems that I didn't have the knowledge to design good programs for them. In spite of this, I loved my work and saw some growth in the children's academic abilities.

"I returned to school the following year for a master's degree at the University of Alberta in Edmonton, Alberta, Canada. I was determined to learn more about teaching children to read, for I had discovered in the Arctic that it was a far more complex task than I had ever realized. I completed the degree at the University of Nevada at Reno and then worked with children who had serious difficulties with reading. It was in Reno that I began my writing career by submitting short stories and articles to children's magazines. When I moved to Syracuse, New York, a few years later, I decided to study journalism at the University of Syracuse. I began writing newspaper articles, and they were published in the local papers.

"I left the classroom to pursue my writing career and continued publishing articles, stories, and poems in children's magazines. At this time, I also began working as a journalist for educational publications. As I wrote about my experiences as an educator, I began to understand my career in ways that I never had before. Even though I enjoyed writing, I found the life of an author far too lonely, and I ached to be in the classroom again. I accepted a position to teach at Manlius Pebble Hill School in Dewitt, New York. When I walked into that school for the first time after my years as a writer, I started seeing stories everywhere—in the hallways, the cafeteria, the classrooms, the playground, the library, the gym ... even in the bathrooms. My new school was a gold mine of writing opportunities, and I delighted in the incredible, crazy stories I found there.

"It seemed as if most of the tales fit best in poetry, so I wrote 'Hiding in the Bathroom,' 'The Perfect Class,' 'A Teacher's Lament,' 'Happy Hiccup to You,' 'There's a Cockroach Lurking Inside My Desk,' and many, many others. The students were the best editors of all, helping me to rewrite, revise, and select their favorites for publication. Before I knew it, the students were also writing poems and sharing them for the pure joy of it.

"I began submitting the poems about elementary school life for publication. Even though many people expressed interest and seemed to enjoy them, it wasn't until Cindy Kane, the editor-in-chief at Four Winds Press at the time, took the gamble on a basically unknown writer and decided to publish *If You're Not Here, Please Raise Your Hand: Poems about School.*

"Teachers and students loved the poems, and I began visiting schools everywhere as an author. My goal was to help teachers and children realize how exciting their lives were if only they looked at life as if they were wearing *magic glasses* and listened as if they were wearing *magic ears.* I developed a program that I called 'A Celebration of Life in the Classroom.' It involved student participation, chanting, echoing, theatrics, and toys—lots of toys to bring the poems and stories to life, and to pull in even the most reluctant readers and writers. I visited schools with magic glasses, magic ears, giant pencils, dancing coke bottles, Miss Piggy's head, worms, snakes, centipedes, toy microphones, and other crazy toys. Even though we have a lot of fun, my main goal is still academic. I want children and teachers to see that there is so much to write about in their own lives."

Dakos's collections of poems are often considered humorous and apt depictions of life in the classroom. In a review of an early effort, *Don't Read This Book, Whatever You Do!, Booklist* reviewer Hazel Rochman contended that Dakos ably captures the fun as well as the more serious side of the times teachers and children share, a sentiment expressed by other reviewers of Dakos's books. More importantly, however, according to Rochman, the poems in *Don't Read This Book* "show kids that their world is something to write about." Betty Teague, a reviewer for *School Library Journal,* commented: "Dakos has a lighthearted style and shows much warmth and understanding of her audience."

In her first book, *If You're Not Here, Please Raise Your Hand,* Dakos established the formula she would rely upon for the next three: it contains about thirty-five short poems, both rhymed and free-verse, celebrating and sometimes lamenting, the kinds of things that happen in school from the vantage point of the students, the teachers, and even from the point of view of the furniture. These poems "demonstrate a keen eye for classroom realism," avowed Amy Adler in *School Library Journal. Don't Read This Book, Whatever You Do!* followed. Dubbed a "companion volume" to *If You're Not Here,* by *School Library Journal* reviewer Sally R. Dow, *Don't Read This Book* contains thirty-seven poems that "catch the poignant moments as well as the sensitivities of children." Dakos's choice of language and subject will give this volume "wide appeal," Dow predicted.

In *Mrs. Cole on an Onion Roll,* Dakos's next book, the author geared her subject matter and language for the first-reader audience. The poems here are unfailingly "energetic, upbeat, and have a humorous slant on the trials and triumphs of the primary years," a reviewer for *Kirkus Reviews* stated. Though Dakos chose to leave out the kinds of sad poems she includes in other volumes, discussing the death of a fellow student, for instance, in "Back Away! Back Away!" from her fourth book, *The Goof Who Invented Homework,* the pieces collected in *Mrs. Cole on an Onion Roll* still "reflect Dakos' sensitivity to the behavior and emotions of elementary-

school children," contended Lauren Peterson in *Booklist.* Also for early readers is *The Bug in Teacher's Coffee,* a shorter collection that relies on "simplicity and word repetition," as applied to Dakos's favorite subjects, in order to appeal to a younger audience, noted a reviewer for *Kirkus Reviews.*

In *The Goof Who Invented Homework,* Dakos collected thirty-six predominantly humorous poems. "The subjects are all down-to-earth—the nitty-gritty of life in an elementary school," reported Susan Dove Lempke in *Booklist.* The best pieces in the collection, according to a reviewer in *Kirkus Reviews,* are those such as the title work, which ably conveys a child's point of view in language typical of the age-group of Dakos's audience. As in her earlier volumes, the levity of poems such as "Bonkers," about a teacher driven crazy by a litany of excuses from her students, is balanced by poems that poignantly deal with some of the more serious issues that may be current in a school situation, such as the death of a fellow student, and the experience of poverty. The result is "an effective and welcome collection of verse," the critic from *Kirkus Reviews* concluded.

Works Cited

Adler, Amy, review of *If You're Not Here, School Library Journal,* December, 1990, pp. 114, 116.

Review of *The Bug in Teacher's Coffee, Kirkus Reviews,* July 1, 1999, p. 1052.

Dow, Sally R., review of *Don't Read This Book, School Library Journal,* April, 1993, p. 130.

Review of *The Goof Who Invented Homework, Kirkus Reviews,* July 1, 1996, p. 965.

Lempke, Susan Dove, review of *The Goof Who Invented Homework, Booklist,* September 15, 1996, pp. 234-35.

Review of *Mrs. Cole on an Onion Roll, Kirkus Reviews,* May 1, 1995, p. 632.

Peterson, Lauren, review of *Mrs. Cole on an Onion Roll, Booklist,* June 1, 1995, pp. 1776-77.

Rochman, Hazel, review of *Don't Read This Book, Booklist,* February 15, 1993, p. 1062.

Teague, Betty, review of *The Goof Who Invented Homework, School Library Journal,* September, 1996, p. 213.

For More Information See

PERIODICALS

School Library Journal, August, 1995, p. 133.*

*   *   *

DARROW, Whitney Jr. 1909-1999

OBITUARY NOTICE—See index for *SATA* sketch: Born August 22, 1909, in Princeton, NJ; died August 10, 1999, in Burlington, VT. Cartoonist and illustrator. Darrow's career began at *New Yorker* in 1933 and ended there nearly fifty years later. Darrow grew up in Greenwich, CT, and graduated from Princeton University in 1931. It was while attending Princeton that Darrow

Offering more poems about school life, **Mrs. Cole on an Onion Roll and Other School Poems** *features thirty-two verses for young readers. (Written by Dakos and illustrated by JoAnn Adinolfi.)*

first began considering life as a cartoonist. After graduation he attended classes at the Art Students League in New York and shortly thereafter began selling cartoons to such publications *Judge* and *Life*. He sold his first cartoon to *New Yorker* in 1933, when he was twenty-four. He stayed with *New Yorker* and was one of the most popular contributors to the magazine, which sometimes published as many as fifty cartoons of his a year. Darrow published five cartoon collections: *You're Sitting on My Eyelashes, Give Up?, Stop, Miss!, Hold It, Florence,* and *Please Pass the Hostess.* In addition, he illustrated numerous books, including *Fun on Wheels* (by Joanna Cole), *Misery Is ... A Blind Date* (by Johnny Carson), and *Kids Sure Rite Funny* (by Art Linkletter). Many critics found Darrow's work to be skillful and believed he helped popularize cartoons.

OBITUARIES AND OTHER SOURCES:

PERIODICALS

Chicago Tribune, August 14, 1999, sec. 1, p. 17.
Los Angeles Times, August 13, 1999, p. A30.
New York Times, August 12, 1999, p. C21.
Washington Post, August 16, 1999, p. B7.

*   *   *

DAVIS, Yvonne 1927-

Personal

Born December 5, 1927, in Seattle, WA; daughter of Reginald (an employee of the Seattle school district) and Florence (Stepney) LeBrun; married Kenneth A. Davis, August 22, 1947 (marriage ended June 20, 1964); children: Kim, Shannon, Rebecca, Seth. *Education:* Attended high school. *Politics:* Democrat.

Addresses

Home and office—5405 Edens Rd., Anacortes, WA.

Career

Mill Pond Press, printmaker in Florida for five years; Island International, Guemes Island, WA, printmaker for twenty-five years.

Writings

ILLUSTRATOR

Bobbie Coffin, *Rider or Horseman?,* Arco (New York City), 1978.
Margaret Reed MacDonald, *Tuck Me In Tales: Bedtime Stories from around the World,* August House (Little Rock, AR), 1996.
MacDonald, reteller, *Slop! A Welsh Folktale,* Fulcrum Kids (Golden, CO), 1997.
MacDonald, reteller, *The Girl Who Wore Too Much: A Folktale from Thailand,* Thai text by Supaporn Vathanaprida, August House, 1998.

Yvonne Davis

MacDonald and Winifred Jaeger, compilers, *The Round Book: Rounds Kids Love to Sing,* Linnet Books (North Haven, CT), 1999.

Sidelights

Yvonne Davis told *SATA:* "According to my parents I showed signs of being artistic by moving my crib close to my mother's dressing table and illustrating everything in sight with her lipstick.

"After high school I married an army officer, and I have the good fortune to have four great kids and grandchildren. We lived in Nuremberg, Germany, for three years, and later lived in Taiwan. I now live on Guemes Island in Puget Sound. I built a small Japanese-style house and a print studio, also a large barn. Presently my daughter's dressage horses reside there.

"Every opportunity to illustrate that has come my way started with a phone call asking if I'd be interested. Naively, I say 'sure.' The great thing about these opportunities is that I was pushed in new directions and toward discoveries. I am grateful to the publishers and authors who have given me a chance."

For More Information See

PERIODICALS

Booklist, October 1, 1996, p. 355.

de HUGO, Pierre
See BRACKERS de HUGO, Pierre

*   *   *

de LINT, Charles (Henri Diederick Hoefsmit) 1951-
(Samuel M. Key)

Personal

Born December 22, 1951, in Bussum, Netherlands; immigrated to Canada, 1952, naturalized citizen, 1961; son of Frederick Charles (a navigator and survey project manager) Hoefsmit and Gerardina Margaretha (a high school teacher) Hoefsmit-de Lint; married MaryAnn Harris (an artist), September 15, 1980. *Education:* Attended Aylmer and Philemen Wright high schools. *Hobbies and other interests:* Music, fine arts.

Addresses

Home—Ottawa, Ontario, Canada. *Office*—P.O. Box 9480, Ottawa, Ontario, Canada K1G 3V2. *E-mail*—cdl@cyberus.ca.

Career

Worked in various clerical and construction positions, 1967-71, and as retail clerk and manager of record stores, 1971-83; writer in Ottawa, Ontario, 1983—. Owner and editor of Triskell Press; juror for William L. Crawford Award, Canadian SF/Fantasy Award, World Fantasy Award, Theodore Sturgeon Memorial Short Fiction Award, Horror Writers of America Award, and Nebula Short Fiction Award; member of Wickentree, a traditional Celtic folk music band in Ottawa, 1972-85, and Jump at the Sun, a Celtic/Americana folk band in Ottawa. *Member:* Science Fiction Writers of America, SF Canada.

Awards, Honors

William L. Crawford Award for best new fantasy author from International Association for the Fantastic in the Arts, 1984; Canadian SF/Fantasy Award ("Casper") nominations, 1986, for *Mulengro,* and 1987, for *Yarrow;* Casper Award for best work in English, 1988, for *Jack the Giant-Killer;* Readercon Small Press Award for Best Short Work, 1989, for short story, "The Drowned Man's Reel"; Reality I Commendations, Best Fantasy Author Award, 1991; New York Public Library's Best Books for the Teen Age list, and CompuServe Science Fiction and Fantasy Forum Homer Award for Best Fantasy Novel, both 1992, for *The Little Country;* Prix Ozone for Best Foreign Fantasy Short Story, 1997, for "Timeskip"; Young Adult Library Services Association of the American Library Association, Best Books for Young Adults, 1998, for *Trader.*

Writings

FICTION, AS CHARLES de LINT

"The Fane of the Grey Rose" (novelette), published in *Swords Against Darkness IV,* edited by Andrew J. Offutt, Zebra, 1979.

De Grijze Roos (title means "The Grey Rose"; short stories), Een Exa Uitgave, 1983.

The Riddle of the Wren, Ace Books, 1984.

Moonheart: A Romance, Ace Books, 1984.

The Harp of the Grey Rose, Starblaze, 1985.

Mulengro: A Romany Tale, Ace Books, 1985.

Yarrow: An Autumn Tale, Ace Books, 1986.

Stick (novella), published in *Borderland,* edited by Terri Windling and Mark Arnold, Signet, 1986.

Ascian in Rose (novella), Axolotl Press, 1987.

Jack the Giant-Killer: A Novel of Urban Faerie, Armadillo-Ace, 1987.

Greenmantle, Ace Books, 1988.

Wolf Moon, New American Library, 1988.

Westlin Wind (novella), Axolotl Press, 1988, Tor, 1993.

(Contributor) *The Annual Review of Fantasy and Science Fiction,* Meckler Publishing, 1988.

Set in modern-day Ottawa, Charles de Lint's unique fantasy novel blends Native Indian mythology with Welsh Druidism to create a tale of horror, suspense, and romance. (Cover illustration by David Bergen.)

Philip Jose Farmer's The Dungeon: Book Three, Byron Preiss/Bantam, 1988.

Philip Jose Farmer's The Dungeon: Book Five, Byron Preiss/Bantam, 1988.

Svaha, Ace Books, 1989, Tor, 1994.

Berlin (novella), Fourth Avenue Press, 1989, reprinted in *Life on the Border,* Tor, 1991.

The Fair in Emain Macha (novella), *Tor SF Double #19,* Tor, 1990.

Drink Down the Moon: A Novel of Urban Faerie, Ace, 1990, Tor, 1995.

The Dreaming Place, illustrated by Brian Froud, Atheneum, 1990.

Ghostwood, illustration by Donna Gordon, Axolotl Press, 1990.

Paperjack (novella), illustrated by Judy J. King, Cheap Street, 1991.

Ghosts of Wind and Shadow (novella), Axolotl Press, 1991.

The Little Country, Morrow, 1991, Tor, 1993.

(With others) *Death Leaves an Echo* (novella) in *Cafe Purgatorium,* Tor Horror, 1991.

Spiritwalk, Tor, 1992.

Into the Green, Tor, 1993.

Dreams Underfoot: The Newford Collection, Tor, 1993.

The Wild Wood, Bantam Books, 1994.

Memory and Dream, Tor, 1994.

The Ivory and the Horn, Tor, 1995.

Jack of Kinrowan, Tor, 1995.

Trader, Tor, 1997.

Someplace to Be Flying, Tor, 1998.

Moonlight and Vines, Tor, 1999.

The Newford Stories, SF Book Club, 1999.

Forests of the Heart, Tor, in press.

FICTION, AS SAMUEL M. KEY

Angel of Darkness, Jove, 1990.

From a Whisper to a Scream, Berkley, 1992.

I'll Be Watching You, Jove, 1994.

Also author of poetry. Work represented in anthologies, including *The Year's Best Fantasy Stories: 8,* edited by Arthur W. Saha, DAW, 1982; *Dragons and Dreams* and *Spaceships and Spells,* both edited by Jane Yolen, Martin H. Greenberg, and Charles G. Waugh, Harper, 1986 and 1987. Author of columns in horror and science fiction magazines, including a monthly book review column in the *Magazine of Fantasy and Science Fiction;* "Urban Thrills: Reviews of Short Horror and Contemporary Fantasy Fiction," in *Short Form,* "Behind the Darkness: Profiles of the Writers of Horror Fiction," in *Horrorstruck,* "Scattered Gold," in *OtherRealms,* and "Night Journeys," in *Mystery Scene,* and "The Eclectic Muse," in *Pulphouse.* Contributor to periodicals, including *Isaac Asimov's Science Fiction Magazine.*

Adaptations

"The Sacred Fire" from *Dreams Underfoot* is being filmed for an episode of *The Hunger* for the Showtime channel.

Work in Progress

A Newford novel, for Tor; short stories for various publications.

Sidelights

Canadian author Charles de Lint is a pioneer of modern fantasy, melding Faerie with the inner city. No fey, upland greenery for him; no cavorting elves or fire-breathing dragons. De Lint blends a potent brew of contemporary realism, characters that live and breathe right off the page, fast-paced plotting, and thought-provoking messages that has captured a wide and loyal readership as well as critical raves. Gary Westfahl, in a *Los Angeles Times Book Review* piece on de Lint's *The Little Country,* warns the reader off easy assumptions vis-a-vis fantasy: "In a genre choking to death on regurgitated Tolkien, de Lint does research and imbues his story with an unusual, authentic atmosphere." Westfahl continued, "In a genre of elaborately mapped Neverlands," de Lint's tales take place in a "contemporary world" that is "no less magical." No Neverland for de Lint, but he has created an intricately mapped region of his own, described in the Newford books; not dew-filled nature, but an urban environment peopled by folks like us, and others not quite like us—crow people, shape-changers, tricksters and grifters gussied up in fantastical finery.

"If ... Charles de Lint didn't create the contemporary fantasy," announced Tanya Huff in *Quill and Quire,* "he certainly defined it.... Unlike most fantasy writers who deal with battles between ultimate good and evil, de Lint concentrates on smaller, very personal conflicts." This may be the reason he appeals to all types of readers, both devoted fans and other audiences. Descriptives like "master of the genre" and "gifted storyteller" pepper reviews of de Lint's work, but de Lint himself is low-key about his achievements. In an interview with *Authors and Artists for Young Adults,* he described himself simply as a "writer of mythic fiction. It's basically mainstream writing, but with elements of myth and folktale. Not the more usual secondary-world fantasy. Some reviewers have described me as a writer who creates fantasy for people who don't normally read fantasy."

From his first publication in 1979, the novelette "The Fane of the Grey Rose," through the 1999 publication of his Newford collection of short stories, *Moonlight and Vines,* de Lint has proven himself to be a versatile and most prolific author, with over 40 books to his credit and an arm's-length list of awards and honors to his credit, including a Canadian SF/Fantasy Award, the Prix Ozone from France, and a YALSA for Best Book in 1998. Apart from a few early books in the standard high fantasy format, de Lint's output has been mainly in urban fantasy or mythic fiction, bringing quotidian magic to the streets of contemporary North America. Folk tale and myth—local variants of same, including Amerindian and Celtic (from that group of early settlers to Canada)—inform his novels and short stories, forming a bass line for a higher melody line that often includes themes of music (de Lint himself is a musician) and artists and other creative people as bridges to a deeper insight into the world. Many of de Lint's tales are set in his freshly minted city of Newford: the novels such as *Someplace to Be Flying, Trader,* and *Memory and Dream,* and the inter-connected short story collections *Dreams Underfoot, The Ivory and the Horn,* and *Moonlight and Vines.* De Lint is also known for such titles as the cult classic *Moonheart,* as well as for *Yarrow* and *The Little Country,* books that, as de Lint puts it, "convey a sort of everyday magic, that show the inexplicable connectedness we sometimes experience with places, people, works of art. I believe in these sorts of daily magic that most of us overlook in the hurried pace of modern urban life. We take these magics for granted, such as the bonds of friendship that connect us with other people and places. We have words for magic and explain it away: synchronicity, coincidence, deja vu. But it's magic nonetheless. That's really what I'm attempting to do with my books, to show simple magics in everyday life. To make us remember, observe, see the world again."

Born in Bussum, Netherlands, on December 22, 1951, de Lint immigrated with his family to Canada when he was four months old. His father worked with a surveying company, a job that took the family from Ontario to Western Canada to Quebec and on to Turkey and Lebanon until they finally settled near Ottawa. During these years of uprootedness, de Lint found stability in books, reading widely in myth and folklore. He lists Mallory, E. B. White, Tolkien, Dunsany, Lovecraft, William Morris, and Mervyn Peake among other authors whom he delighted in reading. But though he loved books, he never thought of becoming a writer. For the young de Lint, it was music that beckoned, and growing up he formed a love for Celtic music long before it became a fashionable address on the world beat map. Leaving high school two credits short of graduation, de Lint took a variety of jobs to support his music, primary among them working as a clerk at a record store.

"I don't advise my academic route to young kids," de Lint once said, "but it is important that they know there are many paths you can take in this world. Now it is increasingly difficult to get ahead without an education, but I'm the sort who learns on his own. It is ironic though that now I do for a living all those things I hated doing in school. I loved to write back then, but not the prescribed compositions and book reports. Now I write columns and book reviews in several magazines. I hated history and geography; now I research all my novels thoroughly."

Increasingly, especially on his days off from the record store, de Lint began concentrating on fiction, writing fantasy short stories that a friend illustrated. Initially this was a pastime; but when a writer saw the stories and recommended submission, avocation quickly turned to vocation. "I sold these first stories for the princely sum of $10.00 each and the proverbial light went on in my head," de Lint wrote on his Web site. "Here was

something that I loved to do and people would actually pay me to do it." Over the next six or seven years de Lint continued to play gigs on the weekend and write stories that he submitted to small magazines. His first success with a larger market was publication of "The Fane of the Grey Rose" in a Zebra collection. De Lint later expanded this short story into the novel *The Harp of the Grey Rose.*

Married in 1980 to MaryAnn Harris, de Lint continued clerking, playing music—in part with his wife—and writing. When he lost his job at the record shop in 1983, his wife encouraged him to write full time. It was wise advice: de Lint sold three manuscripts that first year of full-time writing.

One of these early books was *Riddle of the Wren,* a title that won de Lint much critical attention despite the fact that it plows the Tolkien furrow, as did his re-worked short story, *The Harp of the Grey Rose.* Writing in *Twentieth-Century Science Fiction Writers,* Maureen Speller commented that in these derivative novels "de Lint's fascination for the humbler creatures of folktale and legend, and for the darker side of magic, is also evident, and this mitigates against the more sentimental aspects . . . ." But with publication of *Moonheart,* de Lint was already moving away from the typical imaginary landscape of fantasy to an urban environment. Working on further advice from his wife, he decided to set his fantasy fiction in a realistic environment, opting for modern Ottawa, as it was the locale he knew best. With this novel de Lint began also his peculiar blending of Canadian mythologies, using traditions found in Native Indian shamanism and in Welsh Druidism. Called "a milestone of modern fantasy writing" by Speller, *Moonheart* also blends suspense, horror, and romance in the tale of an Ottawa mansion that proves to be linked to an old battle between good and evil. Tamson House is actually a gate between our world and a magical realm. De Lint's cast of characters ranges from a mage's apprentice, a reformed biker, and an inspector for the Canadian Mounted Police, to the magical little people called manitous and legendary figures out of Welsh and Celtic myth.

Writing in *Voice of Youth Advocates,* David Snider called *Moonheart* "a fascinating and enthralling work that should be in every YA collection," while *Booklist*'s Roland Green commented that the book was "[a] very good and distinctly unconventional fantasy novel." De Lint had found his territory and his voice. "This was really my first successful blend of mythic fiction and fantasy," de Lint commented. Over the next several years he wrote several more loosely linked novels and stories in the "Moonheart" series: *Ascian in Rose, Westlin Wind,* and *Ghostwood,* later collected in *Spiritwalk.* Reviewing that collection in *Quill and Quire,* Michelle Sagara noted that de Lint explores not only the "brightness of magic," but also "its shadow," and that with his multi-layered characters thrown into the mix, "magic becomes choice and consequence, an echo of reality, not an escape from it." Sagara concluded that

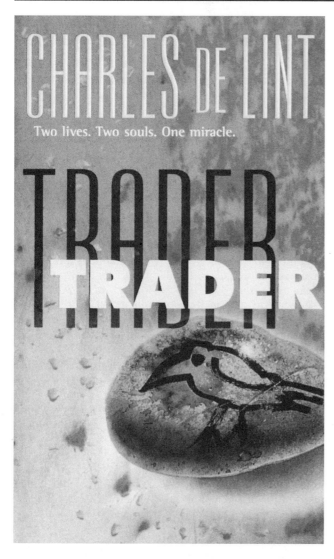

In this unusual coming-of-age story, Max Trader wakes up one morning in the body of a shiftless drunk and must cross into an otherworld to discover why he is no longer himself. (Cover illustration by John Howe.)

"there are very few fantasists today who write with such poetic simplicity and skill."

De Lint turned his fictional eye to Romany culture for *Mulengro,* a book that is a hybrid of horror and fantasy genres. Set among Canada's modern-day gypsy communities, the book tells the story of a series of bizarre murders that have police baffled. The gypsies, however, know that they are dealing with the mythic Mulengro, "He Who Walks with Ghosts." It is up to a reclusive gypsy man and a young woman to get to the heart of this mythic threat and eliminate it. Gary Farber commented in *S.F. Chronicle* that *Mulengro* is "[s]uspenseful, original, and extremely well written." While some other critics did not find the novel to be as successful in blending magic with urban reality as was *Moonheart,* *Booklist*'s Green noted that de Lint "deserves high marks for his research, storytelling," and for his character descriptions.

Other early books in de Lint's development of his mythic fiction include *Yarrow* and *Jack the Giant-Killer.* The former deals with a young fantasy writer whose work comes from her nightly dreamscape. But when her dreams are increasingly being stolen by a telepathic vampire-type creature, she loses the ability to create. Nancy Choice noted in *Voice of Youth Advocates* that "*Yarrow* is filled with suspense and tension from beginning to end." The protagonist of the novel, Cat, is one of a long line of appealing female characters de Lint has created, a "just plain nice person you would like to have living next door," according to Choice. *Jack the Giant-Killer* continues this two-fold trend of strong female characters and a blend of urban setting with Faerie legend. Part of a series of modern retellings of fairy tales, the novel centers on Jacky Rowan, who develops magical powers through the domain of a red cap. She can see the giant in the city park and the elves in the oaks. Faerie has come to the city. And soon she learns that the good elves are dwindling in number, the bad ones prospering. The only way to stop this process is to set the princess free and recapture the Horn for the forces of good. Identifying with the elves as part of the Kinrowan clan, Jacky takes on the task with a little help from her friends, in a "very satisfying" tale, according to Tom Easton of *Analog Science Fiction/Science Fact,* who also dubbed de Lint "one of Canada's modern masters of fantasy." De Lint reprised Jacky in *Drink Down the Moon,* another blend of fairy-tale motifs and modern settings; both books were later published in the omnibus *Jack of Kinrowan.*

De Lint's intricately plotted and crafted novels are not the result of equally intricate plot outlines, but of a hit-and-miss organic approach to writing, as the author described it. "I like to start out with a sense of theme— basic things like let's treat each other better, or do unto others, or be loyal and true to your friends, or we should pay attention to the world around us, to really see it for the magic it contains. Those are the sorts of messages I deal in. And I also like to have the sense of a few scenes in my head, and of course a few characters that I get to know in the process of writing about them. I don't like writing from an outline; it bores me and it too often makes the writing dead, without spontaneity. Of course this method can lead to dead ends. I sometimes get a hundred or two hundred pages into a novel and then discover that I took a wrong turn ten, twenty, maybe a hundred pages earlier. Then I have to throw it all out and start from where it stopped working."

De Lint once again combined Native American mythology with Celtic in his 1990 novel, *The Dreaming Place,* with illustrations by Brian Froud. Featuring teenage cousins, Nina and Ashley, and an emphasis on realism, this book "might ... encourage some realistic fiction fans to give ... fantasy a try," according to Kathryn Pierson in *Bulletin of the Center for Children's Books.*

De Lint's next novel, *The Little Country,* is one of his "most complex," as de Lint himself describes it. It is also one of his favorites, a story within a story and a loving exposition of de Lint's own affection for folk music. Set in modern Cornwall, the novel tells the story of Janey Little, a successful musician, who comes back to the village of Mousehole in England. Apart from her music, another major thing that has influenced her life are the writings of Billy Dunthorn, and she soon discovers an unpublished manuscript of Dunthorn's in the family attic. This manuscript tells the story of Jodi and her friend Denzil in the fictional village of Bodbury. As Janey gets further into the book, parallels develop between real life and that of the story in the found manuscript. Outside forces conspire in the form of John Madden of the Order of the Grey Dove who must have the magical Dunthorn manuscript, which can provide the possessor with ultimate power. The reader is soon swept along following two storylines that ultimately converge. As Peter Crowther noted in *St. James Guide to Fantasy Writers,* the book is filled with "charm, excitement, and above all, complete believability." According to Crowther, "it is [de Lint's] unerring knack of concentrating on his characters and filling them out, making them so real, that places his work at the forefront of the field." A *Publishers Weekly* contributor commented that de Lint's "rendering of the small Cornish town of Mousehole and the life of a folk musician rings true."

One of de Lint's most popular fictional conceits has been his creation of a fantasy world for an ensemble cast of characters. But true to de Lint form, this imaginary world is a compilation of urban settings, from London to Los Angeles. "The derivation of Newford was accidental," de Lint told *Authors and Artists for Young Adults.* "It just grew over the course of several stories. I suddenly realized that I had created a new setting all my own with its own geography, commerce, and population. There are a lot of advantages to such a fictional place: I don't have to go out and do research to make sure I've got the right store on the right corner, for example. But Newford has its own headaches for me. It's getting so complex that I need a map and concordance to keep things straight. And I don't have those. It's all in my head."

The first collection of Newford tales, *Dreams Underfoot,* gathered stories published in magazines over several years, and began the building of the ensemble cast of characters that flow in and out of all the Newford stories. There is Jilly, the artist; Lorio, part gypsy and part punk; Lesli, who sets free the Faerie with her music; and a rich assortment of other urban types. One of the outstanding stories in *Dreams Underfoot,* "Timeskip," won France's Prix Ozone. Elizabeth Hand, in the *Washington Post Book World,* called this "a genuinely chilling ghost story as poignant as it is creepy." Further story collections in the Newford series include *The Ivory and the Horn,* a "fanciful and moving collection," according to a *Publishers Weekly* critic, and *Moonlight and Vines,* stories which demonstrated de Lint to be, according to *Booklist*'s Green, "the most literate and ingenious purveyor of urban fantasy."

De Lint has also used his fictional Newford as the setting for four novels: *Memory and Dream, Trader, Someplace to Be Flying,* and *Forests of the Heart.* In the first of these, the painter, Isabelle, learns to paint amazing creatures that unleash ancient spirits into the modern world. "It is hard to imagine urban fantasy done better than it is by de Lint at his best," remarked *Booklist*'s Green. Jodi L. Israel, writing in *Kliatt,* commented that "Charles de Lint is a master of contemporary fantasy," and that his "literate and flowing style makes his words a pleasure to read." Trading places is at the heart of de Lint's 1997 *Trader,* in which a man named Trader awakes to discover he has traded bodies with a reprobate named Johnny Devlin. Trying to reclaim his own life, Trader becomes involved in the lives of all those whom Devlin has injured. Along the way, readers are re-introduced to stock characters out of Newford, including Jilly Coppercorn and street musician Geordie Riddell, as well as the shaman, Bones. "Readers familiar with de Lint's work know that he is a master of imagery and trenchant detail," wrote Donna Scanlon in a *Voice of Youth Advocates* review of *Trader.* "He continues to demonstrate his remarkable ability here," Scanlon concluded, "never los[ing] control of his myriad plot threads or deftly drawn characters."

One of the most popular Newford novels, and de Lint's personal favorite, is *Someplace to Be Flying,* featuring freelance photographer Lily Carson and a gypsy cab driver, Hank Walker. Once again, de Lint draws the reader into a parallel otherworld, a city beneath the city in the Tombs, and into the realm of shape-shifting animal people, who were the original inhabitants of the earth. The original animal people, as de Lint has it, ultimately turned into the separate animals and people we know today, and in his book, the author focuses specifically on corvids—crows and ravens. *Library Journal*'s Jackie Cassada praised de Lint's "elegant prose and effective storytelling" and his "unique" blend of "magical realism" and "multicultural myths." Brian Jacomb concluded a laudatory *Washington Post Book World* review by noting that "*Someplace to Be Flying* is . . . a solid thriller, full of suspense and peppered with villains of various talents and their adversaries, the decent folk who constantly try to thwart their evil intentions."

"As a writer, my first obligation is to entertain," de Lint concluded. "But as an artist, I know that I first have to please myself, to entertain myself. I try to write the sort of book I want to read but have not been able to find. There has to be that sort of energy in the book, or it won't work for others. Along the way, I hope to remind readers about how much everyday magic there is all around us in the world, if we only will take the time to really see." For de Lint, the very process of writing reinforces the overriding theme of his work. "Making things up for a living is a very magical occupation."

Works Cited

Cassada, Jackie, review of *Someplace to Be Flying, Library Journal,* January, 1998, p. 148.

Choice, Nancy, review of *Yarrow, Voice of Youth Advocates,* February, 1987, p. 291.

Crowther, Peter, *St. James Guide to Fantasy Writers,* St. James Press, 1996, pp. 153-55.

De Lint, Charles, interview with *Authors and Artists for Young Adults,* conducted July 23, 1999.

De Lint, Charles, excerpt from author's Web site, located at http://www.cyberus.ca/~cdl/bio.htm.

Easton, Tom, "The Reference Librarian," *Analog Science Fiction/Science Fact,* August, 1988, pp. 137-38.

Farber, Gary, review of *Mulengro, S.F. Chronicle,* July, 1986, p. 41.

Green, Roland, review of *Memory and Dreams, Booklist,* October 1, 1994, p. 246.

Green, Roland, review of *Moonlight and Vines, Booklist,* December 1, 1998, p. 655.

Green, Roland, review of *Moonheart, Booklist,* December 15, 1984, p. 558.

Green, Roland, review of *Mulengro, Booklist,* November 15, 1985, p. 468.

Hand, Elizabeth, review of *Dreams Underfoot, Washington Post Book World,* May 30, 1993, p. 9.

Huff, Tanya, "Rising Stars in Fantasy Worlds," *Quill and Quire,* May, 1993, p. 26.

Israel, Jodi L., review of *Memory and Dreams, Kliatt,* January, 1996, p. 14.

Review of *The Ivory and Horn, Publishers Weekly,* March 27, 1995, p. 77.

Jacomb, Brian, review of *Someplace to Be Flying, Washington Post Book World,* March 15, 1998, p. 9.

Review of *The Little Country, Publishers Weekly,* December 7, 1990, p. 74.

Pierson, Kathryn, review of *The Dreaming Place, Bulletin of the Center for Children's Books,* January, 1991, p. 114.

Sagara, Michelle, review of *Spiritwalk, Quill and Quire,* July, 1992, pp. 37-38.

Scanlon, Donna, review of *Trader, Voice of Youth Advocates,* August, 1997, p. 192.

Snider, David, review of *Moonheart, Voice of Youth Advocates,* February, 1985, pp. 335-36.

Speller, Maureen, essay on de Lint in *Twentieth-Century Science Fiction Writers,* third edition, St. James Press, 1991, pp. 196-98.

Westfahl, Gary, "Orange County Apple and Other Aberrations," *Los Angeles Times Book Review,* February 3, 1991, p. 11.

For More Information See

BOOKS

Clute, John, and Peter Nicholls, editors, *The Encyclopedia of Science Fiction,* St. Martin's Press, 1993.

Science Fiction and Fantasy Literature, 1975-1991, Gale, 1992.

PERIODICALS

Analog Science Fiction/Science Fact, September, 1987, pp. 159-62; November, 1993, pp. 162-69.

Booklist, May 15, 1992, p. 1666; February 1, 1995, p. 993; January 1, 1997, p. 826; December 1, 1998, p. 655.

Library Journal, May 15, 1992, p. 123; February 15, 1999, p. 188.

Locus, October, 1993, p. 33; November, 1994, pp. 52, 68.

Publishers Weekly, October 3, 1994, p. 54; January 26, 1998, p. 74; December 21, 1998, p. 60.

Quill and Quire, January, 1995, p. 35; January, 1997, p. 18; February, 1997, p. 49; February, 1998, p. 35.

School Library Journal, February, 1991, p. 93; December, 1993, pp. 29, 149.

Voice of Youth Advocates, April, 1994, p. 36; April, 1998, pp. 12, 36.

—Sketch by J. Sydney Jones

*   *   *

DENIM, Sue
See PILKEY, Dav

E–F

ELLEN, Jaye
See NIXON, Joan Lowery

*   *   *

ERLBACH, Arlene 1948-

Personal

Born October 8, 1948, in Cleveland, OH; daughter of Morris (in sales) and Lillian (Fried) Faverman; married Herb Erlbach (a computer trainer and consultant), November 27, 1977; children: Matthew. *Education:* Kent State University, B.S. (communications), 1971; Northeastern Illinois University, Chicago, M.S. (special education), 1989. *Politics:* Liberal. *Religion:* "Jewish (non-practicing)." *Hobbies and other interests:* Animals.

Addresses

Home and office—5829 Capulina Ave., Morton Grove, IL 60053. *Agent*—Lettie Lee, The Ann Elmo Agency, Inc., 60 East 42nd St., New York, NY 10165.

Career

Writer. Schoolteacher in Illinois. *Member:* Society of Children's Book Writers and Illustrators, Romance Writers of America, The Young Adult Network, Children's Reading Round Table.

Awards, Honors

Golden Medallion for best young adult novel, Romance Writers of America, 1987, for *Does Your Nose Get in the Way, Too?*

Writings

YOUNG ADULT FICTION

Does Your Nose Get in the Way, Too?, Crosswinds, 1987.
Guys, Dating, and Other Disasters, Crosswinds, 1987.
Drop out Blues, Crosswinds, 1988.
A Little More Love, Bantam, 1994.
The Herbie Hummerston Homework Haters' Club, Willowisp, 1995.
My Pet Rat, illustrated by Andy King, Lerner, 1998.

YOUNG ADULT NONFICTION

Hurricanes, Children's Press, 1993.
Peanut Butter, Lerner Publications, 1994.
Floods, Children's Press, 1994.
Tornadoes, Children's Press, 1994.
Bicycles, illustrated by Jackie Urbanovic, Lerner, 1994.
Soda Pop, Lerner, 1994.
The Best Friends Book: True Stories about Real Best Friends, Fun Things to do with Your Best Friend, Solving Best Friends Problems, Long-Distance Best Friends, Finding New Friends, and More!, Free Spirit, 1994.
Video Games, Lerner, 1995.
Forest Fires, Children's Press, 1995.
Blizzards, Children's Press, 1995.
Wonderful Wolves of the Wild, Willowisp Press, 1996.
The Families Book: True Stories about Real Kids and the People They Live with and Love, Fun Things to Do with Your Family, Making Family Trees and Keeping Family Traditions, Solving Family Problems, Staying Close to Faraway Relatives, and More!, illustrated by Stephen J. Carrera, Free Spirit, 1996.
Teddy Bears, Carolrhoda Books, 1997.
Happy Birthday, Everywhere!, illustrated by Sharon L. Holm, Millbrook, 1997.
The Kids' Invention Book, Lerner, 1997.
Sidewalk Games around the World, illustrated by Sharon L. Holm, Millbrook, 1997.
The Kids' Business Book, Lerner, 1998.
Everything You Need to Know if Your Family Is on Welfare, Rosen Publishing Group, 1998.
The Kids' Volunteering Book, Lerner, 1998.
Bubble Gum, Lerner, 1998.
Kent State, Children's Press, 1998.
Comic Books, Lerner, 1998.
T-Shirts, illustrated by Jackie Urbanovic, Lerner, 1999.

Arlene Erlbach

Worth the Risk: True Stories about Risk Takers Plus How You Can Be One, Too, Free Spirit, 1999.
Working in Education, Lerner, 1999.

Sidelights

"I've always loved to write and make up stories," Arlene Erlbach told *SATA.* "When I was in grade school I'd make up stories about children while I lay in bed." It was not until much later, however, that Erlbach paid attention to the praise her writing had earned from teachers and professors and submitted a novel for publication.

The book, *Does Your Nose Get in the Way Too?,* follows a teenage girl, Henny Zimmerman, through the trials of Highland High School, where her lack of inclusion in fashionable cliques creates a personal crisis for her. In a *Voice of Youth Advocates* review of *Does Your Nose Get in the Way, Too?,* Joan Wilson complimented Erlbach's "genuine sympathy for the heroine." Henny thinks cosmetic surgery to reduce the size of her nose will solve her problems, but her father refuses to permit her to have the operation. Despite her nose, which she finally realizes isn't bad at all, Henny establishes a romantic relationship which relieves her anxiety.

Henny also appears in Erlbach's second book, *Guys, Dating, and Other Disasters,* in which a school assignment dealing with marriage runs a parallel course with the impending marriage of Henny's widowed father. Erlbach's third book, *Drop Out Blues,* is about two cousins who drop out of school and move in together. Commenting on her inspirations for writing, Erlbach related to *SATA:* "I get ideas from my childhood, my son's experiences, the news and kids at the school where I teach. In addition to being an author, I teach elementary school. I am in charge of my school's Young Authors' Program. It gives me great joy to encourage children in reading and writing."

Erlbach is also the author of several nonfiction works for children and young adults covering everything from natural disasters, in *Hurricanes, Blizzards,* and others, to food, in *Soda Pop* and *Bubble Gum,* and fun, in *Bicycles* and *Video Games.* In the latter title, Erlbach provides a concise history of the popular pastime from pinball to the most recent innovations in a book that "should enthrall aficionados," noted Judie Porter in *School Library Journal.* Also for middle-grade readers is Erlbach's *Happy Birthday, Everywhere!,* which surveys the birthday customs from countries around the world and appends a related craft or cooking project to each. *Booklist* reviewer Carolyn Phelan remarked that both children and adults would find "plenty to interest them here" when planning a party. Jane Claes in *School Library Journal* made a similar observation, and in conclusion dubbed *Happy Birthday, Everywhere!* "a solid addition to any collection on a subject that never goes out of fashion."

For young adults, Erlbach has written several books containing information on solving problems, including *The Best Friends Book* and *The Families Book,* both of which have a section on resolving the problems that arise in relationships, *Everything You Need to Know if Your Family Is on Welfare,* and *Worth the Risk,* which teaches young people about predicting the consequences of risky behavior, either positive or negative. In *The Families Book,* the author spotlights the children of numerous families, who describe how they cope with such things as parental differences in religious and cultural backgrounds, the illness of a family member, and step-siblinghood, among other issues that commonly arise in families. Erlbach includes information on projects that tend to encourage family cohesiveness, such as making a family tree, and offers advice on how to call family meetings and how to deal with annoying relatives. The result is certainly praiseworthy, remarked Jerry D. Flack in *School Library Journal,* who stated, "There is not a false note here."

Worth the Risk helps young people evaluate risk-taking behavior and emphasizes the positive results that are possible when the risk is worth taking. The book contains interviews with a number of young people who at some personal risk stood up for themselves or others and found themselves called heroes. "The narratives are sure to provoke discussion about various types of

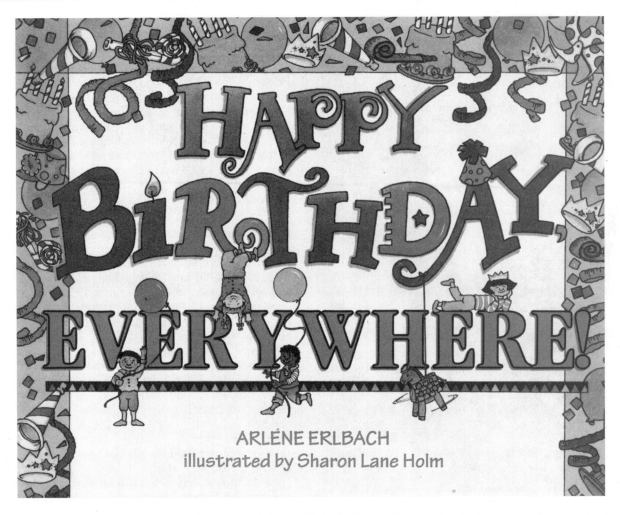

Erlbach discusses birthday traditions from around the world, including crafts to make, food to eat, and games to play. (Cover illustration by Sharon Lane Holm.)

behavior," predicted Lynn W. Zimmerman in *School Library Journal.*

Works Cited

Burner, Joyce Adams, review of *Does Your Nose Get in the Way, Too?*, *School Library Journal*, September, 1987, p. 195.

Claes, Jane, review of *Happy Birthday, Everywhere!*, *School Library Journal*, February, 1998, p. 98.

Flack, Jerry D., review of *The Families Book*, *School Library Journal*, August, 1996, p. 153.

Phelan, Carolyn, review of *Happy Birthday, Everywhere!*, *Booklist*, December 1, 1997, p. 618.

Porter, Judie, review of *Video Games, School Library Journal*, June, 1995, p. 118.

Wilson, Joan, review of *Does Your Nose Get in the Way, Too?*, *Voice of Youth Advocates*, October, 1987, pp. 200-201.

Zimmerman, Lynn W., review of *Worth the Risk, School Library Journal*, August, 1999, pp. 168-69.

For More Information See

PERIODICALS

Booklist, August, 1995, p. 1944; May 1, 1999, p. 1584.
School Library Journal, October, 1987, pp. 149-150.
Voice of Youth Advocates, June, 1988, p. 85; December, 1987, p. 234.

*   *   *

FADIMAN, Clifton (Paul) 1904-1999

OBITUARY NOTICE—See index for *SATA* sketch: Born May 15, 1904, in Brooklyn, NY; died of pancreatic cancer, June 20, 1999, on Sanibel Island, FL. Radio show host, editor, author. Fadiman helped establish the Book-of-the-Month Club and spent more than five decades reviewing books for the group. He loved the written word, having read his first book at age four, and continued his hobby until well into his eighties when he became blind due to acute retinal necrosis. He estimated he had read about 25,000 books in his lifetime and although he lost his sight, he did not lose his interest in books. As a member of the editorial board for Book-of-the-Month he continued reviewing books after listening to them on tape. Fadiman's career included a brief stint as a teacher before he moved to publisher Simon & Schuster, where he was an editor from 1927 to 1935. From there he moved to *New Yorker* magazine, working as book editor. During his tenure at the *New Yorker* he became involved in radio and hosted the "Information Please" show, which ran from 1938 to 1948. The show featured four intellectuals (including Fadiman) who would answer questions sent in by listeners. Anyone who could stump the stars received a free set of *Encyclopedia Britannica*. The show was a success and at one time could claim nine million listeners. Other broadcasts hosted by Fadiman include *Conversation, Mathematics, What's in a Word?, This is Show Business,* and *Quiz Kids.* In 1944 he joined the Book-of-the-Month Club staff and served in a variety of positions until he was named chairman emeritus in 1997. He served on the editorial board for Encyclopaedia Britannica beginning in 1955 and created *Treasury of the Encyclopaedia Britannica,* condensing the company's editions into one volume. A fan of anthologies and treasuries, Fadiman edited more than thirty, including *The Three Readers: An Omnibus of Novels, Stories, Essays and Poems, The Short Stories of Henry James,* and *Party of Twenty: Informal Essays from Holiday Magazine.* Not content to simply edit other people's works and write introductions to them, Fadiman was an author in his own right. He produced a number of books for adults, among them *The Lifetime Reading Plan, Enter, Conversing,* and, with Sam Aaron, *The Joys of Wine* and *The Wine Buyer's Guide.* In addition, Fadiman also wrote several books for children, including *The Voyages of Ulysses, The Adventures of Hercules,* and *The Story of King Arthur.*

OBITUARIES AND OTHER SOURCES:

PERIODICALS

Chicago Tribune, June 21, 1999, sec. 2, p. 7.
Los Angeles Times, June 22, 1999, p. A24.
New York Times, June 21, 1999, p. B8.
USA Today (electronic), June 21, 1999.
Washington Post, June 22, 1999, p. B7.

*   *   *

FORREST, Elizabeth
See SALSITZ, Rhondi Vilott

*   *   *

FUERTES, Gloria 1918-

Personal

Born July 28, 1918, in Madrid, Spain; daughter of a concierge. *Education:* Studied library science, beginning in 1955; attended a trade school for women in Madrid, Spain.

Addresses

Agent—c/o Catedra, Juan Ignacio Luca de Tena, 15-28027 Madrid, Spain.

Career

Pelayo and *Maravilla* (children's magazines), editor and writer, 1940-55; affiliated with the poetry magazine *Arquero,* 1952-55; librarian, beginning in 1960; Bucknell University, Lewisburg, PA, professor of Spanish literature, 1961-64; literature teacher to American students, Madrid, Spain, until 1975; also appeared on children's television programs and worked as a reader and lecturer.

Awards, Honors

Honorable mention, Concurso Internacional de Poesia Lirica Hispana, 1958, for *Todo asusta;* Fulbright fellowship, 1961-64, to teach Spanish at Bucknell University; Guipuzcoa poetry prize, Spain, 1966, for *Ni tiro, ni veneno, ni navaja;* Premio Vizcaya, 1969, for *Como atar los bigotes al tigre;* awards for *Cangura para todo;* Spanish fellowship for authors of children's literature.

Writings

Isla ignorada (title means "Unknown Island"), Musa Nueva (Madrid, Spain), 1950.
Canciones para ninos, Escuela Espanola (Madrid, Spain), 1952.
Aconsejo beber hilo (title means "I Advise Drinking Thread"), Arquero (Madrid, Spain), 1954.
Antologia y poemas del suburbio (title means "Anthology and Poems of the Urban Poor"), Lirica Hispana (Caracas, Venezuela), 1954.
Villancicos, Magisterio Espanol (Madrid, Spain), 1954.
Piruli, Escuela Espanola, 1955.
Todo asusta (title means "Everything Is Frightening"), Lirica Hispana, 1958.
Que estas en la tierra (title means "Who Art on Earth"), Literaturasa (Barcelona, Spain), 1962.
Ni tiro, ni veneno, ni navaja (title means "Not by Gunshot, Nor by Poison, Nor by Razor"), Bardo (Barcelona, Spain), 1966.
Cangura para todo (title means "Kangaroo at Your Service"), Lumen (Barcelona, Spain), 1967.
Poeta de guardia (title means "Poet on Call"), Ciencia Nueva (Madrid, Spain), 1968.
Como atar los bigotes al tigre (title means "How to Tie the Tiger's Whiskers"), Bardo, 1969.
Antologia poetica (1950-1969), edited by Francisco Yndurain, Plaza & Janes (Barcelona, Spain), 1970.
Don Pato y Don Pito, Escuela Espanola, 1970.
Aurora, Brigida y Carlos, Lumen, 1971.
La pajara pinta, Alcala (Madrid, Spain), 1972.
Cuando amas aprendes geografia (title means "When You Love You Learn Geography"), Curso Superior de Filogia (Malaga, Spain), 1973.
El camello-auto de los reyes magos, Igreca (Madrid, Spain), 1973.
El hada acaramelada, Igreca, 1973.

Sola en la sala (title means "Alone in the Living Room"), Javalambre (Zaragoza, Spain), 1973.

La gata Chundarata y otros cuentos, Videosistemas, 1974.

Obras incompletas, Catedra (Madrid, Spain), 1975.

Miguel: Un cuento muy moral en cinco capitulos y un prologo, Alfaguara (Madrid, Spain), 1977.

El libro de los derechos del nino, Nebrija (Leon, Spain), 1978.

Las tres reinas magas: Cuento teatro, Escuela Espanola, 1979.

Historia de Gloria (Amor humor y desamor) (title means "Gloria's Story"), Catedra, 1980.

La ardilla y su pandilla, Escuela Espanola, 1981.

Asi soy yo, Emiliano Escolar (Madrid, Spain), 1982.

Coleta, la poeta, Minon (Valladolid, Spain), 1982.

El abecedario de don Hilario, Minon, 1982.

El dragon tragon, Escuela Espanola, 1982.

Coleta payasa, que pasa?, Minon, 1983.

La momia tiene catarro, Escuela Espanola, 1983.

La oca loca, Escuela Espanola , 1983.

Piopcio Lope, el pollito miope, Escuela Espanola, 1983.

Plumilindo: El cisne que queria ser pato, Escuela Espanola, 1983.

El domador mordio al leon, Escuela Espanola, 1984.

El libro loco de todo un poco: Libro primero (cuentos, versos, aventuras, historietas, fantasias, chistes, acertijos, poesias, botijos, etc.), Escuela Espanola, 1984.

Off the Map, Wesleyan University Press (Middletown, CT), Harper & Row (Scranton, PA), 1984.

Yo contento, tu contenta que bien me sale la cuenta: La tabla en verso, Escuela Espanola, 1984.

Mujer de verso en pecho, Catedra, 1995.

Interviews with Fuertes have been published in *Insula* and *Libro Espanol.* Contributor to periodicals, including *Maravilla* and *Pelayo.*

Sidelights

Gloria Fuertes is a Spanish writer popular with adults and children. From her first book of poems, she has received distinction and praise for her straightforward, often autobiographical verse. Her readings and appearances on children's television have brought her even more devotees. According to *Dictionary of Literary Biography* contributor Martha LaFollette Miller, in an interview with Fuertes translated into English, the author has claimed that her work *Historia de Gloria (Amor humor y desamor)* "isn't a book, but a woman," perhaps indicating how her writings are an extension of her life and personality.

Fuertes was born in Madrid in 1918 to a working-class family. She experienced a childhood filled with poverty and struggle, although she began writing verse during that time and enjoyed sports. She attended a trade school for women where she learned cooking, embroidery, hygiene, child care, and sewing. In 1934 her mother died during the Spanish Civil War, and later, a young man Fuertes loved disappeared. These tragic events and others appear in her poetry.

Throughout her early hardships, Fuertes regularly wrote poetry, which has been published in numerous volumes. She uses humor, wordplay, and slang to address themes of love, death, injustice, and suffering. She has been categorized as a social poet because of her desire to reach as many people as possible. Her professional writing career began as an editor for two children's magazines, *Pelayo* and *Maravilla,* where she also composed weekly stories. Throughout this period she continued writing poetry. In 1950 her poetry volume *Isla Ignorada* ("Unknown Island") was published. Although the pieces in the book do not address the social issues prominent in her later work, they do contain some themes Fuertes uses in future poems as well as autobiographical elements. During the 1950s Fuertes produced books of children's poems and was actively involved in the literary life of Madrid. She then studied library science and became a librarian.

During the 1950s Fuertes also produced new books of poems for adults. *Antologia y poemas del suburbio* ("Anthology and Poems of the Urban Poor") was published in 1954 but was poorly distributed and received little critical attention. According to Francisco Yndurain (cited in the *Dictionary of Literary Biography*), *Antologia y poemas del suburbio* and Fuertes's 1958 volume *Todo asusta* display the hallmarks of Fuertes's later work. Both volumes contain free verse, autobiographical elements, intentionally unpolished writing, and wordplay. Fuertes maintains that poets can help others by addressing social ills. She stresses the healing power of poetry. These convictions further identify Fuertes with the social poetry movement.

Aconsejo beber hilo ("I Advise Drinking Thread") was published in 1954. In this volume, Fuertes's poems are more autobiographical, ranging from a dryly humorous perspective to a surrealistic tone. This book deals with the unique and often maddening nature of various aspects of life. It also reveals Fuertes's thoughts on the nature of existence and death. She uses new poetic techniques in *Aconsejo beber hilo,* imitating the style of advertising slogans, personal letters, and sentences from grammar books. She uses these styles more frequently in later works.

In *Todo asusta* ("Everything Is Frightening"), Fuertes's focus shifts from personal concerns to humanity. She writes about people in need both materially and spiritually and harshly criticizes the problems inherent in Spanish society. According to the *Dictionary of Literary Biography,* in one poem Fuertes "states that she prefers childlessness to raising a child to be cannon fodder." In another, she asserts that a world free of pain can only exist beyond the grave. No one is above Fuertes's criticism in *Todo asusta.* This is evident even in her portrayal of God, depicted in the poem translated as "God Chokes but He Doesn't Squeeze."

In 1962 an anthology of Fuertes's previously published poetry, *Que estas en la tierra* ("Who Art on Earth"), was released. During this time, Fuertes was finally attracting the attention of a wider audience. Fuertes wrote the 1966 volume *Ni tiro, ni veneno, ni navaja* ("Not by Gunshot, Nor by Poison, Nor by Razor") while living in the United States. In the words of Miller, this book "reveals Fuertes's struggle with intensely negative feelings about human existence," and contains more philosophical verse. Fuertes's later work includes the poetry volumes *Poeta de guardia* ("Poet on Call") and *Como atar los bigotes al tigre* ("How to Tie the Tiger's Whiskers").

In *Poeta de guardia,* Fuertes again elaborates on the themes of God, love, and death, addressing these themes in a more positive light and using more humor. She uses extremely brief poetic texts, which she would use more in later volumes. She comments more on current events and uses more colloquial language in the volume. Fuertes also continues to promote poetry's healing effects. Fuertes further experiments with new styles in *Como atar los bigotes al tigre,* alternating tragedy with humor. Along with her usual techniques, she begins to use personification as a tool for expression. This technique is evident in poems such as "La Huespeda" ("The Guest"), where she portrays anguish as an unwelcome squatter.

During the 1970s Fuertes once again concentrated on producing children's literature. By 1975 she quit teaching and reached her audience through her writings, poetry readings, and television appearances. She tried to generate interest in literature by traveling to Spanish provinces in order to read to illiterate people and people who could not afford to buy books. Fuertes's 1980 *Historia de Gloria (Amor humor y desamor)* ("Gloria's Story") contains a more knowledgeable perspective on her usual themes and uses many poems from her personal diary. Some of the verses refer to her difficult early childhood, while others depict her adult life. In these extremely personal pieces and other poems, Fuertes writes of her feelings about life and poetry.

Works Cited

Miller, Martha LaFollette, essay in *Dictionary of Literary Biography,* Volume 108: *Twentieth-Century Spanish Poets,* Gale (Detroit, MI), 1991.

G

GABER, Susan 1956-

Personal

Born June 23, 1956, in Brooklyn, NY; married Richard Barkey, 1988; children: Elias. *Education:* C. W. Post College/Long Island University, BFA, 1978. *Hobbies and other interests:* Gardening and herbology.

Addresses

Home—44 Dunlop Road, Huntington, NY 11743.

Career

Freelance illustrator for accounts including *Newsday,* card company Ellen Anderson Productions, magazines including *Child, Spider, Home, Fifty Plus, House Beautiful,* and for publishers including Scholastic, Dover, Dutton, Knopf, Villard, Pantheon, Doubleday, Workman, Harcourt Brace, Philomel, Putnam, Harper and Row, Orchard, Atheneum, and Farrar, Straus and Giroux, 1978—. *Member:* Graphic Artists' Guild.

Writings

ILLUSTRATOR

Heather Forest, *The Baker's Dozen,* Harcourt Brace Jovanovich, 1988.

Forest, *The Woman Who Flummoxed the Fairies,* Harcourt Brace Jovanovich, 1990.

Jacqueline Briggs Martin, *The Finest Horse in Town,* HarperCollins, 1992.

Briggs Martin, *Good Times on Grandfather Mountain,* Orchard Books, 1992.

Elizabeth Enright, *Zeee,* Harcourt Brace Jovanovich, 1993.

Emma Bull, *The Princess and the Lord of Night,* 1994.

Lee Bennett Hopkins, *Small Talk,* Harcourt Brace, 1995.

Steve Sanfield, *Bit by Bit,* Philomel, 1995.

Alma Flor Ada, *Jordi's Star,* Putnam, 1996.

Liz Rosenberg, *Eli and Uncle Dawn,* Harcourt Brace, 1997.

Rafe Martin, *The Brave Little Parrot,* Putnam, 1997.

Forest, *Stone Soup,* August House, 1998.

Erica Silverman, *Raisel's Riddle,* Farrar, Straus and Giroux, 1998.

Rhonda Growler Greene, *The Stable Where Jesus Was Born,* Atheneum, 1999.

Jennifer Armstrong, *Pierre's Dream,* Dial, 1999.

Martin, *The Language of Birds,* Putnam, 2000.

Nancy Van Laan, *When Winter Comes,* Atheneum, 2000.

Sidelights

Illustrator of a score of children's picture books, Susan Gaber is noted for watercolors and acrylics that at times give a folksy feel to stories, at others impart a lushness and vividness of tone, and at still others become elegant fine art reproductions. Her versatility is well-suited to mythic and folk tales as well as to romantic and fanciful stories.

Born in Brooklyn, New York, Gaber grew up in Wantagh, Long Island. Graduating from high school in 1974, she attended Long Island University where she earned a bachelor of fine arts degree with honors in 1978. That same year she began her freelancing career, working as an illustrator for card companies as well as newspapers and magazines. By 1988 she had enlarged her repertoire to included illustrations for children's books.

Gaber's first children's title was Heather Forest's 1988 traditional tale, *The Baker's Dozen.* That same year Gaber married, and gave birth to a son the following year. She teamed up with Forest again in 1990 for *The Woman Who Flummoxed the Fairies,* and again in 1998 for *Stone Soup,* another traditional tale about two hungry travelers who declare they can make soup from a stone when they are denied food at a mountain village. But they explain they just need a carrot for taste, and then perhaps a little potato would also help. In this way the duo manage to outwit the villagers and create a pot of steaming soup. "Gaber's bold acrylic paintings emphasize the black soup tureen and the brightly colored vegetable ingredients," noted a reviewer for *Publishers Weekly,* while Kathleen Whalin commented in *School*

Susan Gaber illustrated the activities of Old Washburn, content to sit on his porch and whittle, even as disaster strikes all around him. (From Good Times on Grandfather Mountain, *written by Jacqueline Briggs Martin.*)

Library Journal, "Gaber's brilliantly colored paintings illuminate a mountain village with a multicultural population."

Gaber teamed up with the writer Jacqueline Briggs Martin for two titles, *The Finest Horse in Town* and *Good Times on Grandfather Mountain.* The first book, a fictionalized memoir of Martin's two great-aunts, tells of two sisters who run a dry goods store in nineteenth-century Maine and of their carriage horse, Prince. *Publishers Weekly* felt that "Gaber's exquisite watercolors have the naive beauty of early American folk paintings," and Charlene Strickland noted in *School Library Journal* that the "full-color paintings illustrate the mild humor of the incidents and capture the essence of small-town concerns." *Good Times on Grandfather Mountain* tells of Old Washburn who always looks on the bright side of things: when the cow runs off he has a drum instead of milk bucket; when the pig follows suit, the former fence posts become drum sticks. Told in the cadences of a folk tale, the book is a "rustic narrative," according to *Publishers Weekly,* and "Gaber's watercolors imbue this cautionary tale with a folksy flavor that suggest good times indeed." *Horn Book*'s Nancy Vasilakis noted, "The imagery of humans in communal harmony with nature is carried through in illustrations,"

while Kate McClelland remarked in *School Library Journal* on Gaber's watercolors "in a pleasing palette" which "harmoniously depict Washburn's farm as a laissez-faire kind of place."

Gaber turned from rustic to fanciful with illustrations for Elizabeth Enright's *Zeee. Zeee* is the story of an ancient misanthropic fairy whose hatred for humankind changes when he is befriended by young Pandora who offers Zeee the comfort of her dollhouse. Writing of Gaber's illustrations in *School Library Journal,* Valerie F. Patterson noted that they were "colorful and attractive," and "feature colored shadings of brown and green with occasional flashes of red." *Booklist*'s Ellen Mandell commented, "Gaber's lush watercolors delight in their conjuring of Zeee's first tidy home, with its milkweed pod bed, clamshell bathtub, and chrysalis lantern." More fairy tales are served up in Gaber's illustrations for Emma Bull's *The Princess and the Lord of Night.* The eponymous lord puts a curse on the princess at birth, so that if she ever wishes for something she can not have, then the kingdom will fall and her parents will die. Reviewing the book in *School Library Journal,* Lauralyn Persson felt Gaber's "romantic watercolor-and-colored pencil illustrations are lush yet delicate, with clear, rich colors and lovely, flowing lines," while a *Publishers Weekly* reviewer called attention to the "elegant illustrations" which "contain a Renaissance luminosity and precision" as well as "fantasy images." The reviewer for *Publishers Weekly* concluded, "Stylish and visually intriguing, this lyrical fairy tale is enchanting."

Thirty-three short poems are collected by Lee Bennett Hopkins in *Small Talk,* a celebration of simple moments in life for which Gaber contributed the illustrations. The verses deal with the seasons, growing up, the process of a day to night, the birth of a kitten, and dozens of other domestic joys from the pens of poets such as Langston Hughes, Sara Teasdale, and Carl Sandburg, among others. Dot Minzer, reviewing the picture book in *School Library Journal,* felt "Gaber's watercolor and colored-pencil illustrations appear as little gems at the top of many of the poems and as double-page backgrounds for others." Minzer concluded that the Gaber and Hopkins collaboration produced a "stunning little book." *Horn Book*'s Nancy Vasilakis commented, "This small, well-designed book with its lovely watercolor spots and double-page-spread illustrations has copious depths to be mined."

A trio of folktales, two Yiddish, and one Indian, inspired Gaber's brush and palette in collaboration with Steven Sanfield, Erica Silverman, and Rafe Martin. In Sanfield's *Bit by Bit,* a Russian Yiddish folk song was adapted to tell the story of a tailor who wears out his favorite coat and then turns the scraps into further favorite garments which he proceeds to wear out bit by bit. "Imaginative pictures embroider the story line in this suitably homespun adaptation," noted a reviewer for *Publishers Weekly.* Barbara Kiefer, writing in *School Library Journal,* commented, "Gaber's folk-like paintings, done in strong, clear colors, echo the brightly painted threads that are central to the tale." Kiefer went

A young princess, cursed at birth to receive everything she wants or else see her kingdom destroyed, must begin a journey to find true contentment. (From The Princess and the Lord of Night, *written by Emma Bull and illustrated by Gaber.)*

on, "Best of all, Gaber shows us what the words don't tell us, that as [the tailor] Zundel's garments become smaller and smaller, his life becomes richer and fuller." *Booklist*'s Hazel Rochman echoed this sentiment, noting that the "pictures extend the song, showing the tailor with his loving family through the years, as each piece of clothing wears out."

The Cinderella tale got a revamping in Silverman's *Raisel's Tale,* a Yiddish tale from Poland. Finding work in the kitchen of a famed rabbi, Raisel, the orphan of a scholar, is mistreated by the cook and kept from the Purim party. But Raisel disguises herself as Queen Esther, attends the party, and there charms the rabbi's son. *Booklist*'s GraceAnne A. DeCandido commented on Gaber's artwork in a starred review: "The illustrations in velvety, muted colors make use of strong geometric shapes and varying perspectives." DeCandido concluded, "This universal story fits into its Jewish milieu as neatly as a key in a lock." Susan P. Bloom, reviewing the title in *Horn Book,* noted, "Artist Gaber conveys a folkish simplicity with a sophisticated line to evoke a Poland of dreams and reality in which, at book's end, the happy couple float Chagall-like among flower blossoms, living and learning 'happily ever after.'"

A traditional jataka tale from India is at the heart of Martin's *The Brave Little Parrot,* with illustrations by Gaber, in which a small gray parrot takes on a raging forest fire. Watching the spectacle of this hapless parrot trying to battle the fire with minuscule drops of water, a god takes the form of an eagle whose tears ultimately quench the flames. "Gaber's paintings are rich with lush greens and flaming oranges," remarked Judith Gloyer in *School Library Journal.* "The artwork strongly reinforces the message of this lively story," Gloyer concluded. "Gaber's moving, full-page, color illustrations increase the drama of the fire," commented *Booklist*'s Karen Morgan, "showing the seeming impotence of even the most powerful forest creatures and emphasizing the precious beauty of water and its relationship to continued life." Gaber has also teamed up with Martin on *The Language of Birds.*

A further trio of books illustrated by Gaber illuminate the activities of a young boy, his uncle, and his toy elephant in *Eli and Uncle Dawn,* the tireless work of a shepherd in *Jordi's Star,* and the laziest man at a circus in *Pierre's Dream.* In the first book, written by Alma Flor Ada, Jordi, the lonely shepherd, falls in love with the reflection of a star he sees in a well he has dug: simple Jordi actually believes the star has fallen from the sky. "The gently humorous illustrations make the tale of Jordi's spiritual growth shine with joy," commented a reviewer for *Publishers Weekly,* while *Booklist*'s Susan Dove Lempke felt the "touching, lyrically told story is given substance by Gaber's earthy illustrations, which show Jordi as a poignantly real man, his broad face and large hands in sharp contrast to the delicate flowers and twinkling star."

In this Yiddish version of the Cinderella story, a bright young girl relies on her intelligence to find a prince at a Purim celebration. (From Raisel's Riddle, *written by Erica Silverman and illustrated by Gaber.)*

Fantasy takes over in Liz Rosenberg's *Eli and Uncle Dawn* when young Eli understands that his uncle's magic is for real. Forgetting his stuffed elephant at a picnic, the boy is able to float through the night to retrieve him, thanks to Uncle Dawn. A contributor to *Publishers Weekly* commented that Gaber "crafts a stimulating backdrop to this imaginative tale" by deploying "a color-saturated blend of watercolor, acrylic and colored pencil, and setting a lively visual pace that skips from full-page illustrations to small insets...." And in *Pierre's Dream,* by Jennifer Armstrong, another nighttime, dream-like pursuit results in a rescued animal— this time real—when lazy Pierre recaptures a lion from the circus. Reviewing this last title, the *Publishers Weekly* reviewer felt that "Gaber fills in any gaps in narrative logic with a soft impressionistic touch that gracefully moves between the real and imagined."

Whether working in muted impressionistic tones, in more vibrant colors, or in a folksy, homespun medium, Gaber has built an impressive list of illustration credits and has garnered much critical acclaim for her work. Working with watercolors, acrylics, or colored pencils Gaber's illustrations "captivate the eye," as Barbara Elleman noted in *School Library Journal.*

Works Cited

Review of *Bit by Bit, Publishers Weekly,* March 20, 1995, p. 59.

Bloom, Susan P., review of *Raisel's Riddle, Horn Book,* March-April, 1999, p. 215.

DeCandido, GraceAnne A., review of *Raisel's Riddle, Booklist,* May 1, 1999, p. 1590.

Review of *Eli and Uncle Dawn, Publishers Weekly,* February 3, 1997, p. 105.

Elleman, Barbara, review of *Pierre's Dream, School Library Journal,* June, 1999, p. 85.

Review of *The Finest Horse in Town, Publishers Weekly,* June 22, 1992, p. 61.

Gloyer, Judith, review of *The Brave Little Parrot, School Library Journal,* May, 1998, p. 135.

Review of *Good Times on Grandfather Mountain, Publishers Weekly,* February 3, 1992, p. 80.

Review of *Jordi's Star, Publishers Weekly,* November 4, 1996, p. 75.

Kiefer, Barbara, review of *Bit by Bit, School Library Journal,* August, 1995, p. 128.

Lempke, Susan Dove, review of *Jordi's Star, Booklist,* December 1, 1996, p. 652.

Mandell, Ellen, review of *Zeee, Booklist,* June 1 & 15, 1993, pp. 1830-31.

McClelland, Kate, review of *Good Times on Grandfather Mountain, School Library Journal,* August, 1992, p. 144.

Minzer, Dot, review of *Small Talk, School Library Journal,* May, 1995, p. 99.

Morgan, Karen, review of *The Brave Little Parrot, Booklist,* February 15, 1998, pp. 1014, 1016.

Patterson, Valerie F., review of *Zeee, School Library Journal,* June, 1993, pp. 74-75.

Persson, Lauralyn, review of *The Princess and the Lord of Night, School Library Journal,* May, 1994, p. 89.

Review of *Pierre's Dream, Publishers Weekly,* May 31, 1999, p. 92.

Review of *The Princess and the Lord of Night, Publishers Weekly,* February 28, 1994, p. 87.

Rochman, Hazel, review of *Bit by Bit, Booklist,* March 15, 1995, p. 1336.

Review of *Stone Soup, Publishers Weekly,* May 25, 1998, p. 89.

Strickland, Charlene, review of *The Finest Horse in Town, School Library Journal,* August, 1992, p. 144.

Vasilakis, Nancy, review of *Good Times on Grandfather Mountain, Horn Book,* May-June, 1992, pp. 332-33.

Vasilakis, Nancy, review of *Small Talk, Horn Book,* May-June, 1995, pp. 338-39.

Whalin, Kathleen, review of *Stone Soup, School Library Journal,* May, 1998, pp. 131-32.

For More Information See

PERIODICALS

Booklist, February 1, 1992, p. 1041; June 1 & 15, 1994, p. 1824; August, 1995, p. 1953; May 15, 1997, p. 1581.

Publishers Weekly, March 16, 1990, p. 68; December 1, 1997, p. 52; February 22, 1999, p. 94; May 31, 1999, p. 92; August 16, 1999, p. 87.

School Library Journal, April, 1989, p. 96; June, 1990, p. 112; December, 1996, p. 84; June, 1997, p. 100.

Wilson Library Bulletin, December, 1988, p. 88.

—Sketch by J. Sydney Jones

* * *

GONZALEZ, Christina
See GONZALEZ, Maya Christina

* * *

GONZALEZ, Maya
See GONZALEZ, Maya Christina

* * *

GONZALEZ, Maya Christina 1964-
(Christina Gonzalez, Maya Gonzalez)

Personal

Born January 24, 1964, in Lancaster, CA; daughter of Sid (an electrician) and Mary Ellen (self-employed; maiden name, Vensel) Gonzalez; married Wendi Raw (a yoga instructor), May 1, 1989. *Education:* University of Oregon, 1984-87.

Addresses

Home and office—3460 16th St., apt. #2, San Francisco, CA 94114. *E-mail*—mzmaya@dnai.com.

Career

Fearless Art (jewelry business), owner, Eugene, OR, 1988-94; Children's Book Press, San Francisco, CA, illustrator, 1994—. Taught "Fearless Art," University of Oregon, and "Fearless Art for Kids," Maude Kernes Art Center, both Eugene, OR, 1989; National Endowment for the Arts Grant Jury Board, 1992; taught in the Children's Book Press Outreach Program in schools in San Francisco Bay Area and Los Angeles, 1996—; WritersCorps teacher training and student presentations, San Francisco, 1999. *Exhibitions:* Has shown work in solo shows since 1988 in Eugene, OR, and San Francisco, CA, and in group shows since 1991 in Eugene, San Francisco, Fresno, CA, Chicago, IL, Hayward, CA, Oakland, CA, and Los Angeles, CA.

Awards, Honors

Prietita y la llorona won the Americas Honor Award and was named a Smithsonian Notable Book, both in 1994; *Laughing Tomatoes and Other Spring Poems* received the Pura Belpre Honor Award, the National Parenting Publications Gold Medal Award, and was a finalist for the Riverbank Review "Children's Books of Distinction," all in 1996; *From the Bellybutton of the Moon* appeared on the Americas Commended List, won the Skipping Stones Honor Award, and the Choices Award from the Cooperative Children's Book Center, all in 1997.

Writings

ILLUSTRATOR

(As Christina Gonzalez) Gloria Anzaldua, *Prietita and the Ghost Woman/Prietita y la llorona,* Children's Book Press (San Francisco, CA), 1995.
Patricia Almada, *The Crying Mountain,* Rigby, 1997.
I Come from Two Lands, edited by Mary Carden and Mary Cappellini, Rigby, 1997.
Francisco X. Alarcon, *Laughing Tomatoes and Other Spring Poems/Jitomates risuenos y otros poemas de primavera,* Children's Book Press, 1997.
Francisco X. Alarcon, *From the Bellybutton of the Moon and Other Summer Poems/Del ombligo de la luna y otros poemas de verano,* Children's Book Press, 1998.
Francisco X. Alarcon, *Angels Ride Bikes and Other Fall Poems/Los Angeles andan en bicicleta y otros poemas de otono,* Children's Book Press, 1999.
Alba Ambert, *Face Toward the Sky,* Rigby, 1999.
Nicholasa Mohr, *Amigos Inseperables* (for Reading 2000), Simon & Schuster, 2000.
Amanda Perez, *A Room of My Own,* Children's Book Press, in press.

Gonzalez's work is also included in two collections from Children's Book Press: *Just Like Me: Stories and Portraits by 14 Artists,* 1996; and *Honoring Our Ancestors: Stories and Portraits by 14 Artists,* 1998.

Maya Christina Gonzalez

Sidelights

Maya Christina Gonzalez told *SATA:* "I have loved to draw and color for as long as I can remember. As a child I would go looking for my face in my coloring books, in my storybooks ... but I never found my round, chicana face, my long dark hair. So I would go to that blank page in the back or the front of these books and draw my own big face right in where it belonged.

"That's what I tell the kids when I go into the schools. Those empty spots are actually there so that we can draw ourselves in. We belong everywhere. Our face is important. It is a mark of who we are and where we come from. I work almost exclusively with children of color. Children with faces like mine. I teach the kids to claim all that they are: their face, their feelings, their experiences. And express that for all the world to share through art.

"All my books are bilingual. This always seems like a secret prize for me. As a small boy my father was enrolled in an all English speaking school. He spoke only Spanish. I know this was a difficult way for him to learn. It must have affected him because although his family spoke primarily Spanish, I was not raised speaking it at all. In fact I am still learning to speak it. When I am alone in my studio working on one of my books, there is a part of me who is painting for that small boy who became my father."

Maya Christina Gonzalez is known for providing brightly colored paintings that complement and expand upon the themes and emotions evoked by the texts they accompany. In Gonzalez's book, *Prietita and the Ghost Woman,* author Gloria Anzaldua retells a legend about a girl sent by a healer into the forest for a healing plant that will cure her mother. In Anzaldua's version, the lost girl gets no help from the various animals she questions, but finds the plant and makes her way out of the woods aided by La Llorona, the crying woman who lives in the forest, which is a twist on the usual ending of the Prietita legend. "Gonzalez's lovely folk paintings, awash in bright colors, authentically portray the people and native plants and animals of this South Texas locale," observed Marilyn Taniguchi in *School Library Journal.*

Gonzalez has also collaborated with poet Francisco X. Alarcon on several award-winning volumes organized by the seasons. Like *Prietita and the Ghost Woman, Laughing Tomatoes and Other Spring Poems/Jitomates risuenos y otros poemas de primavera* is also a bilingual text published by Children's Book Press. In this work, poet Alarcon provides short, imagistic poems centered on the joys of springtime while artist Gonzalez's abundant illustrations expand upon the themes of the text, according to Annie Ayres in *Booklist.* The effect of Alarcon's "telegraphic one-and two-syllable lines" "is that of quick snapshots of moments in life," wrote Ann Welton in a *School Library Journal* review. Gonzalez's "bold ... paintings" illustrate the poet's bilingual musings on subjects familiar to readers of children's poetry, including food, weather, and dreams, Welton continued. In *From the Bellybutton of the Moon and Other Summer Poems/Del Ombligo de la Luna y otros poemas de verano,* Alarcon and Gonzalez teamed up to produce a similar volume inspired by the joys of summertime in Mexico. As in the earlier volume, to which *From the Bellybutton* was favorably compared, "Alarcon exhibits a tremendous talent for imbuing quotidian objects ... with dignity and jubilation," Denise E. Agosto attested in *School Library Journal.* And again, Gonzalez's brightly colored illustrations featuring Latino children garnered critical acclaim as well. Reviewing *From the Bellybutton of the Moon* for *Booklist,* contributor Annie Ayres concluded, "Gonzalez's happy paintings weave rich waves of color in an exuberant dance between text and design."

Works Cited

Agosto, Denise E., review of *From the Bellybutton of the Moon, School Library Journal,* December, 1998, p. 98.

Ayres, Annie, review of *From the Bellybutton of the Moon, Booklist,* October 15, 1998, p. 423.

Review of *Laughing Tomatoes and Other Spring Poems, Booklist,* June 1, 1997, p. 1707.

Taniguchi, Marilyn, review of *Prietita and the Ghost Woman, School Library Journal,* July, 1996, p. 82.

Welton, Ann, review of *Laughing Tomatoes and Other Spring Poems, School Library Journal,* May, 1997, p. 118.

For More Information See

ON-LINE

Author's internet website, http://www.mayagonzalez. com.

* * *

GORDON, Amy 1949-
(Amy Lawson)

Personal

Born January 22, 1949, in Boston, MA; daughter of Lincoln (a professor, diplomat, and economist) and Allison (an artist, writer, and mother; maiden name, Wright), Gordon; married Richard Lawson (divorced 1995); children: Nicholas Lawson, Hugh Lawson. *Education:* Attended Mary C. Wheeler School, 1968; Bard College, 1972. *Politics:* "Eclectic." *Religion:* "Eclectic." *Hobbies and other interests:* "Writing, reading, mountain climbing, sailing, spending time with people I like, traveling."

Addresses

Home—P.O. Box 186, 2 Old Sunderland Road, Montague, MA 01351. *Office*—Bemeut School, Deerfield, MA. *Literary agent*—George Nicholson, Sterling Lord Literistic, New York, NY.

Career

Bemeut School (K-9 boarding school), Deerfield, MA, drama teacher/director, chair of Fine Arts, 1980—.

Writings

(Under name Amy Lawson) *The Talking Bird and the Story Pouch,* illustrated by Craig McFarland Brown, Harper, 1983.

(Under name Amy Lawson) *Star Baby,* illustrated by Margot Apple, Harcourt Brace Jovanovich (San Diego, CA), 1991.

Midnight Magic, illustrated by Judy Clifford, BridgeWater (Mahwah, NJ), 1995.

When JFK Was My Father, Houghton Mifflin (Boston), 1999.

Sidelights

Amy Gordon told *SATA:* "When I was young, I was a shy person in a verbal, intellectual, talkative family. I discovered that if I *wrote* entertaining stories as Christmas presents, then I could get the entire family to stop talking and pay attention to me. The written word allowed me to have a voice.

"I loved to read when I was young, and spent quite a lot of time pretending. I loved the world of childhood and left it reluctantly. In my adult life, I am very lucky to have a career (teaching drama and directing plays with 6th-9th graders) which allows me to encourage pretending. The creative problem-solving involved in teaching helps my writing, and the kids I teach, also, of course, inspire me. I am a lot less shy, now, but I still feel the written word is my best tool for expressing and sharing my real self."

Amy Gordon's books for children often underline the author's belief in the positive power of imagination. In *Midnight Magic*, Uncle Harry is babysitting Jake and Sam over a weekend when Sam has lost a tooth and Jake's pet hamsters are missing. Uncle Harry distracts the children by enacting their favorite story, "Puss in Boots," and when they wake up on Saturday morning, Sam finds a golden key left under his pillow by the Tooth Fairy. Sam and Jake thus begin to search for the evil Ogre of the "Puss in Boots" story to return the golden key to him, and along the way they find Jake's hamsters. *School Library Journal* reviewer Mary Jo

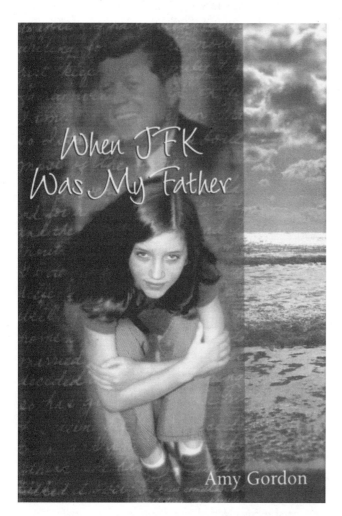

Emotionally neglected by her parents, Georgia Hughes decides to give herself an imaginary father who helps her adjust to the changes in her family life in Amy Gordon's novel. (Cover illustration by Kamil Vojnar.)

Drungil singled out Gordon's "utterly realistic" characterizations of the boys and their "ideal" uncle for special praise. Drungil predicted that *Midnight Magic* is "certain to be appreciated by young fairy-tale fans."

While *Midnight Magic* extols the value and fun of imagination for chapter-book readers, Gordon's novel *When JFK Was My Father* asserts the power of a fantasy life for adolescent readers. This work centers on fourteen-year-old Georgia Hughes, who lives in Brazil with her emotionally remote parents until their marriage breaks apart after Georgia's mother discovers her husband is having an affair. Georgia and mother move to Washington, D.C., and Georgia is deposited in a boarding school in Connecticut, where she feels abandoned by both parents and disconnected from the other students. "It is an inventive and stubborn imagination that keeps Georgia afloat; it is an equally strong and willing heart that brings her back to shore," remarked Patricia McCormick in the *New York Times Book Review*. In Brazil, Georgia had compensated for her cool relationship with her father by pretending that American president John F. Kennedy was her father, and in boarding school in Connecticut, this fantasy offers her a valuable refuge from the stress of her new and lonelier life. Georgia also gets solace from her imagined relationship with the school's long-dead founder, who offers practical advice. "Georgia's account of her virtual abandonment at school by her parents and her barely conscious search for a home is both poignant and gently funny," contended Lauren Adams in *Horn Book*.

When Tim, a friend from Brazil who has run away from his boarding school, invites Georgia to run away with him, Georgia realizes that she no longer wants to leave her school. It has become a home to her and is full of people she cares about and who care for her. "The novel is well paced with moments of dramatic tension," noted Adams, adding that "Georgia's refreshing narrative" ably reveals the cast of interesting secondary characters. "Gordon writes in a vivid, defining style that allows Georgia to emerge as a fresh, fully realized character," attested Ilene Cooper in *Booklist*. Cooper and other critics noted the appeal of Gordon's use of a 1960s setting, remarking that Georgia's attraction to the charismatic, short-lived president mirrors in some regards the emotions he evoked in the nation as a whole. For Connie Tyrrell Burns, writing in *School Library Journal,* the success of *When JFK Was My Father* rests on Gordon's creation of a "likable and well-drawn character [in Georgia], with a wonderful voice." Burns concluded: "Readers will empathize with her and cheer her coming-of-age."

Works Cited

Adams, Lauren, review of *When JFK Was My Father,* in *Horn Book,* July-August, 1999, pp. 463-64.
Burns, Connie Tyrrell, review of *When JFK Was My Father,* in *School Library Journal,* April, 1999, p. 134.
Cooper, Ilene, review of *When JFK Was My Father,* in *Booklist,* June 1, 1999, p. 1813.

Drungil, Mary Jo, review of *Midnight Magic,* in *School Library Journal,* December, 1995, pp. 80-81.
McCormick, Patricia, review of *When JFK Was My Father,* in *New York Times Book Review,* October 17, 1999, p. 31.

*   *   *

GREENWOOD, Pamela D. 1944-
(Ryan Ann Hunter, joint pseudonym)

Personal

Born May 4, 1944, in Great Falls, MT; daughter of Harry Evans (a railroad dispatcher) and Cleo Katherine (a teacher and school principal; maiden name, Hogan) Dickinson; married Walter Bart Greenwood (formerly a reporter, now in public relations), January 23, 1971; children: Anna, Elisabeth, Wynne. *Education:* Settle University, B.A. in English; attended University of Oregon, graduate studies in special education, in the 1970s. *Hobbies and other interests:* Gardening, quilting, sailing and canoeing, hiking, and reading.

Career

Writer. Has taught developmentally disabled preschoolers, worked in a group home for emotionally disabled children, was a nurse's aide at a nursing home, and has worked in a business office; currently teaches writing, gives school presentations and workshops on collaborating. *Member:* Society of Children' Book Writers and Illustrators, Women Who Write (board member).

Awards, Honors

First Prize, *Pockets* Magazine Fiction Writing Contest, 1992, for a short story, "Starting Over"; PTA Golden Acorn Award for volunteer service.

Writings

What about My Goldfish?, Clarion, 1993.
I Found Mouse, Clarion, 1994.

AS RYAN ANN HUNTER, WITH ELIZABETH G. MACALASTER

Cross a Bridge, illustrated by Edward Miller, Holiday House, 1998.
Into the Sky, illustrated by Edward Miller, Holiday House, 1998.
Dig a Tunnel, illustrated by Edward Miller, Holiday House, 1999.

Stories have appeared in *Pockets, Highlights for Children, Junior Trails, Guide Magazine, On the Line, Ladybug,* and *The Friend.*

Work in Progress

Working on a first novel set in Montana, rewriting a beginning reader first composed four years ago; with collaborator Elizabeth G. Macalaster (as Ryan Ann Hunter), working on books on fishing boats, robots, and

Pamela D. Greenwood

undersea technology, revising a manuscript on crows, and collecting a folder of information on buffaloes.

Sidelights

Pamela D. Greenwood told *SATA:* "I am a curious person. To this day my dad says I ask too many questions! But I want to know more about other people, about the world around me, and about myself. Writing is one way of finding things out. In my stories, I put my characters in difficult situations and ask them what they'll do next. While I had a safe and happy childhood, I remember the scariness of not understanding adult things and the frustration of not having everything my own way! We all have problems to solve. I want kids who read my stories to share my characters' experiences from the inside, to get a new perspective on growing up, to feel the power it takes to change or accept things in life.

"I get to ask questions in my nonfiction writing too. What a lucky day for me when, by chance, I met my coauthor, Elizabeth Macalaster. She joined a writing group I was in and we soon discovered that we shared a sense of wonder about the world of nature, science, and technology. We look at things with a child's urgency to know: how? why? so what? One thing that delights me in the school presentations I've given is to have kids ask more questions! I'm glad that our books inspire that.

"I like how it feels to put words together. Now and again a piece of writing seems to flow out almost in finished form, but usually I go through many revisions. I want it

A tree fell across a stream.
Someone chasing an animal
scrambled across it.
This was the first
wood bridge.

Cooperating with Elizabeth G. Macalaster under the pseudonym Ryan Ann Hunter, Greenwood explores the many different types of bridges and how they work. (From Cross a Bridge, *illustrated by Edward Miller.)*

to sound just right. I read my stories out loud, and my coauthor and I read our work out loud too. In fact, we created our pen name, Ryan Ann Hunter, partly to honor the 'voice' that we both hear when we talk our way through a project.

"Do you want to write, too? Choose topics and themes that are important to you. Let your own questions be a starting point."

With Elizabeth G. Macalaster, Pamela D. Greenwood formed the joint pseudonym Ryan Ann Hunter, and together they have created a series of picture books for preschoolers interested in technology-based topics. Their first book, *Cross a Bridge,* in which "young construction and transportation enthusiasts are inducted into the world of bridges," according to a reviewer for *Kirkus Reviews,* was greeted enthusiastically by critics for its exceptionally simple, yet apt, presentation of its subject. In only a brief sentence or two on each page, the authors

discuss the basics of a variety of bridges while emphasizing their usefulness for humans.

In *Into the Sky* Greenwood and Macalaster as Hunter offer a similar treatment of skyscrapers. As in *Cross a Bridge,* the text in *Into the Sky* balances technical information on foundations, walls, windows, and the history of tall buildings, with more poetic prose emphasizing the majesty of skyscrapers. And, like the earlier book, the authors' use of simple but precise language combine with illustrations. For Kathy Piehl, writing in *School Library Journal,* the book effectively captures "the excitement inherent in creating huge structures that soar above their surroundings." A reviewer for the *Times,* published by the Council on Tall Buildings and Urban Habitat, wrote: "*Into the Sky* is a good beginning book for any child with an interest in skyscrapers, cities or construction."

Like Greenwood and Macalaster's first two books, their third, *Dig a Tunnel*, was praised for packing in a lot of information on its topic in a form that is both accessible to the youngest of book audiences and exciting to read. *School Library Journal* reviewer Lee Bock described *Dig a Tunnel* as "filled with useful information expressed in a lively style." In the text, the authors begin with animals and insects who tunnel, then move quickly on to survey a number of human tunnels built to solve a variety of problems, and the uses they have been put to. Reviewers singled out the authors' tactic of inserting interesting details or anecdotes about specific bridges into the text for special praise. "Younger fans of the wheeled vehicles that are visible here in profusion will want repeat readings," concluded a contributor to *Kirkus Reviews*.

Greenwood has also published two fiction books for children under her own name. In *What about My Goldfish*, a little boy whose family is moving across country expresses his anxieties about the changes the move will necessitate through his worries about his goldfish. "First and second graders will follow his narrative intensely," predicted Charlene Strickland in *Wilson Library Bulletin*, "sharing his fears when he tells his friends and teacher he has to move." Greenwood uses contemporary language effectively, and manages to create rounded characters and a well-paced plot in a chapter-book format for first readers, Strickland continued, concluding that the author "tells a universal story that speaks to readers of all ages."

[For more information on Pamela Greenwood, please see the entry on Elizabeth Macalaster in this volume.]

Works Cited

Bock, Lee, review of *Dig a Tunnel, School Library Journal*, April, 1999, p. 114.

Review of *Cross a Bridge, Kirkus Reviews*, February 15, 1998, p. 268.

Review of *Dig a Tunnel, Kirkus Reviews*, January 15, 1999, p. 146.

Review of *Into the Sky, Times* (Council on Tall Buildings and Urban Habitat), September, 1998, p. 2.

Piehl, Kathy, review of *Into the Sky, School Library Journal*, September, 1998, p. 192.

Strickland, Charlene, "Chapter One: Transitional Books for First through Third Grade," *Wilson Library Bulletin*, October, 1993, p. 120.

For More Information See

PERIODICALS

Booklist, April 1, 1998, p. 1326; September 15, 1998, p. 233.

Engineering News-Record, February 22, 1999.

Horn Book Guide, fall, 1998, p. 392; spring, 1999, p. 32.

Kirkus Reviews, August 1, 1998, p. 1118.

Publishers Weekly, October 26, 1998, p. 69; February 8, 1999, p. 212.*

H–I

HAYASHI, Leslie Ann 1954-

Personal

Born August 3, 1954, in Tokyo, Japan; married Alan Van Etten (an attorney), May 10, 1986; children: Justin, Taylor. *Education:* Stanford University, B.A. (with distinction), 1976; Georgetown University, J.D., 1979.

Leslie Ann Hayashi

Addresses

Home—Honolulu, HI. *Office*—District Court of the First Circuit, 1111 Alakea St., Third Floor, Honolulu, HI 96813.

Career

American Judicature Society, Chicago, IL, visiting fellow and staff attorney in Educational Programs Department, 1979-80; Hamilton, Gibson, Nickelsen, Rush & Moore, Honolulu, HI, partner and associate, 1980-88; Hawaii Lawyers Care, Honolulu, HI, executive director, 1988-89; ACRO, Inc., Honolulu, in-house counsel, 1988-90; First Circuit Court, Honolulu, HI, district court judge, 1989—. Hawaii Supreme Court, member of committee on equality and access to the courts, 1990—; vice-chair, 1993; co-chair, 1993—. *Member:* American Bar Association, American Inn of Court (Bencher, 1992—), Hawaii State Bar Association (member of board of directors, 1988-90; member of executive committee, 1990; chairperson of Standing Committee on Law-Related Education, 1994; director of Young Lawyers Division, 1987-88, vice-president of division, 1989, president, 1990), Hawaii State Trial Judges' Association (member of executive committee, 1993-97), Hawaii Women Lawyers (secretary, 1984; vice-president, 1985; president, 1986), Hawaii Women's Legal Fund (director, 1986-88, 1990-94; secretary, 1991), Hawaii Women's Consortium (co-founder; director, 1985), Hawaii Friends for Civic and Law-related Education (founding member; president, 1995-97), Illinois State Bar Association, Judiciary History Center (board member, 1990-93).

Awards, Honors

Named outstanding attorney of the year, Hawaii Women Lawyers, 1989; Justice Award, Young Lawyers Division, Hawaii State Bar Association, 1995; Grand Prize, *Honolulu* Magazine Fiction Contest, 1995, for "Thoughts for a Dead Japanese Fisherman"; Ka Palapala Po'okela Award of Excellence in Illustration in Children's Books and Award of Merit, Hawaii Book

Publishers Association, both 1999, for *Fables from the Garden.*

Writings

JUVENILE

Fables from the Garden, illustrated by Kathleen Wong Bishop, University of Hawaii Press (Honolulu, HI), 1998.

Fables from the Sea, University of Hawaii Press, 2000.

OTHER

(Contributor) *What You Need to Know If You Decide to Go out on Your Own: A Handbook for Solo and Small Firm Practitioners,* Hawaii State Bar Association, 1993.

(Contributor) *Justice for All: Resources for Peace and Law-Related Education,* Department of Education, State of Hawaii, 1994.

Author of legal brochures and guidebooks for the Hawaii court system. Author and presenter of "Legal Line," a regular segment of *KGMB Live at Five News,* 1988-90. Script writer for *Final Verdict,* an educational television series about legal issues, with teacher's guide, 1991-92. Author of "What's the Law?" a column in *Honolulu Advertiser,* 1991-95. Contributor to law jour-nals and popular magazines, including *Honolulu.* Also contributor and co-editor of *Our Rights, Our Lives: A Guide to Women's Legal Rights in Hawaii,* 1990.

Work in Progress

Fables from the Deep, The Chinese Temple, and *The Desert and the Sea.*

Sidelights

Leslie Ann Hayashi told *SATA:* "Ever since I was little, I dreamed of being a writer. When I was in the first grade, I met Kathleen Wong, my best friend. I remember seeing a picture she drew of a girl on a swing. I leaned over and announced firmly, 'I'm going to write the stories, and you're going to do the illustrations.'

"Thirty-seven years later my dream came true. Despite the miles and the years (Kath lives in Phoenix, and I live in Honolulu), we had managed to keep in touch. When I sent her the stories, Kath, who had no formal art training, confessed she couldn't paint. I then reminded her of our agreement made in the first grade. Obligingly she took a few art classes. With just one watercolor class, she produced the most gorgeous works of art.

"I wrote the fables because fables are the archetype of all fiction writing. The lesson in a fable becomes the theme in a short story or novel. The way the lesson is taught becomes the plot in a short story or novel. Fables also remind us of what we share in common and, ultimately, what makes us human.

"The lessons which I have learned during my lifetime are to keep your dream alive and cherish your friend-ships."

For More Information See

PERIODICALS

MultiCultural Review, March, 1999, p. 81.
Star-Bulletin, August 7, 1998, D1, D4.

ON-LINE

University of Hawaii Press website, http://www. uhpress.hawaii.edu.

* * *

Hayashi introduces children to the plants and animals of Hawaii through the telling of ten charming fables. (Cover illustration by Kathleen Wong Bishop.)

HINTON, S(usan) E(loise) 1950-

Personal

Born in 1950, in Tulsa, OK; married David E. Inhofe (in mail order business), September, 1970; children: Nicholas David. *Education:* University of Tulsa, B.S., 1970.

Addresses

Home—Tulsa, OK.

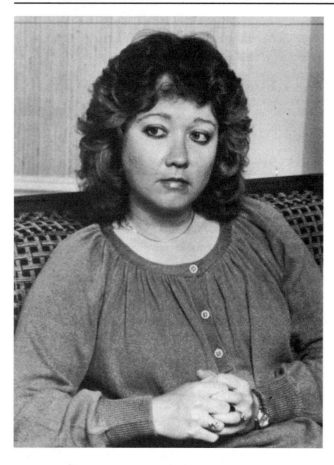

S. E. Hinton

Career

Writer. Consultant on film adaptations of her novels; minor acting roles in some film adaptations of her novels.

Awards, Honors

New York Herald Tribune best teenage books citation, 1967, *Chicago Tribune Book World* Spring Book Festival Honor Book, 1967, *Media & Methods* Maxi Award, American Library Association (ALA) Best Young Adult Books citation, both 1975, and Massachusetts Children's Book Award, 1979, all for *The Outsiders;* ALA Best Books for Young Adults citation, 1971, *Chicago Tribune Book World* Spring Book Festival Award Honor Book, 1971, and Massachusetts Children's Book Award, 1978, all for *That Was Then, This Is Now;* ALA Best Books for Young Adults citation, 1975, *School Library Journal* Best Books of the Year citation, 1975, and Land of Enchantment Book Award, New Mexico Library Association, 1982, all for *Rumble Fish;* ALA Best Books for Young Adults citation, 1979, *School Library Journal* Best Books of the Year citation, 1979, New York Public Library Books for the Teen-Age citation, 1980, American Book Award nomination for children's paperback, 1981, Sue Hefly Award Honor Book, Louisiana Association of School Libraries, 1982, California Young Reader Medal nomination, California Reading Association, 1982, and Sue Hefly Award, 1983,

all for *Tex;* Golden Archer Award, 1983; Recipient of first ALA Young Adult Services Division/*School Library Journal* Margaret A. Edwards Award, 1988, for body of work.

Writings

YOUNG ADULT NOVELS

The Outsiders, Viking (New York City), 1967.
That Was Then, This Is Now, illustrated by Hal Siegel, Viking, 1971.
Rumble Fish (also see below), Delacorte (New York City), 1975.
Tex, Delacorte, 1979.
Taming the Star Runner, Delacorte, 1988.

CHILDREN'S BOOKS

Big David, Little David, illustrated by Alan Daniel, Doubleday, 1995.
The Puppy Sister, illustrated by Jacqueline Rogers, Delacorte, 1995.

OTHER

(With Francis Ford Coppola) *Rumble Fish* (screenplay; adapted from her novel), Universal, 1983.

Adaptations

Film adaptations of Hinton's novels include *Tex,* starring Matt Dillon, Walt Disney Productions, 1982; *The Outsiders,* starring C. Thomas Howell and Matt Dillon, Warner Bros., 1983; and *That Was Then, This Is Now,* starring Emilio Estevez and Craig Sheffer, Paramount, 1985. *The Outsiders* was adapted as a television series by Fox-TV, 1990. Current Affairs and Mark Twain Media adapted *The Outsiders* and *That Was Then, This Is Now* as filmstrips with cassettes, both 1978. *Rumble Fish* was adapted as a record and cassette, Viking, 1977.

Sidelights

Ponyboy. Greasers vs. Socs. For millions of fans around the world, these few words will instantly call up the world of *The Outsiders,* S. E. Hinton's classic novel about teen gangs and the troubled process of fitting in. Since publication of this first novel in 1967, "the world of young adult writing and publishing [has] never [been] the same," according to Jay Daly in the critical study, *Presenting S. E. Hinton.* Daly went on to note that "*The Outsiders* has become the most successful, and the most emulated, young adult book of all time." Ironically, this quiet revolution in book writing and publishing was wrought by a seventeen-year-old girl, who by all rights should have been one of the intended readers of the novel, not its author.

Susan Eloise Hinton was a high school sophomore at Tulsa's Will Rogers High School when she began her novel. At the time she had not the slightest dream in the world that her manuscript would be published, let alone that it would sell millions of copies worldwide, spawn a motion picture, and start a trend in publishing toward gritty realism for younger readers. At the time, young

Susie was simply working out private concerns. Firstly, she was reacting to divisions apparent in her own high school, and secondly, she was filling a void in subject matter that she herself wanted to read. At the time when Hinton began writing, young adult titles were mostly pure as corn and sweetly innocent; tales in which the major problem was which dress to wear to the prom or whether such-and-such a boy would be the date. "Into this sterile chiffon-and-orchids environment then came *The Outsiders*," observed Daly. "Nobody worries about the prom in *The Outsiders;* they're more concerned with just staying alive till June."

If Hinton turned the world of publishing upside down with her youthful title, its publication did the same for her life. As word of mouth slowly made the book a classic (it now has eight million copies in print), Hinton was attempting to develop a normal life, studying education at the University of Tulsa, marrying, and having a family. Writing block settled in and it was four years before her second title, *That Was Then, This Is Now,* came out, another edgy story of teen angst. Two further books were published in four-year intervals: *Rumble Fish* in 1975, and *Tex* in 1979. Then nearly a decade passed before publication of her fifth YA title, *Taming the Star Runner.* Since that time, Hinton has published two titles for younger readers. Small in output, Hinton has nonetheless made a major impact on children's literature, a fact confirmed by the 1988 presentation to her of the first annual Margaret A. Edwards Award for career achievement. Her books now have over ten million copies in print; four of her five YA titles have been filmed; and Hinton still receives bushels of mail from enthusiastic fans for all her books, but especially for *The Outsiders,* now over three decades old, but with a message that continues to speak across the generations.

Hinton was born in 1948, in Tulsa, Oklahoma, but little more is known about her early years, as Hinton herself is a very private person. Indeed, confusion reins around aspects of her life, such as her year of birth as well as her inspiration for beginning to write. What is known is that she grew up a voluntary tomboy in love with horses. That passion has not diminished over the years, and Hinton is still an avid horsewoman. She was able to use her horse lore in the novel, *Taming the Star Runner.* Hinton's tomboy status also brought her closer to male friends than female. She identified more with active males than with the passive role females of the day were encouraged to project.

A self-confessed outsider as a youngster, Hinton did not belong to any one clique in school, but was friends with a wide variety of types. Along with horses Hinton also developed an early love of reading. "I started reading about the same time everyone else did," Hinton wrote in *Fourth Book of Junior Authors,* "and began to write a short time later. The major influence on my writing has been my reading. I read everything, including Comet cans and coffee labels." Her first writing efforts dealt with horses, and her stories were generally told from a boy's point of view. By the time she reached high

school, she was ready to tackle a larger subject, namely the rivalry between two groups in the school, the "greasers" and the affluent "socs" (short for "socials").

In the wake of school shootings across the nation during the 1990s, all Americans have become more sensitive to the outsider groups at schools, to the cruel pecking orders established in the microcosm of schools. In Hinton's day, peer pressure was no less severe and oppressive. "I felt the greasers were getting knocked when they didn't deserve it," Hinton told an interviewer for *Seventeen* shortly after publication of her novel. "The custom for instance, of driving by a shabby boy and screaming 'Greaser!' at him always made me boil. But it was the cold-blooded beating of a friend of mine that gave me the idea of writing a book."

Hinton began the writing in her sophomore year, during the time her father, Grady P. Hinton, was diagnosed with a brain tumor. As Daly put it, "It is not something she talks about, but one gets the impression that his hospitalization, and the inevitable, unavoidable conclusion that his illness promised, were factors in her withdrawing into herself." While her mother spent more and more time at the hospital, Hinton spent more time in her room or at the dining room table working on her novel. "Susie was very close to her father," Hinton's mother told Yvonne Litchfield of the *Tulsa Daily World,* "and I noticed that the sicker he became the harder she worked." Hinton's father died in her junior year, about the time she completed her book.

Hinton worked through four drafts of her story before she was happy with it, but still she gave no thought to publication until the mother of one of her school friends—a professional children's writer—took a look at the manuscript. This reader immediately saw commercial possibilities for the book and urged Hinton to get in touch with her own New York agent. The Oklahoma teenager did just that, and the rest is publishing history.

Hinton's novel was, as Hinton myth has it, accepted for publication the night of her high school graduation, and it appeared in bookstores the spring of her freshman year at college at the University of Tulsa. As the book was written from the male perspective, Hinton's publisher, Viking, prompted her to adapt the more genderless author name of S. E. Hinton. Such a publication was an enormous gamble for a prestigious New York house, but Hinton's book was no overnight success. Slowly and by word of mouth sales grew and continued growing. Letters started arriving at the Hinton household from teenagers all over the country confessing that they never imagined somebody else felt like they did, that they were solaced by the fact that others felt like outsiders just as they did. It was soon apparent that Hinton had touched a raw nerve in American culture.

Hinton's novel deals with a matter of days in the lives of a small group of Tulsa teenagers, loosely modeled after Hinton's own classmates. The book begins and ends with the same lines: "When I stepped out into the bright sunlight from the darkness of the movie house, I had

Mickey Rourke, William Smith, and Matt Dillon star in the 1983 film **Rumblefish,** *adapted from Hinton's novel about a young man wandering aimlessly in a life of violence and tragedy.*

only two things on my mind: Paul Newman and a ride home." In fact the entire book is a composition that the narrator, Ponyboy Curtis, must complete for English class. Trailed home from the movie by a group of Socs (pronounced "soshes" for Socials), Ponyboy is jumped by these rivals, and is saved by his older brothers, Darry and Sodapop, along with other members of his gang, the greasers. These others include the tough guy, Dallas Winston, and the joker who carries a switchblade, Two-Bit Matthews.

Later that night, Ponyboy, Dallas, and another gang member, Johnny, sneak into the drive-in and meet up with two Socs girls, Cherry and Marcia. Confronted after the movie by more Socs, led by Bob Sheldon, their most dangerous fighter, Cherry avoids an altercation by leaving with the Socs. Ruminating about their situation in a vacant lot, Ponyboy and Johnny fall asleep and by the time Ponyboy gets home, he has a run-in with Darry, who has been waiting up for him. Orphaned, the three brothers take care of each other. But Ponyboy has had enough, and decides to run away. Heading off with Johnny, they get only as far as the park before Sheldon and the Socs meet up with them again. In the ensuing fight, Johnny kills Sheldon with a knife.

Heading out is not merely optional now, but vital. Dallas tells the duo of a church hideout in a nearby town, and for the next five days they hole up, reading *Gone with the Wind,* talking about the Robert Frost poem, "Nothing

Gold Can Stay," appreciating sunsets and dawns, and munching on baloney sandwiches. When Dally, or Dallas, comes to visit, Johnny says he's through with running; he's going to turn himself in. On the way home, they go by the church and see that it is burning. Perhaps this is a result of the cigarettes they left inside, but whatever the cause they know that children are trapped inside. Without thinking, both Ponyboy and Johnny rush inside to save them. Though they rescue the children, Johnny is badly hurt when a timber falls on his back. Ponyboy and Dallas are also both badly burned.

Cast in the uncommon role of hero, Ponyboy goes to visit Johnny in critical condition at the hospital. Later that evening there is a big rumble between rival gangs, and even the injured Dallas shows up. Victorious, the greasers are jubilant, and Ponyboy and Dallas rush to the hospital to tell Johnny, only to discover him near death. With his dying words, Johnny tells Ponyboy to "Stay gold," referring to the Frost poem about youth and lost innocence. Johnny's death pushes the edgy Dallas over the line. He robs a grocery store and goes down in a hail of police bullets, an unloaded gun in his hands, his death a rather blindly foolish martyrdom.

Suffering from a concussion incurred at the big rumble, Ponyboy collapses, confined to bed for days. He gets it in his head that he killed Sheldon, not Johnny, and is set to confess at the hearing about the death, but he is acquitted before he has a chance to confess. He remains numb inside, until he discovers another exhortation from Johnny to stay gold, this time in a note left in their copy of *Gone with the Wind.* This breaks through to him and he picks up his pen to start his term paper, writing the first lines of the novel once again.

Critical reception of this publishing phenomenon was mostly laudatory; those with reservations mostly found the book erred on the side of over-sentimentality and cliched writing. "Can sincerity overcome cliches?" asked Thomas Fleming in the *New York Times Book Review.* Fleming answered his own question mostly in the positing: "In this book by a now 17-year-old author, it almost does the trick. By almost any standard, Miss Hinton's performance is impressive." Fleming's view was reflected by other reviewers, both then and now. Writing in *Horn Book,* Jane Manthorne called Hinton's work a "remarkable novel ... a moving, credible view of the outsiders from inside." Lillian N. Gerhardt, reviewing the novel in *School Library Journal,* drew attention to the rare fact in juvenile novels of "confronting the class hostilities which have intensified since the Depression." Gerhardt noted that "Ponyboy ... tells how it looks and feels from the wrong side of the tracks." Reviewing the book in *Atlantic Monthly,* Nat Hentoff lamented the sometimes "factitious" plot, but declared that Hinton, "with an astute ear and a lively sense of the restless rhythms of the young, also explores the tenacious loyalties on both sides of the class divide." Hentoff concluded that the book was so popular among the young "because it stimulates their own feelings and questionings about class and differing life-styles." An English reviewer for the *Times Literary Supplement* cut to the chase when noting that it was largely irrelevant whether adult reviewers found the novel dull, contrived, over-sentimentalized, too violent, or just plain implausible. "Young readers will waive literary discrimination about a book of this kind and adopt Ponyboy as a kind of folk hero for both his exploits and his dialogue," the reviewer concluded.

In the event, this critic was dead on. Once word of mouth was established regarding the youth and gender of the writer of *The Outsiders,* sales continued to grow and grow. It was apparent that Hinton and Viking had struck an entirely untapped readership; young kids aching for their stories to be told from their point of view with their voice. Little matter that Hinton's supposed stark realism was really "mythic" as the critic Michael Malone pointed out in an extended piece on the author in *Nation.* "Far from strikingly realistic in literary form," Malone remarked, "[Hinton's] novels are romances, mythologizing the tragic beauty of violent youth . . . ." Malone and others have rightly pointed out that the vast majority of teenagers personally experience nothing close to the violence of Hinton's characters, nor do they suffer the vacuum of parental supervision of her Peter Pan-like cast of orphans and near orphans who must look after themselves or watch out that alcoholic, abusive parents do not do them harm.

Featuring Matt Dillon, Emilio Estevez, and Meg Tilly, **Tex** *explores the extremes a young man will endure to win back his beloved horse.*

Never mind, either, the fact of Hinton's sometimes "mawkish and ornate" prose, according to Malone who noted that Ponyboy "fling[s] adjectives and archaic phrases ('Hence his name,' 'Heaven forbid') around like Barbara Cartland." Ponyboy, through whose eyes the action is viewed, describes characters with an elevated language that is often inappropriate to his spoken thought; he is also prone to quoting Frost. But never mind any of this; Ponyboy and his cast of friends and foes alike are romantic representations, not the viscerally realistic depictions they are usually labeled. Gene Lyons, writing in *Newsweek,* got it right: "The appeal of Hinton's novels is obvious .... The narrator-hero of each is a tough-tender 14- to 16-year-old loner making his perilous way through a violent, caste-ridden world almost depopulated of grownups. 'It's a kid's fantasy not to have adults around,' says Hinton. While recklessness generally gets punished, her books are never moralistic—all manner of parental rules are broken with impunity."

Royalties from *The Outsiders* helped to finance Hinton's education at the University of Tulsa where she studied education and where she met her husband, David Inhofe. But for several years Hinton suffered from writer's block so severe that, as she told Carol Wallace in the *Daily News,* she "couldn't even write a letter." In an interview with Linda Plemons in the *University of Tulsa Annual,* Hinton confessed that "I couldn't write. I taught myself to type in the sixth grade, and I couldn't even type or use my typewriter to write a letter. Things were pretty bad because I also went to college and started reading good writers and I thought, 'Oh, no.' I read *The Outsiders* again when I was 20, and I thought it was the worst piece of trash I'd ever seen. I magnified all its faults."

Finally, after she decided that teaching was not for her, and with encouragement from Inhofe, Hinton sat down to write a second novel. Setting herself the goal of two pages a day, Hinton had, after a few months, a rough draft of the novel, *That Was Then, This Is Now.* Once again Hinton sets her action in the same Tulsa-like surroundings, and focuses on an orphan, Mark, who has lived with the narrator, Bryon, and Bryon's mother since his own parents killed each other in a fight. It is now over a year since the ending of *The Outsiders,* and the old gang and social rivalries are not as clear-cut as they once were. The days of hippies are at hand; drugs are part of the teen landscape. One of the characters, M&M, is a proto-hippy whose LSD overdose tips the balances between Bryon and Mark. No angel himself, Bryon turns in his foster brother for supplying M&M with drugs. There is gang violence aplenty, teens on the prowl and on their own—Ponyboy Curtis even makes an appearance. Overall the book is more disciplined than Hinton's first title, but as Daly and other critics pointed out, "it lacks something." For Daly, it was the inspirational "spark" missing that kept it from breathing true life as had *The Outsiders.*

Other reviewers, however, found Hinton's second novel a moving and heartfelt cry from yet another teenager in

pain. For Michael Cart, writing in the *New York Times Books Review,* Bryon's struggles with his future and with those he loves form the core of the book. "The phrase, 'if only' is perhaps the most bittersweet in the language," Cart noted, "and Miss Hinton uses it skillfully to underline her theme: growth can be a dangerous process." Though Cart had problems with Bryon's ultimate "life-denying self-pity," turning against his love and life, he concluded that Hinton created "a mature, disciplined novel, which excites a response in the reader. Whatever its faults, her book will be hard to forget." Reviewing the novel in *School Library Journal,* Brooke Anson remarked that the book was an "excellent, insightful mustering of the pressures on some teen-agers today, offering no slick solutions but not without hope, either." *Horn Book*'s Sheryl B. Andrews found that this "disturbing" and "sometimes ugly" book "will speak directly to a large number of teen-agers and does have a place in the understanding of today's cultural problems." Selected a Best Books for Young Adults in 1971, *That Was Then, This Is Now* confirmed Hinton as more than a one-book author.

In Hinton's more recent book for young readers, Nick's initial disappointment that he must settle for a puppy instead of a baby sister disappears when Aleasha begins to take on human qualities. (Cover illustration by Jacqueline Rogers.)

Another four years passed between publication of *That Was Then, This Is Now* and Hinton's third novel, *Rumble Fish*. Hinton's narrator, Rusty-James, is another classic sensitive outsider type, who begins his narrative with the blunt declaration: "I was hanging out at Benny's, playing pool, when I heard Biff Wilcox was looking to kill me." Rusty-James's older brother, Motorcycle Boy, something of a Dallas Winston clone, meets a violent death in the novel, echoes of Dallas's demise in *The Outsiders*. And like Hinton's other novels, *Rumble Fish* takes place in compressed time, focusing on incidents which change the life of the narrator forever. Dubbed Hinton's "most ambitious" novel by Geoff Fox and George Walsh writing in *St. James Guide to Children's Writers,* the novel deals with Rusty-James's attempts to make some meaning of life after the passing of the gang conflicts that made his brother such a hero. Now, however, Motorcycle Boy is disenchanted, without hope, and virtually commits suicide, gunned down breaking into a pet store. By the end of the novel Rusty-James is left on his own, having lost his brother, his reputation, and his girl, and is without direction. As Jane Abramson noted in *School Library Journal,* "it is Rusty-James, emotionally burnt out at 14, who is the ultimate victim." Abramson concluded that the "[s]tylistically superb" *Rumble Fish* "packs a punch that will leave readers of any age reeling." Some reviewers, such as Anita Silvey in *Horn Book,* found the novel unsatisfying and Hinton's further writing potential "unpromising."

Rumble Fish did have admirers both in the United States and abroad. A *Publishers Weekly* contributor declared that "Ms. Hinton is a brilliant novelist," and Margery Fisher, writing in England's *Growing Point,* commented that "once more is the American urban scene in a book as uncompromising in its view of life as it is disciplined." While others complained of too blatant symbolism in the form of Motorcycle Boy and the fighting fish that give the book its title, Fisher concluded that "Of the three striking books by this young author, *Rumble Fish* seems the most carefully structured and the most probing." Exploring themes from aloneness to biological necessity, *Rumble Fish* tackles large questions in a small package. As Daly concluded about this third novel, "In the end we respond to *Rumble Fish* in a much deeper way than we do to *That Was Then, This Is Now*. It's an emotional, almost a physical response, as opposed to the more rational, intellectual reaction that the other book prompted." Daly went on to note that despite its defects in too-obvious symbolism, it "works as a novel . . . . And there is a name usually given to this kind of success. It is called art."

Hinton herself noted that she had been reading a lot about color symbolism and mythology when writing *Rumble Fish,* and that such concerns crept into the writing of the novel, especially in the character of Motorcycle Boy, the alienated, colorblind gang member looking for meaning. Hinton begins with character, as she has often noted in interviews, but in *Production Notes* for *Rumble Fish,* the screenplay of which she co-wrote with Francis Ford Coppola, she remarked that the novel "was a hard book to write because Rusty-James is a simple person, yet the Motorcycle Boy is the most complex character I've ever created. And Rusty-James sees him one way, which is not right, and I had to make that clear . . . . It's about over-identifying with something which you can never understand, which is what Rusty-James is doing. The Motorcycle Boy can't identify with anything."

The standard four years passed again before publication of Hinton's fourth title, *Tex,* which was, according to Daly, "Hinton's most successful effort" to date. Once again the reader is on familiar ground with near-orphan protagonists, and troubled youths. With *Tex,* however, Hinton opts for a more sensitive and perhaps less troubled narrator than before. Tex McCormick is, as Hinton noted in Delacorte Press's notes from the author, "perhaps the most childlike character I've ever done, but the one who makes the biggest strides toward maturity. I have to admit he's a favorite child." Of course this was several years before the birth of Hinton's own son, Nick.

Another fourteen-year-old lacking parental supervision, Tex has his older brother Mason to look after him while their father is on the rodeo circuit. A story of relationships, Hinton's fourth title focuses on the two teenagers at a time when Mason has had to sell off the family horses to pay bills, as no money has come from their father. This includes Tex's own horse, Negrito. Straining already strained relations between the brothers, this loss of a favored animal sets the plot in motion. Tex tries to run off and find the animal. Neither his friend Johnny nor Johnny's sister Jamie (the romantic attachment) is able to talk Tex out of it, but Mason drags him home in the pickup. Johnny and Tex are forever getting in trouble and things get rougher between Mason and Tex by the time the two brothers are kidnapped by a hitchhiker (Mark from *That Was Then, This Is Now,* who has busted out of jail). Tex's presence of mind saves them, but gets Mark, the hitchhiker, killed by the police. Notoriety at this brings the father home, but disappointment follows when he fails to track down Negrito as he promised. More trouble—in company with Johnny and then with a former friend of Mason's who now deals drugs—lands Tex in the hospital with a bullet wound. He learns that his real father was another rodeo rider, gets a visit from Johnny and Jamie, and once recovered and reconciled with Mason, convinces his older brother that he should go on to college as he's wanted to. Tex tells him he's lined up a job working with horses and can take care of himself.

"Hinton's style has matured since she exploded onto the YA scene in 1967," noted Marilyn Kaye in a *School Library Journal* review of *Tex*. Kaye felt that Hinton's "raw energy . . . has not been tamed—its been cultivated." The outcome, said Kaye, "is a fine, solidly constructed, and well-paced story." *Growing Point*'s Fisher once again had high praise for Hinton, concluding that "In this new book Susan Hinton has achieved that illusion of reality which any fiction writer aspires to and which few ever completely achieve."

Nick wonders if his classmate, who has the same name, hair, and glasses as Nick's father, could actually be a miniature version of his dad. (Cover illustration by Alan Daniel.)

Hinton's re-created reality was strong enough to lure Hollywood. Disney productions bought the rights to *Tex,* filming a faithful adaptation of the novel with young Matt Dillon in the lead role, and introducing actors Meg Tilly and Emilio Estevez. Shot in Tulsa, the movie production used Hinton as an advisor, introducing Dillon to her own horse, Toyota, which played the role of Negrito, and teaching the young actor how to ride. It was the beginning of a long and continuing friendship between Hinton and Dillon, who played in three of the four adaptations of her novels. The movie also started a trend of introducing young actors on their way up in her movies.

Next to get a film treatment was *The Outsiders,* though not from Disney this time but from Francis Ford Coppola of *Godfather* fame. Somewhat operatic in its effect, the movie cast Dillon as Dallas Winston, and also starred such future luminaries as Patrick Swayze, Rob Lowe, Tom Cruise, and Estevez. Coppola also filmed *Rumble Fish,* shooting it in black and white to resonate with Motorcycle Boy's color blindness. Once again Dillon starred, with Micky Rourke as Motorcycle Boy. Dennis Hopper, Tom Waits, and Nicolas Cage rounded out the cast. The script was co-written by Hinton and

Coppola. In both the Coppola adaptations, Hinton played bit parts as well as worked closely as an advisor during production. However, with the fourth movie adaptation, from a screenplay by Estevez and starring him, Hinton remained on the sidelines. Thus, within a few short years—from 1982 to 1985—all of Hinton's novels were turned into movies and her popularity was at an all-time high, with movie sales driving up book sales. Hinton had the added plus in that her experience with movies was a very positive one. "I really have had a wonderful time and made some very good friends," Hinton told Dave Smith of the *Los Angeles Times* regarding her work with Coppola. "Like a lot of authors, I'd heard the horror stories about how they buy the property and then want the author to disappear and not meddle around worrying about what they're doing to the book. But that didn't happen at all. They invited me in right from the start, and I helped with the screenplays."

Throughout the early 1980s, then, Hinton was busy with movie adaptations and with her son, born in 1983. It was not until 1988 that she brought out another novel, *Taming the Star Runner.* Earlier that year Hinton became the first recipient of the Young Adult Services Division/*School Library Journal* Author Achievement

Award, otherwise known as the Margaret A. Edwards Award, for career achievement in YA literature. It had been nine years since publication of *Tex;* it was thus fitting that she would have a new title out after receiving such an award. Those first four books had a rough sort of unity to them: a portrayal of the difficult process of sorting through problems of alienation and belonging, with a kind of synthesis if not solution presented by the ending of *Tex.* In other words, that youthful furrow had been plowed, and Hinton was ready, it seemed, to move on to new acreage.

Taming the Star Runner, while dealing with some of the old themes, does set off in new directions. Hinton moves from first- to third-person narration in the story of fifteen-year-old Travis Harris who is sent off to his uncle's Oklahoma ranch in lieu of juvenile hall. He has nearly killed his stepfather with a fireplace poker, an attack not unprovoked by the abusive stepfather. What follows is the classic city-boy-come-to-the-country motif. Unwillingly, Travis learns hard lessons on the ranch, but the change from urban to rural is not a Technicolor idyll. Travis arrives in the middle of his uncle's divorce, and the man is distant from him. He takes to hanging out at a barn on the property which is rented to Casey Kincaid, three years older than Travis and a horse trainer. She is in the process of taming the eponymous stallion, Star Runner. It is the relationship which grows between this unlikely pair that forms the heart of the book. Another major element—a tip of the hat to Hinton's own history—is the acceptance by a New York publisher of a book that young Travis has written. But there are no easy solutions: the stepfather refuses to give permission for publication, as he comes off less than noble in the pages of the manuscript. Finally Travis's mother stands up to the stepfather and signs permission for him. He has grown closer to Casey, as well as his uncle, but there are no completely happy endings for Hinton, either. Star Runner is killed in an electrical storm and Travis and his uncle are forced to move off the ranch to town, but he is now a published author and has made a real friend in Casey.

Reviews of the novel were largely positive. Nancy Vasilakis commented in *Horn Book* that it "has been generally agreed that no one can speak to the adolescent psyche the way S. E. Hinton can," and now with her fifth novel, Vasilakis felt that the author "hasn't lost her touch." In a lengthy critique in the *New York Times Book Review,* Patty Campbell noted that "Hinton has produced another story of a tough young Galahad in black T-shirt and leather jacket. The pattern is familiar, but her genius lies in that she has been able to give each of the five protagonists she has drawn from this mythic model a unique voice and a unique story." Campbell also commented on the "drive and the wry sweetness and authenticity" of the authorial voice, concluding that "S. E. Hinton continues to grow in strength as a young adult novelist." A *Kirkus Reviews* contributor also found much to praise in the novel, remarking that "Hinton continues to grow more reflective in her books, but her great understanding, not of what teen-agers are but of what they can hope to be, is undiminished." Daly, in his critical study, *Presenting S. E. Hinton,* called this fifth novel "Hinton's most mature and accomplished work."

Since publication of *Taming the Star Runner,* Hinton's work has traveled light miles away from her cast of outsiders and bad boys. The year 1995 saw publication of two Hinton titles, both for younger readers. *Big David, Little David* is a picture book based on a joke she and her husband played on their son Nick when the boy was entering kindergarten. In the book, a boy named Nick wonders if a classmate who resembles his father and has the same name could possibly be the same person as his father. Another title inspired by her son is *The Puppy Sister,* about a sibling rivalry between a puppy and an only child, a situation complicated when the puppy slowly changes into a human sister.

Hinton has focused on family in recent years, and on her hobby of horseback riding. She is reportedly at work on another YA novel, though there are no indications whether or not she will return to her outsider themes. "I don't think I have a masterpiece in me," Hinton once told Smith in the *Los Angeles Times,* "but I do know I'm writing well in the area I choose to write in. I understand kids and I really like them. And I have a very good memory. I remember exactly what it was like to be a teenager that nobody listened to or paid attention to or wanted around." In the three-plus decades since Hinton herself was a teenager, things have changed very little. The street kids, the gangs, the cliques at school that drive kids to extremes: these are all still at play, and Hinton's novels speak to teens as strongly now as they did at the time of their publication.

Works Cited

Abramson, Jane, review of *Rumble Fish, School Library Journal,* October, 1975, p. 106.

Andrews, Sheryl B., review of *That Was Then, This Is Now, Horn Book,* July-August, 1971, p. 338.

Anson, Brooke, review of *That Was Then, This Is Now, Library Journal,* June 15, 1971, p. 2138.

Campbell, Patty, review of *Taming the Star Runner, New York Times Book Review,* April 2, 1989, p. 26.

Cart, Michael, review of *That Was Then, This Is Now, New York Times Book Review,* August 8, 1971, p. 8.

Daly, Jay, *Presenting S. E. Hinton,* Twayne, 1987.

de Montreville, Doris, and Elizabeth J. Crawford, editors, *Fourth Book of Junior Authors,* H. W. Wilson, 1978, p. 176.

"Face to Face with a Teen-Age Novelist," *Seventeen,* October, 1967.

Fisher, Margery, review of *Rumble Fish, Growing Point,* May, 1976, p. 2894.

Fisher, Margery, review of *Tex, Growing Point,* May, 1980, pp. 3686-87.

Fleming, Thomas, review of *The Outsiders, New York Times Book Review,* May 7, 1967, part 2, pp. 10-12.

Gerhardt, Lillian N., review of *The Outsiders, School Library Journal,* May 15, 1967, pp. 2028-29.

Hentoff, Nat, review of *The Outsiders, Atlantic Monthly,* December, 1967.

Hinton, S. E., "Rumble Fish," *Production Notes,* No Weather Films, 1983.

Hinton, S. E., "S. E. Hinton: On Writing and *Tex,*" publicity release from Delacorte Press, winter, 1979/ spring, 1980.

Kaye, Marilyn, review of *Tex, School Library Journal,* November, 1979, p. 88.

Litchfield, Yvonne, "Her Book to Be Published Soon, But Tulsa Teen-Ager Keeps Cool," *Tulsa Daily World,* April 7, 1967, p. 20.

Lyons, Gene, "On Tulsa's Mean Streets," *Newsweek,* October 11, 1982, pp. 105-06.

Malone, Michael, "Tough Puppies," *Nation,* March 8, 1986, pp. 276-78, 280.

Manthorne, Jane, review of *The Outsiders, Horn Book,* August, 1967, p. 475.

Review of *The Outsiders, Times Literary Supplement,* October 30, 1970.

Plemons, Linda, "Author Laureate of Adolescent Fiction," *University of Tulsa Annual, 1983-84,* p. 62.

Review of *Rumble Fish, Publishers Weekly,* July 28, 1975, p. 122.

Silvey, Anita, review of *Rumble Fish, Horn Book,* November-December, 1975, p. 601.

Smith, Dave, "Hinton, What Boys Are Made Of," *Los Angeles Times,* July 15, 1982.

St. James Guide to Young Adult Writers, St. James Press, 1999, pp. 454-55.

Review of *Taming the Star Runner, Kirkus Reviews,* August 15, 1988, p. 1241.

Vasilakis, Nancy, review of *Taming the Star Runner, Horn Book,* January-February, 1989, pp. 78-79.

Wallace, Carol, "In Praise of Teenage Outcasts," *Daily News,* September 26, 1982.

For More Information See

BOOKS

Children's Literature Review, Gale, Volume 3, 1978, Volume 23, 1991.

Contemporary Literary Criticism, Volume 30, Gale, 1984.

Stanek, Lou Willett, *A Teacher's Guide to the Paperback Editions of the Novels of S. E. Hinton,* Dell, 1980.

St. James Guide to Young Adult Writers, St. James Press, 1999.

PERIODICALS

American Film, April, 1983.

Booklist, April 1, 1994, p. 1463; October 15, 1994, p. 413; January 15, 1995, p. 936; June 1, 1995, p. 1760.

Bulletin of the Center for Children's Books, February, 1995, p. 200; November, 1995, p. 92.

English Journal, September, 1989, p. 86.

New York Times Book Review, August 27, 1967, pp. 26-29; November 19, 1995, p. 37; November 16, 1997, p. 26.

Publishers Weekly, December 12, 1994, p. 62; July 17, 1995, p. 230; July 28, 1997, p. 77.

Quill & Quire, April, 1995, p. 37.

School Library Journal, December, 1993, p. 70; April, 1995, p. 102; October, 1995, p. 104; May, 1996, p. 76.

Signal, May, 1980, pp. 120-22.

Washington Post Book World, February 12, 1989.*

—Sketch by J. Sydney Jones

* * *

HOOKS, Bell
See WATKINS, Gloria

* * *

HUNTER, Ryan Ann
See GREENWOOD, Pamela D.

* * *

HUNTER, Ryan Ann
See MACALASTER, Elizabeth G.

* * *

INGRID, Charles
See SALSITZ, Rhondi Vilott

J

JACKSON, Ellen B. 1943-

Personal

Born April 27, 1943, in Los Angeles, CA; daughter of Merrill O. (an accountant) and Carol (a children's librarian; maiden name, Goldstein) Jackson. *Education:* University of California, Los Angeles, B.A., 1967; California Family Study Center, M.A., 1977. *Hobbies and other interests:* Hiking, tidepooling and beachcombing after a storm, playing alto and soprano recorder, fiber arts.

Addresses

Home—Santa Barbara, CA. *Agent*—c/o Andrea Brown Literary Agency, P.O. Box 1027, Montara, CA 94037.

Career

Writer. Monte Vista Street School, Los Angeles, CA, kindergarten teacher, 1969-79; Santa Barbara County Schools, Santa Barbara, CA, curriculum writer, 1984-87. *Member:* Society of Children's Book Writers and Illustrators, Authors Guild, Amnesty International.

Awards, Honors

National Writer's Club certificate, 1991; children's choice selection, International Reading Association, 1995, for *The Winter Solstice;* outstanding book designation, *Child* magazine, 1995, for *Brown Cow, Green Grass, Yellow Mellow Sun;* book of the year award, *Family Fun* magazine, 1996, for *Monsters in My Mailbox;* pick of the list designation, American Booksellers Association, and Editor's Choice, *Booklist,* both 1998, for *Turn of the Century.*

Writings

PICTURE BOOKS

The Bear in the Bathtub, illustrated by Margot Apple, Addison-Wesley, 1981.

The Grumpus under the Rug, illustrated by Scott Gustafson, Follett, 1981.

Ants Can't Dance, illustrated by Frank Remkiewicz, Macmillan, 1990.

Boris the Boring Boar, illustrated by Normand Chartier, Macmillan, 1992.

The Tree of Life (nonfiction), illustrated by Judeanne Winter, Prometheus, 1993.

Cinder Edna, illustrated by Kevin O'Malley, Lothrop, Lee & Shepard, 1994.

The Winter Solstice (nonfiction), illustrated by Jan Davey Ellis, Millbrook Press, 1994.

Brown Cow, Green Grass, Yellow Mellow Sun, illustrated by Victoria Raymond, Hyperion Press, 1995.

The Impossible Riddle, illustrated by Alison Winfield, Whispering Coyote Press, 1995.

Monsters in My Mailbox, illustrated by Maxie Chambliss, Troll, 1995.

(Reteller) *The Precious Gift: A Navajo Creation Myth,* illustrated by Woodleigh Marx Hubbard, Simon and Schuster, 1996.

The Wacky Witch War, illustrated by Denise Brunkus, WhistleStop, 1996.

Why Coyote Sings to the Moon, illustrated by Eric Joyner, American Education Publishing, 1996.

The Book of Slime (nonfiction), illustrated by Ellis, Millbrook Press, 1997.

Turn of the Century (nonfiction), illustrated by Ellis, Charlesbridge, 1998.

Here Come the Brides (nonfiction), illustrated by Carol Heyer, Walker, 1998.

The Autumn Equinox (nonfiction), illustrated by Ellis, Millbrook Press, 2000.

OTHER

Stay on the Safe Side (grades 5-6 and 7-8), Office of Criminal Justice Planning (Sacramento, CA), 1985.

Stay on the Safe Side (grades K-4), Office of Criminal Justice Planning (Sacramento, CA), 1987.

Top of the World, Children's Story Scripts, 1991.

Quick Wits and Whiskers, Children's Story Scripts, 1991.

Families Are for Finding, Children's Story Scripts, 1991.

Earthquake Safety, Horizon, 1991.

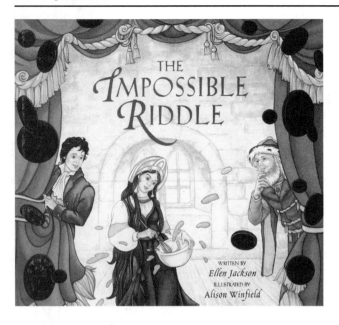

Unable to give up his beloved daughter and the delicious potato pancakes she makes, a jealous tsar makes her suitor answer an impossible riddle to win Princess Katarina's hand. (Cover illustration by Alison Winfield.)

Household Safety, Horizon, 1991.
Stranger Danger (safety advice for kids), Horizon, 1991.

Contributor of articles for adults to newspapers, including *Critical Times,* 1992; also contributor of children's stories to periodicals, including "Dragons in the Drapes," *Humpty Dumpty's,* 1990. Author of the how-to manual *How to Start a Pet Grooming Business.* Also author of multimedia history book for the computer game *Where in Time Is Carmen Sandiego,* v. 3.0, Broderbund Software, 1997.

Work in Progress

The Summer Solstice, for Millbrook Press, due in 2001; a series of twelve books, one on each month of the year, for Charlesbridge, expected in 2001; *Scatterbrain Sam and the Glue Stew,* for Charlesbridge, forthcoming.

Sidelights

Author of a score of children's books that range from cautionary tales to humorous and informative nonfiction picture books, Ellen B. Jackson is noted for a simple, direct style that appeals to very young children and beginning readers. "Jackson is a gifted writer who can make the simplest language rhyming and interesting," noted Lauralyn Persson in *School Library Journal.*

The daughter of a children's librarian, Jackson is well equipped for a career in children's writing. A decade-long career as a kindergarten teacher, as well as a stint as a curriculum writer for the Santa Barbara County Schools, have also helped to prepare her for the job of imparting information to young children concisely and wittily.

Jackson's first book, *The Bear in the Bathtub,* appeared in 1981. It is a funny tale of a young boy, Andrew, who hates to take baths, but learns to appreciate them when a huge bear takes over the bathtub. Unable to bathe for days, Andrew experiences as the consequence of being dirty that his friends no longer want to be near him. Unfortunately, no one, not his parents, the police, or the fire fighters, can remove the bear from the tub. It is Andrew who finally solves the problem. Critics appreciated the humor Jackson imparted in this story. "Jackson accents the mirth by relating the nonsense with a straight face," wrote a contributor to *Publishers Weekly.* "This amusing, well-written story reads aloud well," assessed Pamela Warren Stebbins in a *School Library Journal* review.

Jackson's next book, *The Grumpus under the Rug,* is the tale of a mother who refuses to believe that the Grumpus under the rug is causing the mischief in her house. Even though her little boy keeps assuring his mother that the naughty Grumpus is there, she blames him for the Grumpus' acts. The mother finally discovers the Grumpus by looking under the rug before the Grumpus can disappear, and she throws him into the sky, ridding her house of him. A reviewer for *Booklist* said that Jackson's "spare story, told in mock-tale vein, plunges readers into the crux of its matter."

Another boy has trouble convincing his parents to believe him in *Ants Can't Dance.* Jonathan finds a dancing ant and brings it home to show his parents, but once he is home, the ant refuses to perform. His parents, skeptical to begin with, remain unconvinced, especially when the next day Jonathan brings home a talking peanut that becomes mute in front of them. Jonathan finally discovers a whistling stone that does perform for everybody, even television reporters. A reviewer for *Publishers Weekly* called the book a "whimsical tale" and added that this "lighthearted picture book . . . will be enjoyed by parents and children alike," though the "fresh, witty prose of the opening pages peters out, and the plot and premise become repetitive." Marie Orlando echoed these remarks in a *School Library Journal* review saying "[It is] a slight but amusing story," but concluded, "Colorful cartoon illustrations blend well with the story, and youngsters will enjoy the clever lad's ultimate triumph." John Murray, reviewing *Ants Can't Dance* in *Magpies* found the "[r]epetitive language structures and rhyme accompanying each episode of the story make this a fairly useful book for early reading," while "well marked dialogue and a plot with the three episodes so common in folktales allow for predictability of form and ready dramatization."

There is a lesson in the humor of *Boris the Boring Boar,* in which Boris discovers that it pays to listen. Boris' friends are so tired of his boring monologue about how great he is that no one wants to be around him. Feeling lonely, he meets a smooth-talking wolf who ends up tying him to a tree while preparing to cook him for dinner. Boris, however, uses his wits to save himself by complimenting the wolf on his fine, sharp teeth and handsome coat. The wolf, as lonely as Boris, eats up

"Then one day we had a really rough teaching experience. It seemed as if we were invisible because the students totally ignored us. 'What would it take to get their attention?' we asked. 'I suppose we'd have to grow eight feet, sprout horns and blow smoke before they'd pay attention?' The more we talked, the sillier we became. So we decided to write a story about it. *Vampires Don't Wear Polka Dots,* a story about a really rotten group of students who suspect their new teacher is a vampire, was written in three weeks. Since then, we've published eight companion books. They weren't written as quickly, but they've all been fun!

"Writing is a big part of my life now. It is full of emotion, dreams, and hopes. It challenges me to snip the threads of every day life to weave something new and colorful. Most of all, writing is just plain old fun! That's the message I try to convey to writers at workshops and creative writing classes.

"Once upon a time, I read books that would take me to far away magical lands," Jones told *SATA.* "Now I *write* them!"*

K

KETTEMAN, Helen 1945-

Personal

Born July 1, 1945, in Augusta, Georgia; daughter of Jack (a physician) and Mary Helen (a teacher; maiden name, Walker) Moon; married Charles Harry Ketteman, Jr. (an accountant), in 1969; children: William Gregory, Mark David. *Education:* Young Harris College, A.A., 1965; attended Georgia Southern College, 1965-66; Georgia State University, B.A., 1968.

Addresses

Home—Dallas, TX. *Agent*—Ginger Knowlton, Curtis Brown Ltd., 10 Astor Pl., New York, NY 10003.

Career

Writer.

Awards, Honors

Best books of the year list, *Boston Globe,* 1995, for *Luck with Potatoes;* "Pick of the Lists," American Booksellers Association, 1998, for *I Remember Papa. Bubba, the Cowboy Prince* has been named to the reading award lists in seven states.

Writings

Not Yet, Yvette, illustrated by Irene Trivas, Albert Whitman, 1992.
Aunt Hilarity's Bustle, illustrated by James Warhola, Simon & Schuster, 1992.
The Year of No More Corn, illustrated by Robert Andrew Parker, Orchard, 1993.
One Baby Boy: A Counting Book, illustrated by Maggie Flynn-Staton, Simon & Schuster, 1994.
The Christmas Blizzard, illustrated by Warhola, Scholastic, 1995.
Luck with Potatoes, illustrated by Brian Floca, Orchard Books, 1995.

Grandma's Cat, illustrated by Marsha Lynn Winborn, Houghton Mifflin, 1996.
Bubba, the Cowboy Prince: A Fractured Texas Tale, illustrated by Warhola, Scholastic Press, 1997.
Heat Wave, illustrated by Scott Goto, Walker, 1998.
I Remember Papa, illustrated by Greg Shed, Dial, 1998.
Shoeshine Whittaker, illustrated by Goto, Walker, 1999.
Armadillo Tattletale, illustrated by Keith Graves, Scholastic, 2000.

Also contributor to periodicals, including *Spider* and *Highlights for Children.*

Work in Progress

Mama's Way, for Dial, due in 2001; and many other picture books.

Sidelights

Author of a dozen children's picture books, Helen Ketteman is known for her tall tales and rambunctious protagonists. She weaves stories out of droughts and blizzards, out of bustles and a cowboy prince closely resembling Cinderella. Many of her stories deal with a nostalgia for bygone days and are redolent with the sights and sounds of rural America.

Ketteman's first book, *Not Yet, Yvette,* tells of a girl who waits impatiently while she and her dad busily prepare a surprise birthday party for her mother. Together this African-American father and daughter vacuum, dust, and bake. Excited by the preparations, young Yvette must always be cautioned by her father that it is not yet time for the celebration. "In this homey picture book, excitement and anticipation run high for a girl and her father," according to a reviewer in *Publishers Weekly.* The critic went on to remark, "It would be hard to find more likable party givers ... who aptly illustrate just how much fun giving can be." *Booklist*'s Carolyn Phelan felt that this book "will appeal to any child old enough to enjoy secrets and surprises," while a *Kirkus Reviews* contributor noted that the "simple story is deftly conveyed in natural-sounding dialogue," and that ac-

Wild weather plays a prominent role in Helen Ketteman's Christmastime picture book for young readers. (Cover illustration by James Warhola.)

companied by the illustrations, the book "nicely reflect[s] this black family's warm pleasure in each other's company."

Fashion foibles are put on display in *Aunt Hilarity's Bustle,* a "funny story about a heroine with plenty of spark," according to Michelle M. Strazer writing in *School Library Journal.* Unable to find a high fashion bustle in the backwater town of Willow Flats, Aunt Hilarity determines to make one herself. But her initial creation made out of a hay-filled grain sack has fleas; then she tries paint rags as stuffing for a bustle, but these later cause a fire when Aunt Hilarity stands too close to a candle. A bystander throws punch onto her to extinguish the flames, but unfortunately much of the punch drenches Mrs. Anna Belle Prather, precipitating a food fight of gargantuan proportions. Finally a chicken-wire frame provides support for the bustle worn to a Christmas party, but when the wire begins to unravel, Aunt Hilarity is forced to don the Christmas tree. *Aunt Hilarity's Bustle* "is bound to be a winner with the preschool set and with early readers," commented *Booklist's* Sheilamae O'Hara.

Ketteman serves up more tall tales in such books as *The Year of No More Corn, The Christmas Blizzard, Luck with Potatoes,* and *Heat Wave.* Beanie and his grandfather are at opposite ends of the age cycle in *The Year of No More Corn.* Neither can help out with the corn planting on the family farm this year: one is too young and the other too old. Instead, Old Grampa tells Beanie

of the dreadful year 1928 when local farmers had to plant and replant their corn crop because of weather conditions, until Old Grampa himself finally planted corn kernels carved out of wood. He grew a forest of corncob-bearing trees from such ingenuity and saved the day. *Booklist's* Phelan applauded this wild tall tale, noting, "With its well-written text and accessible story and artwork, this would be a good choice to read aloud, even to somewhat older children studying tall tales." A *Publishers Weekly* reviewer commented that "Ketteman spins her tall tale in a pleasingly folksy deadpan style, her vivid descriptions bringing the old man's outrageous account to life until the reader, like Beanie, would like nothing better than to believe every word." And a *Kirkus Reviews* critic concluded that the book was a "lively, likable tall tale."

The Yuletide is at the center of another Ketteman story, *The Christmas Blizzard,* a "tale taller than the Empire State Building," according to a reviewer in *School Library Journal.* Weather again is a protagonist and the time again the 1920s. The winter of 1922 saw weather so crazy, according to Maynard Jenkins, that the North Pole was a slush pond and Santa had to pull up stakes and set up shop at Maynard's hometown of Lizzard, Indiana. Though cold, there was no snow in Lizzard, but a visit to a local weather spell-caster set that right. "This is a fun-filled story with more hyperbole than a Christmas turkey has stuffing," a critic writing in the *School Library Journal* added. "Ketteman's rollicking original tall tale has a true Christmasy flavor," noted a reviewer for *Publishers Weekly,* while Kay Weisman commented in *Booklist* that the book was an "appealing choice for holiday read-alouds or for older children learning to write their own tall tales."

Weather again goes haywire when a passing heat wave gets snagged on a weather vane at a Kansas farm in Ketteman's *Heat Wave.* It gets so hot on the farm that the corn in the fields starts popping and the cattle are almost cooked. Finally it is left to the young girl of the farm—who has repeatedly been told that girls cannot farm—to save the family by planting iceberg lettuce to cool things off. A critic writing in *Publishers Weekly* called *Heat Wave* a "rollicking original tall tale that would do Paul Bunyan proud. Verbally and visually clever, this is a diverting [tale]." Lee Bock of *School Library Journal* also praised this "rollicking American tall tale" in which "things go from bad to worse," and concluded that "[y]ounger children will enjoy the prescribed exaggeration and silliness, and older children might well be encouraged to create their own."

Farming again provides a venue for a tall tale in *Luck with Potatoes,* in which giant potatoes pop out of the earth at a farm where there was never any luck before. One potato fills the bed of the pick-up; the potatoes cause earthquakes as they grow. In fact, the tubers are so big that the farmer, Clemmon Hardigree, starts cutting them into planks to sell to the local lumber company. "Ketteman has a firm grasp on the humor and stylistic elements of the tall tale," noted Janice Del Negro in a *Booklist* review. "Her narrative voice is bemused yet down-to-earth, retaining its laconic style even as the situation becomes more and more outlandish." *Horn Book*'s Ann A. Flowers called Ketteman's creation a "cheerful story," while Virginia Opocensky, writing in *School Library Journal*, cautioned, "Don't miss the fun!"

In one of her most popular books, Ketteman revises the famous *Cinderella* fairy tale. *Bubba, the Cowboy Prince* tells the story of Bubba, a Texas cowboy who is something of a Cinderella stand-in. The prince charming of the story—or rather *princess* charming—is Miz Lurleen, a rich and feisty young cowgirl who decides it is time to find a husband and throws a ball in order to do so. The fairy godmother's role is taken over by a cow. Poor Bubba is overworked and under-appreciated by his step-dad and no-account stepbrothers, Milton and Dwayne, but manages, Cinderella-like, to attend Lurleen's ball courtesy of his fairy godcow. "Ketteman wisely leaves the [Cinderella] plot unchanged," noted Lauren Peterson of *Booklist*, "but the story has a distinct western flair and a humorous tall-tale feel." A *Kirkus Reviews* contributor remarked that this "Cinderella parody features the off-the-wall, whang-dang Texas hyperbole of Ketteman," while a *Publishers Weekly* critic also joined in the linguistic fun: "Rustler lingo and illustrations chock-ablock with Texas kitsch make this ranch-spun Cinder-fella a knee-slappin' tale . . . . Just the ticket for buckaroos lookin' fer a good read."

When a heat wave hits Kansas, a quick-thinking young girl surprises her family and saves the day by planting a cool crop of iceberg lettuce. (Cover illustration by Scott Goto.)

An Armadillo is at the heart of another Ketteman tale in *Armadillo Tattletale,* a book of animal gossip. His habit of eavesdropping and then spreading gossip makes Armadillo persona non grata to the other animals, until they finally find a way to cure him of listening to private conversations. More mischief is served up in Ketteman's counting book, *One Baby Boy,* in which the baby in question performs a series of rather naughty deeds that introduce, in rhyme, the numbers from one to ten.

In *Grandma's Cat,* a book written from a child's point of view, a little girl visiting her grandmother tries to make a friend of an aloof cat. The girl has no idea how to go about her task, making the cat hiss and spit at her, and pulling its tail. Finally the kindly grandmother intervenes to show her granddaughter how to befriend the animal. It all ends happily with the cat sleeping on the girl's bed at night. "The story will appeal to the many children whose ideas of befriending animals work better in their dreams than in reality," commented *Booklist*'s Phelan. "The story reads aloud well," concluded Phelan, "making this a good choice for storytime." Christina Linz, writing in *School Library Journal,* noted that "*Grandma's Cat* is delightfully told in brief, rhymed sentences that make a charming group or individual read-aloud, yet are simple enough for beginning readers to try on their own." A reviewer for *Publishers Weekly* felt that "Ketteman delivers a full roller coaster of emotion with an economy of words." The same reviewer went on, "Her rhythmic, rhyming (mostly) couplets speak to every child who has tried desperately to express fondness for a pet."

Another family story forms the core of *I Remember Papa,* featuring young Audie who has saved his allowance for months in hopes of buying a baseball mitt. He gets his chance one Saturday when he and his dad take the morning train to Cincinnati to see a Reds game. Before the game Audie sees just the glove for him; his dad also has his eyes on a pair of new workboots for himself. At the game, Audie loses his money, but his dad sacrifices his new boots to buy his son the prized mitt. Christine A. Moesch called the book a "warm story set in the past," in a *School Library Journal* review. Moesch also noted that the story "is warm without being treacly." *Booklist*'s Weisman felt that "baseball fans will appreciate this rich family story," while a *Kirkus Reviews* critic concluded that "the theme at the center of the story is the hallowed relationship between father and son in a bygone era, fondly remembered."

Ketteman returned to tall tales with *Shoeshine Whittaker,* published in 1999. The rag-snapping hero of the tale, Shoeshine Whittaker, discovers the town of Mudville and thinks he found the perfect place to ply his trade. But freshly shined boots are quick to lose their luster on the soggy streets of Mudville, and Shoeshine's satisfaction guarantee soon gets him into trouble. Quick thinking and a creative solution save the day, and in the end Shoeshine manages to satisfy his customers and himself. "Ketteman's colorful yarn is all twang and swagger, sheer catnip to read-aloud enthusiasts," declared a *Publishers Weekly* reviewer.

Miz Lurleen jumped off her horse and ran over to Bubba. "Try this on," she cried.

Bubba took his dirty old boot and pulled it on. "Much obliged, ma'am," he said blushing.

It fit perfectly.

In this Texan version of the Cinderella story, a fairy godcow helps Bubba meet the prettiest rancher in the West. (From Bubba the Cowboy Prince, *written by Ketteman and illustrated by James Warhola.*)

Helen Ketteman once told *SATA:* "I believe children should be exposed to books early and often. If children learn at an early age that books can be fun and entertaining, I think the battle with television and video games can be won. Readers that are created early will be lifelong readers."

Works Cited

Bock, Lee, review of *Heat Wave, School Library Journal,* March, 1998, p. 182.

Review of *Bubba, the Cowboy Prince, Kirkus Reviews,* November 1, 1997, p. 1646.

Review of *Bubba, the Cowboy Prince, Publishers Weekly,* November 17, 1997, p. 61.

Review of *The Christmas Blizzard, Publishers Weekly,* September 18, 1995, p. 100.

Review of *The Christmas Blizzard, School Library Journal,* October, 1995, p. 38.

Del Negro, Janice, review of *Luck with Potatoes, Booklist,* October 1, 1995, p. 326.

Flowers, Ann A., review of *Luck with Potatoes, Horn Book,* January-February, 1996, pp. 64-65.

Review of *Grandma's Cat, Publishers Weekly,* April 15, 1996, p. 67.

Review of *Heat Wave, Publishers Weekly,* December 15, 1997, p. 58.

Review of *I Remember Papa, Kirkus Reviews,* January 15, 1998, p. 114.

Linz, Christina, review of *Grandma's Cat, School Library Journal,* May, 1996, p. 93.

Moesch, Christine A., review of *I Remember Papa, School Library Journal,* June, 1998, p. 112.

Review of *Not Yet, Yvette, Kirkus Reviews,* February 1, 1992, p. 186.

Review of *Not Yet, Yvette, Publishers Weekly,* February 24, 1992, p. 53.

O'Hara, Sheilamae, review of *Aunt Hilarity's Bustle, Booklist,* February 15, 1993, p. 1067.

Opocensky, Virginia, review of *Luck with Potatoes, School Library Journal,* October, 1995, p. 105.

Peterson, Lauren, review of *Bubba, the Cowboy Prince, Booklist,* December 1, 1997, p. 641.

Phelan, Carolyn, review of *Not Yet, Yvette, Booklist,* March 15, 1992, p. 1388.

Phelan, Carolyn, review of *The Year of No More Corn, Booklist,* September 15, 1993, p. 158.

Phelan, Carolyn, review of *Grandma's Cat, Booklist,* April 1, 1996, p. 1372.

Review of *Shoeshine Whittaker, Publishers Weekly,* November 15, 1999, p. 66.

Strazer, Michelle M., review of *Aunt Hilarity's Bustle, School Library Journal,* February, 1993, pp. 72-73.

Weisman, Kay, review of *The Christmas Blizzard, Booklist,* September 15, 1995, p. 170.

Weisman, Kay, review of *I Remember Papa, Booklist,* March 15, 1998, p. 1249.

Review of *The Year of No More Corn, Publishers Weekly,* July 26, 1993, p. 70.

Review of *The Year of No More Corn, Kirkus Reviews,* August 1, 1993, p. 1003.

For More Information See

PERIODICALS

Booklist, February 1, 1998, p. 922.
Bulletin of the Center for Children's Books, June, 1992, p. 265; September, 1993, p. 14; December, 1997, p. 131.
Horn Book Guide, spring, 1998, p. 35; fall, 1998, p. 296.
Kirkus Reviews, December 1, 1997, p. 1776.
Magpies, September, 1993, p. 29.
New York Times Book Review, November 29, 1992, p. 34; August 25, 1996, p. 23.
Publishers Weekly, May 30, 1994, p. 54.
School Library Journal, May, 1992, p. 90.

—*Sketch by J. Sydney Jones*

*   *   *

KEY, Samuel M.
See de LINT, Charles (Henri Diederick Hoefsmit)

KLEIN, James 1932-
(James Kline, Jim Kline)

Personal

Born February 22, 1932, in Beachgrove, IN; son of Charles Raymond (a barber) and Edna Marie (a nurse; maiden name, Pollock) Klein; married Phyllis Dawn Schneider (a homemaker); children: Timson, James, Jr., Peggy, Daniel, Andrew, Mary, John. *Education:* Attended Los Angeles Community College. *Politics:* Democrat. *Religion:* Roman Catholic.

Addresses

Agent—Kazarian, Spencer and Associates, Inc., 11365 Ventura Blvd., Suite 100, P.O. Box 7403, Studio City, CA 91604.

Career

Professional actor, 1955—. Lecturer at schools, outdoor clubs, and museums. Volunteer with programs for the homeless. *Military service:* U.S. Army, 1952-53. *Member:* Screen Actors Guild, American Federation of Television and Radio Artists.

James Klein

Awards, Honors

Community service awards from American Cancer Society and Disneyland.

Writings

Where to Find Gold in Southern California, Ward Ritchie (Pasadena, CA), 1975.

Where to Find Gold in the Desert, P.J. Press (Anaheim, CA), 1975, revised edition, Gem Guides Book (Baldwin Park, CA), 1995.

Where to Find Gold in The Mother Lode, P.J. Press, 1976.

Dry Washing for Gold, with art by Cliff Gamble, P.J. Press, 1980, Gem Guides Book, 1994.

Gold Rush! The Young Prospector's Guide to Striking It Rich (children's book), illustrated by Michael Rohani, Tricycle Press (Berkeley, CA), 1998.

Where to Find Gold in Northern California, Gem Guides Book, 1999.

Other books include *Where to Find Gold in Nevada,* 1985, and *How to Find Gold,* 1994. Contributor to mining magazines. Some writings appear under the names James Kline or Jim Kline.

Sidelights

James Klein told *SATA:* "I have a real love for the history of the West. I hope to make a television video about what remains of the camps and towns of the California Gold Rush. My books are meant to help people enjoy themselves in the outdoors and to really see the land and what it is made of. People soon learn the joy of playing the game with Mother Nature. She's hidden the gold; now try to find it. The game is not about the gold itself; it's about the looking. The real gold is being in the mountains along a stream with the forest all around you."

For More Information See

PERIODICALS

Booklist, April 15, 1998, p. 1442.
Kirkus Reviews, February 15, 1998, p. 269.
Lapidary Journal, February, 1984, p. 1639; February, 1989, p. 88.*

*　　　*　　　*

KLINE, James
See KLEIN, James

*　　　*　　　*

KLINE, Jim
See KLEIN, James

KNUTSON, Kimberley 1963-

Personal

Last name is pronounced NOOT-sun; born February 22, 1963, in Worcester, MA; daughter of Richard (a banker) and Diane (an athletic director and coach) Knutson; married Michael A. McMahon (an account director), July 10, 1993; children: Lukas, Piper Grace. *Education:* Connecticut College, B.A., 1985.

Addresses

Home—112 Parsonage St., Marshfield, MA 02050. *E-mail*—muddigush@aol.com.

Career

Preschool teacher in Andover and Brookline, MA, 1986-90.

Awards, Honors

Muddigush was a Pick of the Lists selection.

Writings

AUTHOR AND ILLUSTRATOR

Muddigush, Macmillan, 1992.
Ska-Tat!, Macmillan, 1993.
Bed Bouncers, Macmillan, 1995.
Beach Babble, Marshall Cavendish, 1998.
Jungle Jamboree, Marshall Cavendish, 1998.

Work in Progress

A winter story.

Sidelights

"I've always loved children's books!" Kimberley Knutson told *SATA.* "I read constantly as a child and also wrote many stories, poems, and plays. In college I took only one English course but I wrote a big collection of silly children's poetry. After teaching preschool for five years I finally submitted my first story for publication, *Muddigush.* It describes a very muddy recess that the children and I celebrated.

"I write about simple childhood pleasures: playing in the mud or at the beach, jumping on the bed ... experiences that I loved as a child. I try to involve all the senses in my description because children use all five senses in their uninhibited approach to life. They look but also touch ... and can tell you how something sounds but also how it feels, smells, and maybe tastes! Then of course we grow older and some of that wonder and exploration begins to fade ... I have to work at staying in touch with that fun part of myself; it is easier now that I have two small inquisitive children of my own!

"My illustration technique originated from *Muddigush*—a story that explored texture needed a tactile form of illustration—collage! Since then, publishers have insisted on it. I admire many illustrators' work. Both Leo Lionni and Ezra Keats are influences, and also Brinton Turkle, whom I met in his Santa Fe home in 1985. I have a paper collection that school children find fascinating. I'm always looking for new paper and its inspiration. First I draw black and white illustrations and then I cut and paste the colored papers—a painstaking process. It is so exciting to switch from black and white to POW! Bright color! So, the first completed picture in each book is a thrilling discovery for me. I feel very much alive and happy when I'm working—some illustrators say it is a lonely process and hard work but I find it exhilarating. I play music and concentrate for 6-14 hours at a time when a deadline is looming.

"My most recent book, *Jungle Jamboree,* started out with the idea of forts—couch cushion forts—the rainy day added a rhythmic beat and soon I was thinking of drums and dancing ... that's how the jamboree idea came!

"I plan on writing a winter story in the near future and certainly hope to be creating books for a long time."

Author and illustrator Kimberley Knutson's picture books celebrate children at play. In her first book, *Muddigush,* Knutson established a reputation for creat-

Knutson fills her picture book with the vivid sounds and sights of children enjoying a summer day at the beach. (From Beach Babble, *written and illustrated by Knutson.*)

ing texts replete with exuberant, imitative wordplay combined with colorful collage depictions of children of various races playing together. *Muddigush* begins with a child dressed in raincoat and boots running outside to play in the mud; he is soon joined by two friends and together the three make mud pies and cakes, form rivers and mountains, and enthusiastically jump in the mud puddles until the sun comes out. "Knutson's onomatopoeic text nicely mimics the rhythm of chanting children at play," observed a reviewer for *Publishers Weekly.* The author's brightly colored cut-paper collages "effectively illustrate this playtime piece," added Janie Schomberg in *School Library Journal.*

Knutson gives new life to another common childhood activity, playing in the autumn leaves that have fallen from the trees, in *Ska-Tat!* In this story, three children run outside to gather up, jump in, and collect the colorful autumn leaves. "Knutson's poetic phrasing is full of action and child-friendly imagery," remarked a reviewer for *Publishers Weekly.* Ilene Cooper, reviewing *Ska-Tat!* for *Booklist,* contended that the author's "delightful collages are the perfect medium to show both the leaves ... and the children." In her next effort, *Bed Bouncers,* Knutson took a leap into fantasy with the story of two children who jump on their bed so long and so well that they are catapulted into space. Here they happily cavort with other children among the moon and stars until an adult voice brings them back to earth. As in her first two books, Knutson's language garnered positive comments from critics who remarked on its bouncy rhythms. *School Library Journal* reviewer Ruth K. MacDonald described *Bed Bouncers* as "a great bedtime story that rollicks along." MacDonald also commented favorably on Knutson's collage technique, comparing her artwork

We peek out the door...

Kimberley Knutson wrote and illustrated this bedtime book about two children who jump to the moon and stars. (From Bed Bouncers.)

to that of Jack Ezra Keats for its reliance upon a variety of textures and designs. MacDonald and other critics praised the multicultural message that arises organically from the material, when the children are joined in space by bed bouncers from all over the world. "The message of universal connections grows right from the action," commended Hazel Rochman in *Booklist.*

In *Beach Babble,* Knutson took a trip to the beach, and her signature onomatopoetic text celebrates the musicality of the ocean as three children play in the surf and make sand castles. "It's a story told with distinct sounds and bright evocative images in a collage of cut paper (the sea is marvelous: pale blue marbleized paper like the endpapers of old books) that pops off the page," enthused Penelope Green in the *New York Times Book Review.* Likewise, *School Library Journal* contributor Lisa Falk concluded that Knutson's artwork and text "capture the essence of a day at the ocean."

Jungle Jamboree is Knutson's fifth tribute to the joyful spirit of children at play. In this book, the author creates a rainy day scenario in which three children create a space of chairs draped with blankets and turn it into a fantasy rainforest complete with monkeys, toucans, and tree frogs who join in the music-making fun. "This romp in the wild is choreographed to rhymed verses that rhythmically pace the pictorial dance," noted Ellen Mandel in *Booklist.* And, as in her earlier books, Knutson's cut-paper collages "show joyous, energetic children of various races romping in a riot of bright colors and patterns," Susan Scheps observed in her review in *School Library Journal.*

Works Cited

Cooper, Ilene, review of *Beach Babble, Booklist,* June 1, 1998, p. 1780.
Cooper, Ilene, review of *Ska-Tat!, Booklist,* December 1, 1993, p. 98.
Falk, Lisa, review of *Beach Babble, School Library Journal,* July, 1998, p. 77.
Green, Penelope, review of *Beach Babble, New York Times Book Review,* July 19, 1998, p. 24.
MacDonald, Ruth K., review of *Bed Bouncers, School Library Journal,* August, 1995, pp. 124-25.
Mandel, Ellen, review of *Jungle Jamboree, Booklist,* September 1, 1998, p. 126.
Review of *Muddigush, Publishers Weekly,* January 20, 1992, p. 64.
Rochman, Hazel, review of *Bed Bouncers, Booklist,* May 15, 1995, p. 1652.
Scheps, Susan, review of *Jungle Jamboree, School Library Journal,* November, 1998, p. 88.
Schomberg, Janie, review of *Muddigush, School Library Journal,* April, 1992, p. 94.
Review of *Ska-Tat!, Publishers Weekly,* October 18, 1993, p. 71.

For More Information See

PERIODICALS

Booklist, February 1, 1992, pp. 1040-41.

KOSS, Amy Goldman 1954-

Personal

Born January 26, 1954, in Detroit, MI; daughter of Max (a juke box man) and Harriet (a teacher) Goldman; married Mitchell Koss (a news producer), August, 1982; two children. *Education:* Attended Wayne State University.

Addresses

Agent—c/o Dial Books for Young Readers, 375 Hudson St., New York, NY 10014.

Career

Writer.

Awards, Honors

Curious Creatures in Peculiar Places won the John Burroughs List Award for outstanding nature books for children, 1989; *How I Saved Hanukkah* was selected by the Bank Street College Children's Book Committee as one of the 1998 Children's Books of the Year in the special interest category; best books of the year list, *School Library Journal,* 1999, for *The Ashwater Experiment.*

Writings

PICTURE BOOKS; SELF-ILLUSTRATED

What Luck! A Duck!, Price, Stern, Sloan (Los Angeles, CA), 1987.
Where Fish Go in Winter and Answers to Other Great Mysteries, Price, Stern, Sloan, 1987.
Curious Creatures in Peculiar Places, Price, Stern, Sloan, 1989.
City Critters around the World, Price, Stern, Sloan, 1991.

INTERMEDIATE NOVELS

The Trouble with Zinny Weston, Dial, 1998.
How I Saved Hanukkah, illustrated by Diane deGroat, Dial, 1998.
The Ashwater Experiment, Dial, 1999.
The Girls, Dial, 2000.
Smoke Screen, American Girl, AG Fiction, 2000.

Work in Progress

Stranger in Dadland, for Dial, due in 2001; *Strike Two!* (working title), for Dial, due in 2002.

Sidelights

Amy Goldman Koss told *SATA:* "I assumed that when I grew up I'd get some miserable job doing something awful and I'd only get to draw pictures and make up stories in my teeny bits of free time. My dad's life was like that. He hated his job as a juke box man so he played violin, painted spooky pictures, and built ornate furniture on his weekends. Perhaps that's why I was a

Amy Goldman Koss

lousy student and never prepared much for adulthood. That is, I went to lots and lots of college, but never graduated and I had many jobs, but no career.

"It didn't occur to me that writing and drawing could be my REAL work until I married a guy who believed it was worth risking humiliation to try to do what we WANTED to with our lives. I figured if he could, I could—so, I began submitting work and getting countless letter-bomb rejections.

"But eventually my drawings, poems, articles, and short stories found their way into newspapers and literary magazines. That was a relief. Then I got my first picture book published and that felt great!

"I spent the next few years writing and illustrating picture books in verse until I started having babies and got so fat my hand could barely hold my drawing pens.

"I took a few years off to change diapers and push strollers then began my rejection collection ALL OVER AGAIN. After eons of disappointment, I was finally yanked out of the slush pile by a fabulous editor at Dial Books for Young Readers. She suggested that I try writing intermediate novels. And that's exactly what I've been doing ever since. And I LOVE it, especially when my characters become so real that I feel them

crowding around my computer, scrutinizing what I say about them.

"Now, I write all day while my kids are in school, and I sometimes sneak in a few hours after everyone else has gone to bed. I know mine is a weird, isolated life—but I also know it's absolutely PERFECT for me."

Amy Goldman Koss began her publishing career as an author and illustrator of picture books with rhyming texts. After the birth of her children, however, she shifted her focus as an author to write novels for middle-graders. Her work has earned high praise from critics for her well-rounded, likable characters, and realistic portrayal of the relationships and problems of the preadolescent set. In her first novel, *The Trouble with Zinny Weston,* fifth-grader Ava tells the story of how she became fast friends with newcomer Zinny Weston, and how everything went wrong after Zinny's mother drowned a raccoon in a garbage can after it had eaten the fish in her backyard pond. Ava and her veterinarian parents are devoted animal lovers, while Zinny and her mother find them dirty and detestable. This difference doesn't bother either girl much until someone reports Zinny's mother to the animal protection agency and Ava is the prime suspect. "Koss clearly knows the dynamics of middle-school friendship and how small misunderstandings can explode into war," averred a reviewer for

Publishers Weekly. Others noted that Ava's consideration of the moral dilemma involved provides readers with a good exposition of this sensitive issue. "Middlegraders will enjoy this first novel for the friend/enemy drama ... and for the sympathetic open discussion of animals rights," predicted Hazel Rochman in *Booklist.* *The Trouble with Zinny Weston* ends with a "believable" resolution to Ava and Zinny's problem, noted Mary M. Hopf in *School Library Journal,* who concluded: "Readers will enjoy meeting these characters."

In Koss's second novel for the middle grades, *How I Saved Hanukkah,* fourth-grader Marla Feinstein is not looking forward to the holiday season. Everyone else in her class celebrates Christmas, but Marla's mother won't let them hang lights on the house because they are Jewish. On the other hand, Mrs. Feinstein is not much interested in staging a festive Hanukkah celebration either, and Mr. Feinstein is out of town on business. It is up to Marla, and her friend Lucy, to inspire Marla's mother to help them make potato pancakes (latkes), play the dreidel game, and dance the hora. Critics concurred that Koss manages to teach readers about this festive Jewish holiday while entertaining them with likable characters and snappy prose. "A witty, warmly realized cast" makes *How I Saved Hanukkah* "fresh and believable," according to a reviewer in *Publishers Weekly.* "The fun and breezy tone and affectionately drawn characters will appeal to readers," Eva Mitnick likewise predicted in *School Library Journal.*

Though Hillary, the protagonist/narrator of *The Ashwater Experiment,* Koss's next novel for middle graders, is only twelve, she has attended eighteen schools while following her parents as they make and sell knickknacks at craft fairs around the country. Faced with the prospect of spending nine consecutive months in Ashwater, California, where she and her parents will housesit for a family on sabbatical, Hillary is dubious that her new life will feel any more real than the blur of the previous eighteen places she has lived. In response to her peripatetic lifestyle, Hillary imagines that the outside world is merely a set put before her by "the Watchers," who are interested in her responses to a variety of situations. "Koss portrays Hillary with such sympathy and wit that readers understand her Watchers game as a comic expression of the loneliness Hillary cannot express," observed a reviewer for *Publishers Weekly.* Of the novel's secondary characters, including the stereotypical class clown, popular girl, and outcast that Hillary has come to expect to find in every school, a contributor to *Kirkus Reviews* remarked: "Undercurrents of humor, and characters who seem typecast initially but develop surprising complexities, give this bittersweet tale unusual depth." A reviewer for *Horn Book* similarly attested: "Koss artfully sidesteps the predictable and crafts a truly original piece of fiction brimming with humor and insight."

Works Cited

Review of *The Ashwater Experiment, Horn Book,* July-August, 1999, p. 385.

Review of *The Ashwater Experiment, Kirkus Reviews,* May 1, 1999.

Review of *The Ashwater Experiment, Publishers Weekly,* June 14, 1999, p. 71.

Hopf, Mary M., review of *The Trouble with Zinny Weston, School Library Journal,* July, 1998, p. 96.

Review of *How I Saved Hanukkah, Publishers Weekly,* September 28, 1998, p. 54.

Mitnick, Eva, review of *How I Saved Hanukkah, School Library Journal,* October, 1998, p. 38.

Rochman, Hazel, review of *The Trouble with Zinny Weston, Booklist,* May 15, 1998, p. 1626.

Review of *The Trouble with Zinny Weston, Publishers Weekly,* June 29, 1998, p. 59.

For More Information See

PERIODICALS

Booklist, October 1, 1998, p. 330.

School Library Journal, August, 1999, p. 158.

L

LaROCHELLE, David 1960-

Personal

Surname is pronounced La-row-*shell;* born October 26, 1960, in Minneapolis, MN; son of Roger (a welder and construction worker) and Ruth (Bonrud) LaRochelle.

Education: St. Olaf College, B.A., 1983; University of Minnesota, B.S., 1984. *Hobbies and other interests:* Entering contests, orienteering, camping, travel, participating in local book club discussions, coaching and judging events for Odyssey of the Mind/Destination Imagination (a creative problem solving program for children).

David LaRochelle

Addresses

Home—4791 Stewart Ave., White Bear Lake, MN 55110. *E-mail*—talldave@ix.netcom.com.

Career

Teacher of fourth grade at a school in Coon Rapids, MN, 1984-88; freelance illustrator and writer, 1988—.

Awards, Honors

Parents' Choice Award for the book *Prime Time Together ... with Kids.*

Writings

A Christmas Guest, illustrated by Martin Skoro, Carolrhoda (Minneapolis, MN), 1988.
The Evening King, illustrated by Catherine Stock, Atheneum (New York City), 1993.

Contributor of stories, poems, puzzles, and illustrations to magazines, including *Spider* and *Cricket.*

AUTHOR AND ILLUSTRATOR; PUZZLE BOOKS

The Case of the Missing Lynx, Price, Stern, Sloan (Los Angeles, CA), 1995.
The Invisible Suit Case, Price, Stern, Sloan, 1995.
A Dog Gone Dilemma, Price, Stern, Sloan, 1996.
Trapped in Hill House!, Price, Stern, Sloan, 1996.
The Pirate's Yo-Ho-Hoax, Price, Stern, Sloan, 1997.
Detective Dave's Bummer Vacation, Price, Stern, Sloan, 1997.
Miss Taken's Identity, Price, Stern, Sloan, 1998.
Detective Dave: Space Case, Price, Stern, Sloan, 1998.

ILLUSTRATOR

Donna Erickson, *Prime Time Together ... with Kids,* Augsburg (Minneapolis), 1989.
Janet Greeson, reteller, *The Stingy Baker,* Carolrhoda, 1990.
Debbie Trafton O'Neal, *Before and after Christmas: Activities and Ideas for Advent and Epiphany,* Augsburg, 1991.
Erickson, *More Prime Time Activities with Kids,* Augsburg, 1992.
O'Neal, *Before and after Easter: Activities and Ideas for Lent to Pentecost,* Augsburg, 1993.
Jill Westburg McNamara, *My Mom Is Dying: A Child's Diary,* Augsburg, 1994.
Erickson, *Donna Erickson's Rainy Day Fun Book,* Augsburg, 1996.
Erickson, *Donna Erickson's Year-Round Holiday Fun Book,* Augsburg, 1996.
Erickson, *Donna Erickson's Great Outdoors Fun Book,* Augsburg, 1997.
Erickson, *Donna Erickson's Travel Fun Book,* Augsburg, 1997.
Erickson, *Donna's Day,* HarperCollins (New York City), 1998.
Joyce Bumgardner, *The New My Writing Book,* Froggie Press, 1998.

Illustrator of "Donna's Day," a nationally syndicated newspaper column by Donna Erickson.

Sidelights

David LaRochelle told *SATA:* "I love children's books. Few things give me greater joy than reading a good children's book. Maybe I haven't completely grown up because I still prefer children's books to books for adults.

"Some of my favorite authors when I was growing up were E. L. Konigsburg, Edward Eager, E. Nesbit, and C. S. Lewis. Their stories were an important part of my life. That is one of the magical things about books: an author can write a story that will move, inspire, or entertain people s/he has never met. I hope that someday I will be able to create books that will be important to other readers."

For More Information See

PERIODICALS

Booklist, December 1, 1993, p. 699.
Horn Book Guide, spring, 1994, p. 42.
Publishers Weekly, November 11, 1988, p. 55.
School Library Journal, July, 1990, p. 60; November, 1993, p. 85.

*   *   *

LAWSON, Amy
See GORDON, Amy

*   *   *

LEE, Hector Viveros 1962-

Personal

Born December 30, 1962, in Calexico, CA; son of Hector Garcia and Teresa Viveros Lee. *Education:* St. John's College (Camarillo, CA), B.A. in philosophy and Spanish, 1985; Academy of Art College (San Francisco, CA), B.F.A. in illustration, 1993.

Addresses

Home—San Francisco, CA.

Career

Has worked as a teacher in Parlier, CA, San Francisco, CA, and New York City; illustrator, San Francisco, 1992—. *Exhibitions:* Sheraton Palace Hotel, San Francisco, 1993; Thatcher Gallery at University of San Francisco, 1999. *Member:* Society of Children's Book Writers and Illustrators.

Writings

I Had a Hippopotamus, Lee and Low, 1996.

But I gave it to my grandma.

A box of animal crackers comes alive in Hector Viveros Lee's self-illustrated picture book, **I Had a Hippopotamus.**

ILLUSTRATOR

Por algo son los amigos, Houghton Mifflin, 1996.
America, My Land, Your Land, Our Land, Lee and Low, 1997.
Jeannine Atkins, *Get Set! Swim!,* Lee and Low, 1998.
Flores para Abuela, Scott-Foresman, 1999.
W. Nikola-Lisa, *Can You Top That?,* Lee and Low, 2000.

I Had a Hippopotamus has been translated into Spanish; Lee's illustrations have appeared in *Cricket Magazine, Spider Magazine,* and *Ladybug Magazine;* and on the covers of books published by Crossroad, Studio Goodwin Sturges for Houghton Mifflin, Wordsmith, and Hispanex for Scott-Foresman.

Sidelights

Hector Viveros Lee told *SATA:* "I was born to Mexican parents in Calexico, California, and was raised in Parlier, near Fresno, in the San Joaquin Valley. This small town in the fertile agricultural region provided my early experiences. Being immigrants, my parents were initially employed as farmworkers, which gave me a taste of the toil and honor of such labor and how life was tied to the land and its seasons. Having grandparents, uncles, and cousins living in the same town, I had the luxury of growing up in an extended family that prized its values and cultural heritage.

"My higher education began as an art major at Fresno State, but a year later I entered St. John's Seminary College in southern California, where I earned a Liberal Arts degree. I had the benefit of a well-rounded education. I returned to Fresno, where I secured a teaching credential and began teaching in Parlier in the very school I attended as a child. While working there, I became familiar with the development of children and rediscovered children's literature. Good children's books spoke to human issues beyond any age bracket; I was amazed how a child and an adult could enjoy a children's book on different levels. I began to create books to assist my students to read, one which served as the beginnings of my first book. I moved to San Francisco in 1990, where I enrolled in the Academy of Art College, earning a second degree in illustration.

"I continue to teach and since 1992 have worked as a freelance artist. I enjoy depicting a variety of subjects that appeal to children and adults. I especially enjoy drawing animals, which have been a constant source of wonder and admiration since I was young. On occasion I draw on my particular Latino experience to create pictures with universal appeal. Imaginary and fantastical elements are part of my work. I believe they are an integral part of living; they provide links to our interior reality. I draw with the conviction that art taps into our paradoxical and wonderful humanity—both in the simple and the complex, ordinary and the magical, the particular and the universal."

Hector Viveros Lee has written and illustrated one picture book, and illustrated several children's books written by others. In his illustration, Lee uses India ink, gouache, and watercolor in layers, creating an effect that has been likened to the look of woodcuts. The author relied on this method for the illustrations in his picture book, *I Had a Hippopotamus,* in which a little boy bestows on others the cookies from his box of animal crackers, and one by one the animals come alive. The kangaroo he gives his grandmother helps her in the kitchen by stowing her utensils in its pocket; the coyote he gives to his uncle howls along with his uncle's guitar playing. Critics admired the author's deadpan delivery of the humorous text, combined with illustrations done in what a reviewer for *Publishers Weekly* dubbed "a wildly vivid palette." A contributor to *Kirkus Reviews* noted that Lee's illustrations "require—and reward—careful scrutiny." *I Had a Hippopotamus* is "a winning spin on the notion that 'tis better to give than to receive ... an anaconda," the reviewer for *Publishers Weekly* concluded.

Lee has also contributed the illustrations to several children's books written by others. Among these is Jeannine Atkins's *Get Set! Swim!,* in which a young girl nervously prepares to participate in a swim meet in the suburbs against a winning team with a large, new pool. For her mother, the meet conjures up memories of swimming in the ocean in Puerto Rico. Though Jessenia wins her match her team loses the meet, inspiring a mixture of feelings which Lee conveys in artwork that "is strong in both design and color," according to Ilene Cooper in *Booklist. Get Set! Swim!* was particularly recommended for libraries in search of materials that focus on Hispanic families.

Works Cited

Cooper, Ilene, review of *Get Set! Swim!, Booklist,* May 15, 1998, p. 1629.

Review of *I Had a Hippopotamus, Kirkus Reviews,* March 15, 1996, p. 455

Review of *I Had a Hippopotamus, Publishers Weekly,* February 26, 1996, p. 104.*

LEHMAN, Barbara 1963-

Personal

Born December 14, 1963, in Chicago, IL; daughter of Donald and Patricia (maiden name, Dupont) Lehman. *Education:* Pratt Institute, B.F.A. in illustration. *Hobbies and other interests:* Letterpress printing, Aikido, gardening, bookbinding.

Addresses

Agent—c/o Candlewick Press, 2067 Massachusetts Ave., 5th Floor, Cambridge, MA 02140.

Career

Self-employed freelance artist, clients include *New York Times,* New York City Transit Authority, and McGraw-Hill.

Awards, Honors

Parents' Choice illustration award, 1993, for *Moonfall.*

Writings

ILLUSTRATOR

Nancy Lecourt, *Abracadabra to Zigzag: An Alphabet Book,* Lothrop Lee and Shepard, 1991.

Marsha Wilson Chall, *Mattie,* Lothrop Lee and Shepard, 1992.

Florence Parry Heide and Roxanne Heide Pierce, *Timothy Twinge,* Lothrop Lee and Shepard, 1993.

Susan Whitcher, *Moonfall,* Farrar Straus & Giroux, 1993.

Lynda Graham Barber, *A Chartreuse Leotard in a Magenta Limousine and Other Words Named after People and Places,* Hyperion, 1994.

Susan Whitcher, *Something for Everyone,* Farrar Straus & Giroux, 1995.

Lynda Graham-Barber, *Say Boo!,* Candlewick, 1996.

Sidelights

Barbara Lehman told *SATA:* "Like many people in publishing I grew up loving books, and reading, and I 'always knew' I wanted to work professionally with books. Illustrating books gives me great pleasure. As a hobby I also do letterpress printing, using metal type and wood and linoleum cuts, as well as hand bookbinding. And I also read a lot—books for all age groups. My most favorite illustrators are: Herge, Winsor McKay, and George Merriman."

Critics have praised Barbara Lehman's illustrations for picture books. In Nancy Lecourt's unusual alphabet book, *Abracadabra to Zigzag,* reviewers noted that Lehman's illustrations bring to the life the abstract concepts explained by the author in a text that introduces children to some of the more colorful expressions in the English language. "The clever and colorful watercolors make the title much more accessible than might be expected given the words involved," asserted Kathy

Piehl in *School Library Journal.* Lehman exploits both variety and identity to increase the appeal of the illustrations—varying the layout of the pictures but including a yellow dog somewhere in each in order to help sustain the interest of young audiences.

Lehman also provided the illustrations for *Mattie,* a first chapter book of three related stories featuring "an impulsive yet appealing second-grader," according to Kay Weisman in *Booklist.* In the first story, Mattie plays a Valentine's Day trick on the class clown that backfires; in the second tale, she sells her little brother and then tries to buy him back.

For the picture book audience, Lehman produced humorous watercolor illustrations for Florence Parry Heide and Roxanne Heide Pierce's *Timothy Twinge,* in which a little boy who worries about everything learns to be brave when his fear that aliens come out in his room at night comes true. "Lehman's bright cartoon-style watercolors will have plenty of appeal for children," predicted Janice Del Negro in *Booklist.*

Lehman's signature watercolor cartoons in bright colors won the Parents' Choice illustration award for the 1993 publication *Moonfall,* written by Susan Whitcher. Critics admired this seriously magical story of Sylvie, who sees the moon fall into the neighbor's lilac bushes one night. After fifteen nights without a moon in the sky, the pragmatic Sylvie goes into the neighbor's garden to rescue the moon and finds it tarnished and dented. When she washes it in Magic Bubble solution, the moon dissolves, but Sylvie blows a bubble with the solution and a pearly one floats up into the sky as the new moon. Critics were equally enchanted by Whitcher's whimsical story and Lehman's illustrations. "Whitcher's deceptively simple, effective text is engagingly partnered by Lehman's pleasantly satisfying watercolors," remarked Janice Del Negro in *Booklist.* Susan Scheps's review in *School Library Journal* concurred: "This delightful combination ... is destined to become a read-aloud favorite in many a household."

Works Cited

Del Negro, Janice, review of *Moonfall, Booklist,* July, 1993, p. 1978.

Del Negro, review of *Timothy Twinge, Booklist,* September 15, 1993, p. 157.

Piehl, Kathy, review of *Abracadabra to Zigzag, School Library Journal,* June, 1991, p. 84.

Scheps, Susan, review of *Moonfall, School Library Journal,* October, 1993, p. 114.

Weisman, Kay, review of *Mattie, Booklist,* April 15, 1992, p. 1527.

For More Information See

PERIODICALS

Publishers Weekly, April 26, 1991, p. 59; June 14, 1993, p. 69.

School Library Journal, August, 1992, p. 134.*

Autobiography Feature

Betsy Lewin

1937-

I was born on May 12, 1937, with a fistful of family names, Elizabeth Patchin Dowler Reilly. But I was never called anything but Betsy.

My mother's family helped to settle the area around where we lived, and there's evidence of that in the names of Patchinville and Dowler junction. I grew up in Clearfield, Pennsylvania, a little town nestled in an Allegheny valley. No matter where I stood in town, I could see the hills and watch the seasons change with a drama unique to the northeast. From the hills I could see the entire town and listen to its muffled voices: the thwack of an ax chopping wood, a barking dog, an occasional car horn. I could see all the church steeples, the river and its bridges, and the railroad tracks where steam engines pulled both passenger and freight cars.

Coal Hill rose up at the end of our street, and its woods were full of magic and mystery, fertile ground for my imagination. There I played with all my book friends, from Winnie-the-Pooh to Robin Hood. I even found the exact tree where Pooh lived under the name of Sanders. Shaft mining and then strip-mining had shaped and reshaped the hill, but I could still find solitude in the woods and thrill to my first encounters with wildlife. Years later while visiting my family, I took an early morning walk on Coal Hill with my husband, Ted. New houses had claimed a little more of

Betsy Lewin in India, 1996.

the hillside, but from the ridge of the old mine we watched deer and wild turkey feeding together in the woods below.

In the center of town, at the corner of East Market and Second streets, stood the county courthouse. A horn on its roof blew at noon every day. The horn was called the Mooley—no one seemed to know why—and if you were anywhere near it when it went off, it would stop your heart and freeze your blood, even when you expected it. People on the street would stop, hunch their shoulders, and grimace the second before it blew. The courthouse still stands today, but the Mooley is long gone. I can't think of one good reason why, but I kind of miss it.

The Susquehanna

The West Branch of the Susquehanna River runs through Clearfield, cutting it in two. We lived on West Market Street and had to cross the bridge to get to shops, church, and school. In the summer, I would stand on the bridge and watch the river grass slowly wave in shallow water like the tresses of drowned women. In the winter, the groans of ice breaking up in the river were music to my ears—they meant that spring was on its way. And all year long, I loved to look down from the bridge at the ducks gathering on the river below.

Only once did the river show me its dark side. I was ten years old, walking home from school on a brilliant March day. When I reached the middle of the bridge, I saw a boy walking across the river on the ice. I wanted to do

that, too. Without thinking, I ran back across the bridge and down the east bank. The boy had already scaled the west bank and disappeared from view. I'd taken no more than twenty steps out onto the frozen river when the ice caved in under me. I dropped hip-deep into the ice-cold water, my chest flat on the surface of the ice, my mittened hands digging into the snowy crust. The current snatched at my ankles, thrusting my legs forward, bending me in half. In tears and terror, I thought the words, "no use." I don't know how I heaved myself up and out. I remember crawling on my hands and knees back to the bank where I sat, amazed at the fact that I was still alive. I never told my parents what had happened.

To this day, when I stand in the middle of that bridge and look down at the waving river grass, I can still feel the pull of the current on my legs.

Childhood Fantasy

I suppose every child has what I call a "save the world" fantasy in which she averts a disaster and emerges the hero. I used to entertain mine on my way to Leonard Grade School, waddling along in galoshes and snowpants. The scene is the school auditorium, where all the teachers, students, and parents are assembled for a school play. Suddenly, out of nowhere, a gorilla bursts onto the stage, roaring and beating his chest. Pandemonium! The screaming, hysterical crowd tries to escape. Calmly, I make my way backstage, climb a ladder, grab the curtain ropes and swing, Tarzan style, out over the stage. I drop onto the back of the raging brute and wrestle him into submission to the wild cheers of the admiring, grateful crowd.

Then I would suddenly snap out of it, saying to myself, "How can I do all that in these stupid old snowpants?"

As I write this, I'm about to fulfill another childhood fantasy: a chance to see real mountain gorillas in Uganda's Impenetrable Forest. I'll be armed with a camera and a better understanding of the gorilla's true, gentle nature, and, of course, I'll be looking for a story.

Mother and Daddy

My mother's name was Winifred, but everyone called her Winnie. She had black hair and dark-brown eyes and great personal style. I wanted to look like her. My brother thought she looked like a Spanish princess.

Mother is responsible for my love of children's books. She read to my brother and me every night: *Winnie-the-Pooh, The Adventures of Babar, The Tales of Uncle Remus,* and all the fairy tales. The illustrators Ernest Shepard and A. B. Frost were among my earliest heroes. Later on, when I started illustrating for children, I realized how strongly I'd been influenced by the gentle watercolors of Beatrix Potter and the energetic line and zany humor of James Stevenson and Quentin Blake.

Mother's sense of humor was always unexpected. One night she came into my bedroom to say goodnight wearing a long satin robe with shoulder pads and satin piping. I thought it was an evening gown and asked if she was going out. "Yes," she said, "like a light." She loved to garden and worked like a horse planting and weeding, turning as brown as a walnut in the sun. A row of purple flags, or popcorn iris, at the far end of our backyard were her pride and joy.

Portulaca lined the flower beds, and I remember Japanese lanterns, gooseberry bushes, and a rose arbor. During the Second World War we planted Victory gardens.

Spring meant the smell of Kemtone paint, because in spring Mother painted the walls. She also cleaned the wallpaper with a big soft wad of something that looked like an enormous kneaded eraser. This needed to be done every spring because of the grime from our coal furnace.

Mother gave teas and luncheons, and she and Daddy loved to play cards: bridge and pinochle and—so my brother and I could play too—hearts. Daddy always said she played best when she didn't think about what she was doing. She usually beat him.

Before Mother married Daddy, she was a teacher. When my brother and I were grown and away at school, she decided to start a kindergarten since there wasn't one in the area public schools. Our dining room was transformed. Lilliputian tables and chairs borrowed from a Sunday school, stacks and stacks of picture books, and mounds of toys replaced the dining room furniture. Mother was in seventh heaven.

Today I am a very early riser, but when I was a Pratt student I stayed up late and slept late if I could. One time I was home for a holiday and still asleep at noon when I heard little footsteps coming up the stairs and into my bedroom. I opened my eyes and looked into the solemn face of a kindergartner who said, "Mrs. Reilly wants to know if you're ever going to get up?" My father's name was John Kennedy Reilly, but everyone knew him as Pat. My brother and I called him Daddy. He was a sweet, crazy Irishman, as dashing as F. Scott Fitzgerald, and a natural storyteller. His wonderful stories of his own childhood in a Pennsylvania mining town were filled with hilarious turns and wacky accents. I inherited his sense of humor, and I hope it's evident in my art. He loved to recite poetry, and he loved to sing—everything from Irish ditties to operatic arias. He used to do little tap dances the way most people absently drum their fingers or rub their chins. Daddy worked for a coal casualty insurance firm. He'd traveled everywhere in Pennsylvania and knew the names of hundreds of towns. He was an excellent driver, but he did get impatient with drivers in front of him, especially at traffic lights. If they didn't move fast enough, Daddy would bark, "It won't get any greener, Bub!" or "What's the matter, don't they have any colors you like?"

Mother used to tell a story about Daddy when they were courting. He took mother and his future mother-in-law for a drive. As they drove by houses in neighboring towns, Daddy would say, "I see the Andersons are at home today," or "The Joneses must be out. Their car isn't in the driveway." Finally my mother's mother was impressed. "My goodness, Pat," she said, "you must know everyone in these parts!" Daddy had simply been reading the names on people's mailboxes.

We loved to sit on the front porch on hot summer evenings with big bowls of Clearfield Dairy ice cream and homemade chocolate sauce. The only flaw in this scene was a new streetlight that shone right in our faces. Daddy bought an awning and tacked it up along the edge of the porch ceiling. He was really pleased with his solution to the problem, but that night when we sat on the porch we found that the awning was just not quite long enough to block the light. No one had the heart to mention it.

One summer we visited friends who had rented a cottage on Chautauqua Lake. I was eight. Our friend's son, who was only nine, took my brother and me out on the lake in a boat with an outboard motor without his parents' permission. The weather turned nasty, and the lake got really choppy. We made it back to the dock, where the grim-faced adults, including Daddy, were waiting. Another boat had been sent out to look for us. Daddy jumped into our boat and gave us each a firm hand up onto the dock. I never saw him so angry. My uncle Harold, who had been holding the rope to steady the boat, forgot to tie it up once all the kids were safe on the dock. "HELP!" we heard and turned to see Daddy stretched out like a gangplank, his feet in the drifting boat and his hands gripping the dock. He took a dunking, which cooled him (and everyone else) off, so we never got the spanking and lecture we deserved.

Daddy never in his life laid a hand on us, and Mother spanked us only once when one day we strayed too far from home. My brother and I were always made to feel ashamed of ourselves more than to fear punishment.

My Brother

My brother John and I are eighteen months apart in age. I was his kid sister. We had normal sibling spats, but mostly I remember getting along with each other. There were lots of kids in our neighborhood when we were growing up, and we all played together. One time when my mother was sick in the hospital, a neighbor's boy threw a toy gun at John, giving him a bad cut over his eye. I went with Daddy to visit Mother and was told to say nothing of the incident. When Mother asked how everything was at home, I said: "Something terrible happened, but I'm not allowed to tell you." While I was spending my hours drawing pictures, John was building model airplanes. He

Betsy with Sport and Trippy in their backyard, 1951.

"My brother, John, in Shriner band costume."

knew the names of all the airplanes of World War II and what all the insignias meant. I was very impressed.

We loved to play counting games when we rode in the family car. We counted cows and Mail Pouch Tobacco signs on the sides of barns. We counted service stars in the windows of homes where one or more family members were serving in World War II, and when we couldn't think of anything else to count, we counted telephone poles.

We both loved the movies and were—and still are—insatiable horror fans: *Frankenstein* and *The Wolf Man, Count Dracula,* and any other chillers that Hollywood churned out. Later we shared goose bumps over Stephen King's *The Shining* and Peter Straub's *Ghost Story.*

While I went to art school, John went to Penn State, then on to law school. He still lives in our hometown of Clearfield, where he's serving his third term as county judge. He marches all over the country with a Shriner band in parades, in which he sheds the somber robes of a judge and bursts forth a giant, turbaned sultan in sequins and gold lamé pantaloons, curled-toe slippers, and his wife's earring, and leads the band, brandishing a rubber scimitar.

Grandparents

My mother's father, Harry Patton Dowler, lived with us in the house he had originally owned. He occupied a room at the top of the stairs. Once he had been a strong man, well over six feet tall, and he was nicknamed "Horse Power Dowler" when he played football at Penn State. But now he was old and stooped, nearly deaf, and he limped around with a cane due to a broken hip suffered in an auto accident. He was a Victorian man who wrote poetry and could draw the most beautiful eagles. He was also a wood-carver and cabinetmaker. He had owned a logging company and had ridden the last great log raft on the Susquehanna from Clearfield to Shawville. He had been a contractor and was active in the Civilian Conservation Corps, planting trees around the area. I remember in particular a magnificent stand of oaks—every time we drove past them my mother would say, "Your grandfather planted those trees." Mother loved to tell about the time Grandpa, angry with neighbor kids for stepping in his fresh cement sidewalk, told their parents, "I love children in the abstract, but not in the concrete."

My mother's mother died before I was born, but I have photographs and my mother's stories about her and something else that I treasure: a collection of exquisitely hand-painted china signed by her—Emma Patchin, 1892. Nana and Dada, as we called my father's parents, lived some forty miles from us in the little coal mining town of Spangler, where Dada owned a partnership in a mine operation. We used to visit them on summer weekends in their comfortable little house on a corner. I remember Dada's big armchair that sat between two windows, a pipe stand, a cribbage set, a model of the Santa Maria, and the rosaries and crucifixes that made it a Catholic home. There was an endless supply of Nana's sand dollar cookies and a passel of second cousins to play with. We found our first family dog there, a little white-and-black fox terrier that appeared on Nana's back porch one day. My brother and I thought he was an escaped circus dog because he chased his tail. We named him Sport.

When I was twelve, Nana and Dada died within weeks of each other. It was my first experience with the anger and hurt of irretrievable loss.

Aunt Betty and Uncle Harold

Mother's sister, Betty, and her husband, my uncle Harold, lived down the block from us in a big old Victorian house.

Uncle Harold loved to hunt game birds and owned several English setters. From the time I was a little girl until I went away to Pratt, I loved to follow him into the field when he worked the dogs. Mack and Lady were two of his favorites. Mack had a "soft mouth" and always retrieved birds intact, but Lady sometimes delivered her birds in less than perfect condition.

Sometimes other hunters would come to the same area to work their dogs. Once there was a van with five or six dogs in the back. The dogs bounced around inside with such energy and enthusiasm it sounded like a drummer doing a solo inside a steel drum. The owner stood off to the side when he opened the back door so he wouldn't get flattened when the dogs burst out.

I longed to go with Uncle Harold to the field trials where the dogs were put through their paces and judged on their skills, but that was out of the question. That was a man's world then.

"With Ethel (left) and my mother behind me, my father and Trippy in front, on our back porch," 1958.

Sometimes my brother and I would sleep overnight at Aunt Betty and Uncle Harold's house. I loved the guest room! It looked like a set for a Jean Harlow movie, with pink satin bedspreads and a monogrammed, mirror-glass wastepaper basket next to a dressing table that held an ivory-handled dresser set including everything from a button hook to a nail buffer.

Aunt Betty made the best spaghetti and meatballs in the world. I remember her best in her kitchen, wading through a pack of milling dogs, carrying a big kettle of spaghetti sauce from the stove to the table. The dogs would knock me down, and the smell of the sauce would knock me out. It was Heaven.

Uncle Aaron

Visits with Uncle Aaron, Mother's handsome bachelor older brother, were always unforgettable. Uncle Aaron moved from New York to Philadelphia at about the time I went to Pratt, but he occasionally returned to New York on business, and he'd always take me out to dinner. He loved to stride down the street with me on his arm and boom out, "Don't worry, Honey, age doesn't matter. We'll make it work." He thought that was the funniest thing in the world. I would cringe and grin sheepishly at passersby.

One time when I was taking the train home from school, he decided to hop the train in Philadelphia and join

me. The train stood for a long time in the Harrisburg Station, so we stepped down to the platform to stretch our legs. Suddenly Uncle Aaron started dragging me toward the front of the train. He called up to the engineer, "How about letting my niece ride up there with you?" The engineer smiled and threw down a pair of work gloves, beckoning me to climb up the steel ladder. I declined the offer and dragged Uncle Aaron back to our seats while he tried out his "Don't worry, Honey, age doesn't matter" routine on the other passengers.

Daddy's Brothers

Uncle Bob, Daddy's older brother, seemed the epitome of normalcy to me. I had heard stories of his youthful escapades, running away to join the circus or the army, only to be retrieved by Dada. One time Dada supposedly dragged him by the ear from a boxing ring, thus ending yet another attempt at a nonconventional career. But to me he seemed a contented and loving family man with no hint of his earlier wanderlust.

Uncle Joe, on the other hand, was a wild man with both Daddy's quirky sense of humor and Uncle Bob's abandoned wanderlust. When my brother and I were little, Uncle Joe used to frizzle his hair into a mad tangle, cross his eyes, and chase us around the house, his unhinged lower plate protruding menacingly. We would squeal in delighted horror until Mother finally called a halt and demanded that we settle down—all three of us.

Sometimes Uncle Joe would ring our door bell at one o'clock in the morning with a huge bucket of shrimp in his arms. John and I would be awakened to join the surprise feast. Mother would whip up a batch of cocktail sauce, and we would all sit in the kitchen, laughing and talking and savoring the delicious shrimp. Then Uncle Joe would disappear into his mysterious, private life until one day he would pop up again, sometimes with a bucket of shrimp.

Ethel

Ethel Fulton was one of seven children whose family lived on a farm. When she was sixteen, she went to live with my grandmother Dowler. Besides doing the cooking and helping with the housework, she also helped raise my mother and her brother and sister. When Mother and Daddy married, Ethel came to live with them and helped raise my brother and me.

She was a short woman, nearly as wide as she was high, with white hair pulled into a little bun at the back of her neck. She wore white, lace-up shoes and spoke in a sweet, gentle voice—unless she was shooing the dog off the couch. She did the laundry every Monday, come what may. Mother always said, "I hope I don't die on a Monday, because Ethel won't come to my funeral."

Ethel was a superb cook, and a tyrant in the kitchen. She allowed no one to help her, but I was content just to watch her. I especially liked how she whipped egg whites for an angel food cake. She would tilt an oval platter at a right angle to the table, and her wire whisk would go at lightning speed, in ever widening arcs, whipping the egg whites into a silvery froth. The tip of her tongue would slip through her tightly closed lips and slowly curve upward, toward her nose.

Christmas and Easter were the most special holidays in our house, and Ethel created some incredible delicacies for them. At Christmas time, the kitchen smelled of citrus, cinnamon, and cloves. Candied orange and grapefruit rinds, gingerbread, and apple, mincemeat, and pumpkin pies were in endless supply. At Easter there were chocolate-covered fondant eggs and fondant-stuffed dates topped with walnuts.

Ethel was an expert seamstress, sewing everything from pinafores to patchwork quilts. I still have two quilts that she made for me to take with me when I went to Pratt.

Daddy was Catholic, but Mother, John and I, and Ethel were all Presbyterians. Ethel had a friend named Margaret who was exactly the same size and shape as Ethel. On summer Sundays, we often walked to church. Ethel and Margaret walked together, rocking to port and starboard like two chubby sailors in their flowered straw hats. The two of them sat together in the pew behind us. Ethel sang the hymns sweetly, but Margaret crowed them out like a rooster, raising the hair on the back of my neck.

Mother said that when Ethel was a young lady, she had a beau. He was a doctor, and he came by horse and buggy to court her. He gave her a puppy once, for her birthday, and eventually he proposed to her, but she refused. She was a member of our family and shared our lives until she died.

Betsy Lewin in her studio, 1996.

Best Friends

I've lost touch with my oldest friend, Marywynn, whom I'd known since we were five years old. We both loved horses and galloped around the neighborhood on homemade steeds. We'd cut holes large enough to fit around our waists in the tops of big boxes. Straps on either side slipped over our shoulders to keep the boxes in place. We painted horse faces on smaller boxes, which we attached to the big boxes with broomstick "necks." We painted legs and feet in stirrups on each side of the big boxes and attached reins to the horses' box heads. A bit of black yarn for the tail, and we were off, our own two feet doing the work of four. Neither of us ever owned a real horse.

We also shared a love for drawing and painting. For me there was never anything else in my future, but Marywynn was also talented in music, and eventually music won out. She went to Oberlin, and I went to Pratt. Our lives touched briefly after that, once or twice. As far as I know, she is still a violist with a symphony orchestra.

I met Donna, the daughter of a Methodist minister, in junior high school. We loved words, made lists of words we loved the sound of, and discovered poetry. We were both good language students and were always the last ones standing in spelling bees, in both English and Spanish.

We pledged each other to follow our dreams, went off to college, then went our separate ways. But I think of her every time I open a book of Old Master paintings she once gave me for Christmas. She signed it "With love and hope."

Art

For as long as I can remember, I drew pictures. I drew in the blank pages of books, on napkins and paper bags, in notebooks, in sketch pads, and on the sidewalk. At school I made drawings for anyone who asked, of whatever they wanted.

Sylvia Breth, my elementary school art teacher, would give us a project, pass out sheets of paper, and say, "Get rid of all your corny ideas first. Then give me your best." In junior high school, Mr. Dominick tried to instill in his students a keen sense of observation and artistic appreciation. Most of the kids elected art class as the least of the evils available to them, but two or three of us were really interested.

At some point in my early years, I realized that my artistic ability could serve me well in crisis situations. Notes of apology accompanied by sketches were especially effective.

In my eighth-grade biology class, each student was asked to write an essay on the subject of his or her choice. I panicked at the thought of having to write a scientific paper, until I decided to write it in story form: "Esmerelda: The Life Cycle of a Tapeworm." Much thought and care went into the cover art, a portrait of Esmerelda, who looked like a long, skinny Carmen Miranda with a head full of fruit. The paper earned me an above average grade, more for its humor and originality than scientific merit. Mrs. Snyder, my teacher, read it aloud to the class and said, with gentle sarcasm, "Well, Miss Betsy, I hope to see your name in lights someday."

Lewin on Isabella Island, Galapagos, doing research for **Booby Hatch**, *1993.*

The same ploy worked in college English when faced with an analytical paper. I dissected and analyzed the layers of an artist's wastepaper basket. (Write about what you know.)

Math was never my best subject, and even the magic of art failed me there. Mr. Smith, my high school math teacher, was passionate about his subject and as patient a man as ever lived. He called his students "people." "People, I don't care what walk of life you choose, whether it be engineering or art (with a meaningful glance at me), someday you are going to need math." He was right. After graduating from Pratt, I worked as an assistant art director at a greeting card company. One day the art director told me to enlarge a card size one-half up for a third reduction. He might just as well have been speaking Hindi. I figured it out, though, and I hope Mr. Smith knows it somehow. I never wield a ruler without thinking of him.

There was no art education in high school, but I took private lessons with a local artist, Nonny Soderlund, and spent Tuesdays after school happily daubing away in oils and pastels in her kitchen. She was very encouraging and urged my parents to consider sending me to art school. She cut out an ad for Pratt Institute from a magazine and told us that this was the best—indeed the only—school to consider.

I had an easel and a set of paints at home, too. The local house-paint store supplied me with stretched canvases, and I painted whatever came into my head, always from memory. I really had no idea how to use paint, but I entered my work in the annual art exhibit at the county fair and won every color ribbon there was on the strength of whatever raw talent the judges recognized.

One year some Pratt instructors were in town and happened into the exhibit. Sylvia Breth engaged them in conversation, showed them my entries, and told them that I might submit an application to Pratt. They had some kind words for my work and suggested that I use alizarin crimson with a little more restraint.

Mother and Daddy never discouraged me from drawing and painting, but they were bewildered by it. "Where did this talent come from?" they wondered. "Certainly not from either of us." But their faith in my ability did not extend to art school and the possibility of a career. Does anyone really make a living as an artist ... especially a woman? They wanted me to go to a college, take a liberal arts course, think about becoming a teacher. After all, I had taken the college preparatory course in high school. But I persisted, and eventually they gave in. I suspect my brother said a word or two on my behalf.

I filled out the application form and completed the required aptitude test, which included drawing a section of a room in my house and depicting a memorable incident in my life. Then I dropped my hopes for the future, in the form of a fifteen-by-twenty yellow envelope, into the mailbox.

Official acceptance came by telephone. It was a long time in coming because they had confused me with another applicant, Patricia Reilly. But now I could exhale, and at last, in the fall of 1955, I was off to New York City and art school.

I arrived with almost no knowledge of art or art history. But that was what the freshman foundation course, which everyone had to take, was all about. It was designed to teach the basics, preparing students for whatever course they wished to follow, such as architecture, industrial design, or, as in my case, illustration.

The instructors who taught illustration were the best in their field and passionate about sharing their knowledge. Richard Lindner, a painter, taught me to look with my own eyes and interpret what I saw in my own, personal way. Calvin Albert taught sculpture and figure drawing. He told his students: "Don't worry if it doesn't all sink in right this minute. One day it will all fall into place." I dedicated a picture book to him. Kosrov Ajootian, my anatomy instructor, taught me to observe closely, trust what I saw, and record it accurately. His affectionate name for his students was "Puppy." "Nice bit of observation there, Puppy," he would say, pointing at a student's drawing of an ankle and foot with all the bones, tendons, and muscles well realized. I remember John Groth, a former war correspondent with a bristling white moustache, bounding around the classroom in a Norfolk jacket booming, "Draw, draw, draw, everyday, everywhere!" He taught me to throw myself at a blank page with all the emotion and action I could summon, and how to tell a story with drawings in sequential order.

The Pennsylvania Railroad

"All aboard for Philadelphia, Paoli, Coatesville and Harr-is-burg Sta-shun!" I listened to that announcement echo through cavernous Penn Station every time I went home from Pratt. Penn Station created its own atmosphere. The voices and footsteps of throngs of travelers rose in a ghostly chorus that dissolved in the permanent white haze that filled the air beneath the skylighted cathedral ceiling. Standing there with my grandfather Dowler's old cloth-covered, monogrammed suitcase and a portfolio crammed with a semester's work to show the folks at home, I waited for the track number of the General or the Broadway Limited to be called over the loudspeaker. The sense of

Illustration from unpublished work, "Hounds and Hunter."

excitement and adventure in that grand old station was palpable.

Once aboard, I'd settle myself into a window seat and watch the scenery change from the train yards and the spiny edges of the city to the serene stretches of the Susquehanna River and the rolling hills and farmlands of Pennsylvania. With a six-hour journey ahead of me, there was plenty of time to read or sketch ("Draw, draw, draw!" ringing in my ear) and, best of all, time to have dinner in the dining car. Leaving a magazine, hat, or jacket on my seat to show that it was occupied, I made my way through the chair car, the sleeper car, and the lounge car into the dining car with its white linen tablecloths, heavy pewter flatware and coffeepots, and smiling waiters.

Boston baked beans, Canadian bacon, and brown bread—a round loaf baked in a coffee can—was the specialty. Did you know that if you plunk a spoon in your cup, the coffee won't spill when the train rocks? Warm apple pie topped with a slice of Vermont cheddar, or saltine crackers and Roquefort cheese, or plain old vanilla and chocolate ice cream for dessert. It all tasted so good, your eyes would roll right back in your head.

Then back to my seat. If it was Christmas time, it would be dark outside by now, and the train lights would be on. Drowsy from my culinary experience, I would watch the Christmas lights float by and let the hours rumble on. The conductor would call out the stops, "Lew-is-town, Hunt-ing-ton," and finally my destination, "Tyrone Station." Through the window I would see Mother and Daddy standing on the platform, framed by the old, red-brick, Victorian station house.

Ted

When I was a sophomore at Pratt I met Ted Lewin. He had graduated the year before and was already finding his way as a freelance illustrator. Our first date was at his apartment. I arrived promptly at six (promptness is one of the things we have in common) and knocked on the door. Ted's roommate answered, dressed as a waiter complete with a little towel draped over one arm. He bowed gracefully and led me to a table with a red-checkered tablecloth in the middle of their living room. He lit a half-burned candle stuck in an ashtray and disappeared into the kitchen. Moments later Ted appeared, a red-checkered napkin tied, gypsy style, around his head, a red sash at his waist, and his childhood violin poised under his chin. He squeaked out a rendition of "Dark Eyes" that set my teeth on edge. It was terrible, but the pasta was great.

Ted captured my heart with stories and pictures of his family's menagerie of exotic pets, from Sheba the lion cub to Jago the chimpanzee. Besides a mutual love of animals, we found that we loved the same books and movies, enjoyed each other's sense of humor, and could spend countless hours talking about our longing to travel to the world's wild places.

New Beginnings

After graduation, my job as assistant art director at a greeting card company led to freelance work doing color separations by hand for several other card companies. I also "pounded the pavement" with my portfolio, accepting whatever assignments were offered, mostly spot drawings for magazines and brochures. I was determined to become a freelance illustrator.

After Ted and I were married, I continued to do color separations by hand for card companies until that method was replaced by a photographic process. Ted had an agent then and was doing a lot of elementary textbook illustration and young-adult book jackets. When his agent retired, I began to represent Ted myself. I had become good friends with the agent, and she was very helpful, introducing me to her contacts and freely offering her knowledge and advice. Soon I was expanding Ted's opportunities to include magazine illustration, some corporate and advertising art, and assignments for *Reader's Digest* Condensed Books.

But though I continued to draw and paint, I wasn't contributing much professionally to the field beyond an occasional illustrated story or poem for a children's magazine. This was a growing frustration to me.

In the early seventies, I began to explore the field of children's picture books for Ted. We became very good friends with Rosemary Casey, a children's book editor at Dodd, Mead and Company. She had seen one of my illustrated poems and asked me to expand it into a picture book. I jumped at the chance, and produced my first picture book, *Cat Count*. That was followed by *Hip, Hippo,*

Hooray, a subtraction book (the one I dedicated to Calvin Albert, my instructor at Pratt). My love of picture books was rekindled, but this time I was writing and illustrating my own.

One day I got a call from Barbara Lalicki, who was then an editor at Lothrop, Lee and Shepard. She had seen a drawing of a cat that I had given as a gift to a retiring editor, and she offered me *Furlie Cat,* by Berniece Freschet, to illustrate, and after that, Beatrice Schenk de Regniers's *Penny.*

But things weren't moving fast enough for me. I found it impossible to represent myself, carrying my own portfolio from one publisher to another, and I was uncomfortable promoting my own work. Then Dilys Evans, who is active in many areas of children's literature including representing illustrators, founded The Original Art, an annual exhibition of children's book art. Two pieces from *Cat Count* were included in the show, and that's when I first met Dilys. I liked her immediately and decided to ask her to represent me. She agreed, and I've been doing picture books ever since, and loving it.

Travel

In 1970, seven years after Ted and I were married, we invested nearly all our savings in a trip to East Africa to see the wildlife of Kenya, Tanzania, and Uganda. It was the beginning of Travel as a Way of Life. Our travels have enriched every aspect of our lives, and they've added exciting dimension to our books for children.

Booby Hatch, published by Clarion Books, was my first travel-inspired picture book, inspired by our visit to the Galapagos Islands. I was struck by the comic appearance and touching behavior of the blue-footed booby. The fact that this species breeds all year round made it possible to observe the birds in all stages of their development. My book follows the progress of Peppe, a booby chick, from hatching to fledging to finally meeting Tina, his mate, with whom he performs their enchanting courtship dance. The book ends with an egg in their nest, ensuring that the life cycle will continue. The watercolor illustrations are naturalistic but slightly anthropomorphized, a departure from the brush or pen line and watercolor style that I normally use.

Chubbo's Pool, also published by Clarion, is a fanciful story about a selfish hippo who refuses to share his pool with other animals. It's based on my real-life experience with a hippo I encountered in the Okavango Delta in Botswana. Again, the illustrations are naturalistic, but the animals are endowed with recognizable human expressions.

Walk a Green Path, a Lothrop, Lee and Shepard book, evolved in a very different way in that the pictures came first, inspiring the text. I've always loved doing botanical water colors, and I have quite a collection hanging on our walls that I've done over a period of years. Some were done right in my own backyard, others as far away as Africa, Australia, and South America. Some were done on location, others back in my studio from either memory or photo references. One day I stood all the paintings up in my studio, and they spoke to me. In the book, I express my love for the natural world through poetry that accompanies each of the paintings. The lush garden landscapes of Childe Hassam, the intimate flower portraits of John La Farge, and the magical woods of my childhood all inspire me.

One of my current projects is an example of how story ideas can come from unexpected sources. Recently Ted and I were presenters at a teachers' conference in Cairo, Egypt. Part of my program included involving my audience in the writing and illustrating of a picture book. I asked them to choose a main character (in this case they chose a camel), and together we developed a story line that I illustrated for them, on the spot, on a blackboard or an easel. In this way they saw how story and pictures combine to create a third entity—the book. While in Egypt, I also had an opportunity to ride a camel and to talk to the camel driver. When I returned home, I took the germ of the story that the conference delegates had helped to develop, stirred it together with my own camel episode, and *What's the Matter, Habibi?* was born, a story about a camel with a mysterious ailment and his worried, bewildered owner. It was published by Clarion in the fall of 1997.

Technique

Although I've tried working in other mediums, I'm most comfortable working in watercolor. I love its capricious nature and the way I almost have to chase it over the paper to make it do what I want. In fact, sometimes it refuses. Then I either have to try to make the mistake look like something I intended, or abandon the whole thing and start over again. Making a mistake work for you is called a "happy accident."

I use mostly Windsor Newton tube watercolors and Windsor Newton Series Seven red sable brushes, a number 3 or 4 for small areas and details, and a number 6 or 7 for large areas of wash. I mix paint on a glass palette or a scrap of watercolor paper. I almost never work larger than actual book size. Sometimes I use a toothbrush or crumpled tissues to get certain effects, and I use a liquid mask to preserve areas where I want the white of the paper to show or to protect certain areas from a surrounding wash. Once the paint dries, the mask is peeled off.

When I'm painting in a naturalistic style, I work from slides that I project onto a screen, moving the images into position, making them larger or smaller as needed. I compose my sketches on tracing paper using a number 2 Mongol pencil, then the finished drawings on five-ply Strathmore bristol paper using a number 4H or 5H Berol Turquoise pencil to refine the sketch. Sometimes I incorporate elements from as many as fifteen slides into a single composition. It may take me two or three days to complete a drawing, and another two to three days to paint it. When painting, I again project the slides on a screen so I can refer to them as I paint, working flat on my drawing table. It's almost like painting from life except that you have the luxury of a constant light source and models that do not wilt.

My favorite way to draw is with a pen or brush and ink, with overlays of watercolor washes. I may use picture references or pose in a mirror to get a particular gesture, but for the most part I draw from memory and I draw fast. I love the immediacy and freshness of drawing like this. It's like liquid thought. The images flow through my hand and onto the paper almost before I know they are in my head. I may draw the same character dozens of times before it has the exact expression or gesture I'm looking for. Often I'll combine parts of many different drawings—a head from

one, a body, a hand, a foot, even eyebrows, from others. The finished drawing may look a bit like a Frankenstein monster, all stuck together with daubs of rubber cement and bits of magic tape. But then I have it copied onto one-ply Strathmore bristol and, Presto!—a perfect drawing with all the verve and spirit of the original sketches. I can make as many copies as I want and experiment with the color, choosing the one I like best.

I find illustrating other people's stories just as exciting as writing and illustrating my own. Reading someone else's story for the first time holds all the anticipation and delight of unwrapping a present. I always sit at my drawing table when I first read a story, with tracing pad and pens handy so I can jot down editorial details I might want to refer to later. I also make quick sketches of my first impressions of characters, settings, and situations. Many of these initial drawings become part of the final work. After several readings, I begin to look for the special touches that I, as the illustrator, can employ to enhance the words. I might add a pet, or a toy that isn't mentioned in the text but that will lend a warm, sympathetic note and perhaps reflect the emotions of the main character. For instance, in *What if the Shark Wears Tennis Shoes?* by Winifred Morris, the expressions on the face of a toy octopus reflect the anxiety of a little boy who is afraid that a shark is coming to eat him. In Grace Maccarone's stories *Itchy, Itchy Chicken Pox* and *My Tooth Is about to Fall Out,* a puppy and a kitten are sympathetic to the plights of their young owners.

There are always places in a story where the author makes such vivid word pictures that illustrating them would be superfluous. Instead, I try to illustrate "between the lines," finding drawing opportunities that enhance the text rather than compete with it. I find the most wonderful thing about illustrating another's words is that together you create a third entity—the book.

Home

Ted and I live in Brooklyn near the Pratt campus in an old brownstone house. Ted's studio is on the top floor, and mine is on the floor below. Besides the usual clutter of pencils and pens, paint tubes and brushes, drawing papers, and, of course, books, we surround ourselves with mementos of our travels: peacock feathers from India, Herero dolls from Botswana, galimoto toys from Namibia and Brazil, brass pots from Egypt, postcards and snapshots, and countless stones and seashells and bits of cloth that transport us back to lands we've visited. Our two cats, Slick and Chopper, can usually be found napping on our drawing tables.

Fortunately, we both like to start working early in the morning and are up by seven. A stroll to the corner luncheonette for breakfast gets us some fresh air and a chance to chat with friends and neighbors before our workday begins. Once we retire to our studios, the outside world ceases to exist until one or two in the afternoon, though once in a while we'll take a break and visit each other's studios to see what the other is doing. Sometimes it's easy to forget that there is life beyond my studio. Once I leave it for the day, though, I try not to return until the next morning. Even if I think I feel like working later, chances are I'll regret it when I look with a fresh eye the next day. But I never stop looking for stories and thinking in pictures. Whenever I get together with other children's book writers and illustrators (which isn't often), we always eagerly ask one another, "What are you working on?" I hope I'll never want for an answer to that question!

Writings

FOR CHILDREN; WRITTEN AND ILLLUSTRATED BY LEWIN

Animal Snackers, Dodd, 1980.
Cat Count, Dodd, 1981.
Hip, Hippo, Hooray, Dodd, 1982.
Booby Hatch, Houghton, 1995.
Walk a Green Path, Lothrop, 1995.
Chubbo's Pool, Houghton, 1997.
What's the Matter, Habibi?, Clarion, 1997.
Wiley Learns to Spell, Scholastic, 1998.
With Ted Lewin, *Gorilla Walk,* Lothrop, Lee & Shepard, 1999.
With Ted Lewin, *Elephant Quest,* HarperCollins, 2000.
Groundhog Day, Scholastic, 2000.

FOR CHILDREN: ILLUSTRATED BY LEWIN

Helen Kronberg Olson, *The Strange Thing That Happened to Oliver Wendell Iscovitch,* Dodd, 1983.
Berniece Freschet, *Furlie Cat,* Lothrop, 1986.
Beatrice Schenk de Regniers, *Penny,* Lothrop, 1987.
Arnold Adoff, *Greens: Poems,* Lothrop, 1988.
Maria Polushkin, *Kitten in Trouble,* Bradbury Press, 1988.
Maria Polushkin, *Here's That Kitten,* Bradbury Press, 1989.
Peter Limberg, *Weird: The Complete Book of Halloween Words,* Bradbury Press, 1989.
Karen Ackerman, *Araminta's Paintbox,* Atheneum, 1990.
Lynda Graham Barber, *Mushy: The Complete Book of Valentine's Words,* Bradbury Press, 1990.
Winifred Morris, *What If the Shark Wears Tennis Shoes?,* Atheneum, 1990.
Lynda Graham Barber, *Gobble: The Complete Book of Thanksgiving Words,* Bradbury Press, 1991.
Harry Allard, *The Hummingbirds' Day,* Houghton, 1991.
Patricia Reilly Giff, *The War Began at Supper: Letters to Miss Loria,* Dell, 1991,
Carolyn Haywood, *Eddie and the Fire Engine,* Beach Tree, 1992.
Grace Maccarone, *Itchy, Itchy Chicken Pox,* Scholastic, 1992.
Russell Hoban, *Jim Hedgehog and the Lonesome Tower,* Houghton, 1992.
Russell Hoban, *Jim Hedgehog's Supernatural Christmas,* Houghton, 1992.

Lynda Graham Barber, *Doodle Dandy: The Complete Book of Independence Day Words,* Bradbury Press, 1993.
Joanne Ryder, *First Grade Elves,* Troll, 1993.
Joanne Ryder, *First Grade Ladybugs,* Troll, 1993.
Joanne Ryder, *First Grade Valentines,* Troll, 1993.
Stephen Krensky, *Fraidy Cats,* Scholastic, 1993.
Joanne Ryder, *Hello, First Grade,* Troll, 1993.
Lynda Graham Barber, *Ho! Ho! Ho! The Complete Book of Christmas Words,* Bradbury Press, 1993.
Ida Luttrell, *Mattie's Little Possum Pet,* Atheneum, 1993.
David L. Harrison, *Somebody Catch My Homework: Poems,* Boyds Mills, 1993.
David Vozar, *Yo! Hungry Wolf: A Nursery Rap,* Doubleday, 1993.
David L. Harrison, *The Boy Who Counted Stars: Poems,* Boyds Mills, 1994.
Caroline A. Levine, *The Detective Stars and the Case of the Super Soccer Team,* Dutton, 1994.
Steven Kroll, *I'm George Washington and You're Not!,* Hyperion, 1994.
Evan Levine, *What's Black and White and Came to Visit?,* Orchard Books, 1994.
Grace Maccarone, *The Classroom Pet,* Scholastic, 1995.
Grace Maccarone, *The Lunch Box Surprise,* Scholastic, 1995.
Grace Maccarone, *My Tooth Is about to Fall Out,* Scholastic, 1995.
David Vozar, *M. C. Turtle and the Hip Hop Hare: A Nursery Rap,* Doubleday, 1995.
Grace Maccarone, *The Gym Day Winner,* Scholastic, 1996.
Grace Maccarone, *The Recess Mess,* Scholastic, 1996.
Grace Maccarone, *Sharing Time Troubles,* Scholastic, 1996.
David L. Harrison, *A Thousand Cousins, Poems of Family Life,* St. Martin's Press, 1996.
Carol Sonenklar, *Bug Boy,* Holt, 1997.
Jackie French Koller, *No Such Thing,* Boyds Mills, 1997.
Carol Sonenklar, *Bug Girl,* Holt, 1998.
David Vozar, *RAPunzel: A Happenin' Rap,* Doubleday, 1998.
Grace Maccarone, *I Have a Cold,* Scholastic, 1998.
Elizabeth Nygaard, *Snake Alley Band,* Doubleday, 1998.
Mary Skillings Prigger, *Aunt Minnie McGranahan,* Clarion Books, 1999.
Grace Maccarone, *The Class Trip,* Scholastic, 1999.
Nikki Grimes, *Is it Far to Zanzibar?: Poems about Tanzania,* Lothrop, Lee & Shepard, 1999.
Grace Maccarone, *First Grade Friends: Softball Practice,* Scholastic, 2000.
Doreen Cronin, *Click, Clack, Moo: Cows that Type,* Simon & Schuster, 2000.
Patricia Lauber, *Purrfectly Purrfect: Life at the Acatemy,* Morrow Junior Books, 2000.
Elizabeth Winthrop, *Dumpy La Rue,* Holt, 2000.
Elizabeth Winthrop, *Promises,* Clarion Books, 2000.

Autobiography Feature

Ted Lewin

1935-

Early Memories

When I was about four years old, I had a serious bout with polio. The doctor came to our house to take a spinal tap, which he did with me spread out on the dining room table, a not unusual practice for the time. I don't remember the pain, but I'm told I screamed a lot. The test showed that I had a bad case and, by all rights, should have ended up in an iron lung for the rest of my life. I was kept in isolation and can remember seeing my parents on the other side of a big, glass wall and my hydrotherapy sessions when I sat in a big tub of water. About two weeks later, weak from being bedridden, I came home to a sunlit bedroom full of new toys, but with no aftereffects. I don't know why I was spared.

When I was about seven years old, some of my most vivid memories are of the censored letters we received from my brother Donn, who was then a marine serving in the Pacific in World War II. The letters had been so cut up they looked like chains of paper dolls. I remember each of the three telegrams that came to our front door with news of yet another war wound. And most of all, I remember my parents' anguish.

We sent grand packages loaded with goodies overseas to Donn: cookies, booze, chewing tobacco. My father spent hours carefully knotting and double-knotting the stout string that bound them.

And I remember when Donn came home. Nineteen years old, wearing his dress blues, he stood stiffly at the Philadelphia Naval Station to receive his Purple Heart with three clusters. To this day, I can't look at Marine Corps dress blues without crying.

Years later, this time wearing a yellow terry cloth bathrobe, this tough old marine brought tears to my eyes again. After weeks of mercilessly ribbing me about being a "Joe College," Donn handed me an envelope. In it was the money for my first year's tuition.

The Violin

At about age ten I took up the violin. I wasn't very good at it, and my family suffered the squeaking practice sessions for years. I never really learned how to read music, but I got as far as the high school orchestra before anyone discovered this. One day, at orchestra practice, Mr. Jacoy,

the music teacher, said: "Wait, something is wrong in the violin section." He had each of us play a solo. I, of course, couldn't. It was a relief to be found out at last. He tried to help by tutoring me after school, but I was hopeless.

My one moment of glory, musically speaking, came when my sister and I played a duet. During the war, the third-floor apartment in our house was occupied by Bell Aircraft plant workers. One of these roomers, Al, was about to leave for the army. Sallee and I decided to do a little number for his going away party. We practiced diligently, she at the spinet and me squeaking away on the violin. The day of the party—and our big moment—arrived. We played (badly, on my part) a heartfelt rendition of "My Buddy." When we finished, big tears were running down Al's cheeks.

One day I asked my mother why I took violin lessons. "You told me you loved the violin and wanted to learn to play it," she said. I do love the violin, but I sure don't remember the part about asking for lessons.

In high school I went out for the football team—the Lafayette Violets (the color, not the flower). I wasn't any better at football than I was at the violin, but now that my violin charade was over, at least I didn't have to come to school carrying a violin case in one hand and a football helmet in the other. I didn't know then that a mixture of athletics and art was to be a recurring theme in my life.

Shyness

I was painfully shy when I was a kid, a shyness I didn't shake until I went to art school. It really got in the way. When my kid brother Mark and I went anywhere, I would always push him up front to do the talking.

Once I wanted to see a Tarzan movie at the Elmwood Theatre. I had to take two buses to get there, and when I saw the marquee my shoulders drooped. It was a double feature, but neither one was a Tarzan movie. I was so disappointed, I could have cried. Instead I turned around and took the two buses back home. My mother, surprised to see me back so soon, asked what had happened. "The Tarzan movie isn't playing," I said. "One was a Western and the other one was called 'CO-HIT.'" After my mother stopped laughing she told me: "The co-hit is the Tarzan movie. Why didn't you ask the man in the box office?" I

Ted Lewin in India, 1996.

hadn't asked because Mark wasn't along to do the talking for me.

I didn't know it then, but, in a way, I was doing him a favor. His gift of gab as a kid served him well later in the wrestling business.

One time, after watching me draw for a while, Mark said: "See these hands? I can't do anything with them." I did my best to teach him how to draw. He tried, but he couldn't sit still long enough. He never did sit still.

Making Things

I was always making things—model planes, boats, animals—from those kits where you pasted sections of cut out cardboard together until you had a three-dimensional dog or horse. Then you sanded and painted it. My happiest hours were spent painting those things with something called dope. I'm sure now that my euphoria was from the fumes.

Once I got hold of some mannequin heads. Using Plasticine, I sculpted a Ubangi head, complete with lip disk, and a Zulu warrior. I'd seen photographs of them in a book by Martin and Osa Johnson. I also sculpted the head of a mountain gorilla, painted the face, and added fur from my mother's old stole. It was eerily realistic. I put the head on my sister's bed pillow and pulled the covers up around it. She wasn't amused. I kept my "museum" collection until I was a teenager.

I also collected pictures of everything that interested me from magazines, old books, newspapers, anyplace I could find them. They became the basis of my picture reference files, which now fill six big filing cabinets. I still add to them, and, weirdly, I can remember every picture.

Berenece

My mother, Berenece, was the one who made order out of chaos in our household. According to her, it was my father's idea to have a big family. My mother was the general manager of a Western Union office in Buffalo when my father met her; it was the kind of job that not many women held in those years, just after World War I. My father, Sid, courted her by indulging *her* mother in fresh lobsters. I guess the quickest way to Berenece's heart was through her mother's stomach.

They settled down in the Sherwood Apartments in Buffalo. I have an old eight-by-ten print of them in bathrobes lounging with their first two babies, Donn and Sallee. It looks like a movie still from the thirties. There were five kids finally. A sister born before me died, and my name, Ted, which means gift from heaven, came out of their anguish over that loss.

Berenece was a wonderful cook—the meat-and-potatoes kind. Garlic, oil, and exotic spices hadn't yet been discovered in our house. She made roast beef with Yorkshire pudding, spareribs and sauerkraut, and enormous turkeys with stuffing. And she baked apple cream pies, pineapple upside-down cakes, and lemon icebox pies. Butter, sugar, and cream definitely had been discovered in our house.

Mother insisted that we all sat down together at mealtime. There was no "eating and running."

My mother did all the handyman work around the house, fixing the plumbing, hanging the storm windows. Sid tried to fix a window with a broken sash one day, and it fell on his thumb, smashing the nail. My mother wouldn't let him touch a tool after that. This was just the way he wanted it, I'm sure.

Berenece patiently suffered all the exotic creatures that both Sid and Donn brought into the house, everything from lions to chimpanzees. Once she was hanging laundry out in the backyard when Ellie, our pet capuchin monkey, was tied to the pole that held the wash line. Berenece was wearing red slacks that day, and Ellie just hated those red slacks. She climbed down from the top of the pole and bit Berenece on the ankle. It was ironic, because it was Mother who cared for and loved Ellie the most.

On Thursdays, my father's store was open late, so my mother would take Mark and me downtown. She would get "all dolled up," as Sid used to say, and we had to wear suits because: "Your father is in business, and you're not going into the store dressed in jeans and sneakers." We would have dinner in McDole's restaurant. (Mark would always throw a tantrum if they didn't have turkey on the menu.) Then we would go to the movies at the Shea's Buffalo Theater, pick up my father as he closed the store, and all take the streetcar home. Once we went to see *The Picture of Dorian Gray*. In the middle of the movie, a black band appeared across the screen. The white letters on it read, "FDR has just died of a cerebral hemorrhage." My mother gasped as if she'd been struck by lightning. It was my first experience with the impact such an event can have on your life. I felt the same jolt eighteen years later when, on a handball court, I heard the news of JFK's assassination.

My father retired after he lost the lease on his store. The building was being sold, and he didn't want to start in a new location after fifty years. His youthful wanderlust

leg at the Blarney Stone to eat when I got home after the long subway ride on the A train to Brooklyn. The next day: work on the portfolio, wait for the phone to ring, then off again at three or four in the afternoon for the Holland Hotel and a ride to the next wrestling match. It was a merry-go-round, but at least it began to pay off.

A really exciting job came in one day. It was for *Boxing/Wrestling* magazine. They wanted an illustration of the historic Fitzsimmons Jeffries fight. It was right down my alley. I read the story and settled on an incident to illustrate. Fitzsimmons and Jeffries had almost had a fight in the dressing room beforehand, so the story went. I thought that would make an exciting picture. Now where would I get the models for those big, brawny men and the beat up old dressing room where they had had it out?

That night in Hartford I found the perfect dressing room—beat-up, old and dirty—and the wrestlers would make perfect models. Arnold Skaaland, who was wrestling that night, was a perfect Jeffries model and would work for a Fitzsimmons model, too. Karl Von Hess would be perfect as one of the seconds holding the raging fighters apart. He even had a handlebar mustache just right for the period. Larry Simon volunteered to help, too. They all loved the idea of my illustration, and while everyone else got ready for their matches, the three of them restaged that historic brawl from a century before while I snapped the shutter of my camera.

They were wonderful actors; the pictures turned out great; the illustration was a big hit with the client and his readers, and all the guys cherished their copies of the magazine when it was published.

All the wrestlers respected what I was trying to do. They all knew that, although I was one of them and could hold my own in the ring, I was really only passing through. I could see the art and beauty in what they did because I was also an observer—but an inside observer.

I wanted to record that special art of theirs, so I began a series of paintings of my wrestling friends and their lives to try to hold on to that time forever. Many of those paintings hang in my home today, and many are reproduced in my memoir, *I Was a Teenage Professional Wrestler.*

The Neighborhood

For a while there were almost as many wrestlers as art students in the neighborhood around Pratt Institute. Mark and Donn took a room three blocks from my apartment in a great old Victorian mansion turned rooming house, complete with central hall and a magnificent mahogany curving staircase with a single-seat elevator attached. There were dozens of rooms filled with art students—and Mark and Donn. It wasn't long before they were joined by Danny McShain and Handsome Johnny Barend. Wrestlers tend to flock, and they all had a grand old time there.

They had breakfast every morning in the local greasy spoon, gabbed with the local characters on the corner, and then, with nothing much to do, came over to my place, a second-floor rear apartment in an old brownstone. Up the stairs they came like a herd of elephants, and—flop—I had them for the rest of the day.

I lived in one large room with a small kitchen, a darkroom built into a closet, a bed, and an easel set in the middle of the room. Danny would smoke his big cigar, lay on the bed, and take a nap. Johnny Barend had the incredibly irritating habit of singing TV jingles. "Rinso white ... Rinso white. Tide's in, dirt's out ..." over and over and over.

I began to make mistakes on the painting I was working on for the cover of an adventure magazine. Donn, watching over my shoulder, would say, "Gimme the brush, Teddy. Just for a minute. I'll fix it. I know I could do it if you'd just gimme the brush." I just kept painting.

Mark talked endlessly, on the phone or off. I just kept painting.

"Rinso white ... Rinso white." I used to think, "God, I wish there was a gym nearby. That'd keep them busy."

I'd get even, though. I needed models, and they were it. Mark was to be everything from a Nazi general being machine-gunned to young Abe Lincoln "wrassling" back in Springfield to a pirate of the Sulu Sea to a confederate soldier at Vicksburg—all in full costume under hot floodlights. I got Donn and Danny, too. They became New Guinea natives, doughboys, and gunfighters. Sometimes Donn or Mark would take the pictures while I posed as Horatio Hornblower or John Dillinger.

Mark and I had girlfriends who went to Pratt, and they did their share of posing too. They were gored by rhinos, attacked by rogue elephants or crocodiles, or carried off by pirates. We all had great fun acting out those horrors.

Come three o'clock, all the boys would pile in Donn's white Caddy convertible with the big tail fins—his pride and joy—and head for the night's matches: Johnny Barend in the back seat ("Rinso white ... Rinso white ..."), Danny seated stoically next to him, and Mark talking constantly. Mark's favorite joke was taking out his partial upper plate. It was a small metal contraption with two teeth attached and a series of metal prongs that held it onto his own teeth. It looked like a metal spider. He loved to slip it out and set it on your knee. You'd look down, and here was

The Lewin brothers: Ted, Mark, and Donn at Uline Arena, Washington, D.C., about 1965.

this disgusting thing. No one would touch it, so he'd scoop it up quick and pop it back into his mouth. He thought it was great fun.

But one day Donn wasn't in the mood for Mark's humor. Maybe it was the Rinso white. Maybe it was the rain. Anyway, when Mark snuck the plate out of his mouth and set it on Donn's knee, Donn looked at it with utter disgust, picked it up, reached out the side window, and stuck it under the windshield wiper. Mark was horrified. His five hundred dollar partial plate was scraping back and forth, back and forth on the windshield at seventy miles an hour. It cured him.

We'd get home around two or three in the morning. But good old Joe Cino, who had closed up his restaurant at midnight, waited in the kitchen for us. We'd knock on the door of the darkened dining room, and he'd come out of the kitchen wiping his hands on his apron, turn on the lights, and unlock the door. We'd pile in and drop our bags, starving. "I gotta scungilli—hot, the way thissa bum like it," he'd say, grabbing Donn around the waist and leaving a white flour handprint on him. He'd warm up big loaves of Italian bread in the oven. Eventually he'd go into the kitchen and bring out plates of steaming scungilli, veal parmigiana, and big salads. Mark would kid him about the Mafia. Joe would get a no-nonsense look on his face,

"Talking to a Taureg in Morocco while doing research for **Market!,***" 1994.*

glance over both shoulders, then back at Mark, and hold his finger to his lips.

Joe put in long hours in that restaurant, and I'm sure he was exhausted by two in the morning. But he wouldn't have gone home on a bet, knowing we were coming in.

Sometimes, if Joe was off or the restaurant was closed, we'd go next door to Erick's Bar. There never was an Erick, and no one ever knew how it got that name. It was run by two big German guys from the Ridgewood section of Brooklyn. Bill, who was about fifty, bald, and big enough to be a wrestler himself, and Heinrich (or Henry as everyone called him), who was older, had a big belly and a tiny white mustache, and wore small, rimless glasses. The place had its original mahogany bar and mirror, stamped tin ceiling, and white tiled floors. It was usually packed with students and a few neighborhood drunks. The students took the tables in the back room; the locals took the bar. The locals played German oompah music on a big jukebox; the students played the Beatles. Sometimes when the oompah music really got rolling, one of the locals would get up from his bar stool and do a step dance, complete with heel slapping and shrill whistles.

They had wonderful Limburger and raw onion sandwiches, and we'd order pitchers of beer and jump right into whatever parties were in progress: student talk of politics, art, or philosophy, or neighborhood talk about the funeral parlor guy who died or Mrs. Wood's bulldog who'd just had puppies again.

Bill, the bartender, always wanted to arm wrestle with Mark, but Mark would never oblige him. I think he was afraid Bill could have beaten him.

We'd drink pitcher after pitcher and finally close the place at four in the morning. The guys headed home to their "pits" (Donn's word) and me to my "garret" (Donn's word, too). I had to get up early to finish an illustration—like one that showed Mark waist-deep in a swamp, covered with mud, being attacked by a rogue alligator.

Sometimes we'd all walk over to Myrtle Avenue—"The Avenue," it was called. The elevated train had been taken down a few years before, and the street seemed smaller in scale and the buildings squat because of it. I hated to see the El go. It had great charm—Reginald Marsh knew.

The street was lined with Italian restaurants, stores, shops, and outdoor fruit markets with awnings. Many had been there for years, and their Italian owners lived in the neighborhood. We'd all been on TV, and to the local characters along the street we were celebrities. For us, *they* were the celebrities. There was blind Mike, for instance, who ran a junk-antique shop called The Cobweb Shoppe. He could tell you the price of anything in the store or the difference between a five and a ten dollar bill just by the feel of them. He held court in front of the place, which took up two old-fashioned glass store fronts on The Avenue, sitting in a used, overstuffed chair (for sale, of course), surrounded by his cronies. In the window was an old prison electric chair with a female store dummy dressed in an old gown propped in it. Her head was cupped by the metal headpiece, and her wrists were strapped down. Seated on Mike's right was "Lock em up," a fellow who used to blow a policeman's whistle as hard as he could and scream, "Lock em up!" To his left sprawled Big Angie, the only woman in the crowd. She helped out at the nearby

"With Jago, one of our many exotic pets," 1951.

laundromat, which was run by a guy named Seymour who could tell what you did nights by your laundry. Angie weighed two hundred pounds, had a full-grown mustache, and said things like, "It's hot. I'm sweatin' undah de ahms!"

The Sons of Italy was just a few doors down, and the guys who hung there were a tough bunch. Fat Freddie would see us coming and say, "You guys are da wrestlahs, right? I figured, 'cause you're built like bruddahs." Fat Freddie got into an argument once with the Greek guy who ran the corner luncheonette. They had a terrible fight, and Freddie leaped behind the counter and bit the Greek's ear off.

Then there was Tony's Pizzeria. Tony had two huge sheepdogs that he shaved bald every summer and a bunch of chickens he kept in the yard behind the restaurant. He'd walk back through the chicken droppings to feed them, then return to the kitchen, step up on a box, and turn on the vent fan. It was the same box he made the pizza dough on. When he brought the finished pie out, he watched us eat it.

"Come good?" he'd ask. Mark and I thought it was delicious. Donn could never get past the chicken droppings.

At Christmastime, every corner on The Avenue was lined with trees for sale and barrels with fires in them against the cold. The Cobweb Shoppe replaced the electric chair with an elaborately carved and gilded circus wagon wheel. With all the trees and fires and Christmas lights, the wagon wheel looked like an Italian shrine.

Atlantic City

Atlantic City on a Saturday night: What could be better? The boardwalk, the Steel Pier, Diving Horse, Fralinger's Salt Water Taffy, Capt. Starn's, The Globe Burlesque, a ride on Miss Mermaids, or in the Rolling Chairs, and the beach. What a beach! So what if there never was a Marvin Gardens.

I'd walk up Ocean Avenue past the old Victorian, wooden-frame, rinky-dink hotels and foul-smelling alleys to the boardwalk and the clean smell of the ocean. The wide expanse of beach was smartly decorated with neat rows of folding chairs and beach umbrellas. Flags snapped smartly in the breeze. Then into the lobby of the old New Belmont Hotel, past the admiring eyes of the grand dames seated along the wall ("One of the wrestlers," they'd whisper to one another), and up to the desk.

There, set up on the counter next to the bell, was a poster announcing the wrestling matches at Convention Hall that very night. And somewhere near the bottom was *my* name. I looked from the poster into the sweet, smiling face of Minnie Walden, who ran the place and would inherit it if she could only live long enough. (She didn't.) We went through the same little game each time I arrived.

"I don't know if 401 is available," she'd say. I'd get a disappointed look on my face. After all, it was the "Lewin Suite" (stayed at by three generations of us). Then she'd fumble in the key slots. "No, it's booked, but this room is just as nice." She'd stick a key in my hand. I'd say it was all right and take the key without looking at it. Then Jake, the old black bellman, and I would get on the elevator and head for the fourth floor. We always hit the roof because he couldn't stop the elevator fast enough. I'd known Jake since I was a child, and he never did learn how to stop that elevator.... It always scared the hell out of me. He'd do his cackling laugh, and we'd step off the elevator (in my case gladly) at the fourth floor and head straight to 401, both of us knowing all along that Minnie had saved it for me.

The hotel was very old, and the fourth floor listed toward the ocean so you had to walk with a lean to stay upright. But 401 was wonderful: a corner room facing the ocean with windows on two sides. There was a tin box in the corner of the room with a thick rope coiled inside it and attached to the wall with a chain. If the hotel caught fire, you were supposed to shinny down this rope.

The hotel even smelled old, and the furniture was huge, creaky, and gothic. The faucets leaked and were held together by adhesive tape, expertly applied by Charlie, the old black handy man (whom I'd also known since childhood). I wouldn't have stayed anywhere else on a bet. I was home. I'd spend the day on the beach, which I reached by going (at a lean, of course) through the fourth-floor hallway all around the building to the freight elevator, where I'd find Charlie sorting sheets into big canvas carts. He'd drop what he was doing, and we'd both get into the huge open elevator. It took forever to descend four floors. Charlie would lean on the control handle and ask all about the upcoming matches. Finally we'd reach the cellar, where the boiler was. It smelled of sour laundry and steam. I'd exit into the back alley on Ocean Avenue. Across the street the ice cream vendors sat on their boxes, folded bills between their fingers, playing craps. Beneath the boardwalk the immaculate glare of the beach stretched before me.

At three in the afternoon I'd put on a shirt, leave the beach, and head for a place called The Dugout. Three feet below street level, it looked awful, but for a buck and a quarter it served the best grilled steak and home fries in town.

At seven-thirty in the evening, showered and dressed, bag in hand, I'd head for the lobby. There I'd run the gauntlet of ladies who had assembled to wish the resident wrestler good luck, then out onto the jam-packed boardwalk that smelled of saltwater taffy and Twin Kiss Custard.

In front of McCrory's there was a guy selling Slinkys and blowing a water whistle that sounded like a singing canary. I walked past the Mayflower Hotel where you could hear people being paged on the upper deck (my father used to say they had themselves paged to sound important)—past the stalls where Louis the artist would sit with cotton in his ears and do your portrait in three minutes, the same way he did presidents and movie stars—past the Claridge Hotel's illuminated fountains and the wood-frame Brighton Hotel, floating like a riverboat on a sea of manicured grass.

Convention Hall was right on the boardwalk. Mobs of people were going in to the Ice Capades, some to the wrestling matches. We were never there for the Miss America Pageant—instead, we got Mr. America, his bleached blonde head towering over the crowd, signing autographs.

The dressing room was spacious, brightly lighted, and full of frenetic activity: guys getting examined by the doctor, commissioners, officials, referees, wrestling bags and suitcases strewn about, tall tales going back and forth. In one corner Billy Darnell, well on his way to becoming a chiropractor, delivered agonizing, deep massages and adjustments to aching bodies. In another, Mr. America talked about the latest honey-and-lemon high-caloric craze. Antonio Rocca stood there naked, looking like Michelangelo's David except for the enormous cigar in his mouth.

Finally the matches got under way, and as soon as everyone knew the time of his match, we'd head down the cavernous back corridors to a set of fire doors. We'd pound on them until an usher on the other side would open up. He'd gape and stand aside as this strange group of huge men with bleached hair, cauliflower ears, and spangled robes swept past him into the darkened hall to watch the Ice Capades in progress. One by one, as match time came up, the guys would slip back to our hall.

By the time of my match, the house was jam-packed. I'd head from the dressing room to the square of light surrounded by brandy red ropes in the center of the hall. Eager hands reached out of the dark to touch me or plead for autographs. Then into the ring, the bell, and bingo—it was all over like a dream. The roars still in my ears, I jogged back to the dressing room, touching hands as I went.

Loud talk, showers, steam, wet floors, laughter. Then everyone headed out into the night and back to the city or on to the next booking.

But I always stayed over Saturday night in Atlantic City, had a steak at the Ranchhouse and a double Twin Kiss, and sat on a boardwalk bench to watch the people like I used to do with Sid.

Later in my dark room, I lay on my back under the seashore-damp sheets, watching the neon lights from the Million Dollar Pier flash red and green on the gently blowing curtains. I fell asleep to the sound of the ocean breaking on the shore and the whistle that sounded like a singing canary.

End of an Era

In 1967 I had my last professional wrestling match in Sparta, New Jersey. I had become very busy by then with my freelance artwork and could no longer take the time to travel. Once I stopped, I knew I would never see all my close friends again. Our worlds were too far apart. So I sadly retired my high-top wrestling shoes and gear, packed them in my beat-up old wrestling bag, put it on the top shelf in a bedroom closet, and closed the door on that part of my life forever.

Travels with Betsy

When I graduated from Pratt in 1956, all the big magazines that I hoped to work for, *Saturday Evening Post, Collier's, McCall's,* etc., had disappeared. I began freelancing, getting work from *Boys' Life* magazine, men's adventure magazines, greeting card companies, *Reader's Digest* condensed books, and finally for children's publishing and young-adult book jackets.

Soon after, in 1957, I met my wife-to-be, Betsy. She was in her second year at Pratt studying illustration. I wooed her with snapshots of our pet chimp, Jago, and our lion cub, Sheba. We talked endlessly of our yearnings to see Africa and the great herds on the Serengeti plains before they were gone forever. For the next seven years, we were inseparable, and in 1963 we were married, still dreaming of travel. By 1970 we had scraped enough money together for our first big trip to Kenya, Uganda, and Tanzania. That trip was to shape the rest of our lives. We were right to feel the urgency. In 1976 there were thirty thousand black rhino in that part of Africa; by 1996, there were fewer than a thousand.

Not long after our African journey, we began a series of trips to the Florida Everglades, where we canoed, camped, and bird-watched. It was because of those trips that I began to write.

I was having lunch one day with an editor friend at Dodd, Mead and Company, and told her stories of our adventures in the Everglades. She encouraged me to write them down, and the "World within a World" series of books began. First, the *Everglades:*

Florida Bay is where all journeys in the Everglades end and where so much life begins.

I glide in my canoe on placid blue-green water. To the north is an endless wall of mangrove trees; the southern horizon is punctuated by tree-islands. Stilt-like, these trees stand as fragile buffers against the nightmare force of the hurricanes that howl out of the sea, hurling giant sea turtles twenty miles inland and flattening birds like splashes of paint on tree trunks.

The bay is quiet now—but beneath its surface is a stew of life. A great silver tarpon lifts himself from the water and hangs like a trophy in the air before slamming back into the sea. Above, ospreys patrol, hover, dive, and come away rewarded. Their screams, echoing along the three walls and across the shimmering water, carry the sound of heartbreak.

Next came *Baja:*

When the whale breaches, it gleams against the muted gray of sky and sea, lifting tons of sea water in slow motion. Then, the infinitely slow crash back into obscurity, sending great sprays of sea aloft.

Then *Pribilofs:*

An Arctic fox comes down to Big Lake for a drink. He stands shoulder deep in the cow parsnip and brilliant yellow beach fleabane. Suddenly, frightened, he is a gray shadow running lightly through the wet beach rye. He disappears over the dune. A gray mist returns . . . .

On a trip to India in 1983, we watched from elephant-back as a tiger hunted and took a chital fawn. I tried to re-create that amazing experience in *Tiger Trek,* my first full-color, author-illustrated picture book. Out of the same journey to India came *Sacred River,* years later.

The more we traveled, the more stories began to reveal themselves. They were in everything I saw. On the Amazon in Brazil, a little boy in a dugout canoe held up a fish he had just speared on his trident, and *Amazon Boy* was born. In the Pantanal, grazing cattle suddenly appeared out of the jungle and gingerly stepped over toothy caimans—*When the Rivers Go Home.* One night in Norway, a hundred-and-twenty miles above the Arctic Circle and minus forty degrees, I stepped out of a lavu to watch a breathtaking aurora borealis, and later I came upon a reindeer roundup on the frozen Finmark plateau—*Reindeer People.*

There were stories of twenty-foot saltwater crocodiles on Yellow Water Billabong in Australia's Northern Territory (*Billabong,* a work in progress). And in the Galapagos, on top of Alcedo Volcano on remote Isabela Island, I watched a giant tortoise basking in the sun (*Nilo and the Tortoise*).

Searching for an elusive herd of elephants in the flooding Okavango Delta of Botswana, I found *Elephant Quest.* In Morocco I watched an old man and his grandson telling stories and found *The Storytellers.*

While walking through an Indian market high in the Ecuadorian Andes, I thought of all the wonderful markets I'd seen in twenty-five years of traveling. A month later, back home on a subway train, I wrote the introduction to *Market!:*

From the chill highlands of the Andes to the steamy jungles of central Africa, from the fabled souks of Morocco to the tough New York waterfront, people come to market.

They come barefoot and bent with back-breaking loads, walking for days over lonely mountain passes. They come on jungle trails and roads jammed with traffic. They come by dugout canoe from upriver or by trawler after weeks away at sea. They come any way they can.

They come to sell what they grow, catch, or make, and to buy what other people grow, catch, or make.

So come along—let's go to market!

There are still so many stories out there waiting to be found and so many manuscripts by wonderful authors to take me on journeys I might never have made myself.

Research

Some of the places in which I find myself doing research for books amaze me. For instance, following a

Ted with his wife, Betsy, in southern India, 1996.

bunch of Shoshone buckaroos on a roundup in northern Nevada, I was almost trampled trying to photograph them roping and branding for Ann Herbert Scott's *Cowboy Country*.

The following excerpts are from my journals:

Lapland

Ola made it look so easy. He just knelt there on the reindeer hides, broke tiny bits of birch twig and fed them to the fire. It burned clean and hot and without smoke. He nurtured it all through coffee and a big pot of bidus, and it was still hot and smokeless. The temperature inside the lavu was thirty-two degrees. Outside it was falling like an avalanche to thirty below. Ola half stood and swung the door flap back. Cold came in like the edge of an ax. He pointed at the fire, the kindling beside it, the pile of small birch logs outside, an ax imbedded in one of them, and said something in Sami. The look on his face said, "Don't let it go out." He slipped through the opening and closed the flap behind him.

Amazon, Ariau Tower

There is a tower in the middle of the Amazon rain forest where you can climb above the tops of the trees and watch flocks of macaws fly at sunrise.

There is an old man there who takes care of the resident and orphaned animals that hang around the place. There are at least ten big scarlet macaws, and they all fight for the chance to sit on his head.

There is a tiny squirrel monkey who is spoiled rotten, and a small green parrot. The monkey absolutely hates that parrot. One morning I heard terrible screaming. The monkey had the parrot by the throat with both hands and was choking it to death. The old man jumped in and broke it up. He motioned me to follow him. We left the tower and walked a series of elevated walkways through the jungle to a small enclosure with some cages. The squirrel monkey followed us and was sitting on the railings of the walkway snatching big blue morpho butterflies from the air and stuffing them in his mouth, their wings sticking out each side of his face, like a blue mustache. There was a beautiful ocelot chained to the railing, some injured parrots in the cages, and a small, bright blue plastic baby pool filled with water. The old man began to siphon the water out of the pool, revealing a smooth, shiny back. Soon the entire animal lay like a big slug in the empty pool. It was a baby manatee. Its mother had been illegally killed by the local people and it would surely die without care. The old man smiled sweetly at the little, rubber-like creature as he stuck a big bottle with a nippled end into its whiskered mouth. It closed its eyes and sucked contentedly. When it was through, the old man massaged its body the way its mother would have. He refilled the pool with fresh water and the little creature had a look of absolute ecstasy on its face. I wondered what would become of it.

That evening as I climbed the tower, I passed the ten scarlet macaws and, further up, a big spider monkey hung by one arm, staring at me—another of the old man's charges.

The next day my boat was waiting in front of the tower and I was getting ready to leave when the old man motioned to me to wait. He came back with an eight-foot boa constrictor and placed it around my neck like a lei.

Chitwan National Park, Nepal

It was late afternoon when the elephant, a big tusker owned by the Nepalese government, arrived. I climbed a ladder and crawled onto the howdah. A big metal thermos of hot tea was loaded on with me. The mahout urged the huge beast forward with a kick behind its ears, and we crossed the Dungla River into Royal Chitwan National Park. The sun was leaving quickly as we crossed the tall grass, and it was gone completely from the jungle.

Across a clearing in the jungle, high in an old kapok tree, was the machan, an elevated platform originally used for tiger hunting. I was to spend the night here. I entered the platform through a trap door in its floor. The mahout handed me the hot tea, and I pulled up and secured the trap door for the night.

I watched them slowly and silently melt into the darkening jungle. I was alone. I wrapped myself in my sleeping bag, drank some tea, and waited. A bright moon rose above the trees and bathed the clearing beneath me in soft, silver light. I was beginning to nod off when I heard the snapping of twigs, and the scraping and rustling of branches in the forest. Out of the black shadows, into the silver light, came three one-horned rhinos. They grazed as they came. Their thick, armored plating seemed made of hammered silver. In the middle of the clearing they stopped, shaggy ears alert, and sniffed the air. They seemed to be waiting for something. Then they slowly moved off and were swallowed by the inky darkness on the other side.

American Point, Northwest Territories, Canada

Five o'clock the next morning, I awoke in my tent to groaning, grunting and snorting very close by. Still lying in my sleeping bag, I quietly unzipped the tent flap and folded it back. Outside the triangle of the tent opening was a forest of legs and hooves, and huge, shaggy bodies that rose like black mountains above them. My little tent was in the middle of the Bison herd. Through the leg forest I could see the horizon, a cutout of stunted spruce trees against an orange streak where the sun would soon rise.

Smaller legs and hooves of the red-golden calves moved along with the big black ones of the adults. They had churned up the area around the tent into thick, black muck. Long strands of drool that hung from their noses and mouths glinted in the rising sun. Separated only by thin

nylon walls, I knew exactly how it felt to be part of the herd. Big, steaming buffalo chips fell outside my door as if dropped from the sky. I could now see their shadow shapes of Bison through the translucent nylon tent.

The forest of legs and hooves was so thick I could no longer see the horizon. Then suddenly they were all gone, like a clearcut forest.

A lone white wolf stood at the edge of the spruce forest.

Trinidad

I sit among crabs that climb trees and four-eyed fish that walk on land, and wait at sunset for birds the color of scarlet rose petals. They are feeding now out on the mud flats, but as the tide rises, they will fly here to roost.

The first arrivals, just a few scarlet ibi blazing in the light of the setting sun. Then more, six, then a dozen, then flock upon flock all wheeling around and settling onto a small, mangrove island. The green island slowly changes to glowing red. Suddenly, a common black hawk appears and puts them all back up—all at once, thousands of scarlet birds, like someone has tossed rose petals high into the sky.

When they all finally settle, the trees look as if they've suddenly blossomed.

Ecuadorean Andes

Towering above the high, barren plain—Cotopaxi— nineteen-thousand-five-hundred feet of active volcano with a thirty-foot thick cap of ice extending down its black cinder sides. It is a place of condors. A herd of wild mustangs roams the plain. The herd stallion is as black as a cinder and as lean as a jack rabbit. He leads the herd up the sawtooth ridges.

At fourteen thousand feet, the ice wall behind me, I look down on the plain almost a mile below, and can see the whole kingdom of the wild stallion.

India

Big trucks roar by, passing the ox carts and camel carts, and people with bundles on their backs. The trucks carry chemicals and bags of cement. Just down the road the wondrous Taj Mahal, a monument to death, might die itself of the pollution from these trucks and the factories they serve.

The countryside is dusty, broken and used. Close to Delhi, close to Agra. Along the verge stands a Bhalu Wallah and his charge, a half grown sloth bear on a leash. The Bhalu Wallah wears a white shirt, black baggy pants, and slippers. He carries a long bamboo staff. At any sign of interest from passersby he lifts the staff into the air. The bear rises on his hind legs and begins to dance, mouth agape, moaning. He swings his head back and forth. He has no teeth and very loose lips used normally to suck termites from their nests.

The oven-like heat doubles as it rises off the macadam road. The fumes and noise of the trucks are terrible. The bear dances. The Bhalu Wallah has a demonic look in his eyes. The crowd melts away. The bear continues to dance.

Sloth bears live in the quiet deep of the forest where they carry their young on their backs. They are extremely intelligent and have keen knowledge of the seasons and their effect on the food supply. They know the way plants grow, and the habits of the insects they eat. This one dances on the road to Delhi.

Alaska

The trail cuts through a stand of willows alongside the steep bank of a glacial torrent, milky blue-white and cold, out onto an open tundra flat thick with blueberry bushes. The sun is low on the horizon and fall is only hours away.

From out of the sun appear three dark, bear shapes. The largest shape has a golden halo on its shoulders, the grizzle of a grizzly bear. It is a mother and two near-grown cubs that are coming steadily my way.

I can't go back into the willow thicket. That's where they're headed. I can't climb down the steep bank behind me into that glacial rush, I'd never make it across. I want to run, but there's no place to run. So I stand there and wait.

A strange passivity comes over me, I can't swallow, and I'm very frightened. Frightened more of the grizzly's reputation than of this big girl here scraping blueberries off their branches with big sweeps of her open mouth.

I'm rooted to the ground, and my knees are beginning to give way, a fine cowardice, as Kipling called it.

She and the cubs are fifty feet from me now. I know they see me. I don't think they've smelled me, I'm downwind. I wonder what will happen when they do?

They are passing directly in front of me now. I have no place to go. They act as if I'm not there, feeding as they go by. They pass within twenty-five feet and head into the thicket. Just before she's gone from sight, the mother turns her huge head and looks right at me. My heartbeat hurts my ears. She turns, and is gone.

I'm unable to move from that spot for five minutes, and when I do, I'm shaking all over and grinning foolishly, thinking that if I'd worn my bear bell, I might not have seen them at all.

Models

The people who inhabit my pictures are real people—my friends and neighbors and their kids. Sometimes I "curbstone" kids on the street, then go home with them to talk with their parents about the possibility of their modeling for a book. I always pay the kids for their work, and sometimes their parents frame the check. "It's his very first paycheck," they tell me.

Once I've found the perfect models for a story, they come to my studio, which takes up the entire top floor of our Brooklyn brownstone. I get out costumes if it's a period piece or set in a specific locale or country. The costumes come from all over: gellabas from Morocco for a story set

there, long dresses, knickers, and high-button shoes for period stories.

When the models are dressed and ready for action, I pull down a photo backdrop like a giant window blind, set up photo floodlights, assemble any needed props (from chairs and tables to camel saddles, boat railings, and oil lamps). Then I tell the story to the models, reading them salient passages to motivate them. Kids are generally wonderful actors, especially when in costume. An eight-year-old posed for me once wearing knickers, my mug cap, and a change apron. He was supposed to be a 1920s newsboy. His mother told me he had had so much fun that she couldn't get those clothes off him for a week.

Once they're familiar with the story, they're raring to go. I set the lights (firelight, candlelight, late afternoon light, bright sunlight), and the acting begins.

For me, this part of the process is like magic. The story comes alive with real people in a "real" setting. They begin to interact in ways I couldn't imagine.

Once, for a book called *Potato Man* set in the 1920s, I told two kids dressed in knickers, high-top shoes, and caps to go out and steal those potatoes (a line of potatoes that I had set on the floor—in the story they had fallen off the back of a wagon). They ran over to the potatoes and started stuffing them in their pockets—exactly what kids would naturally do. I hadn't thought of that.

Another time, for *Sami and the Time of the Troubles*, a story about a family living in a Beirut basement to escape the war, I set the scene just as described in the text. I arranged Oriental rugs and pillows, a Coleman lantern, and a radio on the floor, turned out the lights, and turned up the lantern. Voila! We were in a basement in Beirut. I told the models that bombs were falling above. We could hear them. Dust was falling on our heads. We were afraid. The boy playing Sami looked up at the ceiling and grabbed his chest in fear. His mother, sitting on the rug near him, reached out for his sister and hugged her close. They were reacting to imaginary bombs. It was wonderful. I walked around them, shooting from all different angles. It was as if we were all really there in that basement.

For *Peppe the Lamplighter*, I assembled a whole family as if from spare parts, none of them related. I dressed them all in period costumes, turned out the lights, and lit an oil lamp. Soft shadows cast on the walls in the orange light. We were back in the time before electricity.

I've used some kids from the time they were toddlers until they went to high school, first as models for picture books, later for young-adult book jackets. One neighbor has a whole shelf of my books featuring her two children as characters. One day a young man with two small children came up to me on the street and said, "Hi, Mr. Lewin. Remember me? When I was about ten, I posed for a book where I was thrown from a horse and befriended a mountain lion."

Watercolor

Watercolor is my medium, but I was never formally trained in the techniques of it. I learned by trial and error. I love it for its refusal to be mastered, though I've learned a few tricks over the years to help tame it. One is the use of liquid mask, a waterproof liquid that is brushed onto the areas of the painting that you wish to be left white; i.e., a

Illustration from unpublished work "Souk in Marrekesh."

figure in front of a cloudy sky. Mask out the figure, lay in the sky, then peel off the mask when the sky area is dry and paint in the figure on the clear, white space. Liquid mask can be used on anywhere you want to keep the white of the paper.

Another trick is called "the happy accident." Sometimes a wash doesn't happen as you'd planned but can be incorporated anyway and put to good use.

Unhappy accidents are another thing altogether: when a painting is overworked and unsalvageable, throw it out and start again. I had an instructor at Pratt who used to tell me it takes two people to make a painting—one to make

the painting and one to hit you over the head when it's time to stop.

I think the most important trick of all is to make a very careful key drawing. I use a 5H pencil and make extremely detailed, finished line drawings, delineating everything. This eliminates any guesswork when I finally apply the watercolor. A careful drawing allows me great freedom in handling the paint.

I use 500-pound Strathmore bristol paper, which is stiff enough not to buckle too much when wet and flexible enough to wrap around the scanning drum in the reproduction process. It has a slight tooth and takes the paint beautifully.

I use Windsor Newton tube watercolors, about ten or twelve colors usually, adding specific others if needed. I don't own a tube of white paint. Windsor Newton red sable brushes, numbers three and ten, and a big, mop-type brush are my tools. I work on a clear glass palette sitting on a white surface. I paint in a pretty straightforward style. I don't worry about wet on wet, or scumbling, or dry brush. The technique happens naturally, according to what I'm painting. A rainy sky is wet. The bristles on a capybara's back are dry brush.

My work day runs from eight in the morning till one in the afternoon without a break, almost every day. My studio is on the top floor of our hundred-and-fifteen-year-old brownstone. It's a large, fourteen-by-forty-eight-foot room that doubles as a photo studio for models when needed. Betsy works in her own studio one floor below. I work from slides, using a projector to compose and make my final line drawings. Then I project slides on the screen and paint from them, just as if I were painting from life, working flat on a drawing table, sometimes standing up. The finished painting, just the painting part, takes me anywhere from one hour to five days. I work directly and don't "go back in" a lot, so the painting moves along quickly. But a finished line drawing can take a whole day if it is complicated subject matter. I almost never make color sketches. The entire painting is pretty much finished in my head before I begin anyway.

When I get to a difficult point, I need an unbiased opinion. I'm lucky I have Betsy. "Come up and look at this," I call down the stairs. She usually calls back, "You come down here and look at this first." Having each other to look with a "fresh eye" is invaluable, though sometimes tricky. Saying "it looks great" doesn't mean much when the "great" doesn't sound enthusiastic enough.

In a sense, children's book writers and illustrators seem always to be working. It's impossible to have a conversation without some one commenting, "Hey, that would make a great book!" Whenever that happens, the other is likely to retort, "Get a life!"

Writings

FOR CHILDREN; WRITTEN AND ILLUSTRATED BY LEWIN

World within a World: Everglades, introduction by Don R. Eckelberry, Dodd, 1976.
World within a World: Baja, Dodd, 1978.
World within a World: Pribilofs, Dodd, 1980.
Tiger Trek, Macmillan, 1990.
When the Rivers Go Home, Macmillan, 1992.
Amazon Boy, Macmillan, 1993.
I Was a Teenage Professional Wrestler, Orchard Books, 1993.
The Reindeer People, Macmillan, 1994.
Sacred River, Clarion, 1995.
Market!, Lothrop, 1996.
Fair!, Lothrop, Lee & Shepard, 1997.
The Storytellers, Lothrop, Lee & Shepard, 1998.
Nilo and the Tortoise, Scholastic, 1999.

Touch and Go: Travels of a Children's Book Illustrator, Lothrop, Lee & Shepard, 1999.
With Betsy Lewin, *Gorilla Walk,* Lothrop, Lee & Shepard 1999.
With Betsy Lewin, *Elephant Quest,* HarperCollins Publishers, 2000.

FOR CHILDREN; ILLUSTRATED BY LEWIN

Jack McClellan, Millard Black, and Sid Norris, adapters, *A Blind Man Can!,* Houghton, 1968.
Wyatt Blassinghame, *The Look-It-Up Book of Presidents,* Random House, 1968.
George S. Trow, *Meet Robert E. Lee,* Random House, 1969.
Margaret T. Burroughs, *Jasper the Drummin' Boy,* Follett, 1970.
Janet H. Ervin, *More Than Half Way There,* Follett, 1970.
Donald Cox, *Pioneers of Ecology,* Hammond, 1971.
Nellie Burchardt, *Surprise for Carlotta,* F. Watts, 1971.
Gene Smith, *Visitor,* Cowles, 1971.
Betty Horvath, *Not Enough Indians,* F. Watts, 1971.
Maurine H. Gee, *Chicano, Amigo,* Morrow, 1972.
Rose Blue, *Grandma Didn't Wave Back,* F. Watts, 1972.
Michael Capizzi, *Getting It All Together,* Delacorte, 1972.
Rose Blue, *A Month of Sundays,* F. Watts, 1972.
Rita Micklish, *Sugar Bee,* Delacorte, 1972.
Darrell A. Rolerson, *In Sheep's Clothing,* Dodd, 1972.
Charlotte Gantz, *Boy with Three Names,* Houghton, 1973.
William MacKellar, *The Ghost of Grannoch Moor,* Dodd, 1973.
Marian Rumsey, *Lion on the Run,* Morrow, 1973.
Rose Blue, *Nikki 108,* F. Watts, 1973.
Marjorie M. Prince, *The Cheese Stands Alone,* Houghton, 1973.
Darrell A. Rolerson, *A Boy Called Plum,* Dodd, 1974.
Jean Slaughter Doty, *Gabriel,* Macmillan, 1974.
Gene Smith, *The Hayburners,* Delacorte, 1974.
Matt Christopher, *Earthquake,* Little, Brown, 1975.
Patricia Beatty, *Rufus, Red Rufus,* Morrow, 1975.
Charles Ferry, *Up in Sister Bay,* Houghton, 1975.
Jean Slaughter Doty, *Winter Pony,* Macmillan, 1975.
Rose Blue, *The Preacher's Kid,* F. Watts, 1975.
S. T. Tung, *One Small Dog,* Dodd, 1975.
Scott O'Dell, *Zia,* Houghton, 1976.
Lynne Martin, *Puffin: Bird of the Open Seas,* Morrow, 1976.
Laurence Pringle, *Listen to the Crows,* Crowell, 1976.
Patricia Edwards Clyne, *Ghostly Animals of America,* Dodd, 1977.
Mildred Teal, *Bird of Passage,* Little, Brown, 1977.
Marian Rumsey, *Carolina Hurricane,* Morrow, 1977.
Nigel Gray, *The Deserter,* Harper, 1977.
Robert Newton Peck, *Patooie,* Knopf, 1977.
Philippa Pearce, *The Shadow-Cage and Other Tales of the Supernatural,* Crowell, 1977.
Helen Hill, Agnes Perkins, and Althea Helbig, compilers, *Straight on Till Morning: Poems of the Imaginary World,* Crowell, 1977.
Rose Blue, *The Thirteenth Year: A Bar Mitzvah Story,* F. Watts, 1977.
Lee Bennett Hopkins, *Mama,* Knopf, 1977.
Leslie Norris, *Merlin and the Snake's Egg: Poems,* Viking, 1978.

William MacKellar, *The Silent Bells,* Dodd, 1978.

Robert Newton Peck, *Soup for President,* Knopf, 1978.

William MacKellar, *The Witch of Glen Gowrie,* Dodd, 1978.

Anne E. Crompton, *A Woman's Place,* Little Brown, 1978.

David Stemple, *High Ridge Gobbler: A.Story of the American Wild Turkey,* Collins & World, 1979.

Margaret Goff Clark, *Barney and the UFO,* Dodd, 1979.

Patricia Edwards Clyne, *Strange and Supernatural Animals,* Dodd, 1979.

Robert Newton Peck, *Hub,* Knopf, 1979.

Jean Slaughter Doty, *Can I Get There by Candlelight?,* Macmillan, 1980.

Rose Blue, *My Mother the Witch,* McGraw, 1980.

Francine Jacobs, *Bermuda Petrel: The Bird That Would Not Die,* Morrow, 1981.

Margaret Goff Clark, *The Boy from the UFO Returns,* Scholastic Book Services, 1981.

Mark Twain, *The Adventures of Tom Sawyer,* Wanderer, 1982.

Margaret Goff Clark, *Barney on Mars,* Dodd, 1983.

Eleanor Clymer, *The Horse in the Attic,* Bradbury, 1983.

Priscilla Homola, *The Willow Whistle,* Dodd, 1983.

Mary Francis Shura, *The Search for Grissi,* Dodd, 1985.

R. R. Knudson, *Babe Didrikson: Athlete of the Century,* Viking, 1985.

Enid Bagnold, *National Velvet,* Morrow, 1985.

Frances Wosmek, *A Brown Bird Singing,* Lothrop, 1986.

Elizabeth Simpson Smith, *A Dolphin Goes to School: The Story of Squirt, a Trained Dolphin,* Morrow, 1986.

P. R. Giff, *Mother Teresa,* Viking, 1986.

Susan Saunders, *Margaret Mead,* Viking, 1987.

Scott O'Dell, *The Serpent Never Sleeps,* Houghton 1987.

Yukio Tsuchiya, *Faithful Elephants: A True Story of Animals, People, and War,* Houghton, 1988.

Kathleen Kudlinski, *Rachel Carson,* Viking, 1988.

Bruce Coville, *Herds of Thunder, Manes of Gold,* Doubleday, 1989.

Scott O'Dell, *Island of the Blue Dolphins,* Houghton, 1990.

Jane Yolen, *Bird Watch,* Philomel, 1990.

F.P. Heide and J. H. Gilliland, *The Day of Ahmed's Secret,* Lothrop, 1990.

Frances Ward Weller, *I Wonder If I'll See a Whale?,* Philomel, 1991.

Megan McDonald, *The Potato Man,* Orchard Books, 1991.

Margaret Hodges, *Brother Francis and the Friendly Beasts,* Scribner, 1991.

F. P. Heide and J. H. Gilliland, *Sami and the Time of the Troubles,* Clarion, 1992.

Corinna Damas Bliss, *Matthews Meadow,* Harcourt, 1992.

Frances Ward Weller, *Matthew Wheelock's Wall,* Macmillan, 1992.

Megan McDonald, *The Great Pumpkin Switch,* Orchard Books, 1992.

Elisa Bartone, *Peppe the Lamplighter,* Lothrop, 1993.

Ann Herbert Scott, *Cowboy Country,* Clarion, 1993.

Sheldon Oberman, *The Always Prayer Shaw,* Boyds Mills, 1993.

Louise Borden, *Just in Time for Christmas,* Scholastic, 1994.

Jan Slepian, *Lost Moose,* Philomel, 1994.

Elisa Bartone, *American, Too,* Lothrop, 1996.

Mary Kay Kroeger and Louise Borden, *Paperboy,* Clarion Books, 1996.

Jane Yolen, *The Originals,* Philomel, 1998.

Louise Borden, *A. Lincoln and Me,* Scholastic, 2000.

Corinne Demas Bliss, *The Disappearing Island,* Simon & Schuster, 2000.

Edward Grimm, *The Doorman,* Orchard Books, 2000.

LORENZ, Albert 1941-

Personal

Born December 9, 1941, in New York City; son of Albert (a police officer) and Josephine (a housewife) Lorenz; married Maureen McCartney (a housewife and business manager), October 19, 1965; children: Margaret Lorenz, Kirsten Lorenz Guerin. *Education:* Pratt Institute, B.Arch., 1965; Columbia University, M.S. Arch., 1970; pursued doctorate degree in anthropology at Princeton University. *Politics:* "Agnostic." *Religion:* "Roman Catholic (fallen)."

Addresses

Home and office—49 Pine Ave, Floral Park, NY 11001.

Career

Curtis & Davis Architects, architectural designer, 1965-66; Katz-Waisman-Weber-Strauss, AIA, architectural designer, 1968-69; founder and principal, The Albert Lorenz Studio, 1969—; freelance illustrator, 1971—; Pratt Institute, professor of Media and Communication, 1972—, coordinator of Media, 1980—; has also taught at Tuskegee Institute, Southern University, Auburn University, University of Louisiana, all 1972; New York School of Interior Design, 1972-81; University of Alabama and Tulane University, both 1973; New York Institute of Technology, 1985-86; Society of Illustrators, 1988; Connecticut AIA Chapter, 1991; and at Adelphi University, 1992-95. *Military service:* United States Infantry, 1966-68, achieved rank of first lieutenant. *Exhibitions:* Has participated in the Society of Illustrators Annual Exhibit, 1990-99; other shows include

Albert Lorenz

Museum of Modern Art Architectural Exhibit, 1974; National Gallery of Art, 1975; Meet the Illustrators at Pratt Institute Gallery, 1977; Society of Typographic Arts 100, 1980; Art Directors' Show, 1985; New York Society of Renderers, 1987; Society of Illustrators, 1987; Carlson Gallery at University of Bridgeport, 1988; The Illustrator's Art at Sabbeth Art Gallery, 1991; Smithtown Arts Council Annual Exhibit at Mills Pond House, 1990; New York School of Interior Design Gallery, 1990, 1995; Art Director's Show, 1991; Tiffany's "New York Landmarks" window exhibit, 1993; Society of Illustrator's Traveling Exhibition, 1993; Recent Visions: One man show at Adelphi University Center Gallery, 1994; The Artist and the Baseball Card Traveling Exhibition, 1995; Smithsonian Institute National Museum of the American Indian Permanent Collection, 1995; The Visual Club: Illustrators Only Exhibit, 1996; Smithtown Arts Council: Society of Illustrators Show, 1996; Society of Illustrators Traveling Show, 1997-98. *Member:* Society of Illustrators (president of New York City chapter, 1999-2000), Association of Collegiate Schools of Architecture, National Institute for Architectural Education.

Awards, Honors

Kinne Traveling Fellowship, Columbia University, 1969; Design Award, *Progressive Architecture,* 1972;

Chicago Publishers Guild award, 1976; certificate of excellence, AIGA, 1978; exceptional achievement, *PRINT,* 1981; Society of Illustrators Annual Exhibit, certificate of merit, 1982, 1984, 1990-91, 1994, 1996-98 (New York chapter), silver medal, 1993, gold medal, 1995, 1996 (both Los Angeles chapter); award of excellence, *Communication Arts,* 1983; New York Art Directors' Show, silver medal, 1985; *Graphic Design USA,* DESI Award, 1985; first place award, National Newspaper of Admissions Marketing, 1991; merit award and bronze award, both from *Admissions Marketing Report,* 1995; Prix Nautile de Cristal Award, 1996, for *Metropolis;* Vernacular Architecture Forum, 1999, for *House.*

Writings

AUTHOR AND ILLUSTRATOR

Illustrating Architecture, Van Nostrand Reinhold, 1985.
(With Leonard Lizak) *Architectural Illustration Inside and Out,* Whitney Library of Design, 1988.
(With Stanley Salzman) *Drawing in Color: Rendering Techniques Architects and Illustrators,* Whitney Library of Design, 1991.
(With Peter Primak and others) *Trace: 3,000 Drawings from the Al Lorenz Entourage File for Architects, Designers, and Illustrators,* Whitney Library of Design, 1993.
(With Joy Schleh) *Metropolis: Ten Cities, Ten Centuries,* Harry N. Abrams, 1996.
(With Joy Schleh) *House: Showing How People Have Lived throughout History with Examples Drawn from the Lives of Legendary Men and Women,* Harry N. Abrams, 1998.
(With Joy Schleh) *Buried Blueprints: Maps and Sketches of Lost Worlds and Mysterious Places,* Abrams, 1999.

ILLUSTRATOR

Phyllis R. Fenner (selector) *Lift Line: Stories of Downhill and Cross-Country Skiing,* Morrow, 1976,
Eve Merriman, *AB to Zogg: A Lexicon for Science-Fiction and Fantasy Readers,* Atheneum, 1977.
The Dictionary of American English, Longman, 1983.
The Terra Beyond, Atheneum, 1984.
The Bible for Students, Tyndale, 1988.
Barbaralee Diamonstein, *Landmarks: Eighteen Wonders of the New York World,* Abrams, 1993.
Readers' Digest Bible, Readers Digest, 1993.

Illustrations also appear in the following books: *Architectural Rendering,* Burden, 1975; *Architectural Illustration,* Halse, 1978; *Communication Arts Annual,* 1978; *Outstanding American Illustrators Today,* Graphic-Sha, 1980; *Print Casebooks 5: The Best in Covers & Posters,* 1983; *Listening to American Jews,* Sh'ma, 1986; *Society of Illustrators Annual,* 1986-94; *Pictorial Maps,* Watson-Guptill, 1991; *The Technical Pen,* Watson-Guptill, 1992; *Sketching Your Favorite Subject in Pen & Ink,* North Light Books, 1993; *The Best in Diagrammatic Graphics,* Quarto, 1993; *Infinite Worlds: A History of Science Fiction Illustration,* Vincent DiFate, 1998; and in the following newspapers, journals, and magazines: *New York Times, National Geographic, National Geo-*

Selecting one significant event for each of the last ten centuries, Lorenz presents an illustrative account of the last one-thousand years on earth. (Cover illustration by Lorenz.)

graphic Traveler, Travel & Leisure, American Illustration, Architectural Forum, Architectural Record, Interiors, Newsweek, and Progressive Architecture.

Work in Progress

Jack and the Beanstalk, for Abrams, due in 2000.

Sidelights

"I began my career as an architect," Albert Lorenz told *SATA,* "but soon ... (almost immediately) realized architecture was *not* for me. Since I always loved to draw I decided to become a freelance illustrator. (Arrogance!) Calling yourself a freelance illustrator and supporting a family of three are two very different things. Luckily, *very luckily,* I landed a teaching job, and was able to make ends meet (almost).

"Slowly, very slowly, my wife (she is our business manager) and I began to make professional progress. In 1977 I was hired to illustrate a book called *AB to Zogg* by Eve Merriman published by Atheneum. The illustra-

tions and the book won a few awards. It wasn't long after this that Van Nostrand Reinhold asked me to write a book about my work. This was followed by several other 'How To' books that appealed to architects and designers.

"In 1993 I got a really big break. The publisher Abrams approached me to illustrate a book: *Landmarks: Eighteen Wonders of the New York World* by Barbaralee Diamonstein. Abrams was pleased with my work, and encouraged me to write and illustrate my own book. It took a year to come up with the idea for *Metropolis.* The book took two years of intense work. It was well reviewed and followed by *House* in 1998, and *Buried Blueprints* in 1999. That brings us to the present. I am currently working on a book of fairy tales. I consider myself very lucky to have worked at home (my studio is attached to my house) for the past thirty years. My wife and my two daughters have helped to make my choice of a freelance career especially rewarding. Without them I would not be writing this paragraph."

Albert Lorenz is a trained architect who makes his living teaching architectural drawing and writing and illustrating books. His finely detailed illustrations have been called dazzling by reviewers intrigued by his renderings of abodes both humble and historic. Lorenz's illustrations for Barbaralee Diamonstein's *Landmarks: Eighteen Wonders of the New York World* were commended for both architectural accuracy and artistic vitality. The text, written by the chair of the New York City Landmarks Preservation Foundation, emphasizes the historical, cultural, or architectural significance of such well-known New York City landmarks as Central Park and Grand Central Station as well as several lesser-known sites. As for the illustrations, "Lorenz's drawings impart the refreshing immediacy of sketches yet are satisfyingly accurate," according to Edward B. Cone in *Library Journal.*

In *Metropolis: Ten Cities, Ten Centuries,* the author/ illustrator created a unique vision of a thousand years of history by depicting ten significant events or series of events as they occurred in a particular city in a particular century. These and smaller associated drawings and a timeline offer a snapshot of the culture, highlighting events of historical significance in other locations throughout the world. Thus the construction of Notre Dame in Paris exemplifies the twelfth century, while a castle under siege in Osaka, Japan, is showcased for the seventeenth century. "Lorenz dazzles readers with his extraordinary visual depictions of some of the greatest defining moments in human history," remarked a reviewer for *Art and Architecture.* Others emphasized both the details of individual drawings and the artist's ability to contextualize information by juxtaposing images. "Lorenz conveys an architect's sense of how his subject ties into its surrounding environment on a human scale," noted a contributor to *Kirkus Reviews.* Lorenz's visual approach to history was considered appropriate for young adult readers as a supplementary text. "[The pages of this book] are sure to stimulate questions not only about familiar places but also those that are, for most American children, supremely exotic, if they know them at all—places like Mozambique or a tent city of the Mongol empire," observed John Cesh in the *Washington Post Book World.* A reviewer for *Publishers Weekly* simply dubbed *Metropolis* "an eclectic look at past and present civilizations."

In *House: Showing How People Have Lived throughout History with Examples Drawn from the Lives of Legendary Men and Women,* Lorenz adapted the format of *Metropolis* to show a wide variety of human domiciles, including the womb, the belly of the Trojan Horse, space station *Mir,* and more expected places such as a serf's cabin, Thomas Jefferson's historic plantation Monticello, and Sherlock Holmes's famous Baker Street address, among others. Through this spectrum of abodes, the author surveys the history of design and offers anecdotes about famous historical and literary figures. "The artwork is deeply satisfying," a critic for *Kirkus Reviews* intoned, concluding that *House* is a volume "to savor slowly or devour in one sitting."

Works Cited

Cesh, John, review of *Metropolis, Washington Post Book World,* December 8, 1996, p. 23.

Cone, Edward B., review of *Landmarks, Library Journal,* November 1, 1992, p. 82.

Review of *House, Kirkus Reviews,* November 15, 1998, p. 1670.

Review of *Metropolis, Art and Architecture,* July 1, 1997.

Review of *Metropolis, Kirkus Reviews,* November 1, 1996, p. 1603.

Review of *Metropolis, Publishers Weekly,* November 18, 1996, p. 75.

For More Information See

PERIODICALS

Booklist, February 15, 1993, pp. 1046-47.

Horn Book, spring, 1997, p. 164.

Publishers Weekly, July 15, 1996, p. 23.

M

MACALASTER, Elizabeth G. 1951-
(Ryan Ann Hunter, joint pseudonym)

Personal

Born October 10, 1951, in Laconia, NH; daughter of Gordon G. and Jane (Hunter) Macalaster; married Daniel K. Sayner (an F.B.I. agent), May 29, 1982; children: Jack, Jane. *Education:* Goucher College, B.A. in Biology, 1973; Dalhousie University, M.Sc. in Biology, 1976; Boston University, M.S. in Science Communications, 1978. *Hobbies and other interests:* Hiking, beach combing, sailing, birdwatching, and reading.

Addresses

Home—1076 Brookview Ave., Westlake Village, CA 91361. *E-mail*—lizdan@gte.net.

Career

Dalhousie University, Halifax, NS, Canada, teaching assistant, 1974-76; U.S. Department of the Interior, Washington, DC, writer/editor, 1978-79; U.S. Environmental Protection Agency, Annapolis, MD, writer/editor, 1979-82. Since 1990 has volunteered as a science specialist at elementary schools in New Jersey and California, helping teachers with labs and hands-on activities and designing specific science units. *Member:* Society of Children's Book Writers and Illustrators.

Awards, Honors

Society of Children's Book Writers and Illustrators, Ventura/Santa Barbara Chapter, 13th Annual Writer's Day, Picture Book and Poetry Awards of Excellence, 1998.

Writings

UNDER PSEUDONYM RYAN ANN HUNTER, WITH PAMELA D. GREENWOOD

Cross a Bridge, illustrated by Edward Miller, Holiday House, 1998.
Into the Sky, illustrated by Edward Miller, Holiday House, 1998.
Dig a Tunnel, illustrated by Edward Miller, Holiday House, 1999.
Take Off!, illustrated by Edward Miller, Holiday House, 2000.

Articles have appeared in *Highlights for Children, Sea Frontiers,* and *Issues for the Chesapeake;* reviews of nonfiction books for Children's Department Bulletin at the New Providence (NJ) Memorial Library, 1995-97; contributor to *Earth Science, Physical Science,* and *Life Science,* textbooks for Silver Burdett, and to *Cephalopod Life Cycles,* edited by Peter Boyle, Academic Press, 1983.

Work in Progress

A series of books on the ocean, spin-off magazine articles from the Ryan Ann Hunter books, poetry, in particular writing about endangered species using the cinquain format; with co-author P. D. Greenwood, books on fishing boats, robots, trains, aquariums, buffaloes, and undersea technology.

Sidelights

Elizabeth Macalaster told *SATA:* "I grew up in New England surrounded by woods, mountains, and water. I feel like it was always summer (or winter) camp at my house, with my father the head counselor. Our backyard was always full of pets and animals others found or discarded. So, an appreciation for animals and the outdoors came easily.

"I wasn't read to very much, that is, except for poetry. My parents read it out loud to my sister and me early on.

Elizabeth G. Macalaster

They also played records of poetry. I remember crying every time 'Little Boy blue' was recited.

"Writing poetry was a natural start to writing for me, and I still write it. I love searching for that right word or two to express a complex thought or feeling.

"But, in preparing reports and articles in my field of marine biology, I started to focus more on nonfiction. Writing for lay people about the undersea world I was studying grew on me. For me, the real world is every bit as amazing and inspiring as make-believe, and I am constantly awed by what goes on just in my yard. Walt Whitman says it well:

To me, every hour of the light and dark is a miracle.

Every cubic inch of space is a miracle.

And so we believe, inch by inch.

"In writing children's literature, it's been my goal to capture for children that miracle of the world around us and illuminate our connection to it."

Macalaster has co-authored her work with Pamela D. Greenwood under the joint pseudonym Ryan Ann Hunter.

[For more information on Elizabeth Macalaster, please see the entry on Pamela D. Greenwood in this volume.]

For More Information See

PERIODICALS

Booklist, April 1, 1998, p. 1326; September 15, 1998, p. 233.
Engineering News-Record, February 22, 1999.
Horn Book, fall, 1998, p. 392; spring, 1999, p. 32.
Kirkus Reviews, August 1, 1998, p. 1118.
Publishers Weekly, October 26, 1998, p. 69; February 8, 1999, p. 212.

*   *   *

MANSON, Ainslie Kertland 1938-

Personal

Born October 31, 1938, in Montreal, Quebec, Canada; daughter of Donald Montseratt and Kathleen Winnifred

(Oliver) Kertland; married Arthur David Currie Manson, December, 1962; children: Graeme, Murray, Gavin. *Religion:* Anglican. *Hobbies and other interests:* Reading, quilting, dog walking, hiking, cross country skiing, horse back riding, canoeing and kayaking.

Addresses

Home—4768 The Highway, West Vancouver, British Columbia, V7W 1J5. *E-mail*—amanson@istar.ca.

Career

Writer. *Member:* Writers' Union of Canada, Canadian Society of Children's Authors, Illustrators, and Performers, Childrens' Writers and Illustrators of British Columbia, British Columbia Writers' Federation, Alexander Mackenzie Voyageur Association, IBBY, PEN, Canadian Children's Book Centre, Vancouver Children's Literature Roundtable.

Awards, Honors

A Dog Came Too was named to the shortlist for the Sheila A. Egoff Children's Prize, British Columbia Book Prizes, Geoffrey Bilson Award for Historical Fiction for Young People, 1993, and a Tiny Torgi Award from the Canadian National Institute for the Blind, 1994. *Just Like New* received an Amelia Francis Gibbon Award for illustration, The Five Owls Book of Merit, and was shortlisted for the Mr. Christie Award, 1994.

Writings

Mr. McUmphie of Caulfield Cove, illustrated by Janet Stethem, Queenston House (Winnipeg, Manitoba), 1982.

A Dog Came, Too: A True Story, illustrated by Ann Blades, Macmillan International (New York City), 1993.

Just Like New, illustrated by Karen Reczuch, Groundwood Books (Toronto, ON), 1996.

Baboo: The Story of Sir John A. Macdonald's Daughter, illustrated by Bill Wand, Groundwood Books (Toronto, ON), 1998.

Ballerinas Don't Wear Glasses, illustrated by Dean Griffiths, Orca Book Publishers (Victoria, B.C.), 2000.

Work in Progress

The Bonfire House, for Groundwood.

Sidelights

Ainslie Kertland Manson is known for writing historical picture books for children. Her genre of books was described by Jonathan F. Vance in *Canadian Children's Literature:* "Another variety of history for children begins with a conventional story line, but places it in a historical context. It encourages children to envision what it was like to live in the past by presenting them with a situation in which they can easily see themselves. They are invited to occupy the shoes of the characters, and imagine what they would do in similar circumstances."

Mr. McUmphie of Caulfield Cove, published in 1982, tells the story of an old sea captain who lives in a cave in a park in a suburb of West Vancouver. Two children, Jill and Gordon, make friends with him on their first trip to the beach alone, and help him protect his home from a winter clean-up crew. In return, he teaches them valuable lessons about life and nature, including how to tie knots, how to be resourceful, how to deal with emergencies, and how to be happy about the new twin brother and sister in their family. In a review of *Mr. McUmphie of Caulfield Cove* for *Quill and Quire,* critic Joan McGrath declared: "This mild, pleasant little story has a regional flavour of [British Columbia]."

Manson's 1993 volume *A Dog Came, Too,* which was named to the 1993 shortlist for the Sheila A. Egoff Children's Prize, relates the fictional adventures of a dog who really existed—the dog that accompanied explorer Alexander Mackenzie's exploration group on their 1793 trek across Canada to the Pacific Ocean. Known simply as "Our Dog," in Manson's narrative the canine helps the explorers hunt for food, retrieves lost canoe paddles, watches over them at night, and is their constant companion, trotting along on the rocky river bank because there is no room for him in the expedition's canoes. When the group is close to the Pacific coast, Our Dog becomes lost. The men eventually find him on their return trip back from the ocean, but by then he is very weak from exposure. He recovers and returns with them to the East. The dog is the main character in this book; none of the people, except for the explorer Alexander Mackenzie, are named. Critical response to *A Dog Came, Too* was highly favorable. Though Deborah Stevenson, in her review for *Bulletin of the Center for Children's Books,* said that the book "occasionally ascribes unprovable thoughts to Our Dog" and "tells as fact undocumentable actions" of the dog, she also commented that *A Dog Came, Too* is "an intriguing story with an adventurous backdrop."

Just Like New, published in 1996, is set in Canada during World War II, when rationing and shortages meant that many children in England did not get Christmas presents. Sally is a girl living in Canada, and she is distressed by this shortage of gifts. When she is asked to donate a gift for English children, something that is both well-loved by her and "just like new," she decides to give away the doll she loves the most, Ann Marie. *Canadian Children's Literature* contributor Jonathan F. Vance wrote that the book "is elevated above the commonplace by its magical details." A reviewer in *Quill and Quire* remarked that Manson "successfully evokes the young girl's struggle, the tense wartime atmosphere, and the loving but not always kind relationship of an older brother and younger sister." Sally and her family follow Ann Marie's trip across the ocean on a map, and wonder where she will go. Eventually, Sally receives a letter from Deborah, the English girl who received Ann Marie.

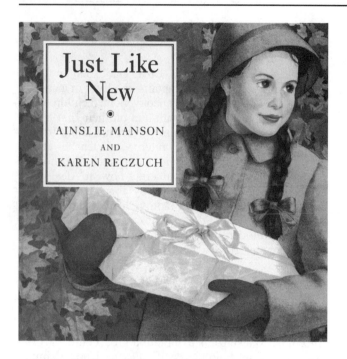

In Ainslie Kertland Manson's touching picture book, a Canadian girl is saddened to discover that some English children will not have gifts for Christmas because of the war, and unselfishly decides to give away her favorite doll. (Cover illustration by Karen Reczuch.)

Baboo: The Story of Sir John A. Macdonald's Daughter, is a picture-book biography of Macdonald's daughter, Mary, whose nickname was Baboo. Baboo was born with brain damage and could not walk or talk clearly, and she spent her life in a wheelchair. The book tells the story of her life through anecdotes, as well as a series of letters between Baboo and her father. In her review of *Baboo* for *Quill and Quire,* Annette Goldsmith noted problematic elements in the illustrations by Bill Wand, but remarked: "We learn about [Baboo] through well-chosen anecdotes in this carefully researched account."

For her next book, *Ballerinas Don't Wear Glasses,* Manson drew inspiration from memories of her own experience in childhood dance classes to create a story that *Quill & Quire* contributor Sherie Posesorski declared "will immediately strike a chord with many children and parents." Young Allison's dance class is set to perform *Swan Lake* for a recital, and Allison has to wear the ugliest of the swan costumes. She knows she's as good as the rest of her classmates, but her confidence is shaken by constant reminders of how she's different: she's the only one in the group who wears glasses. The story is told through the eyes of Allison's older brother, Ben, who at first resents having to look after her the day of the recital. But soon he begins to feel badly for her, and starts helping her prepare for the performance. His solutions to her worries and fears are both funny and creative. According to Posesorski, "the book's a delightful demonstration of how, with a bit of ingenuity, too different can be transformed into winningly distinctive."

When asked about her favorite book as a child, Manson answered to *SATA:* "Because of the war, I had very few books when I was a child. I adored them all—equally! I discovered our small local library, at about the same time that my family discovered my sight was poor. An eccentric eye doctor informed my mother that I should be reading nothing but essential school work! I didn't go blind, but I don't think it had anything to do with his outlandish treatment. I now read voraciously—probably because of that skimpy beginning!"

Discussing role models, Manson told *SATA:* "I'd say my Mum was my role model. She was the most thoughtful, nonjudgmental and incredibly wise person I've ever known! She wrote, too, but I guess you'd call her a 'closet poet!' She would send her poems to magazines and newspapers and though they were often published, she would only sign her initials. Her mother before her, also had a fair amount of poetry published, but she was even more secretive! SHE wouldn't even sign her initials! Times change, or do they ... my eldest son Graeme is now a film writer."

Asked if she had a quote she would like to share with children, Manson answered to *SATA:* "Yes, this is from Goethe. I keep it above my desk: 'Are you in earnest? Seize this very minute! What you can do, or dream you can, BEGIN IT! Boldness has genius, power and magic in it. Only engage, and then ... the mind grows heated. BEGIN, and then the work will be completed.'"

Manson told *SATA:* "When I was growing up, I didn't have the faintest idea that writing was something that I might choose for a career. In my school days, I spent a great deal of time staring out the window, deep in daydreams. My report cards always said things like 'Ainslie is doing all right, but I know she could do better.' I was happiest in school when we had a subject called 'Composition' ... I found I could 'talk it all out' in my diary ... I could sort out things that happened to me. I was extremely shy when I was young—people who didn't know me then find that hard to believe.

"By the time I was in High School I'd found another subject that I loved ... history. I think a few keen, enthusiastic teachers looked at me, shook their heads and said, 'Well, she's near hopeless, but let's push her as HARD as we can in creative writing and history!'

"After high school I could have (and probably should have) gone on to university, but they insisted on more Math, and I couldn't have faced that at the time. Instead, I decided to specialize in Travel. I worked, and when I'd earned enough money—I set off ... not exactly ALL 'round the world, but I covered a good part of it, and I wrote about my experiences every night. I did well in Travel! I expect I got about 99% in that.

"I really only settled on writing as a career after I was married. I took a three year creative writing course, working on it at home in the evenings ... because I had a day job.

"My first attempts were quite hopeless articles for magazines. It wasn't until after I had children that I realized I'd been writing in the wrong genre, writing for the wrong audience. I discovered I loved telling stories to children. And the rest is history ... quite literally. My stories that have been most successful are stories connected with some aspect of history.

"I write in a little back room in our house. We live in the older part of Caulfeild, in West Vancouver, British Columbia. I can see the sea from my window ... so I still stare out the window and dream a lot because I love the sea.

"On my favorite kind of day, I get up early, walk my two dogs along the sea or through a wonderful rainforest park near our house. Then I come home and sit down at my computer with my dogs contentedly snoring by my side ... and I write. Usually until lunch time or a little beyond. If it's a good day, I grab a sandwich and go BACK to my computer. I expect I'll go on like this forever, because I don't think writers retire."

Works Cited

Goldsmith, Annette, review of *Baboo: The Story of Sir John A. Macdonald's Daughter, Quill and Quire,* September, 1998, p. 66.

Review of *Just Like New, Quill and Quire,* August, 1995, p. 33.

McGrath, Joan, review of *Mr. McUmphie of Caulfield Cove, Quill and Quire,* April, 1982, p. 28.

Posesorski, Sherie, review of *Ballerinas Don't Wear Glasses, Quill and Quire,* March, 2000, p. 67.

Stevenson, Deborah, review of *A Dog Came, Too: A True Story, Bulletin of the Center for Children's Books,* March, 1993, pp. 219-20.

Vance, Jonathan F., review of *Just Like New, Canadian Children's Literature,* winter, 1996, p. 122.

For More Information See

PERIODICALS

Booklist, May 1, 1993, p. 1599; November 15, 1996, p. 594.

Books in Canada, March, 1982, p. 25.

Bulletin of the Center for Children's Books, January, 1997, p. 180.

Canadian Book Review Annual, 1995, p. 477.

Children's Book News, spring, 1997, p. 34.

Children's Book Watch, spring, 1996, p. 7.

Five Owls, March, 1993, p. 97.

Horn Book Guide, fall, 1993, p. 268.

New Advocate, spring, 1994, p. 143.

Quill and Quire, February, 1995, p. 35.

School Library Journal, December, 1996, p. 100.

McDONNELL, Christine 1949-

Personal

Born July 3, 1949, in Southampton, NY; daughter of Peter Joseph (in public relations) and Margaret (Doyle) McDonnell; married Terry Shaneyfelt (an artist and baker), December 8, 1979; children: Garth (stepson), Soo Ae, Joseph Doo Wook. *Education:* Barnard College, B.A., 1972; Columbia University, M.L.S., 1973; graduate study at Simmons College, 1979-81.

Addresses

Home—117 Pembroke St., Boston, MA 02118.

Career

New York Public Library, New York City, children's librarian, 1972-75; junior high school librarian in Arlington, MA, 1976-79; Simmons College, Boston, MA, assistant professor of education, 1979-82, director of community programs at Center for the Study of Children's Literature, 1979-80, acting director, 1981. Pierce School, Brookline, MA, teacher, 1982—.

Writings

Don't Be Mad, Ivy, illustrated by Diane de Groat, Dial, 1981.

Toad Food and Measle Soup, illustrated by de Groat, Dial, 1982.

Lucky Charms and Birthday Wishes, illustrated by de Groat, Viking, 1984.

Count Me In, illustrated by de Groat, Viking, 1986.

Just for the Summer, illustrated by de Groat, Viking, 1987.

It's a Deal, Dogboy, illustrated by G. Brian Karas, Viking, 1988.

Friends First, illustrated by de Groat, Viking, 1990.

Trouble Times 2, Viking, 1999.

Contributor of articles and reviews to magazines and newspapers, including *Horn Book.* In 1994 *Friends First* appeared in Spanish translation as *Los Amigos Primero.*

Sidelights

Beginning her involvement with children's literature while working as a librarian at the New York Public Library in New York City, teacher and author Christine McDonnell has gone on to contribute several titles to both library and bookstore shelves, among them *Toad Food and Measle Soup, Count Me In,* and *It's a Deal, Dogboy.* Each of McDonnell's books deals with experiences to which many of her young readers can easily relate. As she once told *SATA:* "I am interested in the importance of little events in children's lives—birthday parties, new pets, spelling bees, and special toys. To children these are not insignificant: they are the stuff of real life. I look for the drama in everyday happenings. I am interested in the issues that concern children at different ages: the need for independence, self-respect, friends, security. I also like dualities—simple but complex, serious but funny." McDonnell's books have been consistently praised for their realistic plots and characters. As Karen Jameson commented in *Horn Book,* McDonnell's "quiet stories reflect the author's sense of the working of young minds and her ability to write sensitively about everyday events." Likewise, Ellen D. Warwick noted in a review of *Just for the Summer* for *School Library Journal,* "Once again, McDonnell displays her special gift for authentic dialogue and warm family relationships."

Born in Southampton, New York, in 1949, McDonnell grew up around books and around enthusiastic readers of books of all sorts. She began writing after earning her degree in library science at Columbia University and starting a job working in a junior high school library. While she first wrote book reviews and short fiction for adult readers, her exposure to children soon inspired McDonnell to begin gearing her fiction for younger, emergent readers. Most of her book-length fiction has been crafted for beginning readers in the elementary grades and incorporates short chapters and simple vocabulary into an engaging plot.

In her first published book, McDonnell introduced readers to six-year-old Ivy Adams. Ivy is a typical young girl whose life is punctuated with numerous activities, many involving fellow six-year-old best friends Emily Mott and Lydia, as well as eight-year-old Leo Nolan. In *Don't Be Mad, Ivy,* McDonnell entertains beginning readers with six short episodes in Ivy's life. While the majority of them—"The Birthday Present," "The Swimming Pool," and "The Borrowed Bear," among them— were based on the author's own childhood, others were inspired by McDonnell's stepson, Garth. Describing Ivy as "independent and ingenious," *Horn Book* contributor Mary M. Burns added that the young protagonist's "triumphs and trials are appropriately scaled to younger readers," and McDonnell's tone is "warm and reassuring."

Other books by McDonnell feature easy-to-relate-to situations encountered by Ivy, Emily, Lydia, Leo, and their friends. In *Just for the Summer* Lydia visits Ivy and Emily's neighborhood, staying with aunts May and Connie while her father recovers from a serious illness at a hospital back home. Although worried about her father, Lydia takes her mind off his condition by making new friends in summer camp, starting a toddler day-care business, and braving the swimming hole to learn a new skill. Describing *Just for the Summer, Publishers Weekly* reviewer Diane Roback called the book "a gem of a story, a well-written and fully-faceted reflection of one young girl's life."

In *Lucky Charms and Birthday Wishes,* McDonnell presented five stories in which readers follow Emily through what turns out to be a fantastic school year. While nervous about whether she will fit in or not, Emily finds she can cope with the changes the year brings, as she comes to terms with the school bully, supports friend Lydia in dealing with Lydia's father's continued illness, and comes to appreciate a birthday gift that holds special significance.

Leo returns to entertain eager readers in *Toad Food and Measle Soup,* as he rescues a lost puppy, survives his mother's attempts to turn Leo's family into tofu-eaters, and presents an amazing book report in front of his class. Describing Leo as "gentle, imaginative, [and] cheerful . . . [as well as] a daydreamer," Elizabeth Holtze added in her *School Library Journal* review of *Toad Food and Measle Soup* that McDonnell "presents a very human boy, beset by the insecurities of youth . . . [and] does so with clever, gentle humor." *It's a Deal, Dogboy* also features Leo—dubbed "Dogboy" by his older sister. Leo is not-so-eagerly awaiting the beginning of fourth grade and spends his summer playing baseball with his best buddy Johnny and several—ick!—girls, outfitting a newly acquired tree house, getting a new dog, and putting up with his annoying, "punked-out" older sister Eleanor and whiny younger cousin Tim. "Leo and his misadventures are lively and credible," noted *Horn Book* reviewer Nancy Vasilakis, who added that "fans of the series—as well as new friends—should find [*It's a Deal, Dogboy*] a briskly engaging diversion." Calling the chapter book a "springboard into summer" for beginning readers, *School Library Journal* reviewer Janet M. Bair added that with the book "the stories could be used to start some lively classroom discussions," for children will easily empathize with Leo's problems.

While most of McDonnell's books deal with the same popular cast of characters, she wrote several novels with young adult readers in mind. *Friends First* finds Miranda confused about her changing feelings toward Gus, a neighbor and classmate who has been Miranda's best buddy since they were both toddlers. A frightening encounter with a local street gang further deters Miranda from a blossoming adolescent love affair with her best friend until she learns to deal with her changing feelings and her initial fear of men. In the 1986 novel *Count Me In,* thirteen-year-old Katie confronts the possibility that she might no longer be the sole apple of her mother's eye after her newly remarried mother and stepfather Steve let slip the news that they are expecting a baby. While fantasizing that she will find a secure place with her divorced father, Katie is disappointed to find her father distracted and emotionally unavailable to her due to the hectic pace of his job and his preoccupation with a new girlfriend. *Count Me In* "is a book about new shapes of families," McDonnell once told *SATA,* "and the struggle that all of us have in finding a place for ourselves within our family." Praising *Count Me In* as "a very human story with an underlying warmth that is extremely appealing," *Horn Book* contributor Elizabeth S. Watson added that "the gradual growth of Katie's role within each of her families is skillfully drawn and believable." In her review for *Publishers Weekly,* Genevieve Stuttaford also deemed *Count Me In* "sensitive" and "satisfying," adding that McDonnell "handles a familiar subject well, with characters real enough to make the point" that people create their own definitions of family.

McDonnell, who now works as a teacher in both middle school and high schools in Brookline, Massachusetts, has described her chapter-book fiction as "episodic." As she once explained to *SATA:* "I enjoy the unfolding of character through separate events. I think such a style is well suited to the needs of younger readers, who may have difficulty following a continuous long story. But the style may be related to my erratic writing schedule, since I have to work writing around my teaching.

"I believe in strong characters, straightforward stories, and clean, simple, evocative writing." McDonnell added. "The children's authors I admire most are E. B. White, Eleanor Estes, Paula Fox, and Katherine Paterson." The books that influenced her most as a child included *Charlotte's Web, Stuart Little,* and novels by nineteenth-century writers Louisa May Alcott and Edith Nesbit.

Works Cited

Bair, Janet M., review of *It's a Deal, Dogboy, School Library Journal,* November, 1998, p. 90.

Burns, Mary M., review of *Don't Be Mad, Ivy, Horn Book,* April, 1982, p. 167.

Holtze, Elizabeth, review of *Toad Food and Measle Soup, School Library Journal,* October, 1982, p. 143.

Jameson, Karen, review of *Lucky Charms and Birthday Wishes, Horn Book,* June, 1984, p. 331.

Roback, Diane, review of *Just for the Summer, Publishers Weekly,* October 9, 1987, p. 88.

Stuttaford, Genevieve, review of *Count Me In, Publishers Weekly,* June 27, 1986, p. 94.

Vasilakis, Nancy, review of *It's A Deal, Dogboy, Horn Book,* November-December, 1998, pp. 735-36.

Warwick, Ellen D., review of *Just for the Summer, School Library Journal,* October, 1987, p. 127.

Watson, Elizabeth S., review of *Count Me In, Horn Book,* July-August, 1986, pp. 449-50.

For More Information See

PERIODICALS

Booklist, November 1, 1998, p. 493.

Horn Book, December, 1982, p. 651; September-October, 1987, pp. 612-13; July-August, 1990, p. 464.

Publishers Weekly, May 11, 1990, p. 261.

School Library Journal, December, 1981, pp. 53-54; May, 1984, p. 82; June, 1990, p. 138.*

*   *   *

MITTON, Jacqueline 1948-

Personal

Born July 10, 1948, in Stoke-on-Trent, England; daughter of Charles (a teacher) and Gertrude (Bridgwood) Pardoe; married Simon Mitton (a publisher), June 27, 1970; children: Lavinia, Veronica. *Education:* Oxford University, B.A., 1969; Cambridge University, Ph.D., 1975.

Jacqueline Mitton explores the search by scientists to discover extraterrestrial life. (Cover illustration by Jonathan Hair.)

Addresses

Home—8A Canterbury Close, Cambridge CB4 3QQ, England. *Agent*—Sara Menguc, 4 Hatch Place, Kingston Upon Thames, Surrey, KT2 5NB, England.

Career

Teacher at convent school in Cambridge, England, 1972-74; Cambridge University, Cambridge, researcher in astronomy, 1975-78; writer, 1978—; British Antarctic Survey HQ, Cambridge, head of information, 1981-85; *Journal of the British Astronomical Association,* editor, 1987-93; Cambridge Health Authority, non-executive director, 1993-96; Maris Multimedia Ltd., consultant, 1995-98. Writer/consultant, Nugus Martin Productions, 1998-99. Part-time press officer for the Royal Astronomical Society, 1989—. *Member:* British Astronomical Association (council service, 1994-97, 1998-99), Royal Astronomical Society (fellow), British Association for the Advancement of Science (council member and Physics Section committee), International Astronomical Union, American Astronomical Society (Planetary Sciences division), U.K. Planetary Forum, Association of British Science Writers.

Awards, Honors

Marshall Children's Guide to Astronomy was shortlisted for Rhone-Poulenc Junior Book prize in 1999.

Writings

Astronomy: An Introduction for the Amateur Astronomer, Scribner, 1978.

(With husband, Simon Mitton) *The Prentice-Hall Concise Book of Astronomy,* Prentice-Hall, 1979.

(Co-editor S. Mitton and author of introduction) *Star Atlas,* Crown, 1979.

(Translator from French with S. Mitton) Jean Heidmann, *An Introduction to Cosmology,* Springer-Verlag, 1980.

Key Definitions in Astronomy, Frederick Muller, 1980, published in England as *A Language of Its Own: Astronomy,* Frederick Muller, 1981.

(With S. Mitton) *Invitation to Astronomy,* Basil Blackwell, 1986.

Discovering the Planets (juvenile nonfiction), Troll Associates, 1991, Eagle Books, 1991.

Penguin Dictionary of Astronomy, Penguin, 1991 (published in England as *Concise Dictionary of Astronomy,* Oxford University Press, 1991), 3rd edition, 1998.

(With S. Mitton) *Astronomy* (juvenile), Oxford University Press, 1994, published in England as *The Young Oxford Book of Astronomy,* Oxford University Press, 1994.

(Co-editor with John Spencer, and contributor) *The Great Comet Crash: The Impact of Comet Shoemaker-Levy 9 on Jupiter,* Cambridge University Press, 1995.

(With Stephen Maran) *Gems of Hubble,* Cambridge University Press, 1996.

Galileo: Scientist and Star Gazer (juvenile), illustrated by Gerry Ball, Oxford University Press, 1997.

(With Alan Stern) *Pluto and Charon: Ice Worlds at the Ragged Edge of the Solar System,* Wiley, 1997.

Zoo in the Sky: A Book of Animal Constellations (juvenile), illustrated by Christina Balit, National Geographic, 1998.

Aliens (juvenile), Candlewick Press, 1998, Walker, 1998.

(With S. Mitton) *Marshall Children's Guide to Astronomy,* Marshall, 1998, published in the United States as *Scholastic Encyclopedia of Space,* Scholastic, 1999.

Contributed articles to *Children's Britannica,* 1984; *Oxford Children's Encyclopedia,* 1991.

Work in Progress

Follow up to *Zoo in the Sky* (for Frances Lincoln); *Lifting Time's Veil: Exploring the Giant Moons of Saturn,* with Ralph Lorenz (for Cambridge University Press); *Stars and Planets* volume in *Young Oxford Encyclopedia of Science* (for Oxford University Press).

Sidelights

Jacqueline Mitton once commented: "I doubt whether I would have ever written anything at all if my husband, Simon, had not started writing when we were both graduate students. At the time I thought, 'If he can do it,

I can do it.' My first book, in fact, which was created from an astronomy course I had been teaching, for a while became a standard text for that course in the United Kingdom."

Mitton and her husband have since collaborated on four books. "Our joint efforts have been particularly fruitful since we specialize in separate fields," she explained. "The criticism we offer each other seems to result in something better than we might have produced individually. We have no problems in working together.

"Although people imagine writing for children is easy, there is a real challenge in choosing the few words and ideas carefully."

Jacqueline Mitton, sometimes in association with co-authors, has written books on astronomy for adults, young people, and children. In each case her ability to summarize and lyrically explicate difficult concepts and large amounts of material has been lauded. In a *Nature* review of Mitton's 1991 publication, *A Concise Dictionary of Astronomy,* R. J. Tayler wrote that this book "should be extremely useful to anyone who wishes to find a short definition of a word or phrase relating to astronomy."

Written for a young adult audience, *Aliens* gives an account of the Search for Extraterrestrial Intelligence (SETI), lists aliens from movies, excerpts an issue of *UFOs: The Magazine with All the Answers,* and recounts several tales of encounters with aliens, explaining why the existence of other intelligent life in our solar system is unlikely. "This inviting mix of hype and hypotheses will draw readers like a magnet," predicted John Peters in *School Library Journal.*

Also for the young adult crowd is *Gems of Hubble,* co-written by Mitton and Stephen P. Maran. This work not only discusses the history of the Hubble Space Telescope, but also introduces readers to the history of telescopes themselves, and along the way explains the basics of photo-astronomy, the technique through which much of our current information on space is gained. "Amazingly," noted Darrell G. Ardoin in *School Library Journal,* "in spite of its brevity, the book details a majority of the types of objects in our solar system." Ardoin adds that the stunning photography, accompanied by complete descriptions of cameras, lenses, and filters used in order to achieve the effects shown, add to the "appealing look at our universe" *Gems of Hubble* presents.

For younger children, Mitton has written *Zoo in the Sky,* which pictures the animals of the zodiac as seen in the night sky highlighted in glittering stars and gives the animals bodies through the details of the illustrations. The result is a picture book that "certainly has eye appeal," noted Carolyn Phelan in *Booklist.* Likewise complimentary, Donna L. Scanlon in *School Library Journal* dubbed this a "lovely and unusual offering" that would serve as "an attractive introduction to astronomy" but would also be an effective entree into discussions on mythology and folklore. Mitton has also written a biography of the Renaissance astronomer Galileo for middle-grade readers.

Works Cited

Ardoin, Darrell G., review of *Gems of Hubble, School Library Journal,* July, 1997, p. 118.
Peters, John, review of *Aliens, School Library Journal,* July, 1999, p. 111.
Phelan, Carolyn, review of *Zoo in the Sky, Booklist,* November 1, 1998, p. 498.
Scanlon, Donna L., review of *Zoo in the Sky, School Library Journal,* December, 1998, p. 111.
Tayler, R. J., review of *A Concise Dictionary of Astronomy, Nature,* April 2, 1992, pp. 395-96.

For More Information See

PERIODICALS

Magpies, November, 1992, p. 36.
School Librarian, November, 1997, p. 205.

*   *   *

MORE, Caroline
See CONE, Molly (Lamken)

*   *   *

MURPHY, Stuart J. 1942-

Personal

Born in 1942; married Nancy Kolanko Murphy; children: Randall, Kristin. *Education:* Rhode Island School of Design, B.F.A., 1964; graduate, Harvard Business School, Owner/President Management Program. *Hobbies and other interests:* Sketching, Italian language.

Addresses

Home—1014 Hinman Avenue, Evanston, IL 60202. *Office*—c/o Publicity Director, Children's Books, HarperCollins Publishers, 1350 Avenue of the Americas, New York, NY 10019.

Career

Education research consultant, author of children's books. Art director, *The Art Gallery* magazine, 1964-67; designer and art director, Ginn and Company, educational publishers, 1967-1980; co-founder and president of Ligature, Inc., an educational research and development firm that helped develop the *Houghton Mifflin Social Studies Program* for K-8, 1980-1992; independent author, consultant, and lecturer, 1992—. Serves on the Board of Trustees, Rhode Island School of Design, Committee on Museum Education for the Art Institute of Chicago, Arts Education Advisory Council of Harvard University's Graduate School of Education, and the

Stuart J. Murphy

Board of Governors, Northwestern University's Library Council.

Awards, Honors

Awarded a Xerox Social Service Leave, 1973, to work as Director of Special Projects for the International Fund for Monuments, in Venice, Italy; Mary Alexander Award, Chicago Book Clinic, 1992, for service to the Chicago Book Clinic and the book publishing community; W. A. Daiggin Award, Bookbuilder of Boston, 1993, for excellence in the building of books and the advancement of the book building community; Top Ten Nonfiction Series for Young Children list, *Booklist,* 1999, for "Mathstart" series.

Writings

"MATHSTART" SERIES, ALL PUBLISHED BY HARPERCOLLINS

The Best Bug Parade, illustrated by Holly Keller, 1996.
Give Me Half!, illustrated by G. Brian Karas, 1996.
Ready, Set, Hop!, illustrated by Jon Buller, 1996.
A Pair of Socks, illustrated by Lois Elhert, 1996.
Get Up and Go!, illustrated by Diane Greenseid, 1996.
Too Many Kangaroo Things to Do!, illustrated by Kevin O'Malley, 1996.

The Best Vacation Ever, illustrated by Nadine Bernard Westcott, 1997.

Divide and Ride, illustrated by George Ulrich, 1997.

Every Buddy Counts, illustrated by Fiona Dunbar, 1997.

Betcha!, illustrated by S. D. Schindler, 1997.

Elevator Magic, illustrated by Karas, 1997.

Just Enough Carrots, illustrated by Frank Remkiewicz, 1997.

Lemonade for Sale, illustrated by Tricia Tusa, 1998.

Circus Shapes, illustrated by Edward Miller, 1998.

A Fair Bear Share, illustrated by John Speirs, 1998.

The Greatest Gymnast of All, 1998.

Animals on Board, 1998.

The Penny Pot, 1998.

Henry the Fourth, illustrated by Scott Nash, 1999.

Jump, Kangaroo, Jump!, illustrated by O'Malley, 1999.

Super Sand Castle Saturday, illustrated by Julia Gorton, 1999.

Rabbit's Pajama Party, 1999.

Spunky Monkeys on Parade, 1999.

Room for Ripley, 1999.

Beep Beep, Vroom Vroom, 2000.

Pepper's Journal, 2000.

Dave's Down-to-Earth Rock Shop, 2000.

Also the author of *Elementary Mathematics,* Silver Burdett Ginn, *Integrated Mathematics 1-3,* McDougal Littel, and *The Fat Firm,* McGraw Hill.

Sidelights

Stuart J. Murphy is an education consultant whose MathStart books for HarperCollins have helped kick-start a new approach in teaching math skills. Twenty-seven strong and projected at a total of forty-five, the series is graded in three levels and aimed at young children. Murphy's idea is to present math concepts such as comparing, counting, matching, sequencing, fractions, adding, and subtracting, among dozens of others, in the context of stories. Murphy's stories deal with circuses, vacations, birthdays, shopping, gymnastics, food, and just about any other situation that a young child will encounter in real life. The math concepts are also presented visually through diagrams and illustrations. "I think that most people understand things best when they can see them," Murphy told *Something about the Author* (*SATA*). "It's often better to draw a map then to try and explain where you're going to meet someone. Family trees help to show how people are related to one another. And graphs are usually the easiest way to demonstrate comparisons between two or more things . . . . I also found that stories helped kids to see how math is used in everyday, real-life situations . . . . This is how MathStart was born."

Murphy served a long apprenticeship before inaugurating his popular math series. Graduating from the Rhode Island School of Design in 1964, he served as the art director for the magazine, *The Art Gallery,* for three years before joining the textbook company, Ginn and Company, as a designer. In 1971 he became art director for Ginn, a position he held until 1980. In that year he co-founded Ligature, Inc., an educational research and development firm that worked with publishers to conceptualize and prepare high quality books for the nation's schools. During these years he worked on social studies projects as well as math books. "A number of years ago," Murphy told *SATA,* "I started working with a group of top mathematicians on a major new secondary school program. I found . . . that many of the concepts that students find difficult are easier for them to understand when they are presented visually."

Combining his background in visual arts with his work in educational publishing and research, Murphy began working on the books that would become MathStart. He took as his starting point two principles: first, that many kids are visual learners, and second, that students do not study math the same way they experience it. That is to say that while they study mathematics in terms of word problems or operations symbols and numbers, they experience it directly by telling time, buying things, keeping score, and hundreds of other real-life situations. Murphy put these two principles together and come up with the concept for his narrative and visual approach to teaching math. When he pitched the idea to HarperCollins, they contracted an initial three, then twenty-four books in the series, later expanding it to forty-five.

Written on three levels from preschool through second grade and up, MathStart deals with beginning math concepts such as counting, comparing, and ordering in Level 1; in Level 2 basic math skills such as adding and subtracting are introduced; and in Level 3 multiplying and dividing are demonstrated. As Ian Elliot noted in *Teaching K-8,* "It's easy to see why Murphy is so successful in getting young children turned on to math." Elliot pointed out the "lively but simple story lines," "delightful illustrations," and "visual representations of the math that's involved."

The first three books in the series were some four years in the making, and covered each of the three levels in the MathStart program. *The Best Bug Parade* was aimed at Level 1, *Give Me Half!* was geared for Level 2, and *Ready, Set, Hop!* at Level 3. *The Best Bug Parade* deals with size comparisons, with a red ladybug parade marshal as a constant referent, while a sibling squabble over pizza is the story line in *Give Me Half!* and two frogs debate their estimated length of jump in *Ready, Set, Hop!*. Reviewing the first title in *School Library Journal,* Diane Nunn noted that concepts such as long/short and big/bigger/biggest "are presented by an assortment of cheery insects marching through a colorful environment of flowers and grass," and concluded that "teachers and parents will all find this a useful book, and youngsters will be attracted to the lively illustrations." Reviewing *Give Me Half!,* Carolyn Phelan of *Booklist* felt that it was "[o]ne of the few math concept books with realistic dialogue, authentic emotions, and genuine humor."

Not all reviewers were enthusiastic about the first batch of MathStart titles, however. Elizabeth Bush writing in *Bulletin of the Center for Children's Books* pointed to several inconsistencies and confusions in the books' story lines and illustrations, and concluded, "Wasn't two plus two easier before math was supposed to be fun?" Reviewing *Ready, Set, Hop!* in *School Library Journal,* JoAnn Rees felt, "This series entry flops as a stand-alone title . . . . The story frame is weak and will not hold readers' interest long enough for them to care about which frog wins."

Critical reception improved as the series continued, however. The next three books in the series were *A Pair of Socks, Get Up and Go,* and *Too Many Kangaroo Things to Do.* Reviewing all three in *School Library Journal,* Marsha McGrath noted that each "focuses on a simple math concept: matching, time lines, or multiplication." McGrath went on to comment, "Bright hues of acrylic paint and collage are used in the cartoon illustrations" while the end pages provide "helpful hints about using the books to teach additional concepts." *Booklist*'s Phelan felt that Murphy's *A Pair of Socks* might be the only picture book story "told from the point of view of a sock." Phelan also commented, "Short, snappy rhymes and Ehlert's brilliantly colored collage illustrations combine to make this tale from the Math-Start series an entertaining book."

Publication of six further titles came in 1997. The first three were *Every Buddy Counts, The Best Vacation Ever,* and *Divide and Ride,* followed by *Just Enough Carrots, Elevator Magic,* and *Betcha!.* Reviewing the first three titles in *School Library Journal,* Christine A. Moesch pointed out that they dealt with concepts such as counting, collecting data, and dividing, and concluded that they were an "entertaining approach to progressive levels of math concepts." *Booklist*'s Hazel Rochman, reviewing the first three titles of the 1997 batch, remarked that "these stories use everyday situations and lively line-and-watercolor illustrations to teach math concepts at various levels of difficulty." Noting in particular *Divide and Ride* as "the most sophisticated in math and story," Rochman felt that kids "of all ages will be drawn into the story" of how eleven children at the carnival need to divide up into twos and threes and fours for various rides.

Rochman also had praise for Murphy's second group of 1997 titles, noting that *Betcha!* "is a real winner that will entertain kids with the buddy story and the causal dialogue and with Schindler's bright, active pictures of two boys having fun in the city." Commenting on how the boys in *Betcha!* play at estimating the number of people on the bus as they ride to the city and the number of jellybeans in a window display, a writer for *Kirkus Reviews* noted that all the while readers would be introduced to concepts and techniques such as "rounding off and how to count a small number and apply that to the great, uncounted whole through the use of multiplication, fractions, and simple geometry." The same reviewer concluded that "Murphy's success is in beveling the sharp, unforgiving reputation of math and in showing how numbers can be toyed with."

Murphy expounded on his methodology and writing technique in a *Booklist* interview. Noting that "most people don't see math as part of their daily lives," he explained, in *Booklist,* that the driving force behind his MathStart series was "to draw kids into a story based on their own experiences sorting socks, rushing to get ready for school, fighting for a fair share of a pizza." He went on to explain that his books begin with a concept and that he then searches his mind for a story to fit. "For example, I wanted to do a book on division. I was looking for a model in the daily experiences of children, but I kept coming up with things that were more like fractions. Then I remembered going to the carnival with my kids." At the carnival, Murphy and his children always had the problem of how they were going to divide up to go on rides, and employing this in his story *Divide and Ride,* he provided a very realistic approach to the concept of division.

Murphy, a trained artist, also oversees the early versions of artwork, supplying roughs for the artists to work from. His end-of-the-book suggestions for further reading and extended activities come from his own experience and are also added to and checked by three teachers in the field. Finally, each title is tested in the field with children's workshops at schools. Murphy remarked that kids in these workshops "end up having so much fun giggling and participating and explaining their work that I almost have to remind them that this is math."

Writing in *Teaching K-8,* Elliot noted, "Despite the great success MathStart has enjoyed in the primary grades, there are no plans to extend the series to the middle grades." Murphy explained to Elliot, "'Educators are reluctant to buy picture books for the middle and upper elementary grades, even though kids can benefit from the books . . . . We may end up having to produce visual learning books with a combination of words and pictures.'"

Meanwhile, the series has continued at the primary level, with twenty-seven titles which have earned general praise from reviewers, teachers, and students alike. Reviewing his first group of 1998 titles, *Circus Shapes, A Fair Bear Share,* and *Lemonade for Sale,* a *Publishers Weekly* contributor praised their "disarmingly chipper stories," while a writer for *Kirkus Reviews* called *Lemonade for Sale* a "lively entry" demonstrating the use of bar graphs. The same reviewer concluded, "A winning way to make some basic concepts and techniques less intimidating." Reviewing the 1999 entries, *Henry the Fourth* and *Jump, Kangaroo, Jump!,* *Booklist*'s John Peters felt that the former title had "the more complex story line," but that both titles followed "a winning formula." Writing in *School Library Journal,* Jane Claes reviewed a further 1999 addition to the MathStart series, *Super Sand Castle Saturday.* "Murphy does a good job of imparting the math lesson while delivering a natural story," Claes noted.

"The MathStart series is designed to help children become more fluent in the language of mathematics," Murphy concluded in *SATA,* "be more comfortable with match concepts, and make math part of their system of communication. By presenting math concepts in stories, supporting those stories with high-quality illustrations and carefully-constructed math diagrams, and providing easy-to-accomplish activities that extend the learning of the story at the end of each book, children will realize that math can be easy—and fun!"

Works Cited

Review of *Betcha!, Kirkus Reviews,* September 15, 1997, p. 1460.

"The Booklist Interview: Stuart Murphy," *Booklist,* April 1, 1997, p. 1347.

Bush Elizabeth, review of *The Best Bug Parade* et al, *Bulletin of the Center for Children's Books,* May, 1996, p. 310.

Review of *Circus Shapes* et al, *Publishers Weekly,* January 19, 1998, pp. 379-80.

Claes, Jane, review of *Super Sand Castle Saturday, School Library Journal,* July, 1999, p. 88.

Elliot, Ian, "Murphy's Magical MathStart," *Teaching K-8,* January, 1998, pp. 43-44.

Review of *Lemonade for Sale, Kirkus Reviews,* November 15, 1997, p. 1711.

McGrath, Marsha, review of *A Pair of Socks* et al, *School Library Journal,* December, 1996, p. 116.

Moesch, Christine A., review of *The Best Vacation Ever* et al, *School Library Journal,* March, 1997, pp. 179-80.

Nunn, Diane, review of *The Best Bug Parade, School Library Journal,* June, 1996, pp. 10607.

Peters, John, review of *Henry the Fourth* and *Jump, Kangaroo, Jump!, Booklist,* April 15, 1999, p. 1534.

Phelan, Carolyn, review of *Give Me Half!, Booklist,* May 1, 1996, p. 1510.

Phelan, Carolyn, review of *A Pair of Socks, Booklist,* October 1, 1996, p. 355.

Rees, JoAnn, review of *Ready, Set, Hop!, School Library Journal,* June, 1996, pp. 117-18.

Rochman, Hazel, review of *The Best Vacation Ever* et al, *Booklist,* February 1, 1997, p. 943.

Rochman, Hazel, review of *Betcha!* et al, *Booklist,* October 1, 1997, p. 336.

For More Information See

PERIODICALS

Booklist, March 1, 1998, p. 1142.

Horn Book Guide, fall, 1996, pp. 269, 329; spring, 1997, pp. 110, 111; fall, 1997, p. 254.

School Library Journal, November, 1997, p. 110; December, 1997, p. 113; April, 1998, p. 121; March, 1999, pp. 122-23.

—*Sketch by J. Sydney Jones*

N

NARAHASHI, Keiko 1959-

Personal

Born January 20, 1959, in Japan; daughter of Toshio (a scientist) and Kyoko (a potter) Narahashi; married Peter Belamarich (a pediatrician), June, 1982; children: Micah, Joy. *Education:* Parsons School of Design, B.F.A.; attended Oberlin College, 1977-78.

Addresses

Agent—c/o Publicity Director, Margaret K. McElderry Books, 866 3rd Avenue, New York, NY 10022.

Career

Children's writer and illustrator, 1987—.

Awards, Honors

Parents' Choice Picture Book Award, 1987, for *I Have a Friend.*

Writings

AUTHOR AND ILLUSTRATOR

I Have a Friend, McElderry Books, 1987.
Is That Josie?, McElderry Books, 1994.
Two Girls Can!, McElderry Books, 2000.

ILLUSTRATOR

Mary Serfozo, *Who Said Red,* McElderry Books, 1988.
Serfozo, *Who Wants One,* McElderry Books, 1989.
Serfozo, *Rain Talk,* McElderry Books, 1990.
James Sage, *The Little Band,* McElderry Books, 1991.
Melanie Scheller, *My Grandfather's Hat,* McElderry Books, 1992.
Dee Lillgarde, *Do Not Feed the Table,* Doubleday, 1992.
Yoshiko Uchida, *The Magic Purse,* McElderry Books, 1993.
Serfozo, *What's What?: A Guessing Game,* McElderry Books, 1996.

Marcia K. Vaughan, *Happy Birthday, Mrs. Boedecker,* Celebration Press, 1996.
Norma Farber, *Without Wings, Mother, How Can I Fly?,* Holt, 1998.
Deborah Chandra, *A Is for Amos,* Farrar, Straus and Giroux, 1999.

Sidelights

Keiko Narahashi is an author-illustrator of children's books that feature warm and subtle relationships between friends and family members. Her artwork is noted for its soft-focused quality, sometimes employing a pastiche of Japanese brushwork. Most comfortable in watercolors, Narahashi creates joyful, often playful illustrations in both muted and bright primary hues.

Born in Japan, Narahashi early on developed a love for art from her potter mother. She moved to the United States when still very young. "I grew up in Durham, North Carolina, in a middle-class neighborhood," Narahashi once told *SATA.* "Life was uneventful. I went to the North Carolina School of the Arts in Winston-Salem (which was almost too eventful), where I discovered a world of fascinating people with more gifts and emotional problems than I'd ever encountered before. It was a real eye-opener. I eventually made my way to New York City and to Parsons School of Design where I got my B.F.A.

"While growing up, I never gave much thought to being Japanese. I was too busy trying to conform. Nowadays, I find that it is more and more relevant in my life, especially in my artwork. I have a renewed interest in Japanese and Chinese art, particularly the brush paintings of Chinese monks—Bada Shanren is one of my favorites. As a child, I spent a lot of time looking at Japanese picture books, so it feels like a homecoming to look once again to the Asian masters."

Narahashi married in 1982 and soon became the mother of two children. But by 1987 she was looking for other creative outlets in addition to motherhood. She turned to writing books for children. "There are many different

In Keiko Narahashi's self-illustrated picture book, a young boy has a very special friend who follows him everywhere he goes. (From I Have a Friend.*)*

reasons I ended up in children's books," Narahashi once told *SATA.* "Love of the book form and of narrative; the opportunity to reconcile my two main areas of interest as an artist, illustration and painting; the openness of the audience; memories of my childhood among books, etc. But the main reason remains my arrested development (somewhere around age eight). I think this is probably why I feel a strong empathy with children and why I am attracted to children's books. I don't really have the storytelling impulse, or God forbid, the urge to didacticism. What fascinates me are the various moods of childhood and that is what I like best to evoke."

With her first self-illustrated title, *I Have a Friend,* Narahashi told the story of one young boy's discovery of his shadow. This friend goes with him as the boy walks down the street, goes to the park or to the beach. In a handful of simple, direct sentences, Narahashi describes the boy's fascination with this special friend, and accompanies the text with "deceptively simple" watercolor paintings, according to *Horn Book's* Ellen G. Fader. "Shadows hold fascination for all children," Fader explained, "and this story, with its large watercolor paintings, encourages exploration of the subject." Fader also noted that the book, a Parents' Choice Picture Book award winner, was "more of a poetic exploration than a full-blown story." Judith Gloyer wrote in *School Library Journal* that Narahashi's debut picture book "is as deceptively simple and magical as a shadow." Gloyer pointed to Narahashi's "softly rounded shapes" in her simple illustrations and "slippery, watery colors," and

concluded that the book was a "lovely and subtle match of words and pictures." A reviewer for *Publishers Weekly* felt that "the book remains an intriguing, poetic introduction to the world of shadows."

Narahashi followed up this initial success with illustrative efforts for other writers; her next self-illustrated writing appeared in 1994. *Is That Josie?* is "a simple but effective picture book [that] celebrates the liveliness of a preschool child's imagination," according to Martha V. Parravano writing in *Horn Book.* Josie, a young girl, is shown at play throughout the day, pretending to be various animals. It is not Josie peeking out of the bed in the morning, but a wily fox. Later, in response to her mother's questions, Josie is alternately a turtle, a kangaroo, an ant, a possum, a cheetah, and even an eagle. *Booklist's* Kay Weisman called *Is That Josie?* an "imaginative picture book" that will make a "good choice for story hours, where children will enjoy anticipating the answers to Mommy's questions." A reviewer for *Publishers Weekly* felt that the "spare, glowing pastel watercolors represent Narahashi at her best." And Carolyn Noah, writing in *School Library Journal,* noted the "simple text and watercolor paintings with strokes evocative of Japanese brush work" which lead to a portrayal of an Asian-American family that "is elegantly natural." Narahashi's next solo effort was published in 2000. In *Two Girls Can!,* she tells the story of two girls who celebrate all the things that best friends can do together.

"I try for a loose, unstudied approach in my illustrations," Narahashi once told *SATA,* "and so I really have to fight the need to control every result. This is why I choose watercolor and brush over pencil or pen. In my hand, the pencil gets unbearably tight and dull. Something about the brush and ink, the fluidity of the paint, allows me to take risks with my drawing. I don't know why it is so hard to take these tiny, almost imperceptible risks, all I know is that these small feats are what make for the satisfying pictures."

Narahashi has collaborated on eleven picture books, providing pictures for the words of others, including four books by Mary Serfozo. Her 1996 book with Serfozo, *What's What?: A Guessing Game,* employs a question-and-answer format with rhyming, simple text; Narahashi's pictures provide a counterpoint to each question. For example, a line of boldface black text asks, "What is light?" The answer: "Daytime is light." This is accompanied by "a lovely watercolor illustration of two African American children outdoors at play," according to Jerry D. Flack writing in *School Library Journal.* The question, "What's dark?" is followed by a picture of the same duo huddled under a tent-blanket with a moon and owl gazing down upon them. "Narahashi's splendid watercolors capture all of the joy and sense of wonder of the childhood investigations," Flack concluded. A *Publishers Weekly* critic, reviewing *What's What?,* noted, "As in Serfozo and Narahashi's previous collaborations this book features simple text, appealing watercolors and a surprise ending that is sure to please." *Booklist's* Hazel Rochman noted that *What's What?* is "a simple concept

Pretending she is an animal, Josie imagines creative responses to a grown-up's questions. *(From* Is That Josie?, *written and illustrated by Narahashi.)*

book about physical sensations and about opposites" in which the "story, ideas, design, and illustrations work beautifully together." Rochman concluded, "Narahashi's soft-toned pictures of an African American family are full of hugs and warmth. This is a winner for the lapsit crowd."

Narahashi has also worked with many other authors, including Melanie Scheller on *My Grandfather's Hat,* Norma Farber on *Without Wings, Mother, How Can I Fly?,* and with Deborah Chandra on *A Is for Amos.* Scheller's story tells the tale of little Jason who recalls his special relationship with his grandfather by playing with his grandfather's old hat. Jason's grandfather always tipped his fedora to people passing by; if the hat got crushed he would just pop it back into shape. Now that the old man is dead, Jason uses the hat as a memory-shaper and a solace. "Soft-focused watercolor and pencil illustrations convey the homey, comforting ambience of this subdued story," noted Anna DeWind in *School Library Journal.* A reviewer for *Publishers Weekly* commented that "Narahashi deviates form her familiar style and artfully mimics the pencil drawings of children, subtly suggesting the emotional bond Jason shares with his grandfather." *Booklist*'s Weisman remarked that

"Narahashi's soft watercolor-and-pencil illustrations match the quiet mood of Scheller's text," while *Horn Book*'s Margaret A. Bush called special attention to Narahashi's "broadly drawn watercolor and pencil scenes" whose "crayonlike texture is childlike and reminiscent of the lovely work of Taro Yashima."

Without Wings, Mother, How Can I Fly? is a question-and-answer poem which deals with many of a toddler's questions about the universe. Published after the death of its author, Norma Farber, the poem uses simple language, "while Narahashi's quiet watercolors, as reassuring as a lullaby, capture a safe and homey rural landscape," according to a critic for *Publishers Weekly.* Rochman, writing in *Booklist,* alluded to Narahashi's "joyful watercolors," and concluded that children "will enjoy the playful animal connections, both wild and snugly warm." Martha Topol, reviewing the picture book in *School Library Journal,* commented on Narahashi's "sun-drenched landscapes" which "are rendered in vibrant greens and watery blues." Topol concluded, "The book exudes a sense of security and love between the mother and child that is implied rather than explicitly stated."

Amos takes a rider on his back and travels around the farm, identifying everything from A to Z. (From A Is for Amos, *written by Deborah Chandra and illustrated by Narahashi.)*

Another collaborative effort, this time with Deborah Chandra, produced the alphabet book and storybook *A Is for Amos*. In this "unique combination," as described by a *Publishers Weekly* reviewer, "galloping rhymes and Narahashi's inviting watercolors take an imaginative cowgirl for a memorable ride." *Booklist*'s April Judge felt that Narahashi's "fanciful watercolors capture the fun and excitement of a special ride," while *Horn Book*'s Parravano noted that "Narahashi has conceived many nice touches that make a harmonious whole of the book."

"I'm happiest when working—or completely miserable, depending on how my work is going," Narahashi once concluded to *SATA*. "I'm a real perfectionist and though it has turned me into much more of a professional than I'm inclined to be, it makes for an interesting challenge."

Works Cited

Review of *A Is for Amos, Publishers Weekly*, January 4, 1995, p. 88.

Bush, Margaret A., review of *My Grandfather's Hat, Horn Book*, March-April, 1992, p. 195.

DeWind, Anna, review of *My Grandfather's Hat, School Library Journal*, April, 1992, p. 100.

Fader, Ellen G., review of *I Have a Friend, Horn Book*, September-October, 1987, pp. 601-02.

Flack, Jerry D., review of *What's What?, School Library Journal*, October, 1996, p. 106.

Gloyer, Judith, review of *I Have a Friend, School Library Journal*, October, 1987, pp. 117-18.

Review of *I Have a Friend, Publishers Weekly*, July 24, 1987, pp. 184-85.

Review of *Is That Josie?, Publishers Weekly*, August 22, 1994, p. 55.

Judge, April, review of *A Is for Amos, Booklist*, March 15, 1999, p. 1332.

Review of *My Grandfather's Hat, Publishers Weekly*, March 16, 1992, p. 78.

Noah, Carolyn, review of *Is That Josie?, School Library Journal*, November, 1994, pp. 86-87.

Parravano, Martha V., review of *Is That Josie?, Horn Book*, January-February, 1995, p. 50.

Parravano, review of *A Is for Amos, Horn Book*, March, 1999, p. 185.

Rochman, Hazel, review of *What's What?, Booklist*, October 1, 1996, p. 351.

Rochman, review of *Without Wings, Mother, How Can I Fly?, Booklist,* March 15, 1998, p. 1247.

Serfozo, Mary, *What's What?: A Guessing Game,* McElderry Books, 1996.

Topol, Martha, review of *Without Wings, Mother, How Can I Fly?, School Library Journal,* May, 1998, p.114.

Weisman, Kay, review of *My Grandfather's Hat, Booklist,* May 1, 1992, p. 1610.

Weisman, review of *Is That Josie?, Booklist,* November 1, 1994, p. 508.

Review of *What's What?, Publishers Weekly,* September 2, 1996, p. 130.

Review of *Without Wings, Mother, How Can I Fly?, Publishers Weekly,* March 9, 1998, p. 67.

For More Information See

PERIODICALS

Booklist, October 1, 1993, p. 349.
Bulletin of the Center for Children's Books, October, 1987, p. 35; October, 1994, p. 60.
Horn Book, January-February, 1994, p. 80.
Junior Bookshelf, April, 1989, p. 64.
Los Angeles Times Book Review, February 28, 1988, p. 10.
New York Times Book Review, November 13, 1988, p. 63; May 19, 1991, p. 28; May 17, 1998, p. 30.
School Library Journal, February, 1989, p. 17; November, 1993, p. 103; January, 1994, p. 108; March, 1999, p. 171.*

—*Sketch by J. Sydney Jones*

*   *   *

NIXON, Joan Lowery 1927-
(Jaye Ellen)

Personal

Born February 3, 1927, in Los Angeles, CA; daughter of Joseph Michael (an accountant) and Margaret (Meyer) Lowery; married Hershell H. Nixon (a petroleum geologist), August 6, 1949; children: Kathleen Nixon Brush, Maureen Nixon Quinlan, Joseph Michael, Eileen Nixon McGowan. *Education:* University of Southern California, B.A., 1947; California State College, certificate in elementary education, 1949. *Religion:* Roman Catholic.

Addresses

Home—10215 Cedar Creek Dr., Houston, TX 77042. *Agent*—Amy Berkower, Writers House Inc., 21 West 26th St., New York, NY 10010.

Career

Writer. Elementary school teacher in Los Angeles, CA, 1947-50; Midland College, Midland, TX, instructor in creative writing, 1971-73; University of Houston, Houston, TX, instructor in creative writing, 1974-78; has taught creative writing in two parochial schools in

Joan Lowery Nixon

Texas. *Member:* Authors Guild, Authors League of America, Society of Children's Book Writers and Illustrators (charter member and former member of board of directors), Mystery Writers of America (former national president, regional vice-president of Southwest chapter, and member of national board of directors), Western Writers of America, Women Writing the West, Kappa Delta Alumnae Association.

Awards, Honors

Steck-Vaughn Award, Texas Institute of Letters, 1975, for *The Alligator under the Bed;* Edgar Allan Poe Award nomination, Mystery Writers of America, 1975, for *The Mysterious Red Tape Gang,* 1985, for *The Ghosts of Now,* 1993, for *The Weekend Was Murder!,* and 1995, for *Shadowmaker,* and 1996, for *Spirit Seeker;* Outstanding Science Trade Book for children, National Science Teachers Association and Children's Book Council Joint Committee, 1979, for *Volcanoes: Nature's Fireworks,* 1980, for *Glaciers: Nature's Frozen Rivers,* and 1981, for *Earthquakes: Nature in Motion;* Edgar Allan Poe Award for best juvenile mystery, Mystery Writers of America, 1980, for *The Kidnapping of Christina Lattimore,* 1981, for *The Seance,* 1986, for *The Other Side of Dark,* and 1994, for *The Name of the Game Was Murder;* Crabbery Award, Oxon Hill branch of Prince George's County (MD) Library, 1984, for *Magnolia's Mixed-Up Magic;* Golden Spur, Western Writers of

America, 1988, for *A Family Apart,* and 1989, for *In the Face of Danger;* Indiana's Young Hoosier Award, 1988, for *A Deadly Game of Magic,* and 1989, for *The Dark and Deadly Pool;* Colorado Blue Spruce Young Adult Award, 1988, Virginia Young Adult Silver Cup, 1989, Oklahoma Sequoyah Young Adult Book Award, 1989, Iowa Teen Award, 1989, California Young Readers Medal, 1990, and Utah Young Adult Award, 1991, all for *The Other Side of Dark;* California Young Readers Medal, 1990, for *The Stalker;* Nevada Young Adult Award, 1992, Nebraska Golden Sower Young Adult Award, 1993, and Detroit Public Library Children's Choice Award, 1994, all for *Whispers from the Dead;* Virginia Young Adult Silver Cup, 1993, for *A Family Apart;* Indiana's Young Hoosier Award, 1996, and Arizona Young Readers award, and Maryland's Black-Eyed Susan award, both 1997, all for *The Name of the Game Was Murder.*

Writings

FICTION; FOR YOUNG PEOPLE

The Mystery of Hurricane Castle, illustrated by Velma Ilsley, Criterion, 1964.

The Mystery of the Grinning Idol, illustrated by Alvin Smith, Criterion, 1965.

The Mystery of the Hidden Cockatoo, illustrated by Richard Lewis, Criterion, 1966.

The Mystery of the Haunted Woods (sequel to *The Mystery of Hurricane Castle*), illustrated by Theresa Brudi, Criterion, 1967.

The Mystery of the Secret Stowaway, illustrated by Joan Drescher, Criterion, 1968.

Delbert, the Plainclothes Detective, illustrated by Philip Smith, Criterion, 1971.

The Alligator under the Bed, illustrated by Jan Hughes, Putnam, 1974.

The Mysterious Red Tape Gang, illustrated by Joan Sandin, Putnam, 1974, published in paperback as *The Adventures of the Red Tape Gang,* illustrations by Steven H. Stroud, Scholastic, 1983.

The Secret Box Mystery, illustrated by Leigh Grant, Putnam, 1974.

The Mysterious Prowler, illustrated by Berthe Amoss, Harcourt, 1976.

The Boy Who Could Find Anything, illustrated by Syd Hoff, Harcourt, 1978.

Danger in Dinosaur Valley, illustrated by Marc Simont, Putnam, 1978.

Muffie Mouse and the Busy Birthday, illustrated by Geoffrey Hayes, Seabury, 1978, published as *Muffy and the Birthday Party,* Scholastic, 1979.

Bigfoot Makes a Movie, illustrated by Hoff, Putnam, 1979.

The Kidnapping of Christina Lattimore, Harcourt, 1979.

Gloria Chipmunk, Star!, illustrated by Diane Dawson, Houghton, 1980, published in paperback with illustrations by Hayes, Scholastic, 1980.

Casey and the Great Idea, illustrated by Amy Rowen, Dutton, 1980.

The Seance, Harcourt, 1980.

The Spotlight Gang and the Backstage Ghost, Harlequin, 1981.

The Specter, Delacorte, 1982, published in England as *The Spectre,* Granada, 1983.

(Under pseudonym Jaye Ellen) *The Trouble with Charlie,* Bantam, 1982.

Days of Fear, photographs by Joan Menschenfreund, Dutton, 1983.

The Gift, illustrated by Andrew Glass, Macmillan, 1983.

A Deadly Game of Magic, Harcourt, 1983.

Magnolia's Mixed-Up Magic, illustrated by Linda Bucholtz-Ross, Putnam, 1983.

The Ghosts of Now, Delacorte, 1984.

The House on Hackman's Hill, Scholastic, 1985.

The Stalker, Delacorte, 1985.

The Other Side of Dark, Delacorte, 1986.

Haunted Island, Scholastic, 1987.

Secret, Silent Screams, Delacorte, 1988.

If You Were a Writer (picture book), illustrated by Bruce Degen, Four Winds Press, 1988.

The Island of Dangerous Dreams, Dell, 1989.

Whispers from the Dead, Delacorte, 1989.

A Candidate for Murder, Delacorte, 1991.

High Trail to Danger, Bantam, 1991.

Honeycutt Street Celebrities, Dell, 1991.

The Mystery Box, Dell, 1991.

Watch out for Dinosaurs, Dell, 1991.

The Haunted House on Honeycutt Street, Dell, 1991.

A Deadly Promise (sequel to *High Trail to Danger*), Bantam, 1992.

The Name of the Game Was Murder, Delacorte, 1993.

Will You Give Me a Dream? (picture book), illustrated by Degen, Four Winds Press, 1994.

When I Am Eight (picture book), illustrated by Dick Gackenbach, Dial, 1994.

Shadowmaker (mystery), Delacorte, 1994.

Spirit Seeker, Delacorte, 1995.

House of Fear (young adult mystery), Delacorte, 1995.

Don't Scream, Delacorte, 1996.

Search for the Shadowman, Delacorte, 1996.

Murdered, My Sweet, Delacorte, 1997.

(With Kathleen Nixon Brush), *Champagne at the Murder,* NTC Contemporary Books, 1998.

The Haunting, Delacorte, 1998.

Who Are You?, Delacorte, 1999.

Champagne with a Corpse, NTC Contemporary Books, 1999.

Champagne at Risk, NTC Contemporary Books, 1999.

Nobody's There, Delacorte, 2000.

Ghost Town (short stories), Delacorte, 2000.

Gus and Gertie and the Missing Pearl, Sea Star, North-South Books, 2000.

Also contributor to anthologies, including *Stories for Free Children,* edited by Letty Cottin Pogrebin, McGraw-Hill, 1982; *Short Circuits: Thirteen Shocking Stories by Outstanding Writers for Young Adults,* edited by Donald Gallo, Delacorte, 1992; *Don't Give Up the Ghost,* edited by David Gale, Delacorte, 1993; *Great Writers and Kids Write Mystery Stories* (co-authored with Nicole Marie Brush), edited by Jill Morgan; and *Mothers and Daughters: A Celebration of Love* (co-authored with Eileen Nixon McGowan), edited by Jill Morgan.

"CASEBUSTERS" MYSTERY SERIES

The Statue That Walks at Night, Disney Press, 1995.
The Legend of the Deadman's Mine, Disney Press, 1995.
The Thief at Piney Point Manor, Disney Press, 1995.
Backstage with a Ghost, Disney Press, 1995.
Check in to Danger, Disney Press, 1995.
Beware the Pirate Ghost, Disney Press, 1996.
Catch a Crooked Clown, Disney Press, 1996.
Secret of the Time Capsule, Disney Press, 1996.
Fear Stalks Grizzly Hill, Disney Press, 1996.
The House Has Eyes, Disney Press, 1996.
Sabotage on the Set, Disney Press, 1996.
The Internet Escapade, Disney Press, 1997.
Bait for a Burglar, Disney Press, 1997.

"FIRST READ-ALONE MYSTERIES" SERIES; ILLUSTRATED BY JIM CUMMINS

The New Year's Mystery, Albert Whitman, 1979.
The Halloween Mystery, Albert Whitman, 1979.
The Valentine Mystery, Albert Whitman, 1979.
The Happy Birthday Mystery, Albert Whitman, 1979.
The Thanksgiving Mystery, Albert Whitman, 1980.
The April Fool Mystery, Albert Whitman, 1980.
The Easter Mystery, Albert Whitman, 1981.
The Christmas Eve Mystery, Albert Whitman, 1981.

"CLAUDE AND SHIRLEY" SERIES

If You Say So, Claude, illustrated by Lorinda Bryan Cauley, Warne, 1980.
Beats Me, Claude, illustrated by Tracey Campbell Pearson, Viking, 1986.
Fat Chance, Claude, illustrated by Pearson, Viking Kestrel, 1987.
You Bet Your Britches, Claude, illustrated by Pearson, Viking, 1989.
That's the Spirit, Claude, Viking, 1992.

"KLEEP: SPACE DETECTIVE" SERIES; ILLUSTRATED BY PAUL FRAME

Kidnapped on Astarr, Garrard, 1981.
Mysterious Queen of Magic, Garrard, 1981.
Mystery Dolls from Planet Urd, Garrard, 1981.

"MAGGIE" SERIES; YOUNG ADULT NOVELS

Maggie, Too, illustrated by Darrel Millsap, Harcourt, 1985.
And Maggie Makes Three, Harcourt, 1986.
Maggie Forevermore, Harcourt, 1987.

"ORPHAN TRAIN ADVENTURES"; YOUNG ADULT NOVELS

A Family Apart, Bantam, 1987.
Caught in the Act, Bantam, 1988.
In the Face of Danger, Bantam, 1988.
A Place to Belong, Bantam, 1989.
A Dangerous Promise, Delacorte, 1994.
Keeping Secrets, Delacorte, 1995.
Circle of Love, Delacorte, 1997.

"ORPHAN TRAIN CHILDREN" SERIES; JUVENILE NOVELS

Lucie's Wish, Delacorte, 1998.
Will's Choice, Delacorte, 1998.
Aggie's Home, Delacorte, 1998.
David's Search, Delacorte, 1998.

"HOLLYWOOD DAUGHTERS" TRILOGY; YOUNG ADULT NOVELS

Star Baby, Bantam, 1989.
Overnight Sensation, Bantam, 1990.
Encore, Bantam, 1990.

"MARY ELIZABETH" SERIES; YOUNG ADULT NOVELS

The Dark and Deadly Pool, Delacorte, 1987.
The Weekend Was Murder!, Delacorte, 1992.

"ELLIS ISLAND" SERIES

Land of Hope, Bantam, 1992.
Land of Promise, Bantam, 1993.
Land of Dreams, Bantam, 1994.

"YOUNG AMERICANS" SERIES

Ann's Story, 1746-47, Delacorte, 2000.
Caesar's Story, 1759, Delacorte, 2000.
Nancy's Story, 1765, Delacorte, 2000.

OTHER

(With others) *This I Can Be* (textbook for eighth graders), Benefic, 1975.
(With others) *People and Me* (textbook for seventh graders), Benefic, 1975.
Five Loaves and Two Fishes: Feeding of Five Thousand for Beginning Readers; John 6:1-15 for Children, illustrated by Aline Cunningham, Concordia, 1976.
Who Is My Neighbor?: The Good Samaritan for Beginning Readers; Luke 10:29-37 for Children, illustrated by Cunningham, Concordia, 1976.
The Son Who Came Home Again: The Prodigal Son for Beginning Readers; Luke 15:11-32 for Children, illustrated by Cunningham, Concordia, 1977.
Writing Mysteries for Young People (for adults), The Writer, 1977.
(With husband, Hershell H. Nixon) *Oil and Gas: From Fossils to Fuels* (nonfiction), illustrated by Jean Day Zallinger, Harcourt, 1977.
(With H. Nixon) *Volcanoes: Nature's Fireworks* (nonfiction), Dodd, 1978.
When God Listens, illustrated by James McIlrath, Our Sunday Visitor, 1978.
When God Speaks, illustrated by McIlrath, Our Sunday Visitor, 1978.
The Grandmother's Book (for adults), Abingdon Press, 1979.
The Butterfly Tree, illustrated by McIlrath, Our Sunday Visitor, 1979.
Before You Were Born, illustrated by McIlrath, Our Sunday Visitor, 1980.
(With H. Nixon) *Glaciers: Nature's Frozen Rivers* (nonfiction), Dodd, 1980.
(With H. Nixon) *Earthquakes: Nature in Motion* (nonfiction), Dodd, 1981.
(With H. Nixon) *Land under the Sea* (nonfiction), Dodd, 1985.
(Author of introduction) Cynthia Manson, editor, *Tales from Ellery Queen's Mystery Magazine: Short Stories for Young Adults,* Harcourt, 1986.
My Baby (nonfiction), Mental Health Association (Houston, TX), 1994.

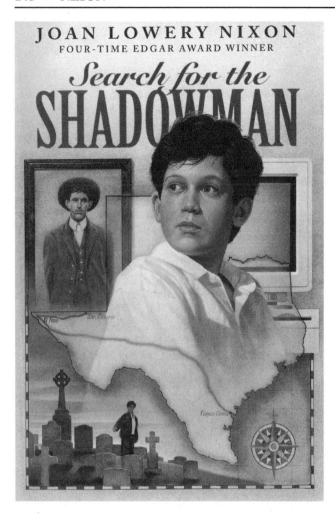

When assigned a school project on his family tree, twelve-year-old Andy Thomas discovers an outcast soul and a desperate warning to stop his research.

Author of introduction to *The Railway Children* by E. Nesbit, Bantam. Also author of nonfiction sections of *The Writer's Handbook,* The Writer, 1978, 1988, and 1992; *Writing Mysteries: A Handbook by the Mystery Writers of America,* edited by Sue Grafton, Writers Digest Books, 1992; and *The Fine Art of Murder, the Mystery Reader's Indispensable Companion,* compiled by the editors of *Mystery Scene* magazine, Carroll & Graf, 1993. Also contributor to magazines, including *West Coast Review of Books, The Writer, American Home, Parents, Woman's Day,* and *Ms.* Humor columnist for the *Houston Post.*

Work in Progress

Three more books in the "Young Americans" series: *Will's Story, 1771; Maria's Story, 1773;* and *Lewis' Story, 1775;* all for Delacorte, all due in 2001.

Sidelights

Joan Lowery Nixon is the undisputed mistress of crime fiction and mysteries for young readers. Over the course of a career spanning almost four decades and comprising more than a hundred books, Nixon has proven time and again that she has what it takes to attract and hold readers of many ages. As Mary Lystad put it in *St. James Guide to Young Adult Writers,* "Nixon's skillful writing and boundless imagination make young readers want to read on, to find out what surprises wait on the next page and discover if their solutions to her never-ending puzzles are the correct one." "In the field of young adult mystery writers, a field crowded with authors," stated Melissa Fletcher Stoeltje in the *Houston Chronicle Magazine,* "she is by all accounts the grande dame."

"Writing is hard," Nixon wrote for *Something about the Author Autobiography Series* (*SAAS*). "It's not easy. But it's such a fulfilling, enjoyable occupation that it's worth all the effort. There are days in which ideas flow and I can hardly type fast enough as I try to get every word down on paper, but there are other days during which I feel as though I'm painfully removing every word from my brain with a pair of pliers." Whether flowing freely or pried with pliers, Nixon's words have already won her the Mystery Writers of America's coveted Edgar Award for best juvenile mystery four times—the first writer to do so—and five of her other works have been nominated for that honor, including her 1996 novel *Spirit Seeker.*

Nixon was born in Los Angeles, California. She lived with her parents, grandparents, and two younger sisters in a large double house. Nixon recalls that at a very young age she wanted to be a writer. When she was three, she began teaching herself to read by memorizing the words in her favorite books. She also followed her mother around, saying, "Write this down. I have a poem." She created verses for every holiday or family celebration. "From the time I discovered mysteries I was in love with them," she said. Her first published work, a poem, appeared in *Children's Playmate* magazine when she was ten years old.

In her childhood home, one of the items that stimulated her imagination in the playroom was a puppet theater for which the young Nixon composed and performed plays with her younger sisters and neighborhood children. "Under my mother's direction," she once told *Something about the Author* (*SATA*), "we wrote our scripts, based on some of the classic fairy tales, such as 'Peter Rabbit' and the traditional 'Punch and Judy,' and took our shows—on a volunteer basis—to children's hospitals and orphanages and schools for many years. One moment I shall always remember: when we put on our puppet show for a group of very young Japanese children, none of whom spoke English. I realized that day the power of 'story telling' and laughter and friendship, as these little ones, unable to understand the dialogue, still responded to the puppets with as much enthusiasm as any audience we had ever met."

Nixon first attended Seventy-fourth Street elementary school in Los Angeles only two blocks from her home, and then Horace Mann Junior High. When she was twelve, her grandfather died and the family moved to a large stucco house in East Hollywood. From her bedroom, which she shared with her grandmother, Nixon could see the lights from the Hollywood theaters. "We had some famous neighbors," she recalled in *SAAS:* "the producer-director, Cecil B. DeMille; the comedian, W. C. Fields; and the champion prizefighter, Jack Dempsey."

After entering ninth grade at Le Conte Junior High in Hollywood, Nixon became interested in journalism and became editor of the school newspaper almost at once. This was in 1941, the year of the attack on Pearl Harbor. Nixon tried to volunteer as a writer of propaganda for the Red Cross, but her offer was ignored. Instead, the next year, when she entered Hollywood High School, she wrote letters to lonely servicemen and helped serve breakfast to them in the school cafeteria. It was also at Hollywood High that Nixon met her favorite teacher, Miss Bertha Standfast. During the next three years, she enrolled in every English class taught by Standfast, seeking her support in her writing. "I treasured the direction and encouragement Miss Standfast gave to me," she declared. "'You have talent,' she'd tell me. 'You're going to be a writer.' It was she who insisted that I major in journalism when I went to college." At the age of seventeen, Nixon wrote her first article for a magazine, selling it to *Ford Times.*

One week after her high school graduation, Nixon entered the University of Southern California as a journalism student. "My training in journalism taught me discipline," she remembered in *SATA.* "For one thing, I learned to create at the typewriter. We took our exams on the typewriter. Journalism taught me to focus because I had to sit down and *write,* whether I felt like it or not—no waiting for inspiration. I learned the skill of finding the important facts in a story, and how to isolate them from all of the unnecessary details."

Nixon's degree in journalism did not lead to a job in that field, partly because of competition from returning war correspondents. However, the Los Angeles School District was in need of teachers, so she found work as a substitute for kindergarten through third grade classes. Soon she received an assignment to teach kindergarten at Ramona Elementary School, at the same time taking night school education courses at nearby Los Angeles City College.

While at USC, Nixon also met her future husband, Hershell "Nick" Nixon, a student majoring in naval science. Two weeks after their first date they became engaged, but, as she stated in *SAAS,* "Nick still had over a year left to serve on his six-year hitch, so off he went to China for ten months. He was back for a few weeks, then off again to Hawaii for a few months." Their marriage was postponed until after he finished his stint in the Navy, but the couple was finally united on August 6, 1949. While Nixon was still teaching at Ramona, the Nixons' first daughter, Kathleen Mary, was born.

In 1952 Nick graduated from USC, having changed his major to geology. His first job, which was with the Shell Oil Company, sent the young family to Billings,

Montana. They later returned to California, but continued to relocate within the state, finally moving to Corpus Christi, Texas. By the time they moved to Corpus Christi, Kathy had been joined by her siblings Maureen, Joe, and the youngest, Eileen. "I shed many tears over that move to Texas," Nixon recalled. "All I knew about the state was that it was full of cattle and cactus, and I didn't want to leave my family, my friends, and my beautiful state of California."

The move to Texas, however, marked an important event in Nixon's life. When she read an announcement of the upcoming Southwest Writers Conference only a little while after her arrival, she became enthusiastic about writing for children. "I had children, I had taught children, and I have the vivid kind of memory which enables me to remember all the details I saw and the emotions I felt when I was a child," she reminisced. "I made a mental note to myself. Maybe I'd try writing something for children." Kathy and Maureen discussed

Tired of waiting for her sweetheart to ask for her hand in marriage, Frances Mary Kelly decides to accompany a train of orphaned children out west to find new homes.

this development and, states the author, announced to their mother, "We've decided. If you're going to write for children, you have to write a book, and it has to be a mystery, and you have to put us in it." Nixon worked every Wednesday from nine a.m. to three p.m. "All week I wrote in my mind, dialogue and scenes coming together, demanding to be written as I shoved them back. 'Not yet!' I'd say with a groan. 'Wait until I can get to my typewriter.'" Each day after school, Nixon read the material she had completed that day to her children. Often she used their suggestions (such as Kathy's "Put something funny in it"). Nixon even joined the Byliners, a local group of writers who read and criticized each other's manuscripts. Despite all this input, *The Mystery of Hurricane Castle* was rejected twelve times by different publishers before Criterion finally accepted it.

The Mystery of Hurricane Castle tells the story of two girls—the Nickson sisters, Kathy and Maureen—and their younger brother, Danny, who are left behind during an evacuation of the Gulf of Texas area just before a hurricane. The book follows them as they seek shelter in a house that, according to local legend, is haunted. Nixon noted in *The Writer* that the plot of the book came from a family experience: "When we moved to Corpus Christi, Texas, we found ourselves in the middle of a hurricane. The eye of the storm missed our city, but the force of the rain, wind, and waves caused tremendous damage ... The area had been evacuated, but I wondered what someone would have done who couldn't leave—who, for some reason, had been left behind in the confusion. The beach houses could not withstand the force of the storm, or stay intact, but what if high on the hill there stood a stone 'castle,' strong enough to survive the storm and to shelter its occupants? And what if this castle were known to have as its only occupant a ghost?" As it turns out, Kathy's interest in painting helps the children to unmask the "ghost." A critic for *Kirkus Reviews* thought that this debut book was a "very friendly, spooky story."

That first book persuaded Nixon to continue writing. After *The Mystery of Hurricane Castle,* she wrote *The Mystery of the Grinning Idol,* a story about smuggling Mexican artifacts (which starred her youngest child, Eileen), and *The Mystery of the Hidden Cockatoo,* about a jeweled pin lost in a house in the French Quarter of New Orleans, before bringing the Nicksons back in *The Mystery of the Haunted Woods.* Son Joe finally got a starring role in *The Mystery of the Secret Stowaway.* Nixon soon found herself busy writing children's books, teaching creative writing classes at local children's schools, libraries, and colleges, and writing a humor column for the *Houston Post.* Nixon said in *SAAS* that it "soon became apparent that I would have to make a decision about the direction of my career ... [because] the careful time I spent on the work from the students in my writing classes subtracted from the time I had for my own writing. It was a difficult decision, but I gave up teaching." This decision allowed her to devote every morning to writing, a hard task, she says in her

autobiographical sketch, "but it's such a fulfilling, enjoyable occupation that it's worth all the effort."

Nixon's earliest work was for young readers; it was not until later in her career that she began writing for young adults. In 1975, Nixon and her daughter Kathy attended the first International Crime Writers Congress in London, England, where a speaker's comment encouraged her to try writing a mystery for young adults. This book became *The Kidnapping of Christina Lattimore,* awarded the Edgar for best juvenile mystery by the Mystery Writers of America in 1980. *The Kidnapping of Christina Lattimore* tells, in the title character's own words, of her ordeal being kidnapped, held for ransom, and then suspected of having engineered the whole project to get money from her grandmother for a school trip. When she is rescued, she dedicates herself to bringing the criminals to justice and proving that she did not try to defraud her grandmother. *New York Times Book Review* contributor Paxton Davis found this part of the novel particularly intriguing, writing that "Christina's inability to persuade the authorities or her family that she was not an accomplice in the crime makes for good narrative." Russ Williams, writing in *Best Sellers,* thought that this book, with its echoes of the Patricia Hearst kidnapping, was "a very hip teenage novel written from the egocentric point-of-view." Williams went on to remark, "All of this is skillfully handled by the author and the reader is ever increasingly enticed deeper within the story." Linda E. Morrell noted in *School Library Journal,* "The heroine grows in strength and maturity through the experiences of being accused of plotting her own abduction ... [and] readers are kept in suspense right up to the final pages as to the identity of the criminals."

One year after *The Kidnapping of Christina Lattimore* won the Edgar, Nixon repeated the accomplishment with *The Seance,* and in 1987 *The Other Side of Dark* made her a three-time recipient of the prize. The latter book presents quite a different type of problem to the reader. Seventeen-year-old Stacy wakes up to find that she has lost four years of her life in a coma after an intruder has shot her and killed her mother. Not only does she have to adapt to a new lifestyle and catch up on the missing years, but she also has to identify the killer before she becomes his next victim. "Stacy is a vivid character," David Gale wrote in *School Library Journal,* "whose need to be brought up to date provides some comic moments." *Booklist's* Hazel Rochman declared, "Nixon has written another compelling page-turner," and Mary L. Adams wrote in *Voice of Youth Advocates,* "Nixon is a master of taking a what-if situation and creating a good story around it."

Nixon has written additional compelling suspense novels, including *The Stalker, Secret, Silent Screams,* and *Whispers from the Dead.* In *Whispers from the Dead,* sixteen-year-old Sarah has a near-death experience swimming, and is haunted thereafter by a ghostly presence. When the family moves to Texas, everyone hopes such memories will be left behind, but the house Sarah and her family move into has a tragic history: the previous owner's son was charged with murdering a delivery girl there. Sara feels the presence of evil, but will she discover who is responsible for it before it is too late? "A master at creating compelling suspense novels, Nixon has written yet another carefully plotted, subtly terrifying thriller," commented a reviewer for *Publishers Weekly* in its review of the novel. "Nixon's reputation as the *grande dame* of mysteries for young readers remains solidly intact with this thriller," announced Jeanette Larson in *School Library Journal.*

In the meantime, Nixon was writing a series of picture-book, beginning-reader mysteries, the "First Read-Alone Mysteries" published by Whitman. Based on various holidays, many of the titles featured siblings Susan, Mike, and Barney. Working with her geologist husband, she also authored several award-winning nonfiction titles, including, *Oil and Gas, Volcanoes,* and *Earthquakes.*

In addition to scientific nonfiction and her acclaimed mysteries, Nixon has won awards for her historical fiction. Two volumes of her "Orphan Train" series, *A Family Apart* and *In the Face of Danger,* won the Golden Spur Award, the Western Writers of America's equivalent of the Edgar. The idea, she said in *Artists and Authors for Young Adults* (*AAYA*), came from a publisher who asked her if she had ever heard of the "Orphan Train Children." The historical Children's Aid Society, an organization of social activists operating between 1854 and 1929, placed more than 100,000 children with foster families in the West. The children—not necessarily orphans—were usually from immigrant families living in slums in New York City.

Such is the case with Nixon's fictional Kelly family, first generation immigrants living in New York shortly before the Civil War. In *A Family Apart,* Nixon tells how, after the oldest boy is arrested for petty robbery, the widowed Mrs. Kelly realizes that she can no longer provide for her six children. She accepts the offer of Reverend Charles Loring Brace, a social activist, to have them placed with other families in the West. When the Kellys reach St. Louis, Missouri, however, they find to their dismay that they will be adopted by different people and must split up. *A Family Apart* shows how Frances Mary, the oldest girl, and Petey, the youngest boy, are adopted by the Cummings, an abolitionist couple living in Kansas, who help escaping slaves flee north. Megan, the second-oldest girl, is chosen by prairie farmers Ben and Emma Browder. *In the Face of Danger* is the story of how she learns to overcome her grief about her family's disintegration and her lack of self-esteem. Ten-year-old Danny and his little sister Peg end up with a family named Swenson in *A Place to Belong,* while Mike, the would-be thief whose activities precipitated the family's exodus, finds a home with a German family named Friedrich in *Caught in the Act.* Reviewing *A Family Apart* in *Voice of Youth Advocates,* Dorothy M. Broderick declared, "This is as close to a perfect book as you'll buy this year. The plot is rational and well paced; the characters are real and believable; the time setting important to U.S. history, and the values all

that anyone could ask for." Broderick concluded, "Buy it, book-talk it, push it." Reviewing *In the Face of Danger* in *School Library Journal,* Janet E. Gelfand called the novel "exciting and touching," with "an aura of historical reality."

Nixon expanded the series with the 1994 title, *A Dangerous Promise,* focusing on Mike Kelly who joins the Union Army with his best friend, only to be horrified by the facts of war at the Battle of Wilson Creek. In *Keeping Secrets,* Peg Kelly is drawn into the dangerous activities of a mysterious young woman who has fled William Quantrill and his raiders, and Frances Kelly is featured in *Circle of Love* when she returns to New York to escort another group of orphans west to new homes. *Booklist*'s Susan DeRonne commented on *Circle of Love,* "Rooted in historical fact, the narrative follows Frances' adventures on the train, the same train that carried her to an adoptive home just six years earlier." DeRonne concluded, "Young readers familiar with the Orphan Train Adventures series will not want to miss this installment." In 1998 Nixon began a series of similar stories for young readers, the "Orphan Train Children" series which branch out from the Kelly family. Included in these are *Lucie's Wish, Will's Choice, Aggie's Home,* and *David's Search.* In *Aggie's Home,* awkward twelve-year-old Aggie is sure no one will want to adopt her when she takes the orphan train, but when she meets the eccentric Bradon family she finds new hope. Reviewing this title in *School Library Journal,* Linda Bindner thought, "Readers will enjoy watching this spirited child stick up for herself despite the consequences." Bindner went on to say, "The addition of historical material on the women's suffrage movement and the orphan trains ... make this book a fulfilling historical adventure."

Nixon's popular "Claude and Shirley" series for younger readers is also set in the American West. In a series of adventures ranging from *If You Say So, Claude,* in which Claude and Shirley, a pioneer couple, leave their noisy mining town for the peace of the Texas frontier, to *You Bet Your Britches, Claude,* in which the couple adopts a little boy and girl, Nixon displays a sense of humor that echoes the West's traditional "tall tales." A reviewer for *Publishers Weekly* appreciated the humor in *Fat Chance, Charlie,* calling it a "rib-tickling yarn," while Betsy Hearne, writing in the *Bulletin of the Center for Children's Books,* further added that it contains "endearing characters, adroit writing, and an action-packed feminist pioneer."

Published in 1991, *High Trail to Danger* originates in nineteenth-century Chicago, where teenage sisters Sarah and Samantha are coping with the death of their mother. When greedy relatives assume control of the family boardinghouse, seventeen-year-old Sarah is encouraged by her younger sister to try to find their father, who left over a decade earlier to try to strike it rich in the silver mines of Colorado. During the journey Sarah confronts a number of seedy characters, as well as a pair of Western suitors. *A Deadly Promise,* published in 1992, continues the story with Sarah summoning her sister to Colorado to help in a quest to restore their father's good name by proving that he was not involved in a murder plot.

"The West to me is a state of mind," Nixon declared in *The Writer.* "While immersed in stories set west of the Mississippi in the last half of the eighteen-hundreds, modern readers are discovering concepts like *sacrifice* and *self-denial* and *unwavering commitment to an ideal*—concepts that are not too common in today's very different world ... Writing western historical novels for young adults is immensely satisfying," she concluded. "It gives me the opportunity to show that history isn't simply a collection of dates and wars and kings and presidents, but that *children* have always helped make history, that *children* are not only important to the past but are helping to shape history being made today."

In 1992, Nixon returned to the setting of New York in *Land of Hope,* the first book in her "Ellis Island" series. The story focuses on Rebekah Levinsky, a Jewish immigrant from Russia who comes to Ellis Island with her family to avoid persecution in her native country. Set in the early 1900s, *Land of Hope* features promises of opportunity for the family when they arrive in the United States. When they arrive in America, however, they find

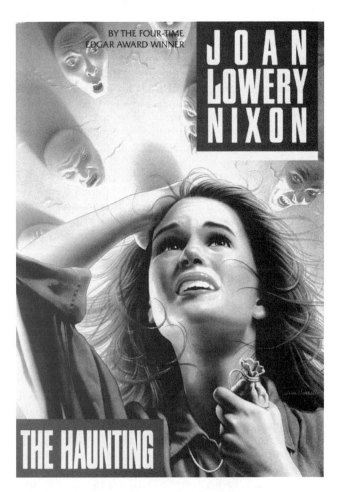

After her family inherits a haunted plantation estate, fifteen-year-old Lia must discover if she has the determination to battle a vengeful ghost. (Cover illustration by Tim Barrall.)

life to be much more difficult than they imagined it would be. This series continued with *Land of Promise,* featuring Rosie, an Irish girl, and *Land of Dreams,* featuring Kristin, a Swedish girl, the three children having met on the boat coming to America. In *Land of Dreams,* Kristin goes to Minnesota with her family and is frustrated by the same gender restrictions that she experienced in Sweden. She rails against tradition and longs for the freedom of Minneapolis, but finally accepts gradual change. "Nixon once again offers a compelling, believable story that gives readers a peek at the past," noted Candace Smith in a *Booklist* review of *Land of Dreams.* "A must for fans of the earlier books," wrote Sally Bates Goodroe in *School Library Journal,* "but one that stands alone as well."

Nixon draws on her own past for inspiration as well. She told *AAYA* that her "Hollywood Daughters" series was based on "some of the kids I knew at Hollywood High during the 1940s—kids who had been stars as children but who were 'has-beens' by the time they were teenagers." Nixon's "Maggie" stories also concern, sometimes tangentially, the world of films, because the eponymous protagonist's father is the famous director, Roger Ledoux, and Maggie must cope with the problems of growing up in an unstable environment. Young Maggie lost her mother in an accident several years before the opening chapters of *Maggie, Too,* and she has little contact with her filmmaker father. Maggie becomes openly resentful when her father announces his plans to marry a twenty-one-year-old starlet and packs her off to spend the summer with her librarian grandmother, also named Maggie, in Texas. Over the course of the book and its two sequels, *And Maggie Makes Three* and *Maggie Forevermore,* Maggie learns to love her grandmother, to lose her resentment toward her father and his new wife, and appreciate her own life. "Nixon is a real pro at delivering likable, true-to-life characters and intriguing plots," a contributor for *Kirkus Reviews* said about *And Maggie Makes Three.* "Readers will sympathize with Maggie from the first and will rejoice at the story's happy ending."

Nixon continues to lead a productive life as a writer, publishing two or more novels a year. In 1995 she began a mystery series for Disney Press, the "Casebusters" books, featuring young detectives Sean and Brian in a bakers dozen of compelling and adventure-filled suspense novels for middle graders. She has also successfully turned her hand to picture books. Her 1994 *When I Am Eight* is an exploration of the "daydreams of a little boy who craves the abilities and privileges that come with age," according to *Booklist*'s Elizabeth Bush. Young Herbie dreams of glory and does not forget his older brother along the way. "Kids will readily empathize with the daydreams of a kindred spirit," commented Bush. Dot Minzer wrote in *School Library Journal,* "Nixon has proved once again that she is not only adept at mystery and adventure for older readers, but also at providing feisty fun for the younger set."

Nixon has continued to write stand-alone volumes of mystery and suspense. In her 1996 *Search for the*

Shadowman, she blends hi-tech (the Internet) with elements of the supernatural to tell the tale of Andy, who is doing a school research project on his family genealogy. Discovering ghosts in the family, Andy must decide whether or not to let the dead lie peacefully or not. Elizabeth S. Watson, writing for *Horn Book,* commented, "The author's latest mystery does not disappoint—in fact, it offers a fresh, tension-packed twist that will appeal to readers as well as their teachers." Julie Halverstadt, reviewing the same book in *School Library Journal,* wrote, "Nixon has once again delivered a riveting tale of suspense set against a background of fascinating historical context, brought up to date through e-mail and the Internet."

In *The Haunting,* published in 1998, Nixon presents a classic haunted house thriller with a twist. Although everyone knows Graymoss mansion is haunted, Lia's mother is still determined to turn it into a foster home. Lia does not want to move there, but after meeting some of the children her mother wants to help, Lia determines to confront the ghosts. With a little help from the stories of Edgar Allan Poe, she succeeds in driving the spirits away. *Booklist*'s Helen Rosenberg called the book "a page-turner that will satisfy mystery and ghost story fans," while *Horn Book*'s Watson summed up the book by saying, "[T]his title has it all—a hint of romance, some really scary scenes, and a plucky heroine who successfully routs both outer and inner demons."

This formula, and variants thereof, have made Nixon one of the most popular children's writers for the last several decades. Commenting on her own writing processes, Nixon wrote in *SAAS,* "Even imaginary characters can have wills of their own," and related that she sees her characters in her dreams and hears them talking about the story. She always has two levels in her mystery novels, "a problem to solve, and a mystery to solve," she stated, "Later the characters can weave them together." In *The Writer* Nixon shared her secret of writing successfully for teenagers: "Appreciating them, really liking them—this, too, I think, is an essential part of the answer." And the secret of her longevity as a writer for an audience known for its fickleness? "Generation to generation, emotions don't change," Nixon stated in *The Writer.* "Loneliness, fear, joy, sorrow, embarrassment ... External situations may differ greatly, but the emotions they cause are always the same. Our basic needs—such as the need to be loved, to be comforted, and to be secure—remain constant."

Works Cited

Adams, Mary L., review of *The Other Side of Dark, Voice of Youth Advocates,* December, 1986, p. 221.

Review of *And Maggie Makes Three, Kirkus Reviews,* April 1, 1986, p. 548.

Bindner, Linda, review of *Aggie's Home, School Library Journal,* December, 1998, p. 129.

Broderick, Dorothy M., review of *A Family Apart, Voice of Youth Advocates,* October, 1987, p. 204.

Bush, Elizabeth, review of *When I Am Eight, Booklist,* January 15, 1994, p. 938.

Davis, Paxton, review of *The Kidnapping of Christina Lattimore, New York Times Book Review,* May 13, 1979, p. 27.

DeRonne, Susan, review of *Circle of Love, Booklist,* April 1, 1997, p. 1334.

Review of *Fat Chance, Claude, Publishers Weekly,* September 25, 1987, p. 107.

Gale, David, review of *The Other Side of Dark, School Library Journal,* September, 1986, pp. 145-146.

Gelfand, Janet E., review of *In the Face of Danger, School Library Journal,* December, 1988, p. 110.

Goodroe, Sally Bates, review of *Land of Dreams, School Library Journal,* February, 1994, p. 104.

Halverstadt, Julie, review of *Search for the Shadowman, School Library Journal,* November, 1996, p. 110.

Hearne, Betsy, review of *Fat Chance, Claude, Bulletin of the Center for Children's Books,* September, 1987, p. 15.

Larson, Jeanette, review of *Whispers from the Dead, School Library Journal,* September, 1989, pp. 275-76.

Lystad, Mary, "Nixon, Joan Lowery," *St. James Guide to Young Adult Writing,* 2nd edition, St. James Press, 1999, pp. 633-36.

Minzer, Dot, review of *When I Am Eight, School Library Journal,* March, 1994, p. 206.

Morrell, Linda E., review of *The Kidnapping of Christina Lattimore, School Library Journal,* September, 1979, p. 160.

Review of *The Mystery of Hurricane Castle, Kirkus Reviews,* May 1, 1964, pp. 452-53.

Nixon, Joan Lowery, "Clues to the Juvenile Mystery," *The Writer,* February, 1977, pp. 23-26.

Nixon, autobiographical sketch in *Something about the Author Autobiography Series,* Volume 9, Gale, 1990, pp. 267-284.

Nixon, "Writing Mysteries Young Adults Want to Read," *The Writer,* July, 1991, pp. 18-20.

Nixon, "Writing the Western Novel for Young Adults," *The Writer,* June, 1992, pp. 21-23.

Nixon, "Joan Lowery Nixon," *Authors and Artists for Young Adults,* Volume 12, Gale, 1994.

Rochman, Hazel, review of *The Other Side of Dark, Booklist,* September 15, 1986, p. 121.

Rosenberg, Helen, review of *The Haunting, Booklist,* July, 1998, p. 1873.

Smith, Candace, review of *Land of Dreams, Booklist,* February 15, 1994, p. 1075.

Stoeltje, Melissa Fletcher, "Murder for Gentle Readers," *Houston Chronicle Magazine,* June 20, 1993, pp. 8-11.

Watson, Elizabeth S., review of *Search for the Shadowman, Horn Book,* January-February, 1997, p. 65.

Watson, review of *The Haunting, Horn Book,* November-December, 1998, p. 737.

Review of *Whispers from the Dead, Publishers Weekly,* October 13, 1989, p. 55.

Williams, Russ, review of *The Kidnapping of Christina Lattimore, Best Sellers,* September, 1977, p. 230.

For More Information See

BOOKS

Children's Literature Review, Volume 24, Gale, 1991.

Ward, Martha E., *Authors of Books for Young People,* 3rd edition, Scarecrow Press, 1990.

PERIODICALS

Booklist, October 1, 1996, p. 352; January 1, 1999, p. 878.
Bulletin of the Center for Children's Books, March, 1992, p. 189.
Horn Book, November, 1986, p. 748.
Los Angeles Times Book Review, November 23, 1986, p. 12.
New York Times Book Review, February 27, 1983, p. 37; October 9, 1988.
Publishers Weekly, February 22, 1980, p. 108; December 5, 1980, p. 52; April 1, 1983, p. 103; April 22, 1983, p. 104; October 5, 1984, p. 91; May 30, 1986, p. 67; November 28, 1986, p. 77; October 9, 1987, p. 89; October 23, 1987, p. 73; December 11, 1987, p. 66; August 12, 1988, p. 462; September 9, 1988, pp. 133-134; September 8, 1989, p. 67; November 10, 1989, p. 62; March 15, 1991, p. 59; June 14, 1991, p. 58; April 27, 1992; April 11, 1994, p. 66, December 12, 1994, p. 63.
School Library Journal, April, 1976, p. 58; January, 1979, p. 45; December, 1979, p. 97; May, 1980, p. 85; September, 1980, p. 62; November, 1980, p. 66; October, 1981, p. 157; December, 1981, p. 82; December, 1982, p. 81; May, 1983, p. 74; October, 1983, p. 152; December, 1984, p. 102; May, 1985, p. 111; September, 1985, pp. 137-138; September, 1986, p. 138; January, 1987; March, 1987, p. 164; May, 1987, p. 102; December, 1987, p. 75; February, 1988, p. 85-86; August, 1988, p. 97; November, 1988, p. 94; September, 1989, pp. 275-276; November, 1989, p. 128; January, 1990, p. 87; May, 1990, p. 126; March, 1991, pp. 194, 216; July, 1991, p. 88; March, 1992, pp. 240, 259; March, 1993, p. 222; May, 1994, p. 117; September, 1997, p. 222; June, 1998, pp. 150-51; August, 1998, p. 164.
Voice of Youth Advocates, December, 1987, p. 236; August, 1988, p. 134; December, 1988, pp. 240-241; February, 1989, p. 288; August, 1989, p. 160; October, 1989, p. 215; June, 1990, p. 108; December, 1990, p. 287; February, 1991, p. 355; August, 1991, p. 174; April, 1992, pp. 18, 34; October, 1992, p. 228; June, 1993, p. 93; February, 1994, p. 371; February, 1998, p. 388.

O

OHMI, Ayano 1959-

Personal

Born August 26, 1959, in Tokyo, Japan; daughter of Masao (a photographer) and Setsuko Ohmi. *Education:* Sophia University (Tokyo, Japan), B.A., 1983, certification of museum study, 1986; City College of New York, M.F.A. in sculpture, 1998.

Ayano Ohmi

Addresses

Home—120 West 78th St., #3B, New York, NY 10024. *Office*—Metropolitan Montessori School, 325 W. 85th St., New York, NY 10024.

Career

Metropolitan Montessori School, New York, NY, art teacher. *Exhibitions:* Has participated in group exhibitions in New York City since 1996.

Awards, Honors

Seymour Peck Scholarship in art, City College of New York, 1996; Therese McCabe Ralston Connor Award for M.F.A./M.A. students, CCNY, 1996, 1997; Best in Show, CCNY Alumni Exhibition at Westbeth Gallery, New York City, 1997; Summer Travel Award, Metropolitan Montessori School, New York City, 1998; Artist Residency Program fellowship, Vermont Studio Center, 1999; Summer Residency Award, Watershed Center, Newcastle, ME, 1999; Notable Children's Book designation, American Library Association, 1999, for *In Search of the Spirit: The Living National Treasures of Japan.*

Writings

(Co-author and calligraphy) Sheila Hamanaka, *In Search of the Spirit: The Living National Treasures of Japan,* Morrow (New York), 1999.

Sidelights

Ayano Ohmi told *SATA:* "I studied journalism and art history at Sophia University in Tokyo. In 1987 I was sent by my corporate employer to the United States to intern at the Philadelphia Museum of Art and the Guggenheim Museum in New York City, where I eventually settled. I received a master of fine arts degree for sculpture from the City College of New York. I now work as a sculptor and teach art at the Metropolitan Montessori School in NYC.

"*In Search of the Spirit* is my first book project with S. Hamanaka. It is an honor to have met Japanese National Treasures and experienced the Japanese traditional art with the masters through this book project. I'm happy to share the master artists' stories with American children and grown-ups. I'm planning to do more book projects some time soon."

For More Information See

PERIODICALS

School Library Journal, May, 1999, p. 138.

*   *   *

ONYEFULU, Ifeoma 1959-

Personal

Name is pronounced "Ee-for-ma Oh-yefulu"; born March 31, 1959, in Onitsha, Nigeria, Africa; daughter of Emmanuel (a lawyer) and Emily (a businesswoman; maiden name, Ekwensi) Onyefulu; married Roger Malbert (an exhibition organizer), June 6, 1988; children: Emeka. *Education:* College of Higher Education (London, England), Higher National Diploma, 1984. *Religion:* Church of England.

Addresses

Home—15 Bickerton Rd., London N19 5JU, England.

Career

Caribbean Times, London, England, staff photographer, 1986-87; *West Africa Magazine,* London, freelancer, 1987-90.

Writings

A Is for Africa: An Alphabet in Words and Pictures, Cobblehill Books, 1993.
Emeka's Gift: An African Counting Story, Cobblehill Books, 1995.
Ogbo: Sharing Life in an African Village, Cobblehill Books, 1996, published in England as *One Big Family: Sharing Life in an African Village,* Frances Lincoln, 1996.
Chidi Only Likes Blue: An African Book of Colors, Cobblehill Books, 1997.
Grandfather's Work: A Traditional Healer in Nigeria, Millbrook, 1998, published in England as *My Grandfather Is a Magician: Work and Wisdom in an African Village,* Frances Lincoln, 1998.
Ebele's Favourite: A Book of African Games, Frances Lincoln (London), 1999.

Sidelights

Ifeoma Onyefulu once told *SATA:* "I love people very much, and having grown up in Nigeria where one is never alone, this type of hunger for company comes

Ifeoma Onyefulu

naturally. Therefore, my interest in people has increased since I left my country twelve years ago.

"I love photographing and documenting the everyday life of people, especially Africans, as we have been portrayed by the media as poor people, constantly in need of the West for everything. As a result, in 1991 I had the idea to do *A Is for Africa* in order to show the African way of life not often seen in the West and in children's books."

The picture books Onyefulu has written and illustrated with her own photographs are widely praised for offering a rarely seen depiction of village life. Her brightly colored photographs evoke the relationships of her subjects, and naturalistically inform readers about customs and realities of life in contemporary Africa.

A Is for Africa provides an overview of Nigerian village life along with the concept of the alphabet for English-speaking audiences. Chris Powling in *Books for Keeps* compared the visual impact of *A Is for Africa* to "stepping from a darkened room straight into noon sunshine so bright and needle-sharp are the author's photographs." Onyefulu has a tendency to choose traditional objects over modern, or Western, artifacts to exemplify each letter, observed Roger Sutton in *Bulletin of the Center for Children's Books,* and these "are simply explained and provide good material for a lapsitting visit."

Onyefulu followed up her alphabet book with a counting book, *Emeka's Gift,* which, like *A Is for Africa,* contains a brightly-lit visual tribute to Nigerian village life that some critics found enchanting. In *Emeka's Gift,* Emeka sets off to buy his grandmother a birthday gift. Along the way to the market he encounters two friends and three women; having reached his destination, he finds four brooms, five hats, and so forth up to ten, but Emeka despairs because he doesn't have enough money to buy any of the items he sees. He goes to his grandmother and tells her what happened, only to be told that he himself is the best gift his grandmother could ever have. *Emeka's Gift* is "a wonderful multidimensional story with universal appeal," according to Barbara Osborne Williams in *School Library Journal. Booklist* contributor Mary Harris Veeder felt that the book succeeds in its mission to teach Western children about Nigerian life because "there is a nice balance between difference and sameness here." Veeder contends that this allows American children to relate to scenes of children playing even if they don't recognize the rules of the game, for example. A reviewer for *Junior Bookshelf* praised Onyefulu for avoiding sentimentality in the telling of her story, displaying instead "honest observation and understanding." The result is "an outstanding counting book."

With her third book, *Ogbo: Sharing Life in an African Village,* Onyefulu left behind the high concepts of her earlier works to tell the story of Nigerian age-sets through the eyes of six-year-old Obioma. An ogbo, or age-set, is a tradition practiced by some Nigerian villages in which each person belongs to a group of people all born within a few years of each other, and as the group ages it attains different responsibilities in service to the community. "As each group is shown working and playing together, readers get a firsthand look at customs" common to Nigerian villagers, noted Loretta Kreider Andrews in *School Library Journal.* Obioma is too young to participate in much of the communal activity she sees around her but serves as the reader's guide to her village: her mother's ogbo ensures the river is kept free of litter; her father's votes on how to get electricity to the village; her uncle's builds houses for those who cannot afford to build their own. "Keep this title in mind when Kwanzaa next comes around or any time you want a little lesson in cooperation," advised Elizabeth Bush in *Bulletin of the Center for Children's Books.*

Sarah Mear, a reviewer for *School Librarian,* described Onyefulu's next book, *Chidi Only Likes Blue,* as "a book of colours with a difference." In this story, narrator Nneka introduces the reader to a spectrum of colors available in her village in Nigeria as she tries to convince her brother Chidi that blue, his favorite, is not the only color of beauty. "This is a quality non-fiction text," averred Roy Blatchford in *Books for Keeps,* "which achieves that singular aim of fiction: allowing the reader to climb inside a character's skin and see life from her point of view." As with her earlier books, Onyefulu effortlessly achieves a lesson in the culture of Nigerian village life, and "viewers will certainly be charmed by the luminous range of tones that sets

Nneka's world aglow," averred Elizabeth Bush in *Bulletin of the Center for Children's Books.*

Onyefulu's fifth book for children, *Grandfather's Work: A Traditional Healer in Nigeria,* achieves a similar goal of introducing the variety of work available to Nigerians, including doctor, lawyer, artisan, and in the second half of the book, focusing on the narrator's grandfather's work as a healer. This section "is fascinating," exclaimed Christine A. Moesch in *School Library Journal,* adding that it leaves "readers hungry for more information on the use of various herbs and roots in healing." An author's note at the end explains that modern Western researchers have investigated the use of some of the traditional herbs grandfather uses and found evidence for their healing properties. "With its possibilities for many cross-curricular uses, the book is a natural for the classroom," concluded Maeve Visser Knoth in *Horn Book.*

Onyefulu is a Nigerian expatriate living in England who in six picture books has successfully introduced English-speaking audiences to the range and variety of village life in her homeland. Illustrated with her own photographs, uniformly described as beautiful by reviewers, Onyefulu's books are considered useful additions to classroom libraries for the lessons they teach about the universality of some experiences.

Works Cited

Andrews, Loretta Kreider, review of *Ogbo, School Library Journal,* April, 1996, p. 127.

Blatchford, Roy, review of *Chidi Only Likes Blue, Books for Keeps,* November, 1997, p. 24.

Bush, Elizabeth, review of *Chidi Only Likes Blue, Bulletin of the Center for Children's Books,* November, 1997, p. 95.

Bush, review of *Ogbo, Bulletin of the Center for Children's Books,* April, 1996, pp. 274-75.

Review of *Emeka's Gift, Junior Bookshelf,* August, 1995, p. 130.

Knoth, Maeve Visser, review of *Grandfather's Work, Horn Book,* January-February, 1999, pp. 83-84.

Mear, Sarah, review of *Chidi Only Likes Blue, School Librarian,* November, 1997, p. 187.

Moesch, Christine A., review of *Grandfather's Work, School Library Journal,* January, 1999, p. 100.

Powling, Chris, review of *A Is for Africa, Books for Keeps,* September, 1993, p. 40.

Sutton, Roger, review of *A Is for Africa, Bulletin of the Center for Children's Books,* September, 1994, pp. 19-20.

Veeder, Mary Harris, review of *Emeka's Gift, Booklist,* June 1-15, 1995, p. 1779.

Williams, Barbara Osborne, review of *Emeka's Gift, School Library Journal,* July, 1995, p. 74.

For More Information See

PERIODICALS

Booklist, August, 1993, p. 2067; April 15, 1996, p. 1444.

Horn Book, September, 1993, p. 627.

Kirkus Reviews, August 15, 1999, p. 1077.
Library Talk, November, 1993, p. 50.
Publishers Weekly, June 28, 1993, p. 75.
School Librarian, November, 1993, p. 150.
School Library Journal, August, 1993, p. 160.

P

PANSY
See ALDEN, Isabella (Macdonald)

* * *

PETERS, Lisa Westberg 1951-

Personal

Born October 19, 1951, in Minneapolis, MN; daughter of Walter M. (an inventor) and Naomi (a nurse; maiden name, Balstad) Westberg; married David G. Peters (a journalist), August 16, 1975; children: Emily, Anna. *Education:* University of Minnesota, B.A., 1974. *Hobbies and other interests:* Hiking, canoeing, swimming, reading, gardening, travel.

Addresses

Home and office—915 West California Ave., St. Paul, MN 55117.

Career

Writer. The Loft and Hamline University, St. Paul, MN, instructor in children's book writing; speaker at conferences; St. Paul Public Schools, volunteer. Como Ordway Japanese Garden, volunteer. *Member:* Society of Children's Book Writers and Illustrators, Geological Society of Minnesota, Science Museum of Minnesota, the Loft.

Awards, Honors

Outstanding science trade book, National Science Teachers Association, and Minnesota Book Award nomination, both 1988, both for *The Sun, the Wind, and the Rain;* notable children's trade book in social studies, Children's Book Council, 1990, for *Good Morning, River!;* Children's Choice Book, Children's Book Council, and Children's Books of the Year list, Child Study Children's Book Committee, both 1992, both for *Water's Way;* Minnesota Book Award nomination, 1992, for *Purple Delicious Blackberry Jam;* Outstanding Science Trade Book, National Science Teachers Association, 1994, for *This Way Home;* Children's Choices list, International Reading Association, 1995, for *This Way Home;* Minnesota Book Award nomination, 1996, for *October Smiled Back.*

Writings

The Sun, the Wind, and the Rain, illustrated by Ted Rand, Holt, 1988.
Serengeti, Macmillan, 1989.
Tania's Trolls, illustrated by Sharon Wooding, Arcade, 1989.
The Condor, Macmillan, 1990.
Good Morning, River!, illustrated by Deborah Kogan Ray, Arcade, 1990.
Water's Way, illustrated by Rand, Arcade, 1991.
Purple Delicious Blackberry Jam, illustrated by Barbara McGregor, Arcade, 1992.
This Way Home, illustrated by Norman Chartier, Holt, 1993.
When the Fly Flew In . . . , illustrated by Brad Sneed, Dial, 1994.
The Hayloft, illustrated by K. D. Plum, Dial, 1995.
Meg and Dad Discover Treasures in the Air, illustrated by Deborah Durland DeSaix, Holt, 1995.
October Smiled Back, illustrated by Ed Young, Holt, 1996.
Cold Little Duck, Duck, Duck, illustrated by Sam Williams, Greenwillow, 2000.

Work in Progress

A picture book, *Our Family Tree,* illustrated by Lauren Stringer, for Harcourt; and a picture book of geology poems for Greenwillow.

Sidelights

Lisa Westberg Peters has written both fiction and nonfiction for eager pre-school listeners and beginning readers. Sharing her enthusiasm for science and nature with her audience, Peters also attempts to bring to life the sights and sounds of country life in such books as *The Hayloft, October Smiled Back, Water's Way,* and *Purple Delicious Blackberry Jam.* "Perhaps because I spent childhood summers on a river, I especially like to write picture books involving nature or the natural sciences," Peters once explained to *SATA.* Her approach has proved successful with critics. Calling it a "beautiful book," *School Library Journal* contributor Paula M. Kiely said of Peters's *October Smiled Back* that the "unique and fleeting qualities of time and nature will ring true to children and will recall childhood experiences in adults."

Born in Minneapolis, Minnesota, in 1951, Peters grew up in the city, but was fortunate to spend summers in wooded regions of her home state as well as in neighboring Wisconsin. "The woods and rivers of [these areas] left a strong impression on me as a child," explained the author once to *SATA.* It was during these summer vacations, when she found herself with time on her hands, that Peters first began to dabble in story

writing. Her interest in writing grew during her high school years, and by the time she enrolled at the University of Minnesota, Peters had decided to make writing her vocation. However, as she once recalled to *SATA,* "I chose the more practical field of journalism."

Graduating from the University of Minnesota with a degree in journalism in 1974, Peters soon found herself married and raising a family of two daughters. Reading aloud to her children caused Peters to develop an interest in the spoken sound of prose, and she became attuned to, as she once told *SATA,* "the sounds, patterns, and rhythms found in children's books."

Peters's first published book, *The Sun, the Wind, and the Rain,* appeared in bookstores in 1988. A picture book, the volume tells parallel tales: one tale describes a young child's attempt to make a sand castle at the beach, the other describes the shifting surface of the earth from the work of the elements—wind, sun, and rain. Praised by reviewers, *The Sun, the Wind, and the Rain* was also

But when January froze all her fingers and toes.
We played jungle inside in our tropical clothes.

Peters gives every month a human characteristic in this picture book about the changing nature of friendship. (From October Smiled Back, *illustrated by Ed Young.)*

awarded an outstanding science trade book designation by the National Science Teachers Association. This recognition encouraged Peters to continue in her story-telling efforts.

"Because I'm not a scientist, I recognize the need to make scientific subjects appealing and understandable," Peters once explained to *SATA* in describing such fact-based works as *The Sun, the Wind, and the Rain, Good Morning, River!,* and *The Condor.* "For the sake of young minds, I blend the facts of science with the pull of story. I also try to use simple and expressive language. My ideas come from my own experiences as a mountain climber, a bird watcher, a fossil finder, and from what I hope is a lifelong curiosity about the earth and its creatures. I'm simply trying to gather kids around and help them discover what I am discovering for myself."

In addition to creating picture books that hope to spark young people's interest in the world around them, Peters has indulged in just-for-fun storytelling for the younger set. Her *Purple Delicious Blackberry Jam,* published in 1992, is about two persistent youngsters coaxing their thoroughly modern Grandma into participating in the old fashioned, "gray-haired Granny-type" activity of making jam. Regarding the jam-making saga, which includes going out on a sunny summer day to pick the sweet purple berries, *Booklist* reviewer Hazel Rochman called *Purple Delicious Blackberry Jam* a "delightfully comic story with words and pictures full of character, slapstick, and funny reversals."

In *When the Fly Flew In...,* Peters tackles perhaps the most dreaded task of childhood: cleaning one's room. In the tale a young boy uses his four sleeping pets as an excuse to postpone the inevitable room-cleaning, but a buzzing fly arouses, by turns, the dog, cat, hamster, and parakeet. Fortunately for the boy, the pets' unsuccessful efforts at capturing the irritating intruder result in a tidy bedroom. Calling Peters's imaginative tale "energetic," "clever," and "amusing," *School Library Journal* contributor Kathy Piehl added that *When the Fly Flew In...* "is the stuff of children's fantasies." Ilene Cooper agreed in her *Booklist* appraisal, noting of Peters's book that "the concept is one kids will adore.... Just one look at the book's cover ... and this will be flying off the shelf."

The sources of Peters's inspiration for her fiction are varied, as she once explained to *SATA;* they are "my childhood, my children, my travels, and from a place in my mind where ideas simmer until they're ready." Her 1995 work, *The Hayloft,* weaves several of these inspirations into a book designed for the novice reader. In it, two sisters discover the joys of living on a farm, where the hayloft in an old barn soon becomes their favorite place. Describing the sisters as "appealing characters," *School Library Journal* reviewer Gale W. Sherman described *The Hayloft* as "right on target for newly independent readers." Sherman's praise was echoed by Hazel Rochman, who commented in *Booklist* that the book's "action is funny, the words are simple and lovely."

In addition to her work as a children's book author, Peters volunteers to work with young people interested in science, and teaches at a local university writing school near her home in St. Paul, Minnesota. She enjoys spending time out of doors, whether hiking in the woods, swimming during the warmer weather, or gardening. Describing her writing process, Peters once told *SATA,* "My inspiration to write often comes from a different source: reading great books or listening to great music."

Works Cited

Cooper, Ilene, review of *When the Fly Flew In ...,* *Booklist,* July, 1994, p. 1944.
Kiely, Paula M., review of *October Smiled Back, School Library Journal,* October, 1996, p. 104.
Piehl, Kathy, review of *When the Fly Flew In ...,* *School Library Journal,* September, 1994, p. 192.
Rochman, Hazel, review of *Purple Delicious Blackberry Jam, Booklist,* December 1, 1992, p. 677.
Rochman, review of *The Hayloft, Booklist,* January 1, 1995, p. 828.
Sherman, Gale W., review of *The Hayloft, School Library Journal,* February, 1995, p. 79.

For More Information See

PERIODICALS

Booklist, November 1, 1996, p. 509.
Kirkus Reviews, September 15, 1994, p. 1278; February 15, 1995, p. 231; September 1, 1996, p. 1332.
Publishers Weekly, August 24, 1992, p. 79; August 15, 1994, p. 95; September 16, 1996, p. 81.
School Library Journal, March, 1993, p. 184.

*   *   *

PILKEY, Dav 1966-
(Sue Denim)

Personal

First name is pronounced "Dave"; full name David Murray Pilkey, Jr.; born March 4, 1966, in Cleveland, OH; son of David Murray (a sales manager) and Barbara (an organist; maiden name, Pembridge) Pilkey. *Education:* Kent State University, A.A.

Addresses

Home—Eugene, OR.

Career

Freelance writer and illustrator, 1986—.

Awards, Honors

Caldecott Honor Book, American Library Association, 1997, for *The Paperboy.*

Writings

CHILDREN'S BOOKS; PICTURE BOOKS AND PRIMARY-GRADE FICTION; SELF-ILLUSTRATED, EXCEPT AS NOTED

World War Won, Landmark Editions (Kansas City, MO), 1987.
'Twas the Night before Thanksgiving, Orchard, 1990.
When Cats Dream, Orchard, 1992.
Dogzilla: Starring Flash, Rabies, Dwayne, and Introducing Leia as the Monster, Harcourt, 1993.
Kat Kong: Starring Flash, Rabies, and Dwayne and Introducing Blueberry as the Monster, Harcourt, 1993.
Dog Breath! The Horrible Trouble with Hally Tosis, Blue Sky, 1994.
The Moonglow Roll-O-Rama, Orchard, 1995.
The Hallo-Wiener, Blue Sky, 1995.
The Paperboy, Orchard, 1996.
God Bless the Gargoyles, Harcourt, 1996.
'Twas the Night Before Christmas 2: The Wrath of Mrs. Claus, Blue Sky, 1998.
The Silly Gooses, Blue Sky, 1998.
The Silly Gooses Build a House, Blue Sky, 1998.
Ricky Ricotta's Giant Robot: An Epic Novel, illustrated by Martin Ontiveros, Blue Sky, 2000.
Ricky Ricotta's Giant Robot vs. the Mutant Mosquitoes from Mercury: An Adventure Novel, illustrated by M. Ontiveros, Blue Sky, 2000.

"DRAGON" SERIES; BEGINNING READERS; PUBLISHED BY ORCHARD

A Friend for Dragon, 1991.
Dragon Gets By, 1991.
Dragon's Merry Christmas: Dragon's Third Tale, 1991.
Dragon's Fat Cat: Dragon's Fourth Tale, 1992.
Dragon's Halloween: Dragon's Fifth Tale, 1993.

"DUMB BUNNIES" SERIES; PICTURE BOOKS; WRITTEN UNDER PSEUDONYM SUE DENIM; PUBLISHED BY BLUE SKY

The Dumb Bunnies, 1994.
The Dumb Bunnies' Easter, 1995.
Make Way for Dumb Bunnies, 1996.
The Dumb Bunnies Go to the Zoo, 1997.

"BIG DOG AND LITTLE DOG" SERIES; BOARD BOOKS; PUBLISHED BY HARCOURT

Big Dog and Little Dog, 1997.
Big Dog and Little Dog Getting in Trouble, 1997.
Big Dog and Little Dog Going for a Walk, 1997.
Big Dog and Little Dog Wearing Sweaters, 1998.
Big Dog and Little Dog Guarding the Picnic, 1998.
Big Dog and Little Dog Making a Mistake, 1999.

"CAPTAIN UNDERPANTS" SERIES; MIDDLE-GRADE FICTION; PUBLISHED BY BLUE SKY

The Adventures of Captain Underpants: An Epic Novel, 1997.
Captain Underpants and the Attack of the Talking Toilets: Another Epic Novel, 1999.
Captain Underpants and the Invasion of the Incredibly Naughty Cafeteria Ladies from Outer Space: A Third Epic Novel, 1999.

Dav Pilkey

Captain Underpants and the Perilous Plot of Professor Poopypants: The Fourth Epic Novel, 2000.

ILLUSTRATOR

Adolph J. Moser, *Don't Pop Your Cork on Mondays! The Children's Anti-Stress Book* (nonfiction), Landmark Editions, 1988.
Jerry Segal, *The Place Where Nobody Stopped* (fiction), Orchard, 1991.
Angela Johnson, *Julius* (picture book), Orchard, 1993.

Adaptations

The "Dumb Bunnies" books were adapted into an animated cartoon series for CBS television.

Work in Progress

Ready, Set, Go!, under pseudonym Sue Denim, for HarperCollins.

Sidelights

An author and illustrator of picture books, fiction, and nonfiction, Dav Pilkey is a versatile and prolific creator of books for children from preschool through the middle grades. Considered one of the most popular contemporary authors for readers in elementary school, he is also regarded as a talented artist and inventive humorist as well as a subtle moralist. Pilkey favors broad parodies and farces of art, literature, and popular culture—his books target monster movies, superhero comic books, modern art, science fiction, and classic folktales, among other genres. The author often fills his works with lowbrow humor that appeals to young readers, such as toilet jokes and plots that revolve around such subjects as the effects of dog breath and a hypnotized school principal who thinks he is a superhero and runs around in his underwear. However, Pilkey is also the creator of sensitive, evocative mood pieces, and he underscores his works—even at their most outrageous—with a philosophy that emphasizes friendship, tolerance, and generosity and celebrates the triumph of the good-hearted. Featuring both human and animal characters, the latter both real and imaginary, Pilkey characteristically depicts sweet, sometimes dim protagonists who are misunderstood but end up on top as well as genuinely silly creatures who are blithely unaffected by the stupid things that they do.

Although he is highly regarded for several of his individual works, Pilkey is perhaps best known for four of his series: "Captain Underpants," the "Dumb Bunnies," "Big Dog and Little Dog," and the "Dragon" books. Directed to middle graders, the best-selling "Captain Underpants" stories describe how two mischievous fourth-graders—creators, like the young Pilkey, of their own comic books—use a 3-D Hypno-Ring to turn their mean principal into their own creation, the bumbling but valiant crusader Captain Underpants. The "Dumb Bunnies"—written by Pilkey as Sue Denim, a play on the word "pseudonym"—depicts a family of roly-poly, bucktoothed rabbits who do everything backwards, while the "Dragon" books, simple stories directed to beginning readers, feature a childlike blue dragon whose innocent, well-meaning nature leads him into humorous situations. The "Big Dog and Little Dog" series are board books for very young children about two canine friends whose playfulness gets them into scrapes.

As a literary stylist, Pilkey favors straightforward but lively narratives that are filled with wordplay, especially puns, and jokes; he has also written some of his books in verse. As an artist, Pilkey creates works that range from campy cartoons in bold fluorescent colors to sumptuous, detailed paintings in muted tones. The artist works in a variety of mediums, including watercolor, colored pencil, acrylics, magic markers, collage, and, according to Pilkey, Hamburger Helper and Dijon mustard. Most of Pilkey's art is light-hearted and carries much of the humor of his books; however, some of his works are darker, more mystical and surreal. As with his texts, Pilkey's illustrations are full of allusions. His works include take-offs on well-known paintings by such artists as da Vinci, Van Gogh, Whistler, Grant Wood, and Edward Hopper while echoing the styles of Picasso, Rousseau, Miro, and Chagall, among others. Pilkey's illustrations are often thought to outshine his texts; in addition, he is accused of labored humor and of including allusions that are beyond the scope of his audience. However, Pilkey is also praised as a writer and artist who understands children and what appeals to them and who expresses his distinctive vision in vibrant,

eclectic art. Writing in the *New York Times Book Review,* James Howe, the author of the popular "Bunnicula" series, recommended, "If it's been a while since you've heard a 5-year-old chortle, you owe it to yourself to think of Dav Pilkey when gift giving time rolls around . . . . [He is] a big . . . talent. I look forward to the dreams he will awaken in me and in those children lucky enough to know him in the years to come."

Born in Cleveland, Ohio, to a steel salesman and a church organist, Pilkey recalled his early life in commentary on his website *About Dav:* "I don't remember much about my early childhood, except that I was almost always happy. My parents tell me that I used to laugh in my sleep all the time, even as an infant. When I wasn't laughing, I kept myself busy by drawing. When the other kids in the neighborhood were outside playing baseball and football, I was inside drawing animals, monsters, and super-hero guys. Life was pretty cool when I was little ... and then school started." Pilkey once told *SATA,* "I was never very good at following the rules. My elementary years were spent in a strict parochial school where everyone was expected to be solemn, self-controlled, and obedient. Naturally, I was the class clown. I quickly became well-versed in the art of spitball shooting, paper airplane throwing, and rude noise-making. In first grade I held the classroom record for the number of crayons I could stick up my nose at one time (six)." After setting the school record for the amount of time spent in the principal's office, Pilkey was diagnosed with Attention Deficit Disorder (ADD) and severe hyperactivity. By second grade, he had spent so much time standing in the school hallway that his teacher moved a desk there just for him. Pilkey once remembered in *SATA,* "I was the only kid in the whole school with my own personal desk out in the hall, and I made good use of it." Keeping his desk—which stayed in the hall through the end of fifth grade—well stocked with pencils, paper, magic markers, and crayons, Pilkey spent his detention time immersed in drawing. He once noted in *SATA,* "I spent so much time drawing out in the hall that I became an artist."

As with art, Pilkey developed an interest in writing while sitting at his desk in the hall. In an interview with Sally Lodge in *Publishers Weekly,* he stated, "I'd draw pictures to relieve my boredom. Then I began making comic books, since they seemed to make my stories come alive." Pilkey stapled together sheets of paper to make his own books, which he filled with the adventures of a group of superheroes; one of these creations was Captain Underpants, who would later surface in his own series. Pilkey once recalled in *SATA,* "These comic books were a real hit with my classmates, but not with my teachers. I remember one teacher who, after furiously ripping up one of my stories, told me I'd better start taking life more seriously, because I couldn't spend the rest of my days making silly books. Lucky for me, I wasn't a very good listener either." After graduating from grade school, Pilkey attended a strict high school where his sense of humor continued to be unappreciated by his teachers. He wrote on his website, "One day my principal took me out of class and said to me, 'I know you think you're special because you can draw, but let me tell you something: artists are a dime-a-dozen. You will *never* make a living as an artist!' Those words haunted me for many years. How delightful it was to prove him wrong."

In 1984, Pilkey began attending Kent State University as an art major. The professor who taught freshman English complimented Pilkey on his creative writing and encouraged him to write books. Thinking that this was an idea with some merit, Pilkey began to work on his first children's book. He entered this book, *World War Won,* in the "National Written and Illustrated By ..." contest, a competition for students sponsored by Landmark Editions of Kansas City, Missouri. The winner of the contest was to have his or her book published. *World War Won* was awarded the grand prize and, at nineteen, Pilkey became a published author. He recalled on his website, "It was the most exciting time in my life. I'll never forget getting off the plane in Kansas City and meeting my new publisher for the first time. I tried to act normal, but I was so excited. It took every bit of self-control I had not to scream, jump up and down, and laugh hysterically ... I was going to be an author!"

A picture book written in verse, *World War Won* describes how the leaders of two animal kingdoms, fighting for power, stockpile weapons to use against each other. The result of their stockpiling is a "nuclear freeze" in which both piles of weapons are sprayed with water and then left at Icicle Springs, which is always frozen. "The moral, of course," according to *School Library Journal* contributor Susan Scheps, "is that peace comes only through understanding and cooperation." Scheps added that Pilkey's full-page colored pencil cartoons "are of professional caliber" and that *World War Won* "provides a model for other hopeful young authors." After the publication of his first book, Pilkey began to research the genre of children's literature more thoroughly. He once recalled to *SATA,* "When I really got serious about writing children's books, I began reading everything I could by my favorite writers, Arnold Lobel, Cynthia Rylant, James Marshall, and Harry Allard. I read *Frog and Toad, Henry and Mudge, George and Martha,* and *The Stupids* over and over again, until I started to pick up rhythms and recognize patterns. Soon I began to see what really *worked* in these books—what made them great pieces of literature." Pilkey met the author of *Henry and Mudge* (and other notable children's books), Cynthia Rylant, in a writer's group in Kent, Ohio, in the late 1980s; they have been companions ever since. In 1990, Pilkey dreamed that he was supposed to move to Oregon, so he and Rylant relocated to Eugene three years later. He wrote on his website, "Moving to Oregon was a great adventure for us, because Cyndi and I had never even seen Oregon before. We kind of felt like the early pioneers who traveled the Oregon Trail for the promise of a better life.

In this Caldecott Honor book, an African-American boy and his dog deliver the Saturday morning newspaper before sunrise then return to bed and dream about flying across the night sky. (From The Paperboy, *written and illustrated by Pilkey.)*

Of course, the pioneers encountered many hardships along the way, including starvation, disease, and death. The only hardship we encountered along the way was once when we got french fries at Burger King, and they were kind of soggy."

In 1991, Pilkey produced the first of his "Dragon" books, *A Friend for Dragon* and *Dragon Gets By.* In *A Friend for Dragon,* the gentle soul is tricked by a snake into believing that an apple is his friend. A hungry walrus eats the apple, and Dragon is crushed. However, after he buries the core, a tree grows that bears a whole crop of new "friends" for Dragon. In *Dragon Gets By,* Dragon spends a day doing everything wrong—for example, he reads an egg, then fries the morning paper—before watering his bed and going to sleep on his plants. In subsequent volumes of the series, Dragon celebrates Halloween and Christmas in his own inimitable way and adopts a stray cat, learning by trial and error how to take care of her. Assessing *A Friend for Dragon* and *Dragon Gets By,* a critic in *Publishers Weekly* stated, "With his excellent vocabulary choices and crafty characterizations—small squiggles carry large meanings—Pilkey has created a positively precious prehistoric prototype." *Booklist* critic Carolyn Phelan, reviewing *Dragon's Fat Cat: Dragon's Fourth Tale,* added, "The Dragon series is fast moving toward that pantheon of children's reading reserved for books that make kids laugh out loud.... [W]hat more could we ask for newcomers than the intrinsic reward of a genuinely funny book? Again and again, Pilkey delivers." In a review of *Dragon's Halloween: Dragon's Fifth Tale,* a critic in *Publishers Weekly* concluded, "Bright blue Dragon never disappoints; Pilkey's series hero is affability incarnate."

In 1994, Pilkey launched his "Dumb Bunnies" series under the non de plume Sue Denim. Created as an homage to Harry Allard and James Marshall, the creators of the "Stupids" books, the series features the adventures of a family of clueless bunnies that are depicted in deadpan text and brightly colored cartoons. Pilkey parodies "The Three Bears" and "Little Red Riding Hood" in the first volume of the series, *The Dumb Bunnies.* In this work, Little Red Goldilocks wreaks havoc until Baby Bunny flushes her down the toilet. Subsequent volumes continue the escapades of the loopy lapins, who confuse holiday customs in *The Dumb Bunnies' Easter,* visit the beach during a storm in *Make Way for Dumb Bunnies,* and cause a riot when they let the animals out of their cages in *The Dumb Bunnies Go to the Zoo.* In his review of *The Dumb Bunnies* in *Bulletin of the Center for Children's Books,* Roger Sutton said that "the Dumb Bunnies are the Stupids in pink fur." Mary Harris Veeder of *Booklist,* reviewing *The Dumb Bunnies' Easter,* claimed, "The Bunny family is a worthy successor to those all-time favorites the Stupids.... This is dumbness supreme and a real treat." *The Dumb Bunnies* became an animated series on CBS television in the late 1990s. At around the same time, Pilkey introduced a new series, the "Silly Gooses," which is akin to the "Dumb Bunnies" in its depiction of anthropomorphic animals who engage in backwards

behavior. The books feature Mr. and Mrs. Goose and their goslings Ketchup and Mustard, named after their parents' favorite ice cream toppings.

In contrast to his humorous books, Pilkey has written and illustrated several picture books that showcase the full range of his talents as an illustrator and present young readers with more serious and meditative subjects. One book of this type, *The Paperboy,* was named a Caldecott Medal Honor Book for its illustrations in 1997. A young African-American boy, accompanied by his dog, rises before dawn to deliver his papers on a Saturday morning; after finishing their job, the pair go back to bed and dream about flying across the night sky. According to *School Library Journal* reviewer Wendy Lukehart, Pilkey "paints their shared experience with a graceful economy of language"; the critic concluded by calling *The Paperboy* "[a] totally satisfying story." Pilkey illustrates his book with acrylic paintings that, according to Carolyn Phelan in *Booklist,* "include beautifully composed landscapes and interiors." *Horn Book* contributor Mary M. Burns added that the emphasis of the pictures "is on balance and geometric form, giving solidity to this celebration of routine (so dear to the heart of preschoolers). Yet this interpretation is never boring, for the palette is rich and inviting, and situations are exotic for children whose days begin in light, not darkness."

With his "Big Dog and Little Dog" series, Pilkey has created a number of books for the youngest child. In these works, picture books with minimal text and large illustrations printed on thick cardboard, two devoted canine companions go for walks, play in puddles, and snuggle together while demonstrating both the sweet and more fun-loving sides of their personalities. The sixth volume of the series, *Big Dog and Little Dog Making a Mistake,* describes what happens when the duo mistake a skunk for a kitten and then disrupt a party. Writing in *School Library Journal,* Maura Bresnahan predicted that babies and toddlers will find "the colorful illustrations appealing but the humor will be better appreciated by older children." The critic added that the simple sentence structure and repetitive text "makes this board book ideal for those just learning to read."

After becoming an author and illustrator, Pilkey began to visit schools in order to talk to children. In his lectures, he would explain how he found his calling while sitting in the hallway of his elementary school. Pilkey told *Publishers Weekly,* "Inevitably, the name 'Captain Underpants' would come up, and though I cracked jokes throughout my presentation, the mention of this name would get by far the biggest laugh. And whenever I mentioned the title of one of my early Captain Underpants comic books, which involved talking toilets, the room would explode with laughter. That's when I knew I had to do a book about him." *The Adventures of Captain Underpants: An Epic Novel* was published in 1997. In this work, two misbehaving fourth graders at Jerome Horwitz Elementary School, introverted Harold Hutchins and extroverted George Beard, write their own comic books; Pilkey described Harold and George in

Using the pseudonym Sue Denim, Pilkey wrote and illustrated this first installment in a series about a family of dim-witted hares. (From Make Way for Dumb Bunnies.*)*

Publishers Weekly as "kind of like the yin and yang of my personality." Their nemesis is the crabby principal, Mr. Krupp. After George and Harold hypnotize Mr. Krupp with a 3-D Hypno-Ring, he becomes one of their comic-book creations, Captain Underpants, whenever he hears fingers snapped. Clad in his briefs and a cape and carrying a roll of toilet paper, Captain Underpants stands for "Truth, Justice, and ALL that is Preshrunk and Cottony." Captain Underpants fights criminals such as bank robbers and robot thieves by giving them wedgies; he then confronts a mad scientist, the evil Dr. Diaper, who is intent on controlling the world. Distracting the doctor with doggy-doo, the boys and Captain Underpants save the planet; Harold and George then de-hypnotize their principal and hustle him back into his street clothes.

Pilkey illustrated *The Adventures of Captain Underpants* with black and white cartoons, but he also animates one chapter by means of what he calls "Flip-O-Rama," a device by which readers can flip the pages back and forth for an animation effect. Writing in *Booklist,* Stephanie Zvirin said that the silliness "goes overboard ... and the many action-packed illustrations rob the plot of some of its zip by commanding more than their share

of attention." Zvirin concluded, "Still, the humor is on target for some kids in this age group...." A critic in *Kirkus Reviews* added, "There'll be no silence in the library once readers get hold of this somewhat classier alternative to Barf-o-Rama," while a reviewer in the *Horn Book Guide* noted that the story "is consistently laugh-out-loud funny." Released simultaneously by Scholastic/Blue Sky Press in both hardcover and paperback editions, *The Adventures of Captain Underpants* has sold more than one million copies.

The second volume of the "Captain Underpants" saga, *Captain Underpants and the Attack of the Talking Toilets: Another Epic Novel,* was released immediately after the publication of its predecessor. Drawing once again from the comic books that he created as a youngster, Pilkey relates how George and Harold use school brain Melvin's science project, a copying machine that changes images into matter, to reproduce their latest comic book. Inadvertently, the boys set loose an army of teacher-eating toilets led by the evil Turbo Toilet 2000. Captain Underpants—with the aid of Wedgie Power and his Incredible Robo-Plunger—saves the school, and the boys get to become principals for a Day. In *Captain Underpants and the Invasion of the*

Incredibly Naughty Cafeteria Ladies from Outer Space: A Third Epic Novel, George and Harold fool the cafeteria staff into baking cupcakes that flood Jerome Horwitz Elementary School with goo. After the staff quits, Principal Krupp mistakenly hires an alien trio to take their place. The aliens begin turning the students into zombie nerds, so Harold, George, and Captain Underpants are called into action and end up saving the world from an alien invasion. In *Captain Underpants and the Perilous Plot of Professor Poopypants: The Fourth Epic Novel,* the boys invoke the wrath of Professor Pippy P. Poopypants, a scientific genius who gets no respect because of his name. When chaos ensues, Captain Underpants dons his undies once again.

Reviewing the second volume of the series, which like the first book was a best-seller and contains chapters done in Flip-O-Rama, *Booklist* critic John Peters said that *Talking Toilets* is "[d]estined to be as popular as the first book," while a reviewer in the *Horn Book Guide* called it "[p]art graphic novel, part tongue-in-cheek parody, ... very hip and funny." In *School Library Journal,* reviewer Marlene Gawron noted, "The fun is in the reading, which is full of puns, rhymes, and nonsense along with enough revenge and wish fulfillment for every downtrodden fun-seeking kid who never wanted to read a book." Adding that the cartoon drawings and Flip-O-Rama pages make the work "so appealing that youngsters won't notice that their vocabulary is stretching," Gawron concluded, "Hooray for Captain Underpants!" Speaking to *Publishers Weekly,* Pilkey stated, "If my books can help kids get excited about writing and reading, that is great, but that really isn't what I was after. Really, I just wanted to make them laugh." Pilkey is also the creator of another series with roots in science fiction, the "Ricky Ricotta" books. In these works, a lonely little mouse befriends a giant robot who takes on the school bullies, rescues the city from an evil rat scientist, and saves the world from an invasion of massive mosquitoes from Mercury.

In addition to the works that he has written and illustrated, Pilkey has provided the pictures for *Don't Pop Your Cork on Mondays! The Children's Anti-Stress Book,* a nonfiction handbook for children on the causes and effects of childhood stress by psychologist Adolph J. Moser; *The Place Where Nobody Stopped,* a folktale-like story by Jerry Segal about how a young Jewish man and his family change the life of a lonely Russian baker when they come to stay with him; and *Julius,* a humorous picture book by Angela Johnson that features an Alaskan pig who lives with an African-American family. Pilkey received special notice for his paintings for this book, multimedia collages that were composed by using fabrics and instant coffee as well as more traditional mediums. Writing in *Horn Book,* Ellen Fader noted that Pilkey's pictures "constitute an evolution from his more modest efforts," while *Bulletin of the Center for Children's Books* reviewer Betsy Hearne concluded that the artist's paintings "are a major factor in the hilarity. He translates a keen sense of the ridiculous into vivacious hues and wildly varied patterns without ever getting cluttered."

Pilkey once observed to *SATA:* "One of my biggest inspirations as an illustrator is the drawings of children. Children often send me pictures that they've drawn, and I'm always amazed at the way they present shape and color. Children are natural impressionists. They're not afraid to make their trees purple and yellow, and it's okay if the sky is green with red stripes.... [W]hen children are drawing, anything goes! Of course, you know that one day an art teacher is going to grab hold of these kids and turn them all into accountants, but while they are still fresh and naive, children can create some of the freshest and most beautiful art there is." He added on his website, "When I was a kid making silly books out in the hall, I never dreamed that one day I'd be making silly books for a living. The coolest thing is that I used to get in trouble for being the class clown ... and now it's my job."

Works Cited

Review of *The Adventures of Captain Underpants: An Epic Novel, Horn Book Guide,* July-December, 1997, p. 79.

Review of *The Adventures of Captain Underpants: An Epic Novel, Kirkus Reviews,* June 1, 1997, p. 678.

Bresnahan, Maura, review of *Big Dog and Little Dog Make a Mistake, School Library Journal,* June, 1999, p. 109.

Burns, Mary M., review of *The Paperboy, Horn Book,* July-August, 1996, p. 453.

Review of *Captain Underpants and the Attack of the Talking Toilets: Another Epic Novel, Horn Book Guide,* January-June, 1999.

Review of *Dragon's Halloween: Dragon's Fifth Tale, Publishers Weekly,* September 20, 1993, p. 30.

Fader, Ellen, review of *Julius, Horn Book,* March-April, 1993, pp. 196-97.

Review of *A Friend for Dragon* and *Dragon Gets By, Publishers Weekly,* December 21, 1990, p. 56.

Gawron, Marlene, review of *Captain Underpants and the Attack of the Talking Toilets: Another Epic Novel, School Library Journal,* June, 1999, p. 136.

Hearne, Betsy, review of *Julius, Bulletin of the Center for Children's Books,* May, 1993, p. 284.

Howe, James, "Perchance to Dream," *New York Times Book Review,* November 8, 1992, p. 57.

Lodge, Sally, "Dav Pilkey's Captain Underpants Wins a Starring Role," *Publishers Weekly,* February 22, 1999, p. 32.

Lukehart, Wendy, review of *The Paperboy, School Library Journal,* March, 1996, pp. 180-81.

Peters, John, review of *Captain Underpants and the Attack of the Talking Toilets: Another Epic Novel, Booklist,* May 1, 1999.

Phelan, Carolyn, review of *Dragon's Fat Cat: Dragon's Fourth Tale, Booklist,* February 1, 1992, p. 1029.

Phelan, Carolyn, review of *The Paperboy, Booklist,* March 1, 1996, p. 1179.

Pilkey, Dav, *The Adventures of Captain Underpants: An Epic Novel,* Blue Sky, 1997.

Pilkey, Dav, "The Almost Completely True Adventures of Dav Pilkey," *About Dav* (website), http://www.pilkey.com/abdavs.htm, January 21, 2000.

Scheps, Susan, review of *World War Won, School Library Journal,* March, 1988, p. 174.

Sutton, Roger, review of *The Dumb Bunnies, Bulletin of the Center for Children's Books,* January, 1994, p. 150.

Veeder, Mary Harris, review of *The Dumb Bunnies' Easter, Booklist,* February 1, 1995, p. 1009.

Zvirin, Stephanie, review of *The Adventures of Captain Underpants: An Epic Novel, Booklist,* July 19, 1997, p. 1819.

For More Information See

BOOKS

Children's Literature Review, Volume 48, Gale, 1998, pp. 99-114.

PERIODICALS

Booklist, October 1, 1996, p. 1406.

Bulletin of the Center for Children's Books, April, 1998, p. 292.

Kirkus Reviews, December 15, 1997, p. 72.

Publishers Weekly, October 14, 1996, p. 82.*

—*Sketch by Gerard J. Senick*

R

RAMSTAD, Ralph L. 1919-

Personal

Born September 15, 1919, in Minneapolis, MN; son of Otto (a high school teacher) and Otilia (a homemaker; maiden name, Ellertson) Ramstad; married Ruth Belton (a homemaker), January 29, 1949; children: Patricia, Marit, Deirdre Ramstad Lotter, Lockie Ramstad Chapman, Holly Ramstad Birkeland, Erik, Roslyn Ramstad Hawley. *Education:* Attended Pratt Institute, 1938-41. *Politics:* "Usually Democrat." *Religion:* "A liberal Protestant."

Addresses

Home and office—4509 Zenith Ave., Minneapolis, MN 55410. *E-mail*—RalphRuth@aol.com.

Career

Freelance illustrator, New York City, 1948-54; advertising and marketing illustrator, including work for Pillsbury Co., General Mills, Inc., and Naegele Outdoor Advertising, Minneapolis, MN, 1954-85; editorial illustrator, 1985—. *Military service:* U.S. Army Air Forces, 1941-46; served in Pacific theater; became first sergeant.

Illustrator

J. Bechtdolt, *Oliver Becomes a Weatherman,* Messner (New York City), 1953.
Bechtdolt, *Oliver Sounds Off,* Messner, 1953.
W. Reiner, *The Flying Rangers,* Messner, 1954.
Julie Dunlap, *Birds in the Bushes: A Story about Margaret Morse Nice,* Carolrhoda (Minneapolis, MN), 1996.
Andy Russell Bowen, *The Back of Beyond: A Story about Lewis and Clark,* Carolrhoda, 1996.
Tekla N. White, *The Flight of the Union,* Carolrhoda, 1998.
Jeri Ferris, *With Open Hands: A Story about Biddy Mason,* Carolrhoda, 1999.
Tom Streissguth, *John Brown,* Carolrhoda, 1999.

Ralph L. Ramstad

Jane A. Schott, *Diane Fossey and the Mountain Gorillas,* Carolrhoda, 1999.

Contributor of illustrations to periodicals, including *Story Parade, Young America,* and *Calling All Girls.*

Work in Progress

Research on the life and works of Jules Verne.

Sidelights

Ralph L. Ramstad told *SATA:* "All my life (well, honestly, from the age of three) I have been drawing pictures. I have attempted to create, first for myself and then for others, visual experiences of times past or robust adventures in faraway places. The story of Peter Pan was my first attempt, after seeing the film in 1924. I believe this imagining of an unattainable world is what brought me into illustration in the first place and what colors my subject preferences and objectives. Histories and biographies, particularly of the eighteenth and nineteenth centuries, the days of the horse, are my great favorites. Research is an obsession with me; it's half the fun of illustrating and certainly the challenge for deserving trust.

"Drawing the horse and other domestic and wild animals has always been my avocation. I learned animal anatomy before that of the human. Then I went to art school and learned many things. Pratt Institute in Brooklyn, New York, was not only where I absorbed basics of figure, perspective, anatomy, and painting, but many popular illustrators of the day were frequent lecturers and instructors. (Norman Rockwell was a frequent guest.) This was the late thirties, and magazine illustration was still at its peak. As students, we each had our favorite illustrators and imagined our careers to follow theirs as our talents matured, but World War II came upon us and changed things in many ways for many people.

"Immediately upon graduating from Pratt in 1941, I served in the Army Air Forces for four-and-a-half years, including service with the 13th 'jungle' air force in New Guinea and the Philippines. Returning to civilian life was a scramble to re-educate, go back to Brooklyn, get married, start a family, and try to catch up with something in the field of illustration.

"I drew adventure strips for comic books, worked for a large display house, and freelanced advertising illustration. Most rewarding for me personally was work in the children's publishing field: notably *Story Parade* magazine from 1948 to 1954, Julian Messner's *Everyday Science Stories* in 1953 and 1954, and *Young America* magazine, a publication of the Boy Scouts of America, also in the fifties.

"Moving to Minnesota in 1954 with a growing family, I found employment, freelance or staff, with (among others) the Pillsbury Company, several art studios, and General Mills. At General Mills, for several years my best contributions to children's illustration were the games and stories on the backs of well known cereal packages.

"At this time I was also active in portraiture for corporations and individuals. I have since found it more rewarding, in every way, to paint only the portraits of horses! I have also worked in the outdoor advertising industry as an illustrator, creating comprehensive layouts for sales. I retired from this work before computers would replace me.

"As to my methods of working: there are few media available that I have not used. When working for reproduction, as in book illustration, I have found acrylic inks to be ideal for me—brush and pen, basically, with possibly oil pastel and wax pencil touches added to get the effect I need. I do use the computer but only, so far, as a sketch tool."

* * *

RICE, Dick
See RICE, R. Hugh

* * *

RICE, R. Hugh 1929-
(Richard H. Rice, Dick Rice)

Personal

Born October 29, 1929, in Ashtabula, OH; son of Harry B. (a cabinet maker) and Helen (a bookkeeper; maiden name, Haller) Rice; married Verda M. Casey (a homemaker), November 20, 1949; children: Richard C., Bonnie Rice Morrow, Bridget Rice Madden, Kimberly. *Education:* Attended Florida State University, 1960; Cochise College, A.A. and A.A.S (with honors), 1980; attended Northern Arizona University, 1981-82. *Religion:* Protestant.

Addresses

Home and office—1152 Lee Ave., Ridgecrest, CA 93555.

Career

U.S. Air Force, career non-commissioned officer as electronic technician, instructor in electronics and weapons, special agent with Office of Special Investigations, and photo-journalist, 1948-72, including chief of civic action team in Vietnam, 1967-68, retiring as master sergeant; worked as photography instructor for civil service unit of U.S. Army; scuba diving instructor, 1977-82; U.S. Marine Corps, director of aquatic sports in Okinawa, 1984-85; photo-journalist with U.S. Marine Corps and U.S. Navy in Okinawa, 1985-86. U.S. Army, water sports supervisor at Fort Huachuca, 1977-78; worked as private detective, 1980-82. *Member:* Society of Children's Book Writers and Illustrators, Professional Association of Diving Instructors (emeritus instructor), Confederation Mondiale des Activites Subaquatiques.

R. Hugh Rice

Awards, Honors

Military—Air Force Commendation Medal, Air Force Outstanding Unit Medal, Vietnamese Cross of Gallantry, and Vietnamese Civil Action Honor Medal.

Writings

(With Walter Deas,) *Underwater Photography,* Ure Smith (Sydney, Australia), 1977.

(Photographer) *Okinawa, the Southern Gateway,* Excel Art Publishers (Okinawa, Japan), 1986.

Dragonflies, illustrated by Gary Torrisi, Richard C. Owen (Katonah, NY), 1996.

Flip Flop, illustrated by Neesa Becker, Richard C. Owen, 1998.

Log Garfish, illustrated by Bruce Macdonald, Richard C. Owen, 2000.

Mother Octopus, illustrated by Jo-Ellen Bosson, Richard C. Owen, 2000.

Hawaiian correspondent, *Dive South Pacific* and *Skindiving in Australia,* 1968-72. Sports columnist for Florida newspapers, including *Alert,* between 1958 and 1964. Contributor to periodicals, including *Writer, All Florida, Ford Times, Our Navy, Paddler, Canoe and Kayak, Triton,* and *Oregon Coast.*

Work in Progress

Sea Lights, Houses under the Sea, The Amazing Hummers, Frogs and Toads, Pico's Message Bottle, Bubble Nose, and *Why Cats Sniff Noses,* all for Richard C. Owen.

Sidelights

R. Hugh Rice told *SATA:* "My first publishing success was at age fifteen, when I had a poem published in the *Monroeville Spectator,* in Monroeville, Ohio. As a youth I was a poor and troubled student. I dropped out of school at age sixteen and didn't complete my education until age fifty-three, when I graduated from college with degrees in journalism and criminal justice. In 1953 I received a high school equivalency certificate from the state of Arizona. In 1959 I passed the Air Universities college-level General Equivalency Diploma and was thus eligible for entry into college and university courses.

"In 1960 I completed a course in creative writing given by Florida State University. In 1971, three years after returning from Vietnam, I completed a course in article writing given by the Writer's Digest School. These simple accomplishments enhanced my confidence in my writing activities. In 1977 I coauthored the book *Underwater Photography* with old friend and mentor, Walt Deas of Sydney, Australia. (Earlier he had connected me with *Dive South Pacific* and *Skindiving in Australia* magazines, and I had become their Hawaiian correspondent.) What success I've had in writing is due in great part to the kindness and encouragement shown me by teachers, author friends, magazine and book editors, and publishers worldwide.

"Being an adventurer and job opportunist (accepting dangerous and challenging jobs in exotic and foreign countries) has filled my memory bank with an infinite source for stories. I have been able to turn the few failures I've had into opportunities. After washing out of two high-tech military courses I gained positions with various Air Force newspapers as a photo-journalist, further enhancing my writing abilities. These experiences paid off years later when I gained employment with the Navy and Marine Corps on Okinawa, Japan, as a photo-journalist. I wrote and edited their sports and entertainment guide.

"Although I have only been writing children's books since 1993, I find the genre enjoyable and satisfying."

*   *   *

RICE, Richard H.
See RICE, R. Hugh

Eileen Ross

ROSS, Eileen 1950-

Personal

Born June 2, 1950, in Denver, CO; daughter of James (a civil engineer) and Doris (a homemaker; maiden name, Spry) Russell; married Peter Ross (a teacher), June 12, 1976; children: Stephanie, David, Annie. *Education:* Attended Knox College, 1968-70; University of Northern Colorado, B.A., 1972, followed by graduate study. *Religion:* Roman Catholic. *Hobbies and other interests:* Reading, oil painting.

Addresses

Home—1307 South Sherman St., Longmont, CO 80501.

Career

Special education teacher at an elementary school in Craig, CO, 1972-79; writer and homemaker, Longmont, CO, 1979-94; teacher of fifth grade at an elementary school in Frederick, CO, 1994—. *Member:* Society of Children's Book Writers and Illustrators.

Writings

Josh, Royal Fireworks Press, 1994.

The Halloween Showdown, illustrated by Lynn Rowe Reed, Holiday House (New York City), 1999.

Contributor of articles, stories, and poems, to magazines, including *Turtle, Humpty Dumpty, Friend,* and *U*S*Kids.*

Sidelights

Eileen Ross told *SATA:* "I don't remember my first experience with writing as a young child, and I can't say that I wanted to be a writer 'all my life.' What I do remember is my love affair with books.

"Every Saturday, my brothers and sisters and I all piled into the family Chevy, and my father took us to the public library. We were allowed only three books, so I dug through the stacks looking for the best possible three. Then, when our books were checked out, we all headed outside to the playground. I remember swings and the merry-go-round and tall shade trees. We played and laughed and chased each other until Daddy finally called out that it was time to leave. We never complained (much!) because our next stop was the grocery store.

"My mother stayed home because she was always recuperating from and caring for a new baby, or so it seemed! (I am second-oldest of nine children.) My father did the grocery shopping, and I can remember watching him pencil out the shopping list before we headed to the library. I still remember learning to read the word 'catsup' which doesn't look at all like the word 'ketchup' sounds, and I learned that 'TP' stands for toilet paper. In my mind, this was my first exposure to some of the quirks of written language.

"In spite of the quirks, my memories of books revolve around eagerly anticipated Saturday mornings, playgrounds, and food—also the sound of Daddy's voice. We'd all cuddle up on the couch or at Daddy's feet, and he'd read aloud to us. I've never met anyone who could become so many different characters just by changing the inflection in his voice. It was magical. Somehow my father's voice actually transported us to wherever the story took place. He was great with the Sunday comics, too, which he read aloud after church.

"It's funny, my mother always read to us, too, but I don't have strong memories of it. My guess is that two-o'clock-in-the-morning feedings and colicky babies in a household of nine kids had a way of taking some of the sparkle out of her voice when she finally sat down to read to us. Nevertheless, I grew up knowing that reading and books were valued, and I was hooked.

"In elementary school, I learned to read easily. One primary teacher told me that I was very 'creative' and 'wrote nice stories.' I don't remember any of the specifics, but I do remember trusting myself when asked to write a story. After all, the teacher told me I was creative, and I believed her. Even so, I never thought too much about writing, because reading was my true

When a witch snatches away her grandkitten, Grandmother Kitt enlists the help of a disgruntled spider, bat, and frog to defeat the evil Grizzorka. (Cover illustration by Lynn Rowe Reed.)

passion. In the beginning, I wrote only what was required and no more.

"Then I got my first job as a teacher of handicapped kids, and I decided to write a book about my experiences. I wrote diligently for about two weeks, but couldn't stand reading what I'd written. It was awful! The only real writing I'd done up to this point (besides required assignments) was in college. I wrote poorly crafted, morose poems to help me get through periods of homesickness and loneliness. They were meant for my eyes alone, so it was okay if they weren't any good. Now I was trying to write a book meant for others to read. I put the whole mess away and didn't try again. I confined my writing to lesson plans and letters to family and friends.

"Then I married and had three children. I wanted to give my kids the same wonderful gift my father had given me—the love of books. So each day I held my children in my lap and read to them ... every single day. It was part of the routine. Then something funny happened. I stopped thinking about the good I was doing my kids, and I started focusing on the books themselves. I must have read thousands. Some were great, some were terrible, but a small kernel of possibility was eating away in my brain. 'Eileen, you can do this! You can

write for children.' I grew up surrounded by children, I'd been teaching children for eight years, and now I had three children of my own.

"It wasn't as easy as I thought. I started writing stories for kids and even had the guts to send them to publishers. The rejections came by return mail. I refused to give up. There were more rejections. Some days I suspected that I was single-handedly keeping the U.S. Postal Service in business.

"I started taking writing classes through correspondence, through continuing education. I read and reread every book about writing I could find. I read children's books. I analyzed them, tore them apart, and then put them back together again, looking for the key to how to write. Mostly I taught myself how to write by the only way that works for me. I learned to write simply by writing.

"Every day when nap time came, I'd take the telephone off the hook and write. When my oldest daughter toddled off to preschool and the baby was asleep—no television for me—I'd write. Kindergarten—half-day of writing—no excuses! When my youngest child was finally in school and no teaching job materialized—write, write, write.

"My mother thought I was nuts, but my husband believed in me. I believed in me. I even had the guts to write the word 'writer' on a loan application. Then I had to prove it, and I did!

"One summer day, I headed out to the mailbox (which I'd grown to hate, yet was drawn to like an addict—how many rejections would there be today?). I opened the letter from the magazine *U*S* Kids.* I sold not one story, but two! I earned five hundred dollars. I was ecstatic! My hands shook. I was a writer. Five hundred dollars, and it only took—how many years?

"That first sale was in 1989. Since then I've sold more than fifty pieces to magazines—nonfiction, poetry, short stories. I sold my first novel, *Josh,* in 1994, and my first picture book, *The Halloween Showdown,* was published in 1999. There is no greater thrill short of having children.

"I have since gone back to teaching. I don't plan on having any more children, but I do plan on having more books—lots of them. On one of them, I'm not sure which one yet, for it has to be my best, I've already planned the dedication. It will read, 'With love and thanks to my dad who took me to the library on Saturdays.'"

For More Information See

PERIODICALS

Publishers Weekly, September 27, 1999, p. 47.
School Library Journal, September, 1999, p. 201.

S

SALSITZ, R.A.V.
See SALSITZ, Rhondi Vilott

* * *

SALSITZ, Rhondi Vilott
(R. A. V. Salsitz, Rhondi Vilott; Elizabeth Forrest, Charles Ingrid, pseudonyms)

Personal

Female; married; four children.

Addresses

Agent—c/o DAW Books, 375 Hudson St., 3rd Floor, New York, NY 10014-3658. *E-mail*—rhondi@ earthlink.net.

Career

Novelist.

Writings

UNDER NAME RHONDI VILOTT

Black Dragon's Curse, Signet Books (New York City), 1984.
Challenge of the Pegasus Grail, Signet Books, 1984.
The Dungeons of Dregnor, Signet Books, 1984.
Spellbound, Signet Books, 1984.
Sword Daughter's Quest, Signet Books, 1984.
The Towers of Rexor, Signet Books, 1984.
The Unicorn Crown, Signet Books, 1984
Aphrodite's Mirror, Signet Books, 1985.
Hall of the Gargoyle King, Signet Books, 1985.
Maiden of Greenwold, Signet Books, 1985.
Pledge of Peril, Signet Books, 1985.
Runesword!, Signet Books, 1985.
Secret of the Sphinx, Signet Books, 1985.

FICTION · 88677-UE2648
(CANADA $6.99) · U.S. $5.99

DEATH WATCH

"I hope that Elizabeth Forrest becomes a household name... as she deserves to be."
—DEAN R. KOONTZ

ELIZABETH FORREST

Written under the pseudonym Elizabeth Forrest, Rhondi Vilott Salsitz's virtual-reality thriller revolves around McKenzie Smith's escape from a vicious serial killer stalking beautiful women in Los Angeles. (Cover illustration by Miles Long.)

Storm Rider, Signet Books, 1985.

UNDER NAME R.A.V. SALSITZ

Where Dragons Lie, Signet Books, 1985.
The Unicorn Dancer, Signet Books, 1986.
Where Dragons Rule, Signet Books, 1986.
Daughter of Destiny, Signet Books, 1988.
Night of Dragons, Roc (New York City), 1990.

UNDER PSEUDONYM CHARLES INGRID

Solar Kill (Sand Wars #1), DAW Books (New York City), 1987.
Celestial Hit List, DAW Books, 1988.
Lasertown Blues (Sand Wars #2), DAW Books, 1988.
Alien Salute, DAW Books, 1989.
Return Fire (Sand Wars #5), DAW Books, 1989.
Challenge Met, DAW Books, 1990.
The Last Recall (Marked Man #1), DAW Books, 1991.
Radius of Doubt (Patterns of Chaos #1), DAW Books, 1991.

UNDER PSEUDONYM ELIZABETH FORREST

Phoenix Fire, DAW Books, 1992.
Dark Tide, DAW Books, 1993.
Death Watch, DAW Books, 1995.
Garbage Boy, Ulverscrof, 1996.
Killjoy, DAW Books, 1996.
Bright Shadow, DAW Books, 1997.
Retribution, DAW Books, 1998.
Whirlwind, DAW Books, 1999.

UNDER NAME RHONDI VILOTT SALSITZ

The Twilight Gate, illustrated by Alan M. Clark, Walker (New York City), 1993.

Sidelights

Rhondi Vilott Salsitz is a prolific writer whose love of writing and books began in childhood, when she spent many hours in the children's library in her hometown. "I read anything and everything I could get my hands on," she told an *Amazon Books* interviewer. "The Children's Library in my hometown was in the basement of the main library and it was an adventure in itself to go in." Salsitz is a disciplined writer, and strives to write ten pages every day. "Some days it's done fairly quickly, other days it's like getting blood from a stone," she told *Amazon Books.* Salsitz likes to write at night, but her husband and four children keep her busy so she writes while the children are in school, from nine in the morning to three in the afternoon. "Distraction don't bother me, although life itself sometimes gobbles up huge blocks of time," she told *Amazon Books.*

Salsitz specializes in fantasy, sometimes blending contemporary characters with fantastic elements, as she does in the young-adult novel *The Twilight Gate.* During her chemotherapy treatment, Caroline Walsh's children visit her Vietnam vet ex-husband for their summer vacation. Her children George, 15, Leigh, 12, and Mindy, 6, soon realize that magical forces are all around them. In the remote farmhouse where they're staying, the children's fears about their mother's illness manifest first as bad dreams, then as fiery-eyed werewolf-like beasts called weevils that kill the farm animals and then pursue the children. Mindy recognizes them as characters from one of her books, and soon another character, a kind unicorn, Rosebud, comes to help the children. Rosebud explains that a gate has opened between the two worlds, and the children must find out how to close it. "Using elements from Buddhism, unicorn lore and archtypal nightmares," explained a *Publishers Weekly* reviewer, Salsitz invents a believable description "of the magic that flows through this gripping fantasy-thriller." The book balances realistic events and fantastic ones, and Sylvia Read in *Voice of Youth Advocates* noted that "[h]ard core fantasy fans might find this too 'real,' while fans of realistic fiction may find this a nice segue into the fantasy genre."

In this Salsitz book written under the Elizabeth Forrest name, Vernon Spenser interrupts an FBI raid on a evangelist's hidden mountain ranch and finds himself risking his life to protect a innocent, genetically altered child from the government and vengeful cult leaders.
(Cover illustration by Don Brautigam.)

Dark Tide stars Parker Solomon, a troubled man who is the only survivor of a tragic accident at an amusement park in Pacific Crest, California. He does not remember the accident, or the rest of his childhood there, and he never wanted to go back and find out why. Thirty years later his real estate investor bosses send him to Pacific Crest to investigate developing some property, but Parker's arrival sets off a chain of frightening events. Something is lurking under the waters offshore, a monster called Leviathan that can breathe life into the dead and force the living to do its will, and it wants Parker. Susan Dunn of *Voice of Youth Advocates* remarked, "Exciting and fast-paced, this book races from incident to incident and always keeps readers in suspense."

In *Death Watch,* an abused woman parts company with her husband, but then is suspected for a crime he actually committed. At the same time, a serial killer has chosen her for his next victim and stalks her through both the real world and the dream world. This virtual-reality thriller was praised by Don D'Ammassa of *Science Fiction Chronicle* as "A well told detective story with scientific and horrific overtones."

Bright Shadow is a frightening thriller in which several children, whose genes have been scientifically modified to have psi powers, are under the sway of an evil evangelist in the remote mountains. When Vernon Spencer rescues Jennifer, one of the children, he finds himself the target of the cult's wrath as well as the government's—both want the child, and the other children are being systematically hunted down and killed. D'Ammassa remarked that the story was similar to Stephen King's *Firestarter,* "but with plenty of original twists and turns of its own."

Retribution stars Charlie, an artist whose paintings of the nightmares that have plagued her since childhood have brought her wealth and recognition. She doesn't understand, however, that the images and events she depicts are true, echoing the past and forecasting the future. A murderer whose crimes may be made known is the first to become aware of Charlie's power, but Charlie may be the killer's next prey.

Works Cited

D'Ammassa, Don, review of *Bright Shadow, Science Fiction Chronicle,* October, 1997, pp. 44-45.

D'Ammassa, review of *Death Watch, Science Fiction Chronicle,* June, 1995, p. 34.

Dunn, Susan, review of *Dark Tide, Voice of Youth Advocates,* December, 1993, p. 308.

Read, Sylvia, review of *The Twilight Gate, Voice of Youth Advocates,* June, 1993, p. 104.

Salsitz, Rhondi Vilott, online interview with *Amazon Books,* http://www.amazon.com (December 7, 1998).

Review of *The Twilight Gate, Publishers Weekly,* May 10, 1993, p. 74.

After a long absence, Charlie's horrific nightmares return, this time giving her visions of a killer who wants her as his next victim in this book by Salsitz written under the pseudonym Elizabeth Forrest. (Cover illustration by Don Brautigam.)

For More Information See

BOOKS

Science Fiction and Fantasy Literature, 1975-1991, Gale (Detroit), 1992.

PERIODICALS

Kliatt, September, 1996, p. 16.

Locus, February, 1992, p. 30.

School Library Journal, May, 1993, p. 108.

Science Fiction Chronicle, August, 1993, p. 38.

Voice of Youth Advocates, August, 1992, pp. 173-174; August, 1996, p. 168.

Wilson Library Bulletin, March, 1994, pp. 124-125.*

SCHINDEL, John 1955-

Personal

Born July 20, 1955, in Norwalk, CT; son of Morton Schindel (a children's film producer) and Ellen (an early childhood education specialist; maiden name, Bamberger) DeFranco; married Linda Fogel (a technical writer and editor); children: Celia, Nina. *Education:* New School for Social Research, B.A., 1981. *Hobbies and other interests:* Cooking, photography, writing letters, and building paper models.

Addresses

Home—4335 Everett Ave., Oakland, CA 94602.

Career

Weston Woods Studios, Weston, CT, voice editor and filmmaker, 1973-82; Magic Lantern Productions and Jester Inc., Asheville, NC, filmmaker, 1983-87; picture book writer, 1988—; University of California, Berkeley Extension, instructor in children's picture book writing, 1992—.

Awards, Honors

Children's Choice Award, International Reading Association, 1992, for *"Who Are You?"*; Pick of the Lists, American Booksellers, 1994, for *What's for Lunch?*

Writings

"Who Are You?", illustrated by James Watts, Margaret K. McElderry Books, 1991.
I'll Meet You Halfway, illustrated by James Watts, Margaret K. McElderry Books, 1993.
Something's Fishy, illustrated by Maryann Cocca-Leffler, Simon & Schuster, 1993.
What's for Lunch?, illustrated by Kevin O'Malley, Lothrop, Lee, and Shepard Books, 1994.
Dear Daddy, illustrated by Dorothy Donohue, A. Whitman, 1995.
Frog Face: My Little Sister and Me, illustrated by Janet Delaney, Holt, 1998.
Busy Penguins, photographs by Jonather Chester, Tricycle Press, 2000.

Also author of screenplays for children's films, including *Paper Wings,* Churchill Films, 1985, and *Waffles,* Churchill Films, 1986.

John Schindel

Sidelights

John Schindel told *SATA:* "I came to write picture books from being a filmmaker. I once worked at Weston Woods Studios (now part of Scholastic, Inc.), producers of book-based films for children, where I was surrounded by some of the best children's books ever written. It was there that I learned what makes a picture book tick.

"I admire the work of many picture book writers: William Steig, Tomi Ungerer, Ruth Krauss, Robert McCloskey, Beatrix Potter, and Arnold Lobel, to name a few. Their stories are timeless and speak to everyone, not just to children. They grab hold of us. Their voices are strong, vibrant, and clear. They are wonderful storytellers and masters of the picture book form.

"When I write, images and scenes appear in my mind as though I am watching a movie. I strive to find just the right words to express what I see and feel, to make my story and characters come alive. When my story is done I tape-record what I've written, then close my eyes and listen. Hopefully the images and scenes will come flowing back to me with the story in focus."

John Schindel has developed a reputation for writing gently humorous picture books that teach children lessons about friendship, families, and siblings, and celebrate small adventures. His first book, *Who Are You?,* centers on Young Brown Bear, who longs to be included in his parents' cocktail party, and so borrows a suit of clothes from his father and arrives at the party disguised as Doctor Doctor, where he is welcomed to join in the dancing and feasting. "Listeners will delight in the playful text and in Brown Bear's disguise," averred Carolyn Noah in *School Library Journal.* The joys of friendship, rather than family relations, are celebrated in Schindel's next book, *I'll Meet You Halfway,* about Titus Turtle and Fuller Frog who decide to meet halfway between their homes for a long overdue visit. Along the way, their gifts for each other are spoiled, but that only makes it all the more clear that "friendship is the best gift of all—that's the moral of this affable tale," remarked a reviewer for *Publishers Weekly.* While similar stories abound in children's literature, *Booklist* reviewer Ilene Cooper allowed, "there is [nonetheless] something eminently likable about Schindel's easy-going text."

Schindel's third picture book, *Something's Fishy,* is similarly "a quietly beguiling story," according to a reviewer for *Publishers Weekly,* centering on a boy and his dog on a fishing expedition to a nearby fishing hole. Instead of fish, however, the boy hooks a table, chairs, dishes, and cutlery, sets the table and then calls out for Gus, the octopus who lives in the fishing hole, who joins his picnic. *What's for Lunch?* resounds a similarly food-oriented theme in this cumulative tale of Sidney Mouse as he prepares to enjoy a picnic when a cat threatens him. Shortly, a dog comes along to chase the cat, then a goose nips the dog, a fox tries to eat the goose, and so on until an elephant who is prepared to sit on the whole lot of them starts a stampede in the other direction when Sidney Mouse's friend Shirley shows up with the picnic basket and scares him. The result is "an entertaining romp for story hours," contended Rosanne Cerny in *School Library Journal.*

On a more serious subject, *Dear Daddy* tells the story of Jesse, whose parents are divorced, and whose father lives far away. Jesse misses his father and is sad when the letter he wrote to him goes unanswered for a long time, but is relieved when a letter arrives explaining that his father had been away, followed by a phone call soon after inviting Jesse for a summertime visit. *Booklist* reviewer April Judge dubbed Schindel's depiction of Jesse's emotions "realistic," and added that "any child who is separated from a parent will easily relate." *Frog Face: My Little Sister and Me,* Schindel's next book, likewise treats a realistic aspect of family life in the range of emotions displayed by Johanna when a baby sister is born. Reviewers highlighted the effectiveness and beauty of illustrator Janet Delaney's accompanying photos. According to a *Publishers Weekly* contributor, "The interplay between text and photographs is as symbiotic as its subjects." The *Publishers Weekly* contributor also declared the book "a rare treat," praising its "intimacy and humor." *Booklist* critic Hazel Rochman observed that "siblings will recognize" Johanna's feelings of jealousy and annoyance as their own.

Works Cited

Cerny, Rosanne, review of *What's for Lunch?, School Library Journal,* September, 1994, p. 193.

Cooper, Ilene, review of *I'll Meet You Halfway, Booklist,* February 15, 1993, p. 1068.

Review of *Frog Face: My Little Sister and Me, Publishers Weekly,* August 3, 1998, p. 83.

Review of *I'll Meet You Halfway, Publishers Weekly,* March 1, 1993, p. 55.

Judge, April, review of *Dear Daddy, Booklist,* May 1, 1995, p. 1580.

Noah, Carolyn, review of *Who Are You?, School Library Journal,* February, 1992, p. 78.

Rochman, Hazel, review of *Frog Face, Booklist,* November 1, 1998, p. 505.

Review of *Something's Fishy, Publishers Weekly,* April 12, 1993, p. 61.

For More Information See

PERIODICALS

Booklist, February 15, 1993, p. 1068.

Horn Book, September-October, 1998, pp. 600-1.

Kirkus Reviews, July 15, 1991, p. 935; July 15, 1994, p. 994.

Publishers Weekly, March 1, 1993, p. 55; April 12, 1993, p. 61; July 11, 1994, p. 77.

Sacramento Bee, March 7, 1992.

San Francisco Examiner, December 10, 1991.

School Library Journal, February, 1992, p. 78; May, 1993, p. 91; September, 1993, p. 218; May, 1995, pp. 94-95; November, 1998, p. 95.

SENN, J(oyce) A(nn) 1941-

Personal

Born February 14, 1941, in Pittsburgh, PA; daughter of Elmer William and Leona (Frey) Senn. *Education:* Wheaton College, Wheaton, IL, B.A.; Trinity College, Hartford, CT, M.A. *Politics:* Democrat. *Hobbies and other interests:* Gardening, her two cats, "enjoying times with young people."

Addresses

Home and office—6-C Barrington Dr., Wethersfield, CT 06109. *E-mail*—JSSSSSS@aol.com.

Career

Xerox Publications, Middletown, CT, advertising copywriter, 1970-74; high school English teacher in Collinsville, CT, 1974-79; Ginn and Co., Lexington, MA, senior editor for language arts, 1979-82; D. C. Heath and Co., Lexington, managing editor for language arts, 1982-83; freelance writer, editor, and educational consultant, 1983—. Gives book presentations and professional workshops throughout the United States. *Member:* National Education Association.

Writings

The Many Faces of Poetry, Xerox Education Publications (Middletown, CT), 1978.
The Wolf King and Other True Animal Stories, Xerox Education Publications, 1978.
The Deadly Dinner and Other Exciting Mysteries, Xerox Education Publications, 1978.
Buried Alive and Other True Stories of Escape, Xerox Education Publications, 1978.
(With Carol Bergman) *Heath Grammar and Composition,* Heath (Lexington, MA), 1986.
The Landmark, Ligature (Chicago, IL), 1987.
325 Creative Prompts for Personal Journals, Scholastic Inc. (New York City), 1993.
Jane Goodall: Naturalist, Blackbirch Press (Woodbury, CT), 1993.
What Should I Write My Report On?, Scholastic Inc., 1994.
(With Patricia Breivik) *Information Literacy: Educating Children for the 21st Century,* Scholastic Inc., 1994, 2nd edition, National Education Association (Washington, DC), 1998.
Lots of Lists for Learning!, Scholastic Inc., 1995.
Teacher's Book of Lists, Scholastic Inc., 1996.
(Compiler and editor) *Quotations for Kids,* illustrated by Steve Pica, Millbrook Press (Brookfield, CT), 1999.

Work in Progress

Another book of quotations.

Sidelights

J. A. Senn told *SATA:* "One of my earliest and loveliest memories is my mother enthralling my older sister and

J. A. Senn

me with her made-up stories about brave princes and beautiful princesses. My mother also took us to the local library where we would spend many enjoyable hours among the books. Looking back, I'm not at all surprised now that my sisters and I developed such a deep love and respect for books that we all ended up writing books.

"Before I wrote any books myself, I became an English teacher. Because writing wasn't stressed so much when I was in school, I guess I learned to write as I taught my students to write. I eventually left teaching because in the early days of my career teachers weren't paid very much. After working in a civilian job for the armed services in Germany for two years, I returned to the states and took a job at a publishing company that produced educational magazines for schools—magazines such as *My Weekly Reader*. After writing advertising for that company for about a year, I became a feature writer for a junior-high publication called *Read* magazine.

"After briefly returning to teaching one more time—because I loved it so much—I eventually took a job as an editor in a Boston-area publishing company that produced educational textbooks. Because I had been an English teacher, I worked on grammar books, literature books, and even a speech book.

"A couple years later, a rival educational publisher offered me a challenging job: to revise and modernize a very old set of grammar books for grades seven through twelve. I realized quickly that the books were too old. The only solution that made sense to me was to develop a brand-new set of books. After the company gave me the go-ahead, I did a lot of research, held focus groups with teachers all across the country, and started to draw up the plans for a new set. Eventually someone had to write some sample chapters that could be sent out to teachers to make sure that the books were turning out to be what they wanted. Since there was no one else to write these chapters, I wrote them myself. When they came back with really positive responses, I decided I wanted to write the grammar sections of the books myself. Pretending to be very confident—but trembling inside—I marched into my boss's office and said that I wanted to be one of the authors of the textbooks. I guess that because he had seen enough of my writing to prove that I could write the chapters, he gave me the chance.

"During the next two and a half years, I did nothing else but write those books. I worked literally twelve or more hours a day, seven days a week, to get all the books written by the deadline. As hard as those years were, I have never regretted my decision because writing the books opened the most glorious door for me: independence! With the cash advances and later with the royalties from those books, I was able to work out of my home and become a full-time writer from that moment until now.

"Because I'm my own boss now, I can work during the hours that suit me—usually from eleven at night until five or six o'clock in the morning. For me, that is a wonderful time to work. There are no interruptions, no phone calls, and there's really nothing else to do during those hours! Then I usually sleep until about eleven o'clock or noon. I still have my afternoons for shopping and errands, and then, after a light dinner, I usually sleep for an hour before I start to work. Since I'm what some people call a 'night person,' I'm never tired during those working hours. In fact, sometimes I stop working only because it is starting to get light outside, but *not* because I'm tired!

"Every so often I speak to young people in the nearby schools. These opportunities bring back my love of teaching, and they give me a chance to spend some time with young people. The visits are always refreshing because most young people I know and meet are so full of hope and enthusiasm about the future and all the possibilities available to them. That wasn't always the case—especially for girls. When I graduated from college, girls could basically become teachers or nurses. Now, along with boys, they can become anything they want to be—such as astronauts, governors, or generals in the military.

"When I talk to students about *Quotations for Kids,* we usually discuss some of the quotations in the book, and I also share with them some of the wonderfully interesting books I read while looking for quotations. I always feel

JANE GOODALL

Naturalist

• • THE LIBRARY OF FAMOUS WOMEN • •

Senn examines the life of noted zoologist Jane Goodall and her work with the chimpanzees of Tanzania. (Cover photograph by Gerry Ellis.)

gratified later when I realize that I have encouraged or inspired some students to read some of the books! I think that reading is extremely important. Good readers are generally good writers; the two go together. However, another important benefit of reading is its stimulation of a person's imagination, and I think an imagination is essential to a really satisfying life! It is especially important during life's hardest times. An imagination can help people 'see' some good that can come out of a bad experience, or it can help them see a future that is worth working toward. Of course, an imagination is also very important for all writers—whether they write fiction or nonfiction.

"Having been in and around education for most of my life, I am always looking for new ways to make learning fun and rewarding. When I was writing a book of prompts for students' personal journals, I wanted to include a section of interesting quotations because I thought young people would enjoy reading them and also enjoy writing about them. It was then that I discovered there was no book of quotations just for young people, in which the quotations were taken directly from young people's literature. Right then and there, I decided that I would compile that first book of quotations for kids. Not only did I think it was a good

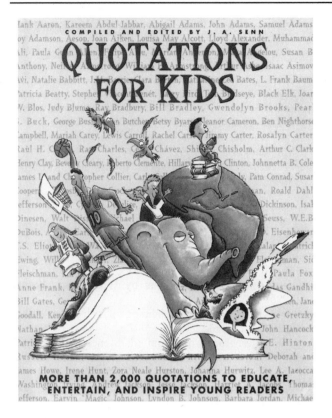

Complete with subject and author indexes, Senn's book offers young readers over two thousand famous quotes taken from children's literature, the Bible, folklore, and other sources. (Cover illustration by Steve Pica.)

idea, but I also knew that it would be enormously fun to do.

"The first thing I had to do, of course, was to read lots and lots of books. I read, and I read, and I read for almost a whole year—more than three hundred seventy-five books. I read classics like Mark Twain's *Tom Sawyer* and even some of Dr. Seuss's familiar books such as *The Cat in the Hat.* I also read many books by current authors such as Jerry Spinelli, Mildred D. Taylor, and Laurence Yep. I loved every minute of the reading! In fact, I was rather sad when I had to stop and start sorting through the five thousand quotations I had gathered.

"After my friends and neighbors helped me paste the quotations onto index cards, I tentatively selected a category for each one—categories I had thought up earlier, such as 'accomplishment,' 'brothers and sisters,' 'courage,' and 'pets.' The subject of some of the quotations themselves created additional categories such as 'death' and 'names.' Originally I thought that I wouldn't have any categories about such sad things as death, but I soon learned that young people are very curious about death; they want to understand it. I also learned that most of the young people's literature I read discussed the importance of people's names. As a result, much to my surprise, 'names' became one of the most interesting categories in the book.

"I also tried to include as many quotations from famous people as I could. In the category for 'democracy,' there are quotations from such people as astronaut Neil Armstrong, Bill Gates of Microsoft, civil rights leader Martin Luther King, Jr., President Abraham Lincoln, and Nelson Mandela, the first freely elected president of South Africa. I included quotations like these in hopes that students would use this book as a source of quotations for reports or biographies they were writing.

"I also hope, of course, that young people will just sit down with *Quotations for Kids* and read it for fun! Throughout my work on this book, I must have read each quotation at least forty or fifty times, but I still chuckle out loud when I read some of them, even now!

"Of the many books that I have written during my career, *Quotations for Kids* certainly was the most satisfying and rewarding because I got to read so many of the wonderful books available to young people today. I loved every minute of the time I spent on the book. Now I can hardly wait to get started on what the movies call 'a sequel.'"

For More Information See

PERIODICALS

Booklist, March 1, 1999.
Kirkus Reviews, February 15, 1999.
School Librarian's Workshop, May, 1999.
School Library Journal, April, 1999, p. 156.

*   *   *

SMITH, Roland 1951

Personal

Born in Portland, OR, 1951; married to Marie Smith. *Education:* Attended Portland State University, studied English and biology.

Addresses

Home—P.O. Box 1611, Wilsonville, OR 97070. *Agent*—Barbara Kouts, P.O. Box 560, Bellport, NY 11713.

Career

Writer. Zoo keeper and senior research biologist for twenty years, Portland Zoo, Portland, OR, and Point Defiance Zoo, Tacoma, WA. *Member:* Society of Children's Book Writers and Illustrators.

Awards, Honors

Outstanding Trade Books for Children list, *Bulletin of the Center for Children's Books* Blue Ribbon Book, both 1990, and both for *Sea Otter Rescue;* Notable Children's Trade Book in the Field of Social Studies, and Notable Books for a Global Society, Children's Literature and Reading Specialist Interest Group of the International

Reading Association, both 1996, and Young Readers Choice Award, 1998, all for *Thunder Cave;* Notable Science Trade Books for Children, National Science Teachers Association/Children's Book Council, and Children's Choices list, IRA/CBC, both 1997, and both for *Journey of the Red Wolf;* IRA Children's Choice Award, 1998, and Young Adult Choice, 1999, Bank Street College of Education's list of Children's Books of the Year, 1999, novel of the year for the Jason Project, all for *Jaguar;* Young Adult Library Services Association Top 10 Quick Picks for Reluctant YA Readers List, Bank Street College of Education's list of Best Children's Books of the Year, and American Library Association Top 10 Quick Picks for Reluctant YA Readers List, all 1999, and all for *Sasquatch;* Bank Street College of Education's list of Best Children's Books of the Year, 1999, for *In the Forest with the Elephants;* Children's Literature Choice List, 1999, for *In the Forest with the Elephants.* Smith's novels and nonfiction books for young readers have also been nominated for numerous state reading awards.

Writings

NOVELS

Thunder Cave, Hyperion, 1995.
Amy's Missing, YS Press, 1996.
Jaguar, Hyperion, 1997.
Sasquatch, Hyperion, 1998.

Roland Smith

The Captain's Dog: My Journey with the Lewis and Clark Tribe, Harcourt Brace, 1999.
The Last Lobo, Hyperion, 1999.

NONFICTION

Sea Otter Rescue: The Aftermath of an Oil Spill, photographs by the author, Cobblehill Books, 1990.
Primates in the Zoo, photographs by William Munoz, Millbrook Press, 1992.
Snakes in the Zoo, photographs by Munoz, Millbrook Press, 1992.
Inside the Zoo Nursery, photographs by Munoz, Cobblehill, 1993.
Cats in the Zoo, photographs by Munoz, Millbrook Press, 1994.
Whales, Dolphins and Porpoises in the Zoo, photographs by Munoz, Millbrook Press, 1994.
African Elephants, photographs by Gerry Ellis, Lerner, 1995.
Journey of the Red Wolf, photographs by the author, Cobblehill Books, 1996.
Vultures, photographs by Lynn M. Stone, Lerner, 1997.
(With Michael J. Schmidt) *In the Forest with the Elephants,* Harcourt Brace, 1998.
Flamingoes, Lerner, 1999.
Pigs, Lerner, 1999.

Contributor of photography to *National Geographic.* Has appeared on national and local television shows including "National Geographic," "Audubon," "Discover the World of Science," and "Northwest Wild."

Adaptations

Thunder Cave has been optioned as a television movie by RHI with a screenplay by Smith and Hunter Clarke

Sidelights

Roland Smith is a zoo keeper turned children's author who has carved a niche for himself both in nonfiction and fiction with such award-winning titles as *Sea Otter Rescue, Journey of the Red Wolf, Thunder Cave, Jaguar,* and *Sasquatch.* Blending action and adventure with accurate scientific detail, Smith's fiction has been praised by critics and applauded by young adult readers, while his nonfiction works are marked by readability as well as detailed insider information told in an accessible manner.

Born in Portland, Oregon, Smith formed a love of reading and writing early in his life. As he noted in a biographical sketch for his web site, he received one of the most memorable presents from his parents for his fifth birthday: "My parents gave me an old manual typewriter that weighed more than I did! It was my favorite possession. I spent hours in my room clacking away on that old typewriter. Of course, when I was five, I didn't know how to spell and I barely knew how to read, but I loved the sound and the look of the letters on the crisp white paper."

Soon thereafter came reading skills and a love for books. After graduating from high school, Smith attended Portland State University, studying English and biology. A work-study program led to part-time work at the Portland's children's zoo, which he thought might provide some interesting material to write about. Instead, the program led to a more than twenty year career in zoo keeping, first at Portland's main zoo, and then at the Point Defiance Zoo in Tacoma, Washington, where he became the curator of mammals and birds.

While at Point Defiance, he also became involved in a project to reintroduce the near extinct red wolf into its native habitat of North Carolina, South Carolina, and Mississippi. Functioning as species coordinator and studbook keeper for the U.S. Fish and Wildlife Service's Red Wolf Recovery Team, he helped oversee the breeding of the last pairs of the endangered wolf, brought to Washington State for that purpose. Once enough litters of new wolves had been born, they were then placed back into the wild with radio transmitters in collars to help with tracking. This successful project would later serve as the basis of one of Smith's most popular nonfiction titles, *Journey of the Red Wolf.* Working in Alaska to help save endangered animals from the 1989 Exxon *Valdez* oil spill would also lead to another title, *Sea Otter Rescue.* Such work led to appearances and interviews on local and national television shows, including "National Geographic," "Audubon," and "Discover the World of Science." Additionally, in his professional capacity, he authored numerous professional papers and presented them at meetings and conferences of scientific organizations as well as to the general public.

While working as a zoo keeper and research biologist, however, Smith never lost his dream of writing. He rose early each morning, trying to teach himself the basics of the writing craft. He read voraciously, up to four books a week, and was a steady consumer of how-to writing books and books about the publishing world. A chance meeting with a well-known children's writer led to the publication of his first title in 1990, *Sea Otter Rescue.* Smith's long-time dream finally became a reality.

With color photographs by Smith, this first book was an "in-depth view of the special care given to 342 sea otters after the Exxon *Valdez* oil spill," according to *Booklist's* Deborah Abbott, who went on to note that the book "reflects the complexity of the operation, which was exacerbated by the geography." Smith recounted in detail how the sea otters were affected by the oil spill, and how they were cleaned and taken care of. "With the environment a top priority of the 1990s, this is an especially useful resource," concluded Abbott. A writer for *Kirkus Reviews* felt Smith's book was unlike "many perfunctory treatments of current events" in that it was written and photographed "by an expert with in-depth knowledge of the *Valdez* oil spill and its effect on wildlife." The same writer continued, "Smith is an experienced zoologist whose writing and color photographs are both clear and immediate, involving readers

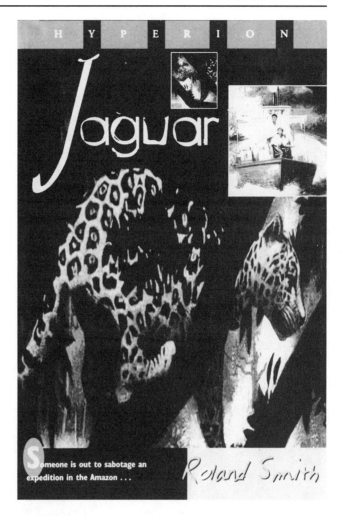

With his father, Jacob Lansa fights ruthless hunters to create a sanctuary for jaguars in Brazil. *(Cover illustration by Dan Brown.)*

in the fate of the sea otters by describing individual animals as well as general rescue operations."

With his first book, Smith created a space for himself in children's literature: eco-books told from an insider's perspective. He has continued to mine this rich vein in subsequent nonfiction and fiction titles. Approaching his new career in a very pragmatic manner, he realized that he had to find new topics or new ways to talk about old topics; he wanted to be able to ultimately support his family with words. Sticking with nonfiction at first, he contracted behind-the-scenes zoo books with Millbrook Press and Cobblehill Books. In 1992 his *Primates in the Zoo* and *Snakes in the Zoo* were published, followed by *Inside the Zoo Nursery* in 1993, and *Cats in the Zoo* and *Whales, Dolphins and Porpoises in the Zoo* in 1994.

Reviewing the first two titles, *Booklist's* Stephanie Zvirin thought that "Smith's conversational tone" would help to make the books "especially appealing to middle graders." Zvirin noted that both books "supply excellent perspectives on how the animals are cared for in a zoo environment." Karey Wehner wrote in *School Library Journal* that the texts for both these "New Zoo" series books "are straightforward, well organized, and contain some interesting anecdotes." Wehner concluded that "Smith's titles will appeal most to youngsters who want to know the nitty-gritty details on zoo routines."

With *Inside the Zoo Nursery,* Smith used the rescue of a newborn baboon as a dramatic narrative thread to connect information on zoo medical facilities. *Horn Book*'s Elizabeth S. Watson felt Smith "created an extremely readable and engaging text that provides excellent information about the complex procedures followed in a zoo nursery." Ruth M. McConnell, writing in *School Library Journal,* called the book a "clear, competent presentation, illustrated with captivating, full-color photographs of the baby animals."

Publication of these early titles and their reception by reviewers and readers encouraged Smith to leave zoo keeping behind and make writing his full time profession. Other nonfiction titles by Smith followed, including several books for the Lerner "Early Bird Nature Series," including *African Elephants* and *Vultures.* In 1996, he published *Journey of the Red Wolf,* in which he recounted the efforts to save the rare red wolf from

Thirteen-year-old Dylan braves a simmering Mount Saint Helens to protect the resident Sasquatch from vicious hunters. (Cover illustration by Dan Brown.)

extinction. In a starred *Booklist* review, Ellen Mandel commented, "Smith delivers behind-the-scenes details about the species-saving effort, generously illustrating his fascinating account with intimate color photographs." Employing dramatized fact, Smith presented the arduous task that confronted him and many other men and women who labored to save the red wolf. Roger Sutton, however, writing in *Bulletin of the Center for Children's Books,* found this fictionalizing technique somewhat confusing: "[I]t is not always clear what really happened," Sutton remarked. Barbara Murphy, on the other hand, noted in *School Library Journal* that "Smith's straightforward style conveys firsthand knowledge."

A 1996 trip to Burma, present-day Myanmar, with fellow zoologist Michael J. Schmidt led to a book on the plight of the Asian elephant, *In the Forest with the Elephants.* Focusing on the Myanmar Forest, where a third of Asia's remaining 35,000 elephants live, Smith and Schmidt tell the story of Won Lin and his elephant, Toe Lai, who have developed a working partnership in harvesting wood. These techniques of partnership may ultimately not only save the dwindling population of elephants, but also the forest. Patricia Manning, writing in *School Library Journal* called this book an "informative and rich cultural experience," while *Horn Book*'s Mary Ann Burns concluded that a "strong ecological theme runs throughout the book, which documents this complex enterprise and relationship between humans and nature."

Meanwhile, Smith has also been developing his writing credits in fiction. His first novel, the 1995 *Thunder Cave,* recounts the adventures of young Jacob Lansa, the half-Italian, half-Native American son of a biologist. When Jacob's mother is killed in traffic, his stepfather wants to send the boy off to relatives, but Jacob has a better idea: he goes to Kenya to find his biologist father, who is doing field research on African elephants. There Jacob hooks up with a Masai trying to bring rain to his draught-ridden country, an experience which helps Jacob examine his Hopi roots. Jacob also battles poachers who threaten elephants with extinction in his adventuresome quest to find his father. "Sparkling detail and vivid realism are keys to *Thunder Cave*'s success," noted Thomas S. Owens in *The Five Owls.* "A boy wanting a dad, elephants eluding capture, and an African exploring tradition combine to create a guaranteed, feel-good thriller," Owens concluded. Sutton commented in *Bulletin of the Center for Children's Books* that *Thunder Cave* "is precisely the kind of book people are thinking of when they ask for a 'boys' book'." As with his nonfiction, Smith played on the ecological theme with his debut novel, and it proved a winner with young readers. He also approaches fiction with the mind of a scientist: for the early drafts of *Thunder Cave* he consulted over 2,000 index cards with bits of information from plot twists to facts about Africa.

Smith followed this adventure novel with a mystery thriller, *Amy's Missing.* In 1997, Smith returned to his protagonist Jacob Lansa with *Jaguar.* This time Jacob follows his dad to Brazil where the biologist is setting up a jaguar preserve. Jake's journey upriver to join his father is beset by danger and violence, and once again Jake comes face to face with those despoiling nature for their own selfish gain. *Booklist*'s Kay Weisman noted, "While Smith's ecological message ... comes through loud and clear, the book's strength lies in strong characterization ... vivid local color, and high adventure." *Kirkus Reviews* called this sequel to *Thunder Cave* a "first-rate adventure about greed, mutual dependence, and family," while Janet Woodward commented in *School Library Journal* that "this fast-paced adventure and survival tale blends enough action, suspense, and legend to keep readers interested until the end."

Smith tackles the Sasquatch or Bigfoot legend in the 1998 *Sasquatch*. Again, a father-son relationship is at the center of an adventure novel in which Dylan must keep his somewhat erratic father in line when his mother leaves for Egypt. The job is made more difficult when the father joins a team hunting the Sasquatch on volcanic Mount St. Helen's. Dylan joins another team shadowing his father's, but soon begins to wonder if his father is crazy after all; the Sasquatch may be more of a reality than he has ever imagined. *Booklist*'s Lauren Peterson dubbed *Sasquatch* "a first-rate thriller," while Elaine E. Knight concluded in *School Library Journal* that with "an exciting climax set amid a Mount Saint-Helen's eruption, this fast-moving, suspenseful story provides lots of action and appeal."

Smith has also written historical fiction, but with a naturalist's eye for detail. In *The Captain's Dog,* he treats the Lewis and Clark Expedition from a dog's point of view, telling the story from the perspective of Seaman, a Newfoundland pup who becomes the companion of Meriwether Lewis. As Smith noted in his web site biographical sketch, "My writing led me to animals and my work with animals led me back to writing. It's funny how things work out. I spent over twenty years working with animals. Now I'm going to spend the next twenty years writing about animals ... as well as a few other things."

Works Cited

Abbott, Deborah, review of *Sea Otter Rescue, Booklist,* September 15, 1990, p. 158.

Burns, Mary M. review of *In the Forest with the Elephants, Horn Book,* March-April, 1998, p. 237.

Review of *Jaguar, Kirkus Reviews,* May 15, 1997, p. 808.

Knight, Elaine E., review of *Sasquatch, School Library Journal,* June, 1998, p. 153.

Mandel, Ellen, review of *Journey of the Red Wolf, Booklist,* May 1, 1996, p. 1504.

Manning, Patricia, review of *In the Forest with the Elephants, School Library Journal,* April, 1998, p. 154.

McConnell, Ruth M., review of *Inside the Zoo Nursery, School Library Journal,* June, 1993, p. 126.

Murphy, Barbara B., review of *Journey of the Red Wolf, School Library Journal,* May, 1996, p. 126.

Owens, Thomas S., review of *Thunder Cave, The Five Owls,* September-October, 1995, p. 18.

Peterson, Lauren, review of *Sasquatch, Booklist,* April 15, 1998, pp. 1446-47.

Review of *Sea Otter Rescue, Kirkus Reviews,* November, 1990, p. 71.

Smith, Roland, "How I Became a Writer," http://www.rolandsmith.com.

Sutton, Roger, review of *Thunder Cave, Bulletin of the Center for Children's Books,* June, 1995, p. 359.

Sutton, Roger, review of *Journey of the Red Wolf, Bulletin of the Center for Children's Books,* February, 1996, p. 20.

Watson, Elizabeth S., review of *Inside the Zoo Nursery, Horn Book,* January-February, 1993, p. 99.

Wehner, Karey, review of *Primates in the Zoo, School Library Journal,* December, 1992, p. 130.

Weisman, Kay, review of *Jaguar, Booklist,* May 15, 1997, p. 1576.

Woodward, Janet, review of *Jaguar, School Library Journal,* June, 1997, p. 128.

Zvirin, Stephanie, review of *Primates in the Zoo, Booklist,* October 15, 1992, p. 427.

For More Information See

PERIODICALS

Appraisal, Spring-Summer, 1993, pp. 105-06.

Booklist, October 1, 1994, p. 323.

Kirkus Reviews, January 1, 1993, p. 68; March 1, 1998, p. 344.

Kliatt, July, 1997, p. 11.

San Diego Union Times, July, 19, 1998.

School Library Journal, November, 1990, p. 133; May, 1995, pp. 122-23; August, 1995, p. 138; March, 1998, pp. 191-92.

Science Books and Films, December, 1995, p. 271.

ON-LINE

Author's web site, http://www.rolandsmith.com.

—*Sketch by J. Sydney Jones*

*   *   *

SORENSEN, Henri 1950-

Personal

Born February 18, 1950, in Aarhus, Denmark; son of Svend Aage (a glazier) and Maren Marie (maiden name, Jensen) Sorensen; married Lise Winther (a college teacher); children: Mathilde Therese, Alexandra Beatrice. *Education:* Attended University of Aarhus, 1974-80; The Academy of Fine Arts in Aarhus, 1980-83.

Addresses

Home—640 Broadway, New York, NY, 10012. *Agent*—Evelyne Johnson Assoc., 201 East 28th Street, New York, NY 10016.

Career

Freelance illustrator, 1985—. Worked as a glazier and at a film company making graphics and models.

Writings

SELF-ILLUSTRATED

New Hope, Lothrop, Lee & Shepard, 1995, Puffin, 1998.
Your First Step, Lothrop, Lee & Shepard, 1996.

ILLUSTRATOR

Alvin Tresselt, *Sun Up,* Lothrop, 1991.
Sheila Cole, *When the Rain Stops,* Lothrop, 1991.
Tresselt, *The Gift of the Tree,* Lothrop, 1992.
Ann W. Dodd, *Footprints and Shadows,* Simon & Schuster, 1992.
Harriet Diller, *Granddaddy's Highway,* Boyds Mills Press, 1992.
Ruth Horowitz, *Mommy's Lap,* Lothrop, 1992.
Nancy W. Carlstrom, *What Does the Rain Play,* Macmillan Children's Book Group, 1993.
Jeff Shepard, *I Know a Bridge,* Macmillan Children's Book Group, 1993.
Laura K. Melmed, *I Love You As Much . . . ,* Lothrop, 1993.
Jane B. Mason, *River Day,* Macmillan, 1994.
Elaine Moore, *Deep River,* Simon & Schuster, 1994.
Robert Frost Poetry for Young People, edited by Gary D. Schmidt, Magnolia, 1994.
Melmed, *Prince Nautilus,* Lothrop, Lee & Shepard, 1994.
Maryann N. Weidt, *Daddy Played Music for the Cows,* Lothrop, Lee & Shepard, 1995.
Bruce Coville, *My Grandfather's House,* BridgeWater Books, 1996.
Peter and Connie Roop, *Take Command, Mr. Farragut,* Lothrop, Lee & Shepard, 1996.
Jean Van Leeuwen, *A Fourth of July on the Plains,* Dial Books, 1997.
Florence Mary Fitch, *A Book about God,* Lothrop, Lee & Shepard, 1998.
Jonathan London, *Hurricane,* Lothrop, Lee & Shepard, 1998.
Melmed, *Jumbo's Lullaby,* Lothrop, Lee & Shepard, 1999.
Carmen Deedy, *The Yellow Star,* Peachtree Publishers, 2000.

Sidelights

Danish-born Henri Sorensen is an author/illustrator whose host of credits have made him one of the most sought-after children's picture book illustrators. His landscapes, family scenes, and nature paintings using watercolor, oil, and pastels "suggest a formality of portraiture that is not usually seen in children's books," as Ruth K. MacDonald noted in *School Library Journal.* Such painterly concerns reflect Sorensen's own development and training as an artist.

"As a child I lived near the Art Museum in Aarhus," Sorensen once told *SATA.* "I went there once or twice a week to look at the paintings from the golden age of Danish painting, which I admired very much. I think that my interest in naturalism and impressionism was formed at that time. When I was a teenager, I was more interested in the non-figurative, abstract expression, but later my interest in naturalism reappeared.

"I knew that I couldn't live as a naturalistic artist in Denmark because it was considered very old fashioned. So after school I was educated as a glazier in my father's company, and later I worked in another company for some years. In my spare time, I always painted. I decided to study art history and went to college and university. During my studies at the university, I found more and more pleasure in painting and less in the theoretical studies, so I decided to study art at the Academy. I had a lot of pleasure painting every day for the next three years. My main interest then, as now, was impressionistic painting. After finishing the Academy, I worked in a film company where I made graphics and models, but mostly studied lighting. I then discovered that there was a market for my kind of art in advertising and publishing and started working as a freelance illustrator in 1985."

Sorensen illustrated his first children's book in 1991 for a re-issue of Alvin Tresselt's *Sun Up,* the lyrical story of a day on a farm, originally published in 1949. Martha Topol, writing in *School Library Journal,* said, "[T]his title is given new life by a newcomer to the field . . . Each expansive page glows with a light so pure that readers can almost feel the heat of the pulsing sun and be relieved once the rain arrives . . . Sorensen's naturalistic oil paintings help children feel a part of this special day-by-day world." Sorensen provided new illustrations for another Tresselt original, *The Gift of the Tree.* "Color tones reflect the seasons, as they are softly muted in fall and winter; more vivid in spring and summer," noted Diane Nunn in a *School Library Journal* review, who also added, "These illustrations are far more vibrant than those in the previous edition." *Booklist*'s Carolyn Phelan lauded the "beautiful woodland paintings stretching across . . . large, double-page spreads."

Among Sorensen's collaborations are two fact books—Anne Westcott Dodge's *Footprints and Shadows,* and Jeff Shepard's *I Know a Bridge. Footprints and Shadows* tells very young readers where footprints and shadows go. Emily Melton, reviewing the title in *Booklist,* thought that the reason the book would appeal to children "is Sorensen's beautifully rendered illustrations, done primarily in soothing, gently washed tones of gold, rust, and blue that emphasize the natural beauty of the seasons." *Booklist*'s Ilene Cooper echoed these comments in reviewing *I Know a Bridge,* "The book's most striking feature is the handsome pictures, some in two-page spreads that fill the pages."

Another of Sorensen's collaborators is Laura Krauss Melmed, with whom he has produced three books. Their first effort, *I Love You As Much . . . ,* uses simple rhymes to express how both human and animal mothers feel about their babies. *Booklist*'s Janice Del Negro commented on Sorensen's "more than agreeably pleasant watercolors" in this book, and MacDonald wrote in

School Library Journal, "Sorensen's paintings are large and bright, spanning double-page spreads and extending to the edge of each page." A reviewer for *Publishers Weekly* called attention to the "grace and drama of Sorensen's light-filled, softly hued impressionistic illustrations," and Lisa Shea, reviewing the title in *New York Times Book Review,* declared that the "light-drenched, golden-toned pictures exert a hypnotic effect on both reader and listener."

Further collaborative efforts with Melmed include *Prince Nautilus* and *Jumbo's Lullaby. Prince Nautilus* is an original fairy tale using a good sister/bad sister theme. A reviewer for *Publishers Weekly* said that "Melmed's fluid, poetic style feels very much at home in the fairy-tale genre, and Sorensen echoes her eloquence in impressionistic acrylics—his sweeping scenes enhance the story's timeless air." Donna L. Scanlon remarked in *School Library Journal* that "Sorensen's double-spread illustrations soar across the pages and are infused with light, evoking the heat of the sun and the glare of the sea;" and *Booklist's* Lauren Peterson wrote that "Sorensen's acrylic paintings are accomplished with gusto." In 1999, Sorensen and Melmed produced *Jumbo's Lullaby,* a bedtime book featuring elephants. "Sorensen dips his brush in the quieter shades of the Serengeti—misty gray-blues, ochre, moss green—for realistic, nuanced animal portraits that reinforce the underlying theme of mother love," remarked Sybil Steinberg in a *Publishers Weekly* review.

Intergenerational themes provide the focus for many of the books Sorensen has illustrated. A new baby and possible sibling jealousy is at the center of Ruth Horowitz's *Mommy's Lap.* Writing for *Booklist,* Del Negro commented on Sorensen's watercolors as "warm and expressive, featuring a traditional family in sun-drenched rooms filled with books and plants." Reviewing the same title in *School Library Journal,* Mary Lou Budd noted, "Realistic watercolor illustrations dramatically portray the emotions of the text." Another of Sorensen's books with an intergenerational theme is *Granddaddy's Highway* by Harriet Diller in which an imaginary road trip brings Maggie and her grandfather together. Hazel Rochman wrote in *Booklist,* "Sorensen's ... watercolor paintings, both realistic and dreamy, capture the country outside, rushing by in the dark, and also the loving bond between the travelers." A *Publishers Weekly* reviewer commented, "Sorensen's painterly illustrations handsomely contrast the grandeur of nature with true-to-life portraits of attractively ordinary folk."

Elaine Moore's *Deep River* and Jane B. Mason's *River Day* are also Sorensen illustrated stories about girls and their grandfathers. Reviewers applauded Sorensen's renderings of nature in both titles. Reviewing *Deep River,* a contributor to *Publishers Weekly* remarked, "Sorensen's lush, sunlit acrylic paintings set a serene summer-day mood, while his cool blues and leafy greens issue a pleasant invitation to the natural world." Writing about *River Day* in *School Library Journal,* Harriet Fargnoli said that Sorensen's acrylic paintings "are rich in color, and in several one can almost feel the water's

wetness, the eagle's shadow, and the hand-lettered name on the canoe." A *Publishers Weekly* reviewer called Sorensen's illustrations in *River Day* "breathtaking," and added, "[T]hey confer grace and intelligence on an otherwise merely serviceable entry."

Sorensen has also used his talents to illustrate poetry. His work accompanying the text of Nancy White Carlstrom's *What Does the Rain Play?* was called "lavish" and "painterly" by a *Publishers Weekly* contributor, while *Booklist's* Melton called them "eye-catching, with bold colors and strong lines soothingly muted to a misty, washed-clean, rain-drenched look." Sorensen also illustrated a collection of Robert Frost's poems and the inspirational verses in Florence Mary Fitch's *A Book about God.* Susan Dove Lempke praised the illustrator's work for the Fitch book saying, "Sorensen's oil paintings capture the majesty evoked by the text, their spaciousness and rich texture filling every page to the edges."

"The thing that means most to me when I read a manuscript is the mood," Sorensen once told *SATA.* "I always see the mood of the pictures in my head before I start illustrating. Moods are difficult to show in lay-outs. Therefore I prefer to do the finished illustrations at once—and change or re-do them if necessary—rather than be stuck with a lay-out that might hinder the creativity and inspiration, resulting in lifeless illustrations."

Sorensen has self-illustrated some of his own books as well. In the first of these, *New Hope,* he tells the story of young Jimmy who is visiting his grandfather in the town of New Hope. Jimmy loves to hear his grandfather's story about the founder of the town, Lars Jensen, who came to New York from his native Denmark and proceeded with his family across America by covered wagon. When a broken axle prompted him to stop in Minnesota, he settled there. Sorensen displays the growth of New Hope from a single cabin to a bustling town with a railroad and many shops, and the arrival of new settlers and offspring. One of these offspring is Jimmy's grandfather, the great-great-grandson of Lars himself.

"The text is simple and straightforward," commented Nancy Palmer in a *School Library Journal* review of *New Hope. Booklist's* Rochman called Sorensen's first solo effort an "archetypal immigration story." Margaret A. Bush, writing in *Horn Book,* remarked, "Family and place are intertwined in a handsome chronicle about the history of a small town.... An immensely appealing book that celebrates small-town Americana and allows children to make personal connections in comprehending the idea of history." A reviewer for *Publishers Weekly* commented, "[Sorensen's] first time out as a writer, speaks volumes about the growth of America, family lineage, and national pride with a fluid tale.... Adding scope and atmosphere to Sorensen's straightforward, affecting narrative are vigorous acrylic paintings."

Another solo effort, *Your First Step,* appeared in 1996. In it Sorensen presents the first steps of babies, both animal and human. A wolf pup plays in the morning sun and an English otter slides down a bank. Set around the globe at the same moment, the visual vignettes also introduce young readers to the relationship of the Earth to the sun. "Lovely, glowing paintings, soft yet precise, are the drawing card in this picture book," remarked *Booklist*'s Julie Corsaro.

Sorensen once commented to *SATA:* "When I illustrate a book, I always hope that my illustrations will appeal both to grown-ups and to children. I'm often surprised to see how much children notice and how important colors are to them. They themselves are extremely good narrative illustrators. Therefore, I disagree with those who think that you have to simplify the mode of expression when illustrating children's books."

Works Cited

Budd, Mary Lou, review of *Mommy's Lap, School Library Journal,* May, 1993, p. 86.

Bush, Margaret A., review of *New Hope, Horn Book,* May-June, 1995, pp. 330-31.

Cooper, Ilene, review of *I Know a Bridge, Booklist,* November 15, 1993.

Corsaro, Julie, review of *Your First Step, Booklist,* August, 1996, p. 1909.

Review of *Deep River, Publishers Weekly,* May 9, 1994, p. 72.

Del Negro, Janice, review of *Mommy's Lap, Booklist,* April 15, 1993, p. 1523.

Del Negro, review of *I Love You As Much ...* , *Booklist,* September 1, 1993, p. 69.

Fargnoli, Harriet, review of *River Day, School Library Journal,* May, 1994, p. 100.

Review of *Granddaddy's Highway, Publishers Weekly,* February 1, 1993, p. 95.

Review of *I Love You As Much ...* , *Publishers Weekly,* August 23, 1993, p. 68.

Lempke, Susan Dove, review of *A Book about God, Booklist,* April 1, 1999, p. 1416.

MacDonald, Ruth K., review of *I Love You As Much ...* , *School Library Journal,* March, 1994, p. 206.

Melton, Emily, review of *Footprints and Shadows, Booklist,* December 1, 1992, p. 674.

Melton, review of *What Does the Rain Play?, Booklist,* April 1, 1993, pp. 1436-37.

Review of *New Hope, Publishers Weekly,* May 15, 1995, p. 72.

Nunn, Diane, review of *The Gift of the Tree, School Library Journal,* June, 1992, p. 111.

Palmer, Nancy, review of *New Hope, School Library Journal,* July, 1995, p. 69.

Peterson, Lauren, review of *Prince Nautilus, Booklist,* November 15, 1994, p. 613.

Phelan, Carolyn, review of *The Gift of the Tree, Booklist,* May 1, 1992, p. 1605.

Review of *Prince Nautilus, Publishers Weekly,* July 4, 1994, p. 63.

Review of *River Day, Publishers Weekly,* January 24, 1994, p. 55.

Rochman, Hazel, review of *Granddaddy's Highway, Booklist,* May 1, 1993, p. 1602.

Rochman, review of *New Hope, Booklist,* June 1, 1995, p. 1789.

Scanlon, Donna L., review of *Prince Nautilus, School Library Journal,* October, 1994, p. 94.

Shea, Lisa, review of *I Love You As Much ...* , *New York Times Book Review,* January 30, 1994, p. 27.

Steinberg, Sybil, review of *Jumbo's Lullaby, Publishers Weekly,* September 20, 1999, p. 86.

Topol, Martha, review of *Sun Up, School Library Journal,* May, 1991, p. 84.

Review of *What Does the Rain Play?, Publishers Weekly,* March 22, 1993, p. 78.

For More Information See

PERIODICALS

Booklist, June 1 & 15, 1994, p. 1842; December 1, 1994, p. 669; October 1, 1995, p. 327; June 1, 1996, p. 1730; May 15, 1997, p. 1582; August, 1998, p. 2015.

New York Times Book Review, July 28, 1996, p. 21.

Publishers Weekly, May 19, 1997, p. 75; July 20, 1998, p. 220.

School Library Journal, July, 1993, pp. 56-57; June, 1996, p. 110; May, 1997, p. 116; May, 1999, p. 105.*

—*Sketch by J. Sydney Jones*

*   *   *

SOVAK, Jan 1953-

Personal

Born February 13, 1953, in Prague, Czechoslovakia (now Czech Republic); son of Miroslav and Dana (Neckar) Sovak; married Daniela Jerie, 1982; children: Adrianne-Monique. *Education:* Attended School of Art, Bechyne, 1968-72, and University of Purkyne, 1972-77.

Addresses

Home—47 Suncastle Bay S.E., Calgary, Alberta, Canada T2X 2MI.

Career

Illustrator.

Awards, Honors

Award of Merit, book illustration category, Canadian Association of Photographers and Illustrators, 1990 and 1992; award for book illustration, Children's Book Centre (Canada), 1991; Golden Bow Award, Czech Ministry of Culture, Young Readers Literature Society, Children's Book Illustrators Society, and Czech section of International Board on Books for Young People, 1995; Illustrator of the Year Award, Rodokaps (Czech publisher), 1995; Choice awards from Young Readers Association (United States), 1997, and Canadian Chil-

Jan Sovak

dren's Book Centre, 1998; nominated for Kentucky Blue Grass Award, 1999.

Writings

AUTHOR AND ILLUSTRATOR

Prehistoric Mammals Coloring Book, Dover (Mineola, NY), 1991.

Great Dinosaurs Poster Book, Red Deer College Press (Red Deer, Alberta), 1992.

Butterflies, Dover, 1992.

Zoo Animals, Dover, 1993.

Insects, Dover, 1994.

Insect Sticker Book, Dover, 1994.

Snakes of the World, Dover, 1995.

Birds of Prey Sticker Book, Dover, 1995.

Realistic Snakes Sticker Book, Dover,, 1995.

Endangered Animals Sticker Book, Dover, 1995.

Pegatinas de Culebras, Dover, 1995.

Desert Sticker Pictures, Dover, 1996.

Wild Cats, Dover, 1996.

Jurassic Dinosaurs Sticker Pictures, Dover, 1997.

Learning about Butterflies, Dover, 1997.

Learning about Cretaceous Dinosaurs, Dover, 1997.

Learning about Insects, Dover, 1997.

(With Phillip J. Currie and Eric P. Felber) *A Moment in Time with: Troodon,* Troodon Productions (Calgary, Alberta), 1997.

Cretaceous Dinosaurs Sticker Pictures, Dover, 1998.

Explore a Coral Reef Sticker Pictures, Dover, 1998.

Learning about Forest Animals, Dover, 1998.

Learning about Snakes, Dover, 1998.

Learning about Tropical Fish, Dover, 1998.

(With Currie and Felber) *A Moment in Time with: Albertosaurus,* Troodon Productions, 1998.

(With Currie and Eva Koppelhus) *A Moment in Time with: Centrosaurus,* Troodon Productions, 1998.

Before the Dinosaurs Coloring Book, Dover, 1999.

Prehistoric Animals Sticker Book, Dover, 1999.

(With Currie and Koppelhus) *A Moment in Time with: Sinosauropteryx,* Troodon Productions, 1999.

ILLUSTRATOR; BOOKS PUBLISHED IN ENGLISH

The Palaeoguide, Government of Alberta (Canada), 1988.

Junior Encyclopedia of Canada, Hurtig (Canada), 1988.

Monty Reid, *The Last Great Dinosaurs: A Guide to the Dinosaurs of Alberta,* Red Deer College Press, 1990.

Currie, *The Flying Dinosaurs: The Illustrated Guide to the Evolution of Flight,* Red Deer College Press, 1991.

Dinosaur World Tour, Ex Terra Foundation (Canada), 1991.

Michael Crichton, *Jurassic Park,* Knopf (New York City), 1993.

The Audubon Society Pocket Guide: Dinosaurs, Knopf, 1993.

The Land before Us, Red Deer College Press, 1994.

Currie and Zdenek V. Spinar, *The Great Dinosaurs: A Story of the Giants' Evolution,* Sunburst Books (London, England), 1994, Longmeadow Publishing (New York City), 1995.

Prehistoric Alaska, Alaska Geographic Society, 1994.

Official Gallery Guide, Royal Tyrrel Museum of Palaentology (Canada), 1994.

Colleayn O. Mastin, *Canadian Wild Animals,* Grasshopper Publishing (Kamloops, British Columbia), 1994.

Mastin, *Canadian Trees,* Grasshopper Publishing, 1994.

Mastin, *Canadian Arctic Animals,* Grasshopper Publishing, 1994, revised edition published as *Canadian Animals of the Arctic,* 1997.

A. Weismann, *Songbirds,* Dover, 1995.

Currie, *Jurassic Dinosaurs,* Dover, 1995.

Dinosaur Safari Guide, Voyager Press, 1996.

Currie, *101 Questions about Dinosaurs,* Dover, 1996.

Currie, *Cretaceous Dinosaurs,* Dover, 1996.

Pacific Rim: National Park Reserve, Blackbird Naturegraphic (Canada), 1996.

M. Jamieson, *Beginnings,* Reidmore Books (Canada), 1996.

(Contributor) *World Book Encyclopedia,* World Book (Chicago, IL), 1997.

What Do We Know, World Book, 1997.

(Contributor) *Kids Encyclopedia,* Kidsbooks Publishers, 1997.

Mastin, *North American Endangered Species,* Grasshopper Publishing, 1997.

Sovak provided the illustrations for Colleayn O. Mastin's natural-history book about animal species threatened with extinction in North America. (From North American Endangered Species.*)*

Mastin, *Canadian Ocean Creatures,* Grasshopper Publishing, 1997.

Mastin, *Canadian Wildflowers and Emblems,* Grasshopper Publishing, 1997.

Mastin, *The Magic of Mythical Creatures,* Grasshopper Publishing, 1997.

Mastin, *North American Animals of the Arctic,* Grasshopper Publishing, 1997.

Ana Adamache, *The Sun King Ray Story,* Astra Books (Calgary), 1997.

Designing Dinosaurs, Bruce Museum (Canada), 1997.

Don Lessem, *The Dinosaurs of Jurassic Park,* Universal City Studios, 1997.

Mastin, *Canadian Birds,* Grasshopper Publishing, 1998.

Mastin, *Newest and Coolest Dinosaurs,* Grasshopper Publishing, 1998.

A Walk through Time, Wiley (New York City), 1998.

Cornerstones, Gage Educational Publishing (Canada), 1998.

Lessem, *Dinosaurs to Dodos: An Encyclopedia of Extinct Animals,* Scholastic Inc. (New York City), 1999.

Canada Revisited, Arnold Publishing (Canada), 1999.

Jerry Hale and Rose Hale, *The Adventures of Muskwa,* Muskwa Trails (Worsley, Alberta), 1999.

Contributor of illustrations to textbooks published by Macmillan (New York City) and McGraw (New York City). Contributor of illustrations to nearly a dozen films, television series, and CD-ROM publications, including *Earth Revealed,* Public Broadcasting Service; *In Steps of Dragons* and *Trip to China: Feathered Dinosaurs,* both for The Discovery Channel; and *Dinosaurs,* The Learning Channel; and *Encarta Yearbook Builder,* Microsoft. Contributor to magazines in the United States and Canada, including *Prehistoric Times, Dinosaur, Canadian Geographic, Earth, Cricket,* and *Canadian Rockies.*

ILLUSTRATOR; FOREIGN-LANGUAGE PUBLICATIONS

A. Barkhausen and Z. Geiser, *Elephanten,* Kinderbuchverlag Luzern (Switzerland), 1992.

L. Dossenbach, *Das Lexikon der Tiere,* Kinderbuchverlag Luzern, 1992.

K. Roberts, *Kapitan Rozmysl,* Touzimsky & Moravec (Prague, Czech Republic), 1992.

J. Henson, *Bin Daa! Wer Noooch?,* Motovun/Disney (Switzerland), 1993.

P. Marc, *Mit Livingstone durch Africa,* Bohema Press (Switzerland), 1993.

Jahrbuch der Coburger Landes Stiftung, DNP Coburg (Germany), 1993.

J. Moravec, *Utek z Onondagy,* Touzimsky & Moravec, 1994.

J. Slade, *Fiesta Smrti,* Rodokaps (Czech Republic), 1994.

M. Wiliamson, *Navrat Rysaveho Johna,* Rodokaps, 1994.

Slade, *Lassiter a Oregonska Mstitelka,* Rodokaps, 1994.

J. M. Adam, *Apacsky Mlyn,* Rodokaps, 1994.

Slade, *Supi z Gila Bendu,* Rodokaps, 1994.

Henson, *Willkommen bei den Sinclairs,* Motovun/Disney, 1994.

Evolution: Life and the Universe, Gakken Publishers (Japan), 1994.

Nature Library, Gakken Publishers, 1994.

Wielkie Dinozaury, Warszawski Dom Wydawniczy (Poland), 1994.
Currie, *Dinosaurs from A to Z,* Yazawa Science Office (Japan), 1995.
From Gaia to Ecopoiesis, Gakken Publishers, 1995.
O. Janka, *Odvedu te k Siouxum,* Touzimsky & Moravec, 1995.
L. Kark, *Sedm z Lancasteru,* Touzimsky & Moravec, 1995.
R. H. Douglas, *O Cest Nepritele,* Rodokaps, 1995.
C. Judd, *Pisen Severu,* Rodokaps, 1995.
Currie, *Giganten der Lufte: Das Grosse Buch der Flugsaurier,* Arena Verlag (Wuerzberg, Germany), 1995.
M. H. Bowery, *Cesta Pres Inferno,* Rodokaps, 1995.
Mass Extinction and Evolution of Life, Gakken Publishers, 1996.
A Biography of the Dinosaur World, A. G. Tokyo Publishers (Japan), 1996.
O. Collins, *Brianuv Mistrovsky Kousek,* Rodokaps, 1996.
J. Fabricius, *Plavcici Kapitana Bontekoea,* Touzimsky & Moravec, 1996.
J. Moravec, *Cteni z Kameni,* Touzimsky & Moravec, 1996.
Bowery, *Muz Ktery Tam Byl,* Rodokaps, 1996.
R. Omphalius, *Planet des Lebens,* Motovun Verlagsgesellschaft (Switzerland), 1996.
Bowery, *Sewardova Lednice,* Rodokaps, 1997.
H. H. Isenbart, *Freude mit Pferden,* Motovum Verlagsgesellschaft, 1997.
Gendai Shinsho, Kodansha (Japan), 1997.
Gizem Dolu Afrika Yolculugu, Turkeiye Yayim Haklari (Turkey), 1997.
Science in Crisis, Gakken Publishers, 1997.
The Dinosaur Handbook, Yazawa Publishing House, 1997.
Currie and Spinar, *De Heersers van Toen,* R & B Productions (Netherlands), 1998.
M. Andera, *Vyhubena Zvirata,* Aventinum Publishing House (Czech Republic), 1998.
V. Hulpach, *Indianske Pribehy,* Aventinum Publishing House, 1998.
Hulpach, *Indianer Geschichte,* Dausien Verlag (Germany), 1998.
Carlsbergfondet Arsskrift, Carlsbergfondet (Denmark), 1998.
Bowery, *Dabluv Kolovrat,* Rodokaps, 1998.
Scientific Controversies, Gakken Publishers, 1998.
A. Stevenson, *Ostrov Pokladu,* Touzimsky & Moravec, 1999.
Praveka More, Granit Publishers (Czech Republic), 1999.

Contributor of illustrations to periodicals.

Work in Progress

Illustrating *Encyclopedia of Dinosaurs* by Don Lessem; working on the "Living Dinosaur" project CD-ROM and book; research on the stories of Genghis-Khan and Alexander the Great.

Sidelights

Jan Sovak told *SATA:* "I was born in a family of book collectors. For as long as I can remember, my favorite refuge was our attic filled with books and old magazines. There I discovered the importance of illustrations for books. I started to write my own stories, so I could illustrate them. The first book I wrote for this purpose was about a Bengal tiger escaping from a circus and learning how to live as a wild animal. I was eight years old.

"My first and foremost wish is to get children interested in books. I want to open a door for endless adventures of the mind that could lead them on the road to discovery of vast horizons of knowledge and to and understanding of nature and history. Maybe that kind of knowledge could give readers an answer about who we are, where we come from, and what it means to share our planet with other forms of live.

"I am happy to see how important children's book publishing has become in the last three decades. The quality of writers and illustrators is higher than ever, and competition is pushing all of us further yet. As for myself, I love going to bookstores to discover new colleagues with a fresh, new outlook on the illustrating process.

"If writing or illustrating is what you want to do in your life more than anything else, then stick with it! It is not easy, and for most of us it has never been, even for established authors! My favorite comparison is about playing a musical instrument. If you want to become a virtuoso, you must spend many hours every day practicing. It is the same with out craft. My teacher used to tell me: 'If you don't want to work fifteen hours a day on your technique, do something else. Right now there are a lot of people around the world who do exactly that.'"

For More Information See

PERIODICALS

Quill and Quire, August, 1991, p. 21.

* * *

STANLEY, Diane 1943- (Diane Stanley Zuromskis, Diane Zuromskis)

Personal

Born December 27, 1943, in Abilene, TX; daughter of Onia Burton, Jr. (a U.S. Navy captain) and Fay (an author, playwright, and copywriter; maiden name, Grissom) Stanley; married Peter Zuromskis, May 30, 1970 (divorced, 1979); married Peter Vennema (a corporation president and editorial consultant), September 8, 1979; children: (first marriage) Catherine, Tamara; (second marriage) John Leslie. *Education:* Trinity University, B.A., 1965; attended Edinburgh College of Art, Scotland, 1966-67; Johns Hopkins University, M.A., 1970. *Politics:* Democrat. *Religion:* Episcopalian. *Hobbies and other interests:* Reading, painting, travel.

Addresses

Home and office—2120 Tangley, Houston, TX 77005.
E-mail—dianley@aol.com.

Career

Author and illustrator of books for children. Freelance medical illustrator, 1970-74; Dell Publishing, New York City, graphic designer, 1977; G. P. Putnam's Sons and Coward, McCann & Geoghegan, New York City, art director of children's books, 1977-79. Full-time author and illustrator, 1979—. *Exhibitions:* Bush Galleries, Norwich, VT, 1987; National Center for Children's Illustrated Literature, Abilene, TX, 1998.

Awards, Honors

Children's Choice Award, American Reading Association, 1979, for *The Farmer in the Dell;* Notable Children's Trade Book in the Field of Social Studies, National Council for the Social Studies, 1983, for *The Month Brothers: A Slavic Tale* and *The Conversation Club,* 1985, for *A Country Tale,* 1986, for *Peter the Great* and *Captain Whiz-Bang,* 1988, for *Shaka: King of the Zulus,* 1990, for *Fortune,* 1991, for *The Last Princess: The Story of Princess Ka'iulani of Hawai'i,* and 1992, for *Bard of Avon: The Story of William Shakespeare;* Outstanding Science Trade Book for Children, Children's Book Council/National Science Teachers Association, 1985, for *All Wet! All Wet!;* Notable Book, American Library Association (ALA), 1986, and Golden Kite Award Honor Book, Society of Children's Book Writers and Illustrators (SCBWI), 1987, both for *Peter the Great;* Notable Book, ALA, and *Boston Globe-Horn Book* Honor Book for Nonfiction, *Boston Globe-Horn Book,* both 1990, both for *Good Queen Bess: The Story of Elizabeth I of England;* Notable Book, ALA, 1991, Children's Choices for 1992, International Reading Association/Children's Book Council (IRA/CBC), and Carter G. Woodson Award, National Council for the Social Studies, both 1992, all for *The Last Princess: The Story of Princess Ka'iulani of Hawai'i;* Children's Choice Award, IRA/CBC, 1992, for *Siegfried;* Notable Book, ALA, and Orbis Pictus Award for Outstanding Nonfiction for Children nominee, National Council of Teachers of English (NCTE), both 1992, and Notable Children's Book in the Language Arts, 1993, all for *Bard of Avon: The Story of William Shakespeare;* Notable Book, ALA, 1994, for *Cleopatra;* Orbis Pictus Award for Outstanding Nonfiction for Children, NCTE, Notable Book, ALA, both 1996, and *Boston Globe/Horn Book* Award for Nonfiction, *Boston Globe-Horn Book,* 1997, all for *Leonardo da Vinci;* Golden Kite Award Honor Book, SCBWI, 1997, for *Saving Sweetness;* Notable Book, ALA, 1998, for *Rumpelstiltskin's Daughter;* Notable Book, ALA, 1998, and Golden Kite Award nominee, SCBWI, 1999, both for *Joan of Arc;* Notable Book, ALA, 2000, for *Raising Sweetness;* Best Books for Young Adults, ALA, for *A Time Apart.*

Writings

The Good-Luck Pencil, illustrated by Bruce Degen, Four Winds, 1986.
Siegfried, illustrated by John Sandford, Bantam, 1991.
Moe the Dog in Tropical Paradise, illustrated by Elise Primavera, Putnam, 1992.
The Gentleman and the Kitchen Maid, illustrated by Dennis Nolan, Dial, 1994.
Woe Is Moe, illustrated by E. Primavera, Putnam, 1995.
(Fictionalized biography) *Elena,* Hyperion, 1996.
Saving Sweetness, illustrated by G. Brian Karas, Putnam, 1996.
Raising Sweetness, illustrated by Karas, Putnam, 1999.
(Young adult novel) *A Time Apart,* Morrow, 1999.
The Time-Traveling Twins: Roughing It on the Oregon Trail, illustrated by Holly Berry, HarperCollins, 2000.

ILLUSTRATOR

(Under name Diane Zuromskis) *The Farmer in the Dell,* Little, Brown, 1978.
(Under name Diane Stanley Zuromskis) Verna Aardema, *Half-a-Ball-of-Kenki: An Ashanti Tale Retold,* Warne, 1979.
Fiddle-I-Fee: A Traditional American Chant, Little, Brown, 1979.
Tony Johnston, *Little Mouse Nibbling,* Putnam, 1979.
M. Jean Craig, *The Man Whose Name Was Not Thomas,* Doubleday, 1981.
Toni Hormann, *Onions, Onions,* Crowell, 1981.
Giambattista Basile, *Petrosinella, a Neapolitan Rapunzel,* adapted from the translation by John Edward Taylor, Warne, 1981; retold by Stanley, Dial, 1995.
Jane Yolen, *Sleeping Ugly,* Coward, 1981.
Jean and Claudio Marzollo, *Robin of Bray,* Dial, 1982.
Joanne Ryder, *Beach Party,* Warne, 1982.
James Whitcomb Riley, *Little Orphant Annie,* Putnam, 1983.
Samuil Yakovlevich Marshak, reteller, *The Month Brothers: A Slavic Tale,* translated by Thomas P. Whitney, Morrow, 1983.
James Skofield, *All Wet! All Wet!,* Harper, 1984.
Fay Grissom Stanley, *The Last Princess: The Story of Princess Ka'iulani of Hawai'i,* Four Winds, 1991.

SELF-ILLUSTRATED PICTURE BOOKS

The Conversation Club, Macmillan, 1983.
Birdsong Lullaby, Morrow, 1985.
A Country Tale, Macmillan, 1985.
Captain Whiz-Bang, Morrow, 1987.
Fortune, Morrow, 1990.
Rumpelstiltskin's Daughter, Morrow, 1997.

SELF-ILLUSTRATED PICTURE BOOK BIOGRAPHIES

Peter the Great, Four Winds, 1986.
(With husband Peter Vennema) *Shaka: King of the Zulus,* Morrow, 1988.
(With Vennema) *Good Queen Bess: The Story of Elizabeth I of England,* Four Winds, 1990.
(With Vennema) *Bard of Avon: The Story of William Shakespeare,* Morrow, 1992.
(With Vennema) *Charles Dickens: The Man Who Had Great Expectations,* Morrow, 1993.

Diane Stanley

(With Vennema) *Cleopatra,* Morrow, 1994.
The True Adventure of Daniel Hall, Dial, 1995.
Leonardo da Vinci, Morrow, 1996.
Joan of Arc, Morrow, 1998.
Michelangelo, HarperCollins, 2000.

OTHER

Stanley also provided jacket art for *Lost Magic,* a young adult novel by Berthe Amoss.

Adaptations

Moe the Dog in Tropical Paradise was released as a video by MCA/Universal Home Video in 1994 and was featured as an animated segment of *Shelly Duvall's Bedtime Stories* on the Showtime Network.

Work in Progress

The Time-Traveling Twins Join the Boston Tea Party, for HarperCollins, 2001.

Sidelights

An American author and illustrator of fiction, nonfiction, and picture books as well as a reteller of folktales from other cultures, Stanley is regarded as an especially talented and versatile creator of literature for children. Although she has written and illustrated a variety of books for primary and middle graders, Stanley is perhaps best known as the writer and artist of picture book biographies of historical and literary figures for readers in the upper grades. These works, which are celebrated as appealing, balanced treatments that do justice to their subjects, profile warriors such as the Russian tsar Peter the Great, the Zulu king Shaka, and the Maid of Orleans, Joan of Arc; women rulers such as Cleopatra and Elizabeth I of England; and creators of art and literature such as Shakespeare, Leonardo da Vinci, Charles Dickens, and Michelangelo. Stanley and her husband, Peter Vennema, both thoroughly research the subjects of Stanley's illustrated biographies. Stanley then writes and illustrates the books, weaving the characteristics and accomplishments of her subjects into a form that resembles a story. Acknowledged for clearly identifying what is known and what is speculative about the lives that she is outlining, Stanley writes her works in concise prose and illustrates them with elegant, detailed watercolor and gouache illustrations that are done in the artistic style of the periods in which her subjects lived. Reviewers note the smoothness and readability of Stanley's prose while lauding her drawings and paintings as both accurate and beautiful. In her review of *Joan of Arc* in *School Library Journal,* Shirley Wilton commended Stanley's "talent for historical research, skill in writing clear and interesting prose, and ability to adapt different art styles and techniques appropriate to her subjects." Bill Ott, assessing *Charles Dickens: The Man Who Had Great Expectations* in *Booklist,* noted that Stanley and Vennema "recognize the demands of their audience as well as any authors in their specialized field."

In addition to her picture book biographies, Stanley has written and illustrated a wide variety of books in various genres. Her picture books range from humorous to gentle to atmospheric and feature children and animals, both real and anthropomorphic. Stanley has also written several longer stories featuring cats as main characters as well a feminist version of the folktale "Rumpelstiltskin," a transformation tale set in ancient Persia, and a fantasy about how two lovers—subjects of paintings by the Dutch Masters—find each other in an art museum. In addition, Stanley is the creator of a young adult novel about an American girl who becomes part of an experimental project that replicates life in an English Iron Age village; two humorous picture books about Moe the Dog and his canine companion Arlene; and two witty stories about Sweetness, a resourceful orphan in the Old West. Stanley is also the reteller of *Petrosinella: A Neapolitan Rapunzel;* the artist supplied pictures for the original version of this book, which was written by Giambattista Basile, and then adapted the text in her own words for the second edition. As with her picture book biographies, Stanley is celebrated for the illustrations that grace her other works; assessing *Fortune,* a critic in *Kirkus Reviews* claimed, "Stanley continues to defy categorization with her art." Using mediums such as colored pencil and collage as well as her characteristic watercolor, the artist creates pictures that range from miniature drawings to soft pastel watercolors and ornate, sumptuous paintings filled with light and intricate geometric shapes. Stanley has also provided well-received pictures for works by such authors as Verna Aardema, Jane Yolen, James Whitcomb Riley, Joanne Ryder, James Skofield, Tony Johnston, and Fay Grissom Stanley, the author's mother. In these works, the artist is generally credited with reflecting the same creativity and attention to detail as in the pictures for her own books. Stanley's works have also been illustrated by other artists, such as Bruce Degen, John Sandford, Elsie Primavera, Dennis Nolan, and G. Brian Karas. Although she is occasionally criticized for the brevity and selective quality of her texts in her picture book biographies as well as for the stiffness of some of the human figures in her illustrations, most observers consider Stanley to be the creator of engaging works that are especially notable for their lucid texts and eye-catching art.

Born in Abilene, Texas, Stanley is the only child of Burt Stanley, a Navy pilot who was a flying ace in World War II and won a Distinguished Flying Cross, and Fay Grissom Stanley, a novelist, playwright, copywriter, and author of nonfiction. Stanley's parents divorced not long after she was born, and Stanley went with her mother to New York City. They lived in a brownstone in Greenwich Village that served as the setting for Fay's first mystery novel, *Murder Leaves a Ring,* which was dedicated to Diane; Stanley returned the favor with the first book that she both wrote and illustrated, *The Conversation Club.* Later, mother and daughter collaborated on the biography *The Last Princess: The Story of Princess Ka'iulani of Hawai'i,* which Fay wrote and Diane illustrated. Writing on her website, *Diane Stanley—Books for Children,* Stanley said, "All this mother-daughter writing and dedicating speaks to the enormous

part that Fay played in my life, and especially in my development as a writer and illustrator. She was a serious lifetime reader, a true lover of words and art. She was also a witty and flamboyant woman with a love of adventure and a broad view of the world.... Fay was addicted to travel, the more exotic and challenging the destinations, the better. A true love and respect of the art and culture of other people and places was part of my family legacy." In her essay in *Something about the Author Autobiography Series (SAAS),* Stanley called her father "neat, precise, conservative, and single-minded. Some of these traits were passed on to me, making me feel at times like a pigeon in an aviary of exotic birds." After his divorce, Burt Stanley remarried and disappeared from Diane's life. She saw him once as a child and then again at sixteen; however, as an adult, she reconciled with her father and saw him more regularly.

Describing herself in *SAAS* as "the one child of a glamorous divorcee living in the artsy West Village of New York in the 1940s...," Stanley ate in elegant restaurants, went to the opera and to Broadway plays, read books by authors such as Oscar Wilde and Hilaire Belloc, and met several artists, actors, and writers. Stanley sang duets from Broadway shows with her mother and acted in both school plays and amateur productions with friends. After completing second grade, Stanley learned that her mother had contracted tuberculosis. During Fay's hospitalization and recuperation, a period that lasted approximately two years, Stanley went back to Abilene to live with her mother's sister Nancy Sayles and her husband Hal. Stanley noted in *SAAS,* "Nancy became my second mother and Martha and Jim, my cousins, were like brother and sister." The Sayles household was a welcoming one: Stanley and her cousins spent a lot of time outdoors, and, when they were inside, Jim Sayles would often tell stories, including one about an adventuresome cat and another about a fairy king who lived in the family backyard. Stanley wrote in *SAAS,* "I was an active, gangly, rumpled, accident-prone sort of child, and I'm very glad I had those years, though I missed my mother very much.... For at least those few years, I was a child among children, and it was fun."

After Fay Grissom Stanley's recovery from tuberculosis, mother and daughter moved to La Jolla, California, where they lived a few blocks from the beach. Diane made and flew kites, rode her bicycle, roller-skated, explored the rocky sections of the beach, and made up plays with her best friend Lynn. Writing in *SAAS,* Stanley revealed, "I might as well say at this point that I was something of a show-off, being once again a child among adults, and anxious to be every bit as intellectual and clever as they were. I doubt if this went down very well with the other children." She added, "I was now growing into an active, gangly, rumpled sort of teenager, advanced intellectually but socially still a child. To make it worse, I skipped the eighth grade and was thus in class with boys and girls a year or two older than I was. I read a lot and was not stylish about my dress. I certainly wasn't popular." In high school, Stanley wrote for the school newspaper, sang in several choral groups, and was president of the drama club, which she described in *SAAS* as "my big interest." At thirteen, Stanley played Puck in a production of *A Midsummer Night's Dream* that was performed at an outdoor theater; in high school, she earned enough points to be a National Thespian and planned on being an actress on Broadway. "It is strange," Stanley noted in *SAAS,* "that once I got to college, I put all thoughts of the theater behind me, so interested did I become in other things."

When Stanley was sixteen, her mother became ill again and had to be hospitalized, so Diane moved back to Abilene and stayed with the Sayles family. After her graduation from Abilene High School, Stanley went to Trinity University, a small, Presbyterian liberal arts college in San Antonio. "I was happy there," Stanley recalled in *SAAS.* She majored in the social sciences but assumed, as she noted, "that I would become a wife and mother, and that it really didn't matter." However, in her senior year, Stanley took two drawing classes. She wrote in *SAAS,* "Though I had had no other art training, I seemed instinctively to know what to do. It felt as if I had been doing it all my life." At the end of the year, Stanley's teacher called her into his office. He told her that she was the only person in the class who was not an art major and that she was also the only person to receive an "A" as a final grade. Stanley stated, "He told me I had talent. This changed my life. I believed him."

In her essay in *SAAS,* Stanley mused that it "seems odd to me that my natural interest and talent in art did not come to the foreground earlier. I certainly shone whenever we had to draw something in school, or carve something out of a bar of soap. I remember taking watercolors down to the beach and attempting to paint the sea. And I was forever making things." Stanley has pointed out that writing is something that she did well, and often. "Because my mother was a writer," she wrote in *SAAS,* "I often thought that I, too, could be a writer." Stanley attributes much of her success in writing to her interest in reading. "I cannot stress enough," she noted in *SAAS,* "what a big part reading has always played in my life. It comforted me when I was sad or lonely, broadened my understanding of the world, enriched my vocabulary, entertained me, made me think, made me laugh, made me cry, helped me grow. I could never have become a writer if I weren't first a reader."

After graduating from college in 1963, Stanley moved to Houston and began working as a lab technician in a hospital; she also took life-drawing classes at night. Stanley recalled in *SAAS,* "Working in a hospital, I learned about medical illustration, a field in which artists are trained in medicine and then do illustrations for medical and scientific books. Being the kind of artist who loves detail and works small, this seemed just right for me." Stanley spent a year at the University of Texas studying art and finishing the pre-med requirements for graduate school. While living in Houston, Stanley met Peter Vennema, a young man who had just graduated from Harvard Business School; the two fell in love, then drifted apart. Fourteen years later, Vennema was to play a prominent role in Stanley's life.

In 1966, Stanley spent a year studying art at the University of Edinburgh; she wrote in *SAAS,* "It turned out to be a wonderful year." When not studying, Stanley traveled to Germany, Italy, Poland, and the Greek Islands. She also went to Russia, which especially fascinated her. Stanley wrote in *SAAS,* "This was the beginning of my 'Russian phase,' in which I read all the great Russian novels, beginning with *War and Peace,* studied Russian art and history, and unknowingly planted the seeds of the first biography I would write years later, *Peter the Great.*" The following summer, Stanley and a friend toured Europe before heading to Israel, where they picked apples in a kibbutz. Returning to the United States, Stanley was accepted for graduate studies at the Johns Hopkins University College of Medicine in Baltimore; she was one of only two students to be accepted that year. She received her master's degree from Johns Hopkins in 1970. The author wrote on her website, "After four years of hard work, I was finally qualified to pursue a profession which I would soon heartlessly abandon—because just a few years later, in my mid-thirties, I suddenly discovered what I wanted to be when I grew up: a children's book illustrator."

Shortly after receiving her master's degree, Stanley married Peter Zuromskis, a fellow classmate who had become a doctor; the couple had two daughters, Catherine and Tamara. "What you do with children, I figured," Stanley noted on her website, "was read to them." She began going to the library and digging through the stacks; a librarian, noting Stanley's keen interest, began setting aside books for her. Stanley noted in *SAAS,* "Without exactly realizing it, I was doing a self-taught course in children's literature." She commented on her website, "I found plenty of good books all right, but I also found a vocation." She stated in *SAAS,* "I'm not sure exactly when I knew that I wanted to become an illustrator of children's books, but this ambition became clear and firm." While researching the field, Stanley began experimenting with watercolors and pen-and-ink drawings; she also taught herself color-separation techniques. Stanley created a portfolio of illustrations for children's books while juggling full-time motherhood and freelance work as a medical illustrator. On a trip to Boston, she made an appointment with John Keller, who was then the editor-in-chief of the publishers Little, Brown and Company. Keller gave Stanley her first book contract; she wrote in *SAAS,* "This was, without a doubt, one of the happiest days of my life."

Keller had suggested to Stanley that she create an illustrated version of the nursery rhyme "The Farmer in the Dell." In 1978, she produced *The Farmer in the Dell* as Diane Zuromskis. In line drawings and pastel watercolors enclosed in circular frames that appear across from the text of the familiar refrain, Stanley depicts the farmer in his bachelor days, at his marriage, with his family, and with his animals. A reviewer in *Publishers Weekly* trumpeted, "Zuromskis's first book suggests that she has begun a rich career." Although a critic in *Kirkus Reviews* called *The Farmer in the Dell* "the sort of nonentity that will circulate—cute and . . .

clever enough to invite a look-through, but too one-dimensional enough to reward it any level," *Booklist* contributor Denise M. Wilms concluded her review by calling the work a "pleasant enough confection for picture book browsers drawn to the familiar lines they can 'read' to themselves." In 1979, Stanley illustrated her first book by another writer, Verna Aardema's *Half-a-Ball-of-Kenki: An Ashanti Tale Retold.* She produced her second adaptation of a familiar song, *Fiddle-I-Fee: A Traditional American Chant,* in the same year. Illustrated with lively four-color drawings, the book depicts a red-haired, freckle-faced girl who has a dinner party in her tree house for all of the animals mentioned in the song. Calling the illustrations "fanciful," *Booklist* reviewer Marilyn Kaye remarked that the book has "an overall look that is dreamy and quietly silly," while Marjorie Lewis wrote in *School Library Journal,* "The sturdy full-color drawings are witty with details and subtleties that amplify the minimal text and manage to give each individual beast ... the attention its idiosyncrasies deserve." *Fiddle-I-Fee* is the first of Stanley's books to be published as Diane Stanley; in the year of its publication, Stanley and Peter Zuromskis were divorced. Stanley wrote on her website, "[M]y daughters and I had moved to New York (does this sound familiar?) where we lived not far from my old childhood apartment in the West Village and my daughters attended the same school I had gone to." During the day, Stanley worked as a publicity designer with Dell Publishing and then as art director in the children's books division for two other publishers, G. P. Putnam's Sons and Coward, McCann & Geoghegan; at night, when her children were asleep, Stanley kept on illustrating. "Somehow," she wrote on her website, "the laundry got done."

Through a series of coincidences, Stanley became reacquainted with Peter Vennema, who was working in engineering and business in Texas. In 1979, Stanley and Vennema married and she moved to Houston, where she became a full-time illustrator. Stanley and Vennema had a son, John Leslie, in 1981; two years later, she produced *The Conversation Club,* the first of her works that she both wrote and illustrated. In this picture book, which is illustrated in alternating spreads of watercolors and black-and-white drawings, Peter Fieldmouse, new in town, is invited to a meeting of the Conversation Club, where everyone converses at once. Peter decides to form his own group, the Listening Club, where one mouse talks at a time. The club becomes a success when the mice experience the joys of listening and of being heard. Writing in *Booklist,* Ilene Cooper called *The Conversation Club* a "cozy little story with pictures to match," adding, "As in other books, [Stanley's] patterning and design work are visual delights." *School Library Journal* critic Pamela Warren Stubbins stated, "The evolution of the club, while predictable, seems natural." Stanley wrote in *SAAS* about the genesis of *The Conversation Club:* "The club of anthropomorphic mice was inspired somewhat by the natural exuberance of my large family. In the story, they all talk at the same time, the result being complete gibberish. This has been known to happen at our dinner table."

In 1986, Stanley published the first of her picture book biographies, *Peter the Great.* Inspired by memories of her travels in Russia and by an adult biography of Peter Alexeevich by Robert K. Massie, Stanley decided to condense the life of the controversial tsar, who opened communication between Russia and the rest of Europe, into a standard thirty-two page text. Stanley emphasizes the events in Peter's life with the most interest for children, such as his boyhood. Through her portrayal, Peter emerges as a visionary and a reformer as well as a tyrant. Stanley illustrated *Peter the Great* with jewel-like, intricately patterned pictures in watercolor and gouache that draw on elements of both Asian and European art. Jean Fritz, an author of nonfiction to whom Stanley is often compared, wrote in the *New York Times Book Review* that *Peter the Great* "stays close to the historical record and turns out to be the strongest story of all.... [Stanley] has the good sense not to embellish his extraordinary life and let it speak for itself." Fritz added that Stanley's "exquisite illustrations hang like framed pictures on her pages." Writing in *Bulletin of the Center for Children's Books,* Betsy Hearne said that Stanley "compressed a good deal of complex information into a compact text while managing to convey some sense of Peter's wildly unique personality and contributions to Russian history. Her illustrations ... offer a visual depth that increases the impact of the book considerably." Ilene Cooper of *Booklist* predicted, "The genre will profit if this is just the first of her forays into biography."

In subsequent biographies, Stanley became, as she stated in *SAAS,* "more thorough and more honest" about revealing the parts of the lives of her subjects that were cruel or shocking. She also continued to search for colorful anecdotes to bring out the personalities of her subjects. "In all my biographies," she noted in *SAAS,* "I now search for the telling anecdote, in hopes that it will capture the child's imagination." Beginning with her second biography, *Shaka: King of the Zulus,* Stanley involved Peter Vennema in the research for her works. Vennema often did the preliminary library work, establishing the bibliography. Both he and Stanley would then read the many sources that he had chosen. Although Stanley did the actual writing, Vennema served as an editorial consultant; consequently, he is listed as co-author on several biographies. Beginning with *Charles Dickens: The Man Who Had Great Expectations,* Stanley and her family began to take research trips for her books. They went to England for *Charles Dickens,* to Egypt for *Cleopatra,* to Italy—twice—for *Leonardo da Vinci* and *Michelangelo,* and to France for *Joan of Arc.* Reviewers consistently praise Stanley for creating exceptional picture books biographies. For example, *Washington Post Book World* critic Phyllis Sidorsky, reviewing *Bard of Avon: The Story of William Shakespeare,* enthused, "What a lucky day for young readers when Diane Stanley and her husband Peter Vennema produce one of their distinguished biographies." A reviewer in *Publishers Weekly* called *Leonardo da Vinci* "[a] virtuosic work," while in *School Library Journal,* Shirley Wilton called *Joan of Arc* a "magnificent picture book" as well as "a work of art, a good story, and a model of historical writing."

Stanley once commented, "With the exception of raising children, [writing picture-book biographies] is the most challenging—and satisfying—work I have ever done. For a year, I am immersed in the life and times of a singular man or woman, and I come to know these people intimately. I not only must learn the details of a life and find a simple and compelling way to convey complex events and ideas, but I also have to understand the architecture and costumes of the period so that I can try to recreate my subject's world in visual terms. One of my favorite aspects of creating these books is choosing something in the art or culture of the subject's country and period to use as a design theme throughout the book—such as the Zulu beadwork in *Shaka* and the mosaics in *Cleopatra*." In an interview with Elizabeth Devereaux in *Publishers Weekly,* Stanley observed that biography "is almost like a collage. You have all these different materials. Your position is not to put words in your subjects' mouths or invent feelings, but to choose from all of these elements, and put them together in such a way that you paint a picture of the person and entertain your reader and give a sense of the person and their world.... That's how you put your stamp on it, in making choices."

In addition to her biographies of well-known international figures, Stanley has created two biographies of lesser-known Americans. The first, *The True Adventure of Daniel Hall,* is a picture book biography published in 1995 about a fourteen-year-old boy from New Bedford, Massachusetts, who ships out to sea on a whaler in 1856. Scheduled to be on the ship for three years, Daniel disembarks in Siberia due to mistreatment by the ship's captain. The boy survives eight months of winter with the help of the Yakut people before returning to New Bedford on another whaler. Writing in *Horn Book,* Elizabeth S. Watson said, "How Daniel survived to finally achieve vindication against the cruel captain makes a wonderful adventure expertly illustrated by the artist's spectacularly rich illustrations." A critic in *Kirkus Reviews* added, "In less adept hands, this would have been but another cruel tale, but Stanley's nimble touch keeps melodrama at bay, provides intriguing glimpses into whaling life, and renders lovely, age-worn pastel illustrations that look as though they were lifted from 19th-century cameos." In *Elena,* a fictionalized biography directed to middle graders, Stanley imagines events in the life of the family history of her mother's friend—portrayed pseudonymously—who fled from Mexico to California during the Mexican Civil War. Elena rejects the traditional passive role assigned to women in her society; she learns to read and do arithmetic and later triumphs over the objections of her father by marrying the man she loves. After her husband dies and war breaks out, Elena takes her children on a dangerous quest to reach the United States. A reviewer in *Publishers Weekly* commented that Stanley's "spare, graceful prose shapes a credible portrait of a person of singular insight and courage."

In 1999, Stanley produced her first book for young adults, the novel *A Time Apart.* In this work, which was inspired by a British Broadcasting Company (BBC) miniseries about an actual Iron Age farm, thirteen-year-old Ginny Dorris leaves Houston to stay in England with her British father while her American mother undergoes treatment for breast cancer. Her father, a professor who is divorced from Ginny's mother, is part of an experimental archaeological project that is replicating an Iron Age village. Battling homesickness and the primitive conditions of her new home, Ginny runs away from the experimental village and books a flight back to Houston with a credit card she has stolen from her father. Her father realizes what she has done and why, and eventually jeopardizes his career by leaving the project to go to Houston after her. After realizing how sick her mother is, Ginny returns to England with her father for a few more months. As the story progresses, Ginny learns to adapt and even flourishes under the difficult conditions of the Iron Age village. As she becomes immersed in the daily life of the community, she discovers hidden strengths and learns to appreciate living a more simple lifestyle; in addition, she becomes closer to her father. Writing in *Booklist,* Sally Estes called *A Time Apart* a "very appealing novel" as well as an "enchanting 'time travel' into reality."

On assessing her life and career, Stanley wrote in *SAAS,* "Looking at the life I have made for myself, I feel terribly grateful to have found work that is satisfying and useful.... The fact is that I love my work. To balance my work is my family life, for which I am also grateful.... For what more could a person ask? Free time, maybe. But that's about all." She once revealed, "I try to approach each new book in a manner that suits the story; consequently, my books are quite different from one another.... Whenever I travel I try to observe such things as how thatched roofs are put together, how period houses are furnished, etc.... I love beautifully designed books and enjoy such extras as ornaments and initial caps. I basically love my work—though it is lonely at times. I feel lucky to earn a living doing something so full of delight!"

Stanley once observed, "Perhaps because I was an only child, reading became my best companion. Today, my life is all about books: writing them, illustrating them, reading them, and sharing them with children. I feel blessed." She added, "I have always admired Mary Catherine Bateson's concept of 'composing a life.' Professionally as well as personally, I have deeply enjoyed moving along the path I set out upon over twenty years ago. Part of the fun is not knowing where it will take me."

Works Cited

Cooper, Ilene, review of *The Conversation Club, Booklist,* September 15, 1983, p. 173.

Cooper, Ilene, review of *Peter the Great, Booklist,* October 1, 1986, p. 275.

Devereaux, Elizabeth, "Diane Stanley: Illustrating a Life," *Publishers Weekly,* July 22, 1996, p. 216.

Review of *Elena, Publishers Weekly,* April 29, 1996, p. 73.

Estes, Sally, review of *A Time Apart, Booklist,* June 1 & 15, 1999, p. 1826.

Review of *The Farmer in the Dell, Kirkus Reviews,* April, 1, 1978, p. 370.

Review of *The Farmer in the Dell, Publishers Weekly,* April 3, 1978, p. 80.

Review of *Fortune, Kirkus Reviews,* February 1, 1990, p. 185.

Fritz, Jean, "The Wedding Gift Had Tusks," *New York Times Book Review,* November 9, 1986, p. 58.

Hearne, Betsy, review of *Peter the Great, Bulletin of the Center for Children's Books,* October, 1986, pp. 37-38.

Kaye, Marilyn, review of *Fiddle-I-Fee: A Traditional American Chant, Booklist,* December 1, 1979, p. 556.

Review of *Leonardo da Vinci, Publishers Weekly,* July 8, 1996, p. 84.

Lewis, Marjorie, review of *Fiddle-I-Fee: A Traditional American Chant, School Library Journal,* January, 1980, p. 55.

Ott, Bill, "Should We Tell the Kids?," *Booklist,* September 1, 1993, p. 56.

Sidorsky, Phyllis, review of *Bard of Avon: The Story of William Shakespeare, Washington Post Book World,* December 6, 1992, p. 18.

Stanley, Diane, entry in *Something about the Author Autobiography Series,* Volume 15, Gale, 1993, pp. 277-91.

Stanley, Diane, "About the Author," *Diane Stanley—Books for Children,* http://www.dianestanley.com, January 14, 2000.

Stubbins, Pamela Warren, review of *The Conversation Club, School Library Journal,* December, 1983, pp. 60-61.

Review of *The True Adventure of Daniel Hall, Kirkus Reviews,* July 15, 1995, p. 1030.

Watson, Elizabeth S., review of *The True Adventure of Daniel Hall, Horn Book,* November-December, 1995, p. 758.

Wilms, Denise M., review of *The Farmer in the Dell, Booklist,* May 15, 1978, p. 1492.

Wilton, Shirley, review of *Joan of Arc, School Library Journal,* September, 1998, pp. 226-27.

For More Information See

BOOKS

Cummins, Julie, editor, *Children's Book Illustration and Design,* PBC International, 1992.

Holtze, Sally Holmes, editor, *Sixth Book of Junior Authors and Illustrators,* H.W. Wilson, 1989.

Pendergast, Sara, and Tom Pendergast, *St. James Guide to Children's Writers,* 5th edition, St. James Press, 1999, pp. 1000-01.

Silvey, Anita, editor, *Children's Books and Their Creators,* Houghton Mifflin, 1995.

PERIODICALS

Bulletin of the Center for Children's Books, July-August, 1997, pp. 414-45.

Horn Book, September-October, 1998, pp. 623, 625.

Publishers Weekly, February 1, 1999, p. 84.

School Library Journal, January, 1999, p. 102.

T

TAKABAYASHI, Mari 1960-

Personal

Born November 20, 1960, in Tokyo, Japan; daughter of Yoshimitsu and Emiko Takabayashi; married Kam Mak (an illustrator); children: Luca, Dylan. *Education:* Otsma Women's College, Japan.

Mari Takabayashi

Addresses

Home—369 Sackett St., Brooklyn, NY 11231.

Writings

Baby's Things, Chronicle, 1994.

ILLUSTRATOR

Christine Loomis, *Rush Hour,* Houghton Mifflin, 1995.
Linda Crotta Brennan, *Flannel Kisses,* Houghton Mifflin, 1997.
Jean Marzollo, *Do You Know New?,* HarperCollins, 1998.
Patricia Hubbell, *Sidewalk Trip,* HarperCollins, 1999.
Brennan, *Marshmellow Kisses,* Houghton Mifflin, 2000.

Also illustrator for more than twenty picture books from Japanese publishers.

Sidelights

Mari Takabayashi told *SATA:* "I moved to New York in 1990, and I started to work for American publishers. I like to work for American publishers because I can draw many races. Also, New York City, where I live, inspires me a lot. My two kids (they are 5 and 2 years old) give me ideas. When I draw pictures for American publishers I always put Asian kids somewhere."

Mari Takabayashi is a Japanese illustrator who has worked on several children's picture books published in the United States. Her illustrations, often executed in pastel watercolors, are praised for imparting energy and depth to the simple, rhyming texts they accompany. In *Rush Hour,* written by Christine Loomis, Takabayashi depicts the varied activities of the masses as they commute to work via car, bus, train, or airplane. Filled with "seemingly inexhaustible, enjoyable details," according to a reviewer for *Publishers Weekly,* Takabayashi's illustrations "are a kaleidoscope of color, pattern and activity." For John Peters in *School Library Journal,* they "effectively capture the hustle and bustle of it all." And because the book ends with the joyful reunion of parents returning home from work to be with their children, the result is "a loving, comforting book for grown-ups to share with their children," contended Stephanie Zvirin in *Booklist*.

For *Flannel Kisses,* a picture book written by Linda Crotta Brennan, Takabayashi contributed a series of nostalgia-imbued illustrations celebrating the kind of fun that may be had on a snowy day. The children in *Flannel Kisses* divide their time between the warmth of their home, depicted as an "idyllic, plank-floored cottage ... decorated with rag rugs, crocheted afghans and toys consisting of a puppet theater and rag dolls," and playing outside in the cold and snow, observed a reviewer in *Publishers Weekly*. The text, written in rhyming couplets, covers the events of the day from climbing out of flannel sheets to touch the cold floor below, to breakfast, playing in the snow, inside for a lunch of hot soup, back outside for making snowmen, then in for dinner and bedtime stories by the fireside. "Matching the text in tone and mood are delightful naive-style pictures," observed Ilene Cooper in *Booklist,* making for "an enjoyable book," especially at the end of a wintry day spent enjoying the types of activities depicted in *Flannel Kisses.*

Works Cited

Cooper, Ilene, review of *Flannel Kisses, Booklist,* October 15, 1997, p. 411.
Review of *Flannel Kisses, Publishers Weekly,* August 25, 1997, p. 71.
Peters, John, review of *Rush Hour, School Library Journal,* September, 1996, p. 184.
Review of *Rush Hour, Publishers Weekly,* August 26, 1996, p. 96.
Zvirin, Stephanie, review of *Rush Hour, Booklist,* July, 1996, p. 1830.

For More Information See

PERIODICALS

School Library Journal, July, 1999, p. 74.

* * *

TIBBLES, Jean-Paul 1958-

Personal

Born February 7, 1958, in the United Kingdom; married, wife's name Annette; children: Marie-Louise, Nicole-Anne. *Education:* Attended Eastbourne College of Art and Design.

Addresses

Home—East Sussex, England. *Agent*—Bernstein & Andriulli, 58 West 40th St., New York, NY.

Career

Illustrator.

Jean-Paul Tibbles provided the illustrations for this installation in the popular "American Girls" series, in which Josefina and her sisters must find a way to persuade their favorite aunt from leaving the rancho. (*From* Changes for Josefina, *written by Valerie Tripp.*)

Illustrator

Valerie Tripp, *Meet Josefina: Am American Girl,* vignettes by Susan McAliley, Pleasant Co. (Middleton, WI), 1997.
Tripp, *Josefina Learns a Lesson: A School Story,* vignettes by McAliley, Pleasant Co., 1997.
Tripp, *Josefina's Surprise: A Christmas Story,* vignettes by McAliley, Pleasant Co., 1997.
Tripp, *Happy Birthday, Josefina! A Springtime Story,* vignettes by McAliley, Pleasant Co., 1998.
Tripp, *Josefina Saves the Day: A Summer Story,* vignettes by McAliley, Pleasant Co., 1998.
Tripp, *Changes for Josefina: A Winter Story,* vignettes by McAliley, Pleasant Co., 1998.
Tripp, *A Reward for Josefina,* vignettes by McAliley, Pleasant Co., 1999.
Tripp, *Again, Josefina!,* vignettes by McAliley, Pleasant Co., 2000.

Sidelights

Jean-Paul Tibbles told *SATA:* "My work was first commissioned while I was in my final year at college in 1979. I have continued to work as an illustrator, working for all the major British book publishers. Often working in advertising, I have many international commissions; in the United States my work has been used by United Airlines, the *New Yorker,* and Puffin."

For More Information See

PERIODICALS

Christian Science Monitor, September 25, 1997, p. B6.
School Library Journal, December, 1997, p. 102; May, 1998, p. 162.

V–W

VILOTT, Rhondi
See SALSITZ, Rhondi Vilott

*   *   *

WARDLAW, Lee 1955-

Personal

Born November 20, 1955, in Salina, KS; daughter of Joseph Patterson (a radio station owner) and Margaret (a homemaker and community volunteer; maiden name, Laux) Wardlaw; married Craig Zeisloft Jaffurs (wine maker), August 27, 1983; children: one son, Patterson Wardlaw Jaffurs. *Education:* California Polytechnic State University, B.A. (with honors), 1977. *Religion:* Atheist. *Hobbies and other interests:* Reading "especially mystery or suspense/thrillers," bodysurfing and swimming, wine tasting, cats, Hawaii; "I also enjoy studying philosophy and chewing bubble gum!"

Addresses

Home—P.O. Box 1452, Summerland, CA 93067. *Agent*—Virginia Knowlton, Curtis Brown Ltd., 10 Astor Pl., New York, NY 10003.

Career

Los Ninos Head Start Pre-School, Santa Barbara, CA, director's assistant, 1977-78; Goleta Head Start Pre-School, Goleta, CA, director/head teacher, 1978-79; Cornelia Moore Memorial Dental Foundation, Santa Barbara, director/teacher, 1979-82; Outlaw Communications, Santa Barbara, owner, 1982-85; children's book author, 1985—. Lecturer, workshop leader at various conferences, schools and associations within California and out of state, 1986—; Santa Barbara Community College, Santa Barbara, writing instructor, 1988—; Mountain View Elementary and Ellwood Elementary, Santa Barbara and Goleta, teacher of creative writing courses for children, 1990-91. KIST radio, Santa Barba-

ra, public ascertainment coordinator, 1974-81; reading tutor, 1975-79; Girl Scout Leader, 1977-78; Montecito Library, storyteller, 1978-79; Peabody Elementary School, library volunteer, 1985-93; Santa Barbara County Schools Library Committee, children's book reviewer, 1986-90. *Member:* Society of Children's Book Writers and Illustrators (Santa Barbara/Ventura Chapter, advisory board, 1996—), California Reading Association, Children's Literature Council of Southern California, Ventura County Reading Association, Cornelia Moore Dental Foundation Board of Directors (education advisor, 1982-1992), Santa Barbara Writers for Children, Cal Poly Alumni Association, Santa Barbara High School Alumni Association, Southern California Children's Booksellers Association, Author's Guild, California Readers, Cat Writer's Association.

Awards, Honors

Creative Service Award, Cornelia Moore Dental Foundation, 1982; selected as Grand Marshal, DownTown Organization/Santa Barbara Chamber of Commerce Christmas Parade, 1989; Best Local Author, Santa Barbara News-Press/KCQR radio community poll, 1990; Recommended for Reluctant Young Adult Readers Award, American Library Association (ALA), and Children's Choice Award, International Reading Association/Children's Book Council, both 1991, both for *Corey's Fire;* Recommended for Reluctant Young Adult Readers Award, ALA, 1992, for *Cowabunga! The Complete Book of Surfing;* Distinguished Alumni Award, Santa Barbara High School Alumni Association, 1993; Texas Lone Star Recommended Reading List, and Florida Sunshine State Young Reader's Award, both 1996, for *Seventh-Grade Weirdo;* Junior Library Guild selection, 1997, Notable Children's Trade Book in the Field of Social Studies, Children's Book Council/National Council of Social Studies, 1998, and nomination for Treasure State (Montana) Children's Choice Award, 2000, all for *Punia and the King of Sharks;* South Carolina Children's Book Award Finalist, Garden State (New Jersey) Children's Book Award Finalist, Florida Sunshine State Young Reader Award, The Great Stone

Lee Wardlaw

Face (New Hampshire) Children's Book Award, and Oklahoma Sequoyah Children's Book Award, all 1999, and nomination for Maryland Black-Eyed Susan Award, 2000, all for *101 Ways to Bug Your Parents.*

Writings

NONFICTION

Giggles & Grins: A Dental Health and Nutrition Curriculum Guide for Pre-School Teachers, C. M. Dental Foundation, 1985.

Cowabunga! The Complete Book of Surfing, Avon Sports, 1991.

Bubblemania: A Kid's Book of Bubble Gum, Aladdin/Simon & Shuster, 1997.

We All Scream for Ice Cream!, HarperCollins, 2000.

FOR CHILDREN

Me + Math = Headache, illustrated by Joanne Hoy, Red Hen Press, 1986, revised edition illustrated by Deborah Stouffer, 1989.

The Eye and I, illustrated by Stouffer, Red Hen Press, 1988.

Operation Rhinoceros, illustrated by Stouffer, Red Hen Press, 1992.

Seventh-Grade Weirdo, Scholastic, 1992, republished as *My Life as a Weirdo,* Troll, 2000.

The Tales of Grandpa Cat, illustrated by Ronald Searle, Dial, 1994; Pavillion Books, Great Britain, 1996.

(Reteller) *Punia and the King of Sharks: A Hawaiian Folktale,* illustrated by Felipe Davalos, Dial, 1995.

101 Ways to Bug Your Parents, Dial, 1996.

The Ghoul Brothers, illustrated by Brian Floca, Troll, 1996.

Dinosaur Pizza, illustrated by Julie Durrell, Troll, 1998.

Bow-Wow Birthday, illustrated by Arden Johnson-Petrov, Boyds Mill Press, 1998.

Hector's Hiccups, illustrated by Joan Holub, Random House, 1999.

First Steps, illustrated by Julie Paschkis, HarperCollins, 1999.

Saturday Night Jamboree, illustrated by Barry Root, Dial, 2000.

FOR YOUNG ADULTS

Alley Cat, Simon & Schuster, 1987.

Corey's Fire, Avon/Flare, 1990.

Don't Look Back, Avon/Flare, 1993.

Alley Cat has been translated into French, German, Italian, and Hungarian. Also contributor of the short story "Shadow Girl" to the anthology *See You in September,* Avon, 1995, and reteller of the "Legend of the Menehune Ditch," published in *Cricket* magazine, September, 1999.

Adaptations

Corey's Fire was recorded for the blind, 1991.

Work in Progress

The Chair Where Bear Sits (picture book) for Winslow Press, due in 2001; *Peek-A-Book* (picture book), for Dial, due in 2002.

Sidelights

Lee Wardlaw is the author of over twenty titles for young readers of all ages. They include coming-of-age novels for young adults, humorous tales for middle graders, and picture books for toddlers. She has also written three popular nonfiction titles extolling the joys of surfing, in *Cowabunga!,* of bubble gum, in *Bubblemania,* and America's favorite dessert in *We All Scream for Ice Cream!* Wardlaw is noted for her humorous viewpoint on growing up and for characters that display inner resiliency and determination in both serious and silly situations.

A long-time resident of Santa Barbara, California, Wardlaw has been an author for much of her life. "I've been writing since age seven, and it was something I always wanted to do," Wardlaw told Russ Spencer of the *Santa Barbara News Press.* She worked as a tutor, a radio commercial copywriter, fashion model, tooth fairy, and a school teacher before committing herself to a career as a writer. As she told Spencer, "I thought if I did it full time it would get boring . . . . I thought that if you did something you really loved, it would get old after a while. But after teaching, I realized writing is really what I should be doing, and I'm still at it."

One of Wardlaw's most celebrated books, *Corey's Fire,* is based on a true story. She once told *SATA* about the pivotal event that changed her life and inspired *Corey's Fire:* "On a hot summer evening in 1977, a young man was flying a kite in the foothills of Santa Barbara, California. A gust of wind tangled the kite in some power lines, showering sparks into the dry weeds below. Although firefighters rushed to the scene, the blaze soon flared out of control. The fire burned for more [than]

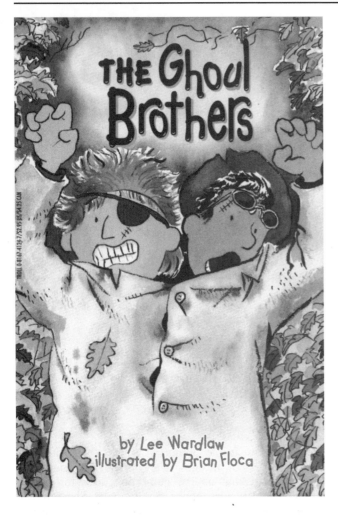

Nick discovers that his pesky little sister can be useful when she helps him win the neighborhood Halloween costume party.

twenty-four hours, destroying 200 homes. My family's home was one of those that burned to the ground. We lost everything—including my cat. Days later, while sifting through the wreckage and ash, I found only two recognizable items: a blackened baby spoon and our front door knob! I kept both as souvenirs of what I call the 'before time.'"

To deal with her feelings about the fire, Wardlaw wrote the story about Corey, the 14-year-old protagonist, who is a dependent, immature girl, full of self-pity. *Corey's Fire* tells of her change after the fire. "It is not the disaster that changes Corey," Wardlaw once explained to *SATA*. "She chooses to change. That's her first step to becoming an independent young woman. And the newfound 'fire' inside her becomes the guiding force behind convincing her parents to rebuild and get on with their lives.

"I started making notes and doing research for *Corey's Fire* in 1978. I interviewed family and friends, re-read newspaper articles, and listened to tape recordings of more than twelve hours of live radio broadcasts from news reporters at the scene. Reliving the fire was

painful—so painful that I was unable to begin writing the book until March of 1982, five years after the disaster. Eight years after that, the book was finally published. I dedicated it to my mother and my two brothers, who also endured the fire."

Romance is at the center of the novel, although next door neighbor Topher (short for Christopher) is anything but romantic at the beginning. Topher is good-looking, but Corey can't stand him because he is sarcastic and chases her cat with his motorcycle. It is Topher, however, who understands Corey's rage when her house is destroyed in a brush fire, and he helps her look for her cat, losing his tough-guy facade in the process. Corey also learns about friendship from her neighbor, Ericka. Ericka sticks by Corey, even when Corey is mean to her because her home was left standing when Corey's was burned. Appreciated by the Santa Barbara community, *Corey's Fire* was praised by critics as well. A reviewer for *Publishers Weekly* described it as a "refreshing twist on the standard love story." The reviewer continued, "The author's unflinching realism in describing the fire and its aftermath adds sizzle to an already appealing romance." Diana Watkins of *Voice of Youth Advocates* wrote, "Middle school students will easily identify with Corey, Christopher West, and Ericka." The International Reading Association/Children's Book Council awarded the book a Children's Choice Award.

Wardlaw has written two other novels for young adults, *Alley Cat* and *Don't Look Back,* neither of which was as well received as *Corey's Fire.* In *Alley Cat,* the author used her experiences in radio to tell the story of an awkward teen, Allison Blake, who finds opportunity and respect for her abilities as a weekend disk jockey on a local radio station. In *Don't Look Back,* Drew faces her inner demons during a summer in Hawaii with her estranged father. A romantic liaison with a sensitive surfer helps her come to terms with her father. A contributor for *Publishers Weekly* commented that "Wardlaw once again combines coming-of-age struggles with a predictable but pleasing romance."

Wardlaw's experience of feeling like a misfit in junior high formed the basis for *Seventh-Grade Weirdo* (later republished as *My Life as a Weirdo*). It tells the story of Christopher Robin, who has a mother who loves Winnie-the-Pooh (hence Rob's name), a father who is a former professional surfer, and a five-year-old sister, Winnie, the family genius, who impersonates story-book characters and invents a game that promises to make her a millionaire. Rob worries that with a family like his, everyone will think he is a weirdo too. To add to his troubles, on the first day of seventh grade, Rob makes an enemy of the school bully, "The Shark," and must, in the end, confront him.

According to Susie Wilde in the *Independent Weekly,* "Wardlaw's masterful dialogue maintains a perfect balance of funny, fresh, realistic kid-talk.... Rob makes a comfortingly comic role model for kids shifting gears into middle school." Carrol McCarthy, writing for *School Library Journal,* said, "This entertaining, sometimes touching story of self-realization is successful despite the exaggerated qualities of the characters." Esther Sinofsky of *Voice of Youth Advocates* wrote that Wardlaw's "light touch keeps a smile on your lips as you read."

Wardlaw has made a minor specialty of middle-grader and beginning reader books that blend humor and realistic situations. In *Me + Math = Headache,* she tells of young Jeffrey who hates math; in *The Eye and I,* Jeffrey is paralyzed with fear when he has to be video-taped giving a speech in front of his fifth-grade class. Jeffrey makes a further appearance in *Operation Rhinoceros,* in which he fears he is losing his friends because the new teacher is none other than his mother. In *The Ghoul Brothers,* two friends dress up as a two-headed monster and get a big surprise from a little sister. Hiccups and their cure form the plot line of *Hector's Hiccups* in which an Hispanic boy is helped by his sister and brother to get rid of his bothersome condition.

Wardlaw introduces twelve-year-old Steve Wyatt, alias Sneeze, an inveterate inventor, in *101 Ways to Bug Your Parents.* His parents deny him the opportunity of attending the annual Invention Conference in San Francisco by enrolling him in a summer writing program, but Sneeze finds a fine way to feel better and make some money at the same time. Out of revenge for his ruined summer, he creates a how-to manual in his writing class, titled *101 Ways to Bug Your Parents.* It is an instant hit with the other kids in the class, and they are desperate to buy copies. "Three-dimensional characters ... populate this fast, fun read," commented Lisa Van Drasek in *School Library Journal,* who added, "Readers will hope for further adventures with Sneeze and his friends." *Booklist*'s Frances Bradburn remarked, "Wardlaw has written a funny story with more substance than is evident initially ... The death of a parent, job insecurity, gifted children, teacher respect, true friendship, and even intellectual freedom all find play here."

Wardlaw told *SATA* the story behind *101 Ways to Bug Your Parents:* "Kids are often surprised to learn that I didn't start writing *101 Ways* when I was a kid. Oh, I definitely had my favorites: I alternated between using #35—'Give them the silent treatment'—and #101: 'Beg them to death.' (Pleasepleaseplease, PUH-LEEEEEZE, Mom?!)

"But the idea for *101 Ways to Bug Your Parents* actually came from an amusing article I read in our local Santa Barbara newspaper.

"The article was called '101 Reasons for Staying Single,' and told the story of a teacher who gave her 4th grade students a unique journal writing assignment: *Write about ten things you've done that really bugged your parents.*

"Immediately the kids started scribbling furiously, and at the end of only 15 minutes, they had hundreds of ideas! The class then compiled 101 of their favorites, and wrote them on the blackboard. A teacher's aide thought the list

was funny, and sent it into the newspaper, which published it the following week ... where I read it and instantly thought: *What a great idea!*

"Of course, no matter how great an idea is, it's not enough to make a great book. I had a title—*101 Ways to Bug Your Parents*—but no story. So the first thing I did was arrange to meet the teacher and the kids who'd written the list.

"I found out from them that the teacher, Nancy Revlin, had been scared to death that she was going to get into trouble. Seems that the newspaper received dozens of letters from parents and one ex-principal, saying things like: 'What a terrible assignment! Is this what our schools are coming to today? This teacher should be fired! Parents have enough trouble raising children without giving them assignments like this!' and blah, blah, blah.

"Poor Mrs. Revlin. This was her first year teaching, and she was really afraid that she'd get fired. But her principal laughed it off. He understood that she'd given the assignment in fun, and that the list wasn't hurting anybody—except maybe a few parents who were getting bugged a little more than usual.

"But the complaints Mrs. Revlin received started me thinking and playing my favorite game: *what if?* What if the teacher *had* gotten into trouble? What if one of her students had turned the writing assingment into an entire book called *101 Ways to Bug Your Parents?* What if he started selling it on school property, causing public outcry against him and the teacher? What if the main theme of this story wasn't just a few kids being obnoxious toward their parents, but one of intellectual freedom? What would happen then?

"The rest, as they say, is history.

"I got the idea for the main character, Sneeze, from another newspaper article, this one about a ten-year-old boy who won a college scholarship for inventing the world's first glow-in-the-dark toilet seat to keep his parents from falling in the you-know-what when they got up in the middle of the night.

"But Sneeze's inventiveness is also based on me. No, I haven't invented a glow-in-the-dark toilet seat, or a Keep Kool Baseball Kap, or bubble gum that never loses it's flavor.

"But I *am* an inventor of stories ... and the passion and pleasure Sneeze has for his crazy creations is exactly how I feel about writing. Sneeze sums it up this way at the end of the book: 'Inventing is who I am, and who I want to be. Always. Sure, making money, being famous and all that stuff is nice. But it's just icing on the cake. Doing something right because you enjoy it, because you believe in it, because it's *right*—that's what counts.

"That's what it feels like to be an author. Yes, I'm a mother, and a teacher, and a wife ... but I'm also a

When her dog reaches the century mark in canine years, Maris invites all her friends over for a birthday celebration. (Cover illustration by Arden Johnson-Petrov.)

writer. I've been a writer since I was seven years old. I enjoy writing more than any other job I've ever had ... and getting to live and work as a writer is a dream come true."

In addition to fiction, Wardlaw has written two nonfiction books, *Cowabunga! The Complete Book of Surfing* and *Bubblemania. Cowabunga!* was inspired by Wardlaw's husband, a surfer for twenty-five years, who suggested that young people would enjoy a book about the sport. Wardlaw found that the only books about surfing available for young people in libraries were "hopelessly out of date," as she told *Los Angeles Times* interviewer Jane Hulse. "Surfboards had one fin, and swimsuits came above the bellybutton." Wardlaw began her research by going through her husband's collection of surfing magazines, interviewing surfers and surfboard makers, and reading about surfing in libraries. After putting together some sample chapters, she contracted with Avon to write the book.

Cowabunga! The Complete Book of Surfing is an overview of the sport rather than a how-to book. "It's difficult to surf by reading a book," she told Hulse. "I'm not a great surfer.... I didn't feel I should teach kids to do it." Wardlaw begins her book with the history of the sport in Polynesia and Hawaii, then describes the culture surrounding it in California in the 1960s, explains the construction of surfboards, lists hot surfing spots, shops, camps, and schools, and even provides a glossary of surfing words. George Delalis, writing for *School Library Journal,* called Wardlaw's book a "comprehensive introduction to the sport," and concluded that the work is "a useful resource for both veterans and

beginners." Writing in *Voice of Youth Advocates,* Drue Wagner-Mees commented, "*Cowabunga!* has just about everything you ever wanted to know about surfing ... The text reads easily, flows, and catches the spirit of the sport."

More playful in spirit, but equally well researched, is Wardlaw's *Bubblemania,* a "zany history of the discovery and development of the bubble-gum industry," according to Jennifer Oyama of *School Library Journal.* Wardlaw traces the history of chewing gum from the tree bark of Mayan Indians to major companies such as Adams, Curtis, and Wrigley. She also details the manufacture and distribution of chewing gum, explains the connection between ball players and bubble gum, and gives handy tips about blowing the perfect bubble. "Young readers will marvel at the detail in this fun book," remarked Susan DeRonne in *Booklist.*

Wardlaw has also found success in writing picture books, such as *The Tales of Grandpa Cat, Punia and the King of Sharks, Bow-Wow Birthday,* and *First Steps.* In *The Tales of Grandpa Cat,* she teamed up with the well-known illustrator Ronald Searle to create a tall tale with a new twist for middle graders. Expecting to be bored out of their wits at a visit to Grandma and Grandpa Cat's retirement home, the grandcats instead are held spellbound by the old cat's tales of former friends and exploits. *Booklist*'s Janice Del Negro said that the book was for "kids ready to venture beyond vocabulary-controlled materials, as well as for those who can't get enough about cats." A reviewer for *Publishers Weekly* wrote, "Antic illustrations by *New Yorker* cover artist Searle accentuate the hilarity of Wardlaw's ... brisk cat-tale." In the opinion of a critic for *Kirkus Reviews,* "The stories are ... playful attention-getters and come to a fine, loopy conclusion."

Describing *Punia and the King of Sharks,* a reviewer for *Publishers Weekly* commented, "Jaunty prose and artwork join forces in this adaptation of a Hawaiian folktale." Punia, a clever boy, outwits the sharks and gets away with some delicious lobsters. "Wardlaw's simple, direct retelling of a little-known Hawaiian folktale combines a popular topic (sharks), an action-filled plot, and the triumph of the weak over the strong," according to *Booklist*'s Julie Corsaro.

On a very different subject, *Bow-Wow Birthday* tells of a party for a favorite pet, a dog who sleeps through its own party. Helen Rosenberg, writing in *Booklist,* commented, "The hilarious story includes a host of children's favorite dog puns ... and Johnson-Petrov's bold illustrations work wonderfully with the humorous text to make the book a fun-filled romp through an unusual birthday party." Personal experiences also figure in Wardlaw's picture books. The birth of her own son inspired Wardlaw to write the briskly rhythmic text of *First Steps,* a 1999 picture book for the very young.

Wardlaw lives in Santa Barbara with her husband Craig, her son, and her two cats, Riesling and Beaujolais. She writes at home, teaches courses on writing for young adults, and visits children in schools throughout California and in other states. She once told *SATA* that the best things about being an author are "working at home, seeing my books in bookstores, creating people I'd like to meet in real life, and getting fan mail." The worst things are "getting bad reviews, not having anybody to talk to during the day (except my cats, who don't say much), [and] waiting two to three years from the time my book is bought by a publisher to when it is actually published." Wardlaw continues to write because "it's fun.... First and foremost, I write to entertain myself. But I also write to show my readers a world they can delight in, a world of wonder and awe, a world where so much is possible. Around any bend, at any moment, might come Mystery! Adventure! Romance!"

Works Cited

Bradburn, Frances, review of *101 Ways to Bug Your Parents, Booklist,* October 1, 1996, p. 128.

Review of *Corey's Fire, Publishers Weekly,* December 22, 1989, p. 57.

Corsaro, Julie, review of *Punia and the King of Sharks, Booklist,* December 1, 1996, p. 667.

Del Negro, Janice, review of *The Tales of Grandpa Cat, Booklist,* October 15, 1994, p. 440.

Delalis, George, review of *Cowabunga! The Complete Book of Surfing, School Library Journal,* February, 1992, p. 117.

DeRonne, Susan, review of *Bubblemania, Booklist,* October 1, 1997, p. 326.

Review of *Don't Look Back, Publishers Weekly,* November 15, 1993, p. 80.

Hulse, Jane, "Hanging 10," *Los Angeles Times,* August 2, 1991.

McCarthy, Carrol, review of *Seventh-Grade Weirdo, School Library Journal,* September, 1992, p. 261.

Oyama, Jennifer, review of *Bubblemania, School Library Journal,* January, 1998, p. 135.

Review of *Punia and the King of Sharks, Publishers Weekly,* December 9, 1996, p. 68.

Rosenberg, Helen, review of *Bow-Wow Birthday, Booklist,* March 1, 1998, p. 1142.

Sinofsky, Esther, review of *Seventh-Grade Weirdo, Voice of Youth Advocates,* April, 1993.

Spencer, Russ, "Catching a New Wave," *Santa Barbara News Press,* March 15, 1991, pp. 25-26.

Review of *The Tales of Grandpa Cat, Kirkus Reviews,* September 15, 1994, p. 1285.

Review of *The Tales of Grandpa Cat, Publishers Weekly,* September 12, 1994, p. 89.

Van Drasek, Lisa, review of *101 Ways to Bug Your Parents, School Library Journal,* October, 1996, p. 128.

Wagner-Mees, Drue, review of *Cowabunga!, Voice of Youth Advocates,* December, 1991, p. 343.

Watkins, Diana, review of *Corey's Fire, Voice of Youth Advocates,* April, 1991, p. 38.

Wilde, Susie, review of *Seventh-Grade Weirdo, The Independent Weekly,* August 19, 1992, p. 21.

For More Information See

PERIODICALS

Booklist, August, 1992.

Bookpage, September, 1992, p. 23.

Camarillo Daily News, March 13, 1992, pp. A1-A2.

Kirkus Reviews, October 1, 1996, p. 1475.

McMahon, Marilyn, "Fiery Inspiration," *Santa Barbara News Press,* July 21, 1987, pp. D1-D2.

Publishers Weekly, June 29, 1992, pp. 63-64.

School Library Journal, February, 1995, p. 83; May, 1998, p. 128.

Voice Literary Supplement, July-August, 1991, p. 15.

Voice of Youth Advocates, August-September, 1987, p. 126.

Wilson Library Bulletin, February, 1995, pp. 94-95.

ON-LINE

Author's website can be found at http://www.leeward law.com.

—*Sketch by J. Sydney Jones*

*   *   *

WATKINS, Gloria Jean 1952- (bell hooks)

Personal

Born September 25, 1952, in Hopkinsville, KY; daughter of Veodis and Rosa Bell Watkins. *Education:* Stanford University, B.A., 1973; University of Wisconsin, M.A. 1976; University of California Santa Cruz, Ph.D. in English, 1987.

Addresses

Home—291 W. 12th St., New York, NY 10031.

Career

Social critic, educator, and writer. Yale University, New Haven, CT, assistant professor of Afro-American studies and English, 1980-85; Oberlin College, OH, associate professor, 1986-94; City College of New York, professor of English, 1995—.

Awards, Honors

Writer's Award, Lila Wallace-Readers Digest Fund, 1994.

Writings

UNDER NAME BELL HOOKS

Ain't I a Woman: Black Women and Feminism, South End Press, 1981.

Feminist Theory: From Margin to Center, South End Press, 1984.

Talking Back: Thinking Feminist, Thinking Black, Between-the-Lines, 1988.

Yearning: Race, Gender, and Cultural Politics, Between-the-Lines, 1990.

(With Cornell West) *Breaking Bread: Insurgent Black Intellectual Life,* South End Press, 1991.

A Woman's Mourning Song (poetry), Writers and Readers, 1992.

Black Looks: Race and Representation, South End Press, 1992.

Sisters of the Yam: Black Women and Self Recovery, South End Press, 1993.

Outlaw Culture: Resisting Representations, Routledge, 1994.

Teaching to Transgress: Education as the Practice of Freedom, Routledge, 1994.

Changing the Subject: Painting and Prints, 1992-94, Art in General, 1994.

Art on My Mind: Visual Politics, New Press, 1995.

Killing Rage: Ending Racism, Holt, 1995.

Reel to Real: Race, Sex and Class at the Movies, Routledge, 1996.

Bone Black: Memories of Girlhood, Holt, 1996.

Wounds of Passion: A Writing Life, Holt, 1997.

Happy to Be Nappy (children's book), Hyperion, 1998.

Remembered Rapture: The Writer at Work, Holt, 1999.

All about Love: New Visions, Morrow, 2000.

Also contributor to *Double Stitch: Black Women Write about Mothers and Daughters,* 1992, *Anthology of Contemporary African-American Women Artists,* 1995, *The Masculine Masquerade,* 1995, *An Elliptical Traverse of 20th Century Art,* 1996, *Spoils of War,* 1997, *Talking about a Revolution,* 1998, and *UpSouth,* 1999. Watkins is a regular contributor to magazines, including *Emerge, Callalo, Utne Reader,* and *Catalyst,* and co-founded the literary magazine, *Hambone.*

Sidelights

Often called one of the foremost black intellectuals in contemporary America, Gloria Jean Watkins has written trenchantly and prolifically about social and cultural topics ranging from racism to feminism to the theory of art and the practice of education. Writing under the name bell hooks, she has authored such popular books as *Ain't I a Woman: Black Women and Feminism; Feminist Theory: From Margin to Center; Yearning: Race, Gender, and Cultural Politics; Black Looks: Race and Representation; Sisters of the Yam: Black Women and Self Recovery;* and *Teaching to Transgress: Education as the Practice of Freedom.* She has also written movingly of her own childhood in the memoir *Bone Black: Memories of Girlhood,* and of writing in *Wounds of Passion: A Writing Life* and *Remembered Rapture: The Writer at Work.* Blending cogent critical analysis with personal experience, hooks has created a distinctive style of essay. Her central tenant is that black women have been marginalized not only by the white, male-dominated power structure, but also the by the feminist and black liberation movements. "At her best she exhibits a command of various voices that range from subtle overlays of the personal and historical to a refreshing public forthrightness that stings," wrote P. Gabrielle Foreman in the *Women's Review of Books.* "Inevitably, a reader will cheer through one essay and scowl through another."

Born Gloria Jean Watkins on September 25, 1952, the author grew up in Kentucky, the daughter of a custodial worker and a homemaker. Poetry was a family-shared interest, and when frequent storms would cause power outages, the family would sit in candlelight and recite poetry to one another. Beginning to write poetry at an early age as a result of this inspiration, hooks was also encouraged by the writings of Emily Dickinson. Additionally, as a young girl, she was committed to the idea of becoming an architect when she grew up. In actuality, the power of words proved more compelling than design, though hooks would later write about both art and design.

Growing up in a segregated community, hooks learned firsthand the effects of racism that would later inform her published work. Additionally, her father's rigid traditional beliefs regarding gender roles made her question, early on, the sexism alive in the black community and in the larger society as well. Strong female role models figured largely in hooks's early life, so much so that she took her great-grandmother's name to write under, in order, according to Paula Giddings in *Ms.,* to "honor the unlettered wisdom of her foremothers." She writes the name in the lower case, as she explained to Michel Marriott in the *New York Times,* "to emphasize her message and not herself."

Gloria Jean Watkins

Hooks graduated from Crispus Attucks High School in Hopkinsville, Kentucky, and entered college at Stanford University. In 1973 she earned her bachelor's degree in English literature and went on to the University of Wisconsin, Madison, to graduate with a master's in English. Her first teaching position took her to the University of Southern California as a lecturer in ethnic studies. After leaving USC in 1979, she taught creative writing, composition, and African-American literature at various universities, including the University of California at Santa Cruz and San Francisco State University, working toward her doctorate at the same time. Her thesis on the works of novelist Toni Morrison earned her a Ph.D. in 1983.

By this time, hooks was already a published author herself, with her initial book appearing in 1981. Black women finding their voices within mainstream feminism is the focus of Watkins's first three works: *Ain't I a Woman, Feminist Theory,* and *Talking Back: Thinking Feminist, Thinking Black. Ain't I a Woman* takes its title from a speech by the nineteenth-century black liberationist Sojourner Truth, and in the book hooks challenges the menial role black women have had in both the feminist and black liberation movements. That black women were treated in such a sexist manner, hooks contended, was proof that the ruling American patriarchal system had been internalized even by the black male leadership. Citing the work of early black feminists, hooks championed the idea of sisterhood among black women. Generally favorable criticism followed publication of this first full-length work, a book hooks had started writing when she was nineteen. Mary Biggs, writing in *Library Journal,* noted, "This exciting book reveals [hooks] to be a lucid, persuasive writer and an extraordinary penetrating and original thinker." Biggs concluded that hooks's book "should be widely read, thoughtfully considered, discussed, and finally acclaimed for the real enlightenment it offers for social change." A reviewer for *Choice* felt that hooks's book was "a provocative, readable, and worthwhile study" despite her "simplified assertion that nineteenth-century black women were more feminist than their twentieth-century counterparts."

Further explorations of the black feminist thesis hooks had begun to develop came in *Feminist Theory,* in which hooks clearly states that the three "isms" (racism, classism, and sexism) have at their root the notion of domination, and also in *Talking Back,* twenty-three essays on different aspects of the black/feminist connection. In these early works, hooks took on large issues with a plethora of voices which some reviewers found disconcerting if not disjointed. A reviewer for *Publishers Weekly,* for example, remarked of *Talking Back* that "although the author makes perceptive and provocative observations, they are diminished by redundancy and weakened by her doctrinaire Marxist rhetoric." In her review of *Feminist Theory,* Giddings pointed out that "Hooks fails to make an important distinction: women on the margin of this society are not necessarily on the margin of feminist aspirations or activism."

Throughout the 1990s, hooks wrote prolifically, publishing a book a year, in addition to teaching as a distinguished professor of English at the City College of New York. In works such as *Yearning, Breaking Bread: Insurgent Black Intellectual Life, Black Looks: Race and Representation, Sisters of the Yam,* and *Outlaw Culture: Resisting Representations,* hooks continued to take on cultural and societal shibboleths: examining not only the black woman's place in the scheme of things, but also that of the black intellectual, and examining the theme of otherness or the role of the outsider in so-called mainstream society. Her books generally met with praise for their dedication and insights, though again reviewers often found her arguments sketchy or formulaic. Reviewing her *Black Looks,* for example, a book that deplores the commodification of the black image, D. Soyini Madison wrote in the *New York Times Book Review* that the essays "are uneven in their analytical complexity and originality of thought" but nevertheless "provide insight into race, representation, and dominance." Reviewing the same title in *Multicultural Review,* Itibari M. Zulu commented, "At times Bell Hooks's essays are a bit preachy (or overly politically correct), but she redeems herself by revealing a witty personal experience related to the sermon that flows through ... her narrative." The twenty-one essays in *Outlaw Culture* would, noted a *Publishers Weekly* reviewer, "enhance ... hooks' reputation as an astute, vigorous and freewheeling critic on matters of race, class and gender" despite being "formulaic at times."

Her 1994 *Teaching to Transgress,* a collection of essays about the power of teaching, was "full of hope and excitement for the possibility of education to liberate and include," as a reviewer for *Publishers Weekly* noted, while her *Art on My Mind,* a book on the impact of black artists, particularly women, was "an odd creature," according to *Kirkus Reviews. Booklist*'s Donna Seaman concluded of that same book that hooks "hones her aesthetic in her adept interpretations of the work and impact of black artists.... As erudite and sophisticated as hooks is, she is also eminently readable, even exhilarating." The lasting effect of white oppression on black society was the theme of a further batch of essays gathered in *Killing Rage,* a book whose message was summed up by Bonnie Smothers in a *Booklist* review: "Hooks contends that racism in the U.S. is as virulent as it has ever been, but that there is a systematic effort, with the media fully engaged, to deny it and to claim equality in our economic and cultural endeavors." The cure hooks proposed was a controlled rage channeled to constructive ends. "Tough antidote," Smothers concluded.

Of particular interest to young readers are hooks's autobiographical writings, chronicling her childhood in *Bone Black,* and her young adulthood beginning with her arrival at Stanford, in *Wounds of Passion.* She has also authored a children's book, *Happy to Be Nappy,* with illustrations by the award-winning Chris Raschka. In *Bone Black,* hooks recalls the formative influences on her youth: the black community, strong women, religion, and the local library. Openly discussing her budding sexuality as well as domestic turbulence in her home, hooks draws an intimate portrait of growing up black in a segregated community. Dottie Kraft, writing in *School Library Journal,* found the book to be a "treasure box of memories" and a "unique autobiography of a contemporary African-American woman that should find a place in all collections," while Ann Burns concluded in *Library Journal* that hooks's was a "sad tale of childhood memories but a winner.... " *Booklist*'s Seaman dubbed the memoir a "lyrical, deeply moving, and brilliantly structured autobiography," and commended hooks's ability "to articulate the sharp, unrelenting anguish of her young self, and her struggle to find comfort and inspiration in books, that elevates her story from simple memoir to a resonant and richly metaphoric portrait.... "

Wounds of Passion takes up hooks's life at the point she leaves Kentucky to enroll at Stanford and has at its heart the long affair with a man who she spent fifteen years with. "In a constantly fresh and bravely honest voice, hooks relates her early development as a feminist writer and scholar," noted a reviewer for *Publishers Weekly.* As in *Bone Black,* hooks employed an episodic style with shifts between first and third person narration. Burns concluded her *Library Journal* review by calling the book an "exceptionally written memoir," while the reviewer for *Publishers Weekly* thought hooks's "greatest achievement here is the open-ended question of whether it is possible to live what we believe." The writing life is also at the heart of essays collected in the 1999 publication *Remembered Rapture,* a celebration of the power of the written word and of some authors who have deeply affected hooks, such as Emily Dickinson, Zora Neale Hurston, and Toni Morrison. *Remembered Rapture* is also an insider's look at the state of publishing. A contributor to *Kirkus Reviews* called the book a "moving testimony to the passion for the written word, and to the inherent difficulties of becoming a purveyor both of language and ideas."

With *Happy to Be Nappy,* hooks took a new direction in her work, creating a children's picture book about the joys of nappy hair. For hooks, such hair is "soft like cotton, / flower petal billowy soft, full of frizz and fuzz." A reviewer for *Publishers Weekly* called the picture book a "joyous ode to hair" and "powerful, uplifting and, above all, buoyantly fun read-aloud." *Booklist*'s Hazel Rochman called the book "a greeting card with just one exuberant message," noting that every page demonstrates "that there are all kinds of ways for small girls to be nappy and happy."

Writing in genres from the essay to poetry to memoir and children's books, bell hooks has created a body of work that questions the dominant power structure, that celebrates black women, and often offers a way out of the racial divide. As Thulani Davis noted in the *New York Times Book Review,* "The only woman in recent years who is readily identified as a member of that select group known as 'black public intellectuals,' Bell Hooks is probably the most provocative and prolific of them all." Though often criticized for being too prolific, hooks

sitting still for hands to brush or braid

In her first book for children, written under the pseudonym bell hooks, Watkins celebrates the uniqueness of kinky hair. (*From* Happy to Be Nappy, *illustrated by Chris Raschka.*)

counters that words are her life. As she told Marriott in the *New York Times,* "It's like Michael Jordan. It's the thing I like to do with a passion."

Works Cited

Review of *Ain't I a Woman, Choice,* April, 1982, p. 1141.

Review of *Art on My Mind, Kirkus Reviews,* April 15, 1995, p. 534.

Biggs, Mary, review of *Ain't I a Woman, Library Journal,* December 1, 1981, p. 2326.

Burns, Ann, review of *Bone Black, Library Journal,* September 15, 1996, p. 75.

Burns, Ann, review of *Wounds of Passion, Library Journal,* October 1, 1997, p. 94.

Davis, Thulani, "Native Daughter," *New York Times Book Review,* December 15, 1996, p. 32.

Foreman, P. Gabrielle, review of *Feminist Theory, Women's Review of Books,* February, 1985, p. 3.

Giddings, Paula, review of *Feminist Theory, Ms.,* October, 1985, p. 25.

Review of *Happy to Be Nappy, Publishers Weekly,* July 19, 1999, p. 194.

hooks, bell, *Happy to Be Nappy,* Hyperion, 1998.

Kraft, Dottie, review of *Bone Black, School Library Journal,* March, 1997, p. 217.

Madison, D. Soyini, review of *Black Looks, New York Times Book Review,* February 29, 1993, p. 23.

Marriott, Michel, "The Eye of the Storm," *New York Times,* November 13, 1997, pp. F1, 4.

Review of *Outlaw Culture, Publishers Weekly,* November 7, 1994, p. 70.

Review of *Remembered Rapture, Kirkus Reviews,* November 15, 1998.

Rochman, Hazel, review of *Happy to Be Nappy, Booklist,* August 19, 1999.

Seaman, Donna, review of *Art on My Mind, Booklist,* June 1, 1995, p. 1715.

Seaman, Donna, review of *Bone Black, Booklist,* September 15, 1996, p. 189.

Smothers, Bonnie, review of *Killing Rage, Booklist,* September 15, 1995, pp. 118, 147.

Review of *Talking Back, Publishers Weekly,* November 18, 1988, p. 72.

Review of *Teaching to Transgress, Publishers Weekly,* November 7, 1994, p. 70.

Review of *Wounds of Passion, Publishers Weekly,* September 22, 1997, p. 64.

Zulu, Itibari M., review of *Black Looks, Multicultural Review,* March, 1993, p. 84.

For More Information See

BOOKS

Contemporary Black Biography, Volume 5, Gale, 1994.
Contemporary Literary Criticism, Volume 94, Gale, 1994.
Feminist Writers, edited by Pamela Kestler-Shelton, St. James Press, 1996.
Florence, Namulundah, *Bell Hooks' Engaged Pedagogy: A Transgressive Education for Critical Consciousness,* Bergin and Garvey, 1998.
Major Twentieth-Century Writers, 2nd edition, Gale, 1999.

PERIODICALS

Black Enterprise, June, 1992, p. 23.
Black Scholar, January, 1983, pp. 38, 46.
Bookwatch, July 1989, p. 4; September, 1992, p. 10.
Choice, July, 1985, p. 1703.
Essence, July, 1989, p. 20.
Library Journal, March 15, 1985, p. 68; December, 1988, p. 126; July, 1992, p. 109.
Ms., July, 1983, p. 24.
Multicultural Review, April, 1992.
New Directions for Women, January, 1992, p. 22.
New Statesman, October 22, 1982, p. 31; November 30, 1990, p. 39.
New York Times Book Review, February 29, 1993, p. 23; December 18, 1994, p. 27; September 17, 1995, p. 25; December 15, 1996, p. 32.
Phylon, March, 1983, p. 85.
Political Science Quarterly, spring, 1983, p. 84.
Progressive, March, 1991, p. 42.
Publishers Weekly, November 22, 1991, p. 49; June 15, 1992, p. 95.
Queen's Quarterly, summer, 1990, p. 318.
Sight and Sound, June, 1991, p. 36; May, 1997, p. 34.
Village Voice Literary Supplement, June, 1982, p. 10; December, 1992, p. 14; November, 1995, p. 19.
West Coast Review of Books, April, 1982, p. 51.
Women's Review of Books, September, 1991, p. 12; October, 1993, p. 12; March, 1995, p. 10.*

—*Sketch by J. Sydney Jones*

WHITE, Tekla N. 1934-

Personal

Born June 3, 1934, in Portland, OR; daughter of Robert William (a barber) and Merle Evelyn (a legal secretary; maiden name, Ramey) Nye; married Donald Olin White, August 10, 1954 (divorced, February, 1987); children: Lara Cecelia, Alyssa Anne. *Education:* Attended Oregon State University; University of Washington, Seattle, B.A., 1956; Holy Names College, M.A., 1980; studied anthropology and archaeology in Mexico. *Politics:* Democrat. *Religion:* Congregational. *Hobbies and other interests:* Photography, reading, pets, people and places, music, family and grandchildren.

Addresses

Home—Woodland, CA. *Office*—P.O. Box 307, Davis, CA 95617. *E-mail*—tnwrites@mother.com.

Career

Worked as a schoolteacher in Prince George's County, MD, and in Fremont, CA; currently a writer. Member of Marine Mammal Center and Oakland's Society for the Prevention of Cruelty to Animals. *Member:* Authors Guild, Society of Children's Book Writers and Illustrators (regional adviser for North Central California), California Reading Association, California Teachers Association, Nye Family Association, Holy Names College Alumni Association, Marine Mammal Center, Society for the Prevention of Cruelty to Animals (Oakland, CA).

Writings

Cultures around the World, Evan-Moor, 1995.
Missions of the San Francisco Bay Area, Lerner Publications (Minneapolis, MN), 1996.
How to Read Nonfiction Books, illustrated by Don Robison, Evan-Moor, 1996.
Survival Reading Skills, illustrated by Robison, Evan-Moor, 1996.
(With Jill Norris and Jeri Nutting) *Thinking Skills Big Book,* Grades 3-4 and 5-6, illustrated by Robison, Evan-Moor, 1997.
The Flight of the Union, illustrated by Ralph Ramstad, Carolrhoda (Minneapolis, MN), 1998.

Author of "Read and Understand" books for Grades 4-6, published by Evan-Moor, 1999. Contributor to textbooks and other educational materials. Contributor of articles and photographs to magazines and newspapers, including *Farm Wife News* and *San Jose Mercury News.*

Work in Progress

Croaker's Song, a picture book about a musical bullfrog; a series of concept books; contributions for the school traffic education program sponsored by the Automobile Association of America, California branch.

Tekla N. White

Sidelights

Tekla N. White told *SATA:* "I loved music and took singing and piano lessons while I was a student in elementary school and high school. I had a great interest in music and wanted to sing in the movies, but I lacked the technical skill and practiced erratically. My other interests were roller-skating, the ocean, sand, saltwater taffy, and sea lions. Every summer we visited the Oregon coast. I spent hours watching the sea lions in the Seaside aquarium.

"I read all the available children's books in the library when I was growing up. It was a family habit. Everyone at home read a great deal. I don't remember learning to read, it just happened before I went to school.

"My literary career began in the fifth grade. The first story I wrote was about a beagle with black ears that went to the moon. I wrote about a beagle because beagles were the only thing I could draw. In the eighth grade I taught a library-literature class for third-grade students on Friday afternoons when the teacher had to leave early. I imagine I was chosen for the task because I had read so many books, and of course my father was on the school board. The students made sure I wasn't bored. They challenged me whenever they could. It was many years past that time before I considered being a teacher.

"I graduated from high school a year early. My parents agreed to an early exit thinking I would go to college in the fall. The thought of school away from home was frightening. I decided to work in a drugstore, so I didn't have to go to college.

"My parents finally sent me off to Oregon State University, where my sister had attended school. There were no majors there that interested me, but my parents were sure I'd find something to study. I tried math. I was the only female student in my classes. I didn't excel in the first-level courses, so I knew it would be impossible to continue. I transferred to different schools, not finding my niche or major anywhere. Looking back, my dear parents had more patience than I deserved.

"I began to write children's stories as I bounced from school to school, and a university librarian, my mentor whose husband was interested in developing my stories into a Saturday-morning television program, encouraged me to continue working on children's books. I married instead, and my writing dreams were set aside while I finished my undergraduate work at the University of Washington.

"When I graduated from the University of Washington, I moved to Virginia and had a brief career in the telephone company's business office in Falls Church. I became an elementary schoolteacher in Prince George's County, Maryland, as there was a shortage of teachers. I took education courses at local universities. After nearly four years I moved to San Francisco, California. I went back to the telephone company while I worked on the requirements for a California teacher's credential. I began teaching in Fremont, California. I went to school in Mexico when I could and studied anthropology and archaeology. I had hoped to work toward an archaeology degree there, but teaching and two children changed my plans. I attended Holy Names College in Oakland and received my master's degree in Spanish literature.

"Except for a few years when my children were babies, I taught in the Fremont Unified School District. I worked with the social science curriculum and literature committees, writing material for the classroom and working with other teachers as a mentor teacher. I taught in the intermediate grades, then taught music and Spanish to all grades, and for the last nine years I taught kindergarten. One of my favorite projects is a monologue as Abraham Lincoln's stepmother. I wanted the young children in the school to learn about the early life of President Lincoln. Even today, I dress up in my long dress and sunbonnet and visit classrooms as Sarah Lincoln.

"I had the opportunity to write for the *San Jose Mercury News* while I was teaching in Fremont, and I couldn't refuse. It was a dream job—an opportunity to interview interesting people and photograph them. I loved the variety of the assignments and worked for the local bureau until they had to limit their work with freelance writers. Even though my first middle-grade novel was not accepted by a publisher, I have been writing and rewriting books and other materials since that time. I hope that, after many revisions, my sixteenth-century Mexican novel for the middle grades will be published.

MISSIONS

Missions of the San Francisco Bay Area

*Santa Clara de Asís · San José · San Francisco de Asís
San Rafael Arcángel · San Francisco Solano*

White retells the history of missions in the San Francisco Bay area and describes the life of Native Americans in the region before the arrival of Spanish settlers.

"I retired in 1994 to devote more time to writing. I worked as a substitute teacher in Fremont until I moved to Woodland, California, in 1996 to be closer to my children and grandchildren. I have worked as a substitute teacher in Davis, California, when my writing schedule allowed it, and I have taught an evening class on writing books for children for the last two years.

"Each writing project I've undertaken has been different and challenging. I hope my stories will open new worlds, past, present, and invented, to young readers.

"Recently I had the opportunity to experiment with a variety of genres. My favorite was inventing a tall tale and adapting tall tales and folk tales. It was fascinating to stretch the truth beyond belief. I loved the humor and special language. I probably wouldn't have attempted a tall tale if I hadn't been compiling the literature material for reading programs.

"Teaching the elements of writing and completing more than seventy stories last year for books in the education field have given me new insights into writing and have improved my work. Writing is a demanding job, but I can't imagine not creating fiction and nonfiction stories for young people. My ideas come from everywhere—trees, animals, the ocean, and most of all from people. I will write as long as I can dream and put stories together."

For More Information See

PERIODICALS

Booklist, September 15, 1996, p. 236.
Horn Book Guide, spring, 1997, p. 172; July-December, 1998, p. 52.

School Library Journal, August, 1996, p. 157.

*   *   *

WILLETT, Edward (C.) 1959-

Personal

Born July 20, 1959, in Silver City, NM; son of James (a teacher) and Nina (a secretary; maiden name, Spears) Willett; married Margaret Anne Hodges (an engineer), September 27, 1997. *Education:* Harding University, B.A. (magna cum laude) in journalism. *Religion:* Christian. *Hobbies and other interests:* Computers, golf, wine.

Addresses

E-mail—ewillett@sk.sympatico.ca.

Career

Weyburn Review, Weyburn, Saskatchewan, Canada, reporter/photographer, 1980-84, editor, 1984-88; Saskatchewan Science Centre, Regina, SK, communications officer, 1988-93; freelance writer, 1993—. Actor, singer. Crocus 80 Theatre, Weyburn, SK, president, 1987-88; Regina Lyric Light Opera Society, president, 1993-96. Contributes a weekly column to the *Regina Leader Post* which is also aired on CBC Radio's *Afternoon Edition;* has been reviews and fiction editor for *Freelance,* the newsletter of the Saskatchewan Writers Guild; host of *net.talk,* a Cable Regina television program about computers and the internet. *Member:* SF Canada, Saskatchewan Writers Guild, Canadian Actors Equity Association, Saskatchewan Motion Picture Industry Association.

Awards, Honors

Best feature story and spot news photo, Saskatchewan Reporters' Association, 1986; winner, Inspiration '86 and Inspiration '87, provincial playwriting competition; Saskatchewan Writers Guild Literary Award, for children's literature, 1991; Saskatchewan Communicators Award of Merit, 1993; third place, 24-hour playwriting competition, Saskatchewan Writers Guild, 1996; short-listed for Brenda Macdonald Riches Award for first book, Saskatchewan Book Awards, 1997, for *Soulworm;* "Strange Harvest," short story named to recommended reading list of science fiction review magazine *Tangent.*

Writings

Soulworm (young adult fantasy novel), Royal Fireworks Press (Unionville, NY), 1997.
The Dark Unicorn (young adult fantasy novel), Royal Fireworks Press, 1998.
Andy Nebula: Interstellar Rock Star (young adult science fiction), Roussan Publishers (Montreal), 1999.
Meningitis (children's nonfiction), Enslow Publishers (Springfield, NJ), 1999.
Comets, Stardust and Supernovas: The Science of Space, Raintree Steck-Vaughn (Austin, TX), 1999.

Edward Willett

OTHER

(With Kathy Ivens) *Using Microsoft Publisher for Windows 95,* Que Corporation (Indianapolis, IN), 1995.
Using Microsoft Publisher 97, Que Corporation, 1997.
America Online's Creating Cool Web Pages, IDG Books (Foster City, CA), 1998.
(With Brian Underdahl) *The Internet Bible,* IDG Books, 1998.
(With Laurie Ann Ulrich) *Using Microsoft PowerPoint 97,* Que Corporation, 1998.
(With others) *The Office 2000 Bible,* IDG Books, 1999.
AOL's Picture This!: Fun and Easy Photo Projects, America Online (Sterling, VA), 1999.
Your Official America Online Guide to Creating Web Pages, IDG Books, 2000.
(With David Crowder, Rhonda Crowder, and David Karlins) *Microsoft Office 2000 Bible,* IDG Books, 2000.

Has contributed to several computer books; short fiction has appeared in *Western People, On Spec, JAM, The Canadian Children's Annual,* and *TransVersions;* has published numerous nonfiction articles.

Scriptwriter for *Western Outlander,* a thirteen-part TV series on wildlife; scriptwriter for Cyberbia segment of CBC series *Utopia Cafe;* writer for *The Dinosaur Hunters,* documentary on the Eastend T-Rex; author of narration for two Regina Symphony Orchestra concerts.

Work in Progress

Andy Nebula: Double Trouble, sequel to *Andy Nebula: Interstellar Rock Star; Razor Wind,* an adult science fiction book; and *Dark Tide,* a young adult fantasy book.

Sidelights

Edward Willett told *SATA:* "I was born July 20, 1959, in Silver City, New Mexico (the town where Billy the Kid shot his first sheriff), and started school in Texas. When I was eight years old, my parents moved to Weyburn, Saskatchewan, where my father taught at Western Christian College. I grew up there, attending public elementary and high school and graduating from Western Christian College in 1976.

"My first complete short story, written when I was about 10, was just something to do on a rainy day. It had the memorable title of *Kastra Glazz: Hypership Test Pilot.* (Thanks to my two older brothers, I was already firmly set on science fiction and fantasy as my genres of choice.) In high school, I was lucky enough to have teachers who really encouraged writing, and a friend who also liked to write. He and I used to get together at the end of the day in an empty classroom, write for a bit, then read back what we'd written, alternating one sentence at a time. Since he was writing a historical drama and I was writing science fiction, the results were interesting!

"I completed three short novels in high school, and they were read by quite a few of my fellow students, but publication was still a long way away. I always said I'd be either a scientist, musician, actor or writer when I grew up, and sometime during high school I chose writing (although I'm also a professional actor and singer and I write about science, so I actually ended up doing a little bit of everything that interested me!). So, off I went to Harding University, in Searcy, Arkansas, to study journalism.

"I returned to Weyburn as a reporter/photographer/editorial cartoonist/columnist and, eventually, news editor, of the weekly *Weyburn Review.* There's nothing like having to turn out a weekly column, several news stories, and two or three feature articles a week to get you over any fears you might have of writer's block! During that time I finally sold my first short story.

"In 1988 I moved to Regina as communications officer for the new Saskatchewan Science Centre. In 1993 I decided it was time to attempt to do what I'd always really wanted to do: be a full-time freelance writer. I quit my job, and, well, so far so good!

"My bread-and-butter is nonfiction writing, including a weekly science column for newspapers and radio and several computer books, but my true love is fiction writing, so I was thrilled, in 1997, to finally see publication of my first novel, *Soulworm,* a fantasy set mostly in Weyburn. *The Dark Unicorn* followed in 1998 and *Andy Nebula: Interstellar Rock Star* in 1999.

"Writers are always asked where they get the ideas for their books. For me, the answer is 'everywhere!' *Soulworm* came about because one day, as I was driving around Weyburn, I looked up at Signal Hill and thought, 'You know, that hill would be a great place for a castle'—and proceeded to write a story about it. *The Dark Unicorn* began with a slip of the tongue by my oldest niece, who, when asked to choose which movie she wanted to watch, mixed up *The Dark Crystal* and *The Last Unicorn* and asked for *The Dark Unicorn.* 'What a great title for a book,' I said ... and wrote it. *Andy Nebula* came from a news item about young female Japanese pop singers who are turned into stars for a few weeks, then forgotten. I took that idea into the far future and turned it into an SF story.

"I write fairly skimpy outlines, which I tend to wander further and further astray from as the actual writing proceeds. The writing itself happens very quickly, almost as fast as I type when things are going really well. Once I have a first draft, I'll show it to some writer friends whose opinions I trust, then I rewrite two or three more times. I try to punch up the language, find and correct inconsistencies, add more detail to scenes that I kind of skated over quickly the first time around, and sometimes cut scenes that are dead weight.

"I'm currently working more on nonfiction than fiction; in addition to computer books, I'm writing some children's science books for Enslow Publishers. They have a series called 'Diseases and People' for which I've already written a book on meningitis (out later this year) and arthritis, and have been contracted to write books on hemophilia, Alzheimer's and Ebola, as well.

"Fiction projects at various stages of completion include an adult science fiction novel called *Razor Wind,* about a very cold planet (much like Saskatchewan in the winter); a sequel to *Andy Nebula: Interstellar Rock Star,* tentatively titled *Andy Nebula: Double Trouble;* and a YA fantasy, *Dark Tide,* set on a world of oceans and islands.

"My primary purpose, always, is to entertain. I want the reader turning pages, anxious to see what happens next. I want them to have as much fun in the world of my imagination as I do.

"But I also hope my young readers will see themselves in my characters. My characters are far from perfect. They're often full of self-doubt. Sometimes their personal situations are quite grim. And yet ... they persevere. They don't give up. And eventually, they come through their trials and tribulations to a new level of maturity and self-confidence. You don't have to be caught up in a fantastic adventure to be facing adversity and feeling unsure of yourself. But if you persevere, do your best, use your head and your heart and your talents to the best of your ability, you'll get through—and emerge a better, stronger person on the other side.

"That's a story worth telling over and over."*

Y–Z

YEE, Wong Herbert 1953-

Personal

Born August 19, 1953, in Detroit, MI; son of Gee Hing and Toy Wun (restaurant owners) Yee; married December 19, 1975; wife's name, Judy Anne; children: Ellen. *Education:* Wayne State University, B.F.A., 1975.

Addresses

Agent—c/o Houghton Mifflin Co., 222 Berkley St., Boston, MA 02116-3764.

Every time Fireman Small tries to get some sleep, an animal emergency arises in this self-illustrated picture book by Wong Herbert Yee. (From Fireman Small.*)*

Career

Writer, artist. *Exhibitions:* The City Gallery, Dearborn, MI, June 19, 1998; Elizabeth Stone Gallery, Birmingham, MI, May 22, 1999; Bookbeat Gallery, one-man show, Oak Park, MI, June 30, 1999.

Awards, Honors

American Bookseller's Pick of the Lists, 1993, for *Big Black Bear,* and 1994, for *Fireman Small;* Parents Choice Award, 1997, for *Fireman Small;* IRA-CBC Children's Choices, 1997, for *Mrs. Brown Went to Town;* National Parenting Publications Honor Award, 1998, for *Fireman Small to the Rescue* and for *Sergeant Hippo's Busy Week.*

Writings

SELF-ILLUSTRATED

Eek! There's a Mouse in the House, Houghton, 1992.
Big Black Bear, Houghton, 1993.
Fireman Small, Houghton Mifflin, 1994.
A Drop of Rain, Houghton Mifflin, 1995.
Mrs. Brown Went to Town, Houghton Mifflin, 1995.
The Officers' Ball, Houghton Mifflin, 1997.
Fireman Small to the Rescue, Houghton Mifflin, 1998.
Sergeant Hippo's Busy Week, Houghton Mifflin, 1998.
Hamburger Heaven, Houghton Mifflin, 1999.
Here Come Trainmice!, Houghton Mifflin, 2000.
Hooray for Truckmice!, Houghton Mifflin, 2000.

Also the illustrator for Erin Douglas's *Get that Pest,* Green Light Readers, 2000.

Work in Progress

Fireman Small: Fire Down Below, for Houghton Mifflin.

Sidelights

Wong Herbert Yee is an author-illustrator of children's books noted for his zany, madcap story lines that are full

A family scurries to comfort a crying infant only to discover that the tear in the baby's eye is actually a raindrop. (From A Drop of Rain, *written and illustrated by Yee.)*

of action and bright colors. Yee writes of rambunctious mice; of a black bear without manners; of raindrops mistaken for tears; an over-worked fireman; a hippo with two left feet; and a clarinet-playing pig with a hamburger dilemma. Employing simple rhyme and repetition, Yee serves up amusing animal characters in his picture books and stories.

Born in Detroit, Michigan, Yee attended Wayne State University, where he earned a B.A. in fine art in 1975. "I remember what an art professor once said when I first started college," Yee once told *SATA*. "'Everybody here is talented and thinks they can cut it. When you graduate, you will find things different; no more support group.' How true. I was cast out in 1975 with a printmaking degree in hand. Like many other fine art graduates, I drifted aimlessly in the world of advertizing." But everything changed with the birth of his daughter. Finally, after many false starts, he found a home in children's book publishing. "My manuscript was plucked out of the slush pile by an editor at Houghton," Yee once told *SATA*. "That's where my story begins."

That first book was *Eek! There's a Mouse in the House,* a "spirited tale of escalating silliness," according to Rachel Fox writing in *School Library Journal,* and a "pandemonium, prepossessing debut," as a reviewer for *Publishers Weekly* described the book. With a mouse in her house, a little girl sends in ever-larger animals to rid her of it, and each new addition causes new silliness and confusion. The girl summons in turn a cat, a dog, a sheep, and a hog, and all three end up in a wild chase hoping to catch the pesky rodent. The hog is soon

wearing a lampshade from the lamp the cat knocked over, and the later also juggles eggs a hen has laid. Fox went on to call Yee's tale an "entertaining first book, filled with the things that children love—silly rhymes and funny, likable characters." A reviewer for the *New York Times Book Review* was appreciative of "the rhyming text" and engaging artwork, while a critic for the *Horn Book Guide* commented on the "bright colors, stylized characters" which "well match the simple and entertaining text." The reviewer for *Publishers Weekly* particularly noted the "[r]iotous colors and patterns" which "provide bright backdrops for Yee's rambunctious menagerie." *Eek!* has also been included in numerous first-grade reading anthologies.

For his next project, Yee devised a bear that has trouble containing his appetite. In *Big Black Bear,* the animal in question ventures out of the forest on the trail of a delicious food smell. This trail leads him to Little Girl's house, where he asks her for food. "'Come in please,'" the girl responds, "'Wipe your paws on the mat.' / 'I'm BIG BLACK BEAR—I don't have to do that,'" he tells her. The contrast between the girl and bear is stark: she has manners and he has none. Not only won't he wipe his feet on the mat, but he also refuses to use a dish or to cover his mouth when he sneezes—all of which prompt criticism from the girl. Finally, put off by her demands, Big Black Bear simply decides to eat Little Girl. But before he has a chance, his mother, an even bigger bear, halts him. She makes him apologize to the girl and clean up the mess he has made.

"The rollicking, rhyming text contains plenty of alliteration," noted *Horn Book*'s Lolly Robinson in a review of

Nervous about an upcoming Officers' Ball, Sergeant Hippo takes dancing lessons which unexpectedly help him become the star of the evening. (From The Officers' Ball, *written and illustrated by Yee.)*

Big Black Bear, "and the strong, flat colors and shapes depict highly appealing characters." *Booklist*'s Ilene Cooper remarked on the combination of "a zippy, rhyming text and eye-catching art that uses cool, pure colorings and simple shapes to appeal to its readers." Mary Lou Budd, writing in *School Library Journal,* felt that the "story projects its message through lilting verse and bold, childlike, tempera illustrations." Budd went on to note that the book was a "good choice for youngsters who need some nudging in the right direction—toward showing consideration for others." And a reviewer for *Kirkus Reviews* concluded, "Big little three-year-olds may not recognize themselves here as quickly as their parents do, but they'll love the funny, rhythmic verse and bold, collage-style illustrations."

The adventures of a diminutive firefighter are recounted in the award-winning *Fireman Small* and its sequel, *Fireman Small to the Rescue.* In the former title, every time Fireman Small goes to sleep he is awakened to rescue some animal in trouble. Some cat, or rabbit, or hippopotamus desperately needs saving, and off goes Fireman Small. Farmer Pig's cat gets stuck in a magnolia tree, and off goes Small; Little Bunny takes a tumble down the well, and it is Small to the rescue. There's even a fire at the bakery, and Small again saves the day. "This short, simple story will delight children with its action, rhyme, and sprightly illustrations," noted *Booklist*'s Lauren Peterson, who also felt that this "charming little book will be a good means of introducing the fire fighting profession." Reviewing *Fireman Small* in the *New York Times Book Review,* Karen W. Gilbert called Yee's picture book "a gem." Gilbert went on to note, "The rhyming repetitive text, the kind that preschool children love, is accompanied by delightful cartoonish watercolor illustrations." Gilbert had only one caution: "young listeners may want to hear the whole tale one more time." A reviewer for *Horn Book Guide* wrote, "The simple, childlike story, told in rhyming couplets, is accompanied by cheerful, stylized illustrations," while Anna DeWind, reviewing the title in *School Library Journal,* concluded that "Fireman Small and his faithful Dalmatian make a charming pair, and this simple rhyming story is endearing." Yee reprised the firefighter in the 1998 *Fireman Small to the Rescue,* a board book, in which Small puts out a fire at Farmer Pig's barn. Everyone at the farm, including a crocodile sporting purple overalls, is in a panic, but Fireman Small remains calm and manages to extinguish the blaze. A critic for *Kirkus Reviews* noted that the book provides "tidbits of information about the civic duties of firefighters," and that Fireman Small "makes a perfect vicarious hero for preschoolers."

In *A Drop of Rain,* Yee recounts a tale of an Asian extended family who feel helpless at a baby's tears—until finally they realize they are tiny drops of rain. Harriet Fargnoli, writing in *School Library Journal,* noted the "[e]xactingly drawn watercolors with just the right amount of detail" which "are appealing in a Grandma Moses-primitive way," while a commentator for *Horn Book Guide* called special attention to the "contemporary Asian-American family" which is portrayed in "simple and charming watercolors."

Another award-winning title from Yee is *Mrs. Brown Went to Town,* the story of Mrs. Brown's visit to the hospital and the subsequent taking over of her house by her farm animals, including a cow, two pigs, three ducks, and a yak. The animals make quite a mess, dressing up, continually flushing the toilet, and raiding the refrigerator before Mrs. Brown is able to oust them. "The artwork is a delight in this silly, rhyming tale," announced Julie Corsaro in a *Booklist* review of the title. "Child-appeal galore," Corsaro concluded. "First-rate silliness," declared a critic for *Kirkus Reviews,* who went on to remark, "the more improbable the situations, the more readers will be laughing out loud." A reviewer for *Horn Book Guide* commented on the "[l]ilting rhyme and rounded, cartoonish illustrations" which "combine to create a playful, nonsensical story."

More animal mayhem and nonsense are served up in twin titles featuring Sergeant Hippo: *The Officers' Ball* and *Sergeant Hippo's Busy Week.* Officer Hippo is nervous about attending the ball in the former title, but his practicing at Madame Lafeet's dance studio and while on duty eventually pays off at the dance. There he asks Officer Mole to dance and they do the hokey-pokey, the jitterbug, disco—you name it. Soon they become the uncrowned royalties of the ball. A reviewer for *Publishers Weekly* felt that "Yee's light-hearted tale handily tackles the feelings of uncertainty and inadequacy that most children—and adults—experience at one time or another." The same reviewer added, "[Yee] creates a jolly world that readers will happily believe in." "A sure bet for story hours," pronounced *Booklist*'s Kay Weisman. Weisman also commented on "Yee's bright watercolor illustrations" which "add humor to the rhymed verses and a visual subtext that children will want to revisit to catch the details." A critic in *Kirkus Reviews* concluded: "Readers won't be surprised by the ending, but it certainly has panache." The portly sergeant makes a further appearance in *Sergeant Hippo's Busy Week,* when the officer goes on highway patrol and apprehends a thieving fox. "Amusing animal characters populate the winsome, color-splashed [book]," according to a reviewer for *Publishers Weekly.*

Pinky Pig takes center stage in Yee's 1999 *Hamburger Heaven,* in which the job of the porker in question is put in jeopardy by a diminished number of customers at her employer's hamburger parlor. Instead of wringing her hands, Pinky Pig, who has taken the after-school job in order to buy a clarinet, sets about adding some zip and sparkle to the menu at Hamburger Heaven. Her "worms lightly fried," "Snailburger Supreme," and "Burger on pine cones," seem to do the trick and in the end Pinky keeps her job and earns enough for her new clarinet. Writing in *School Library Journal,* Marianne Saccardi noted the "fast paced and humorous" rhymed text as well as Yee's watercolor cartoons that "add to the fun," and concluded that the book is a "'heavenly' entrée in which a feisty heroine saves the day." "Yee pens this fable lightly," commented a critic in *Kirkus Reviews,* "but the moral is plain: by putting others first, Pinky attains what she wants."

It is this light touch to his stories which continues to make Yee a popular writer and illustrator of children's books. Yee once told *SATA:* "My advice to people starting out is that being an artist is not a way to make a living, but a way of life. Stick with it—find a way!"

Works Cited

Review of *Big Black Bear, Kirkus Reviews,* September 15, 1993.

Budd, Mary Lou, review of *Big Black Bear, School Library Journal,* October 1993, pp. 14-15.

Cooper, Ilene, review of *Big Black Bear, Booklist,* November 1, 1993, p. 533.

Corsaro, Julie, review of *Mrs. Brown Went to Town, Booklist,* April 1, 1996, p. 1375.

DeWind, Anna, review of *Fireman Small, School Library Journal,* December, 1994, p. 92.

Review of *A Drop of Rain, Horn Book Guide,* Spring, 1996, p. 51.

Review of *Eek! There's a Mouse in the House, Publishers Weekly,* August 12, 1992.

Review of *Eek! There's a Mouse in the House, Horn Book Guide,* Spring, 1993, p. 51.

Review of *Eek! There's a Mouse in the House, New York Times Book Review,* May 8, 1993, p. 24.

Fargnoli, Harriet, review of *A Drop of Rain, School Library Journal,* October, 1995, p. 124.

Review of *Fireman Small, Horn Book Guide,* Spring, 1995, p. 23.

Review of *Fireman Small to the Rescue, Kirkus Reviews,* February 15, 1998, p. 276.

Fox, Rachel, review of *Eek! There's a Mouse in the House, School Library Journal,* October, 1992, pp. 100-01.

Gilbert, Karen W., review of *Fireman Small, New York Times Book Review,* January 29, 1995, p. 20.

Review of *Hamburger Heaven, Kirkus Reviews,* March 19, 1999.

Review of *Mrs. Brown Went to Town, Kirkus Reviews,* February 15, 1996, p. 302.

Review of *Mrs. Brown Went to Town, Horn Book Guide,* Fall, 1996, p. 282.

Review of *The Officers' Ball, Kirkus Reviews,* March 1, 1997, p. 390.

Review of *The Officers' Ball, Publishers Weekly,* March 3, 1997, p. 74.

Peterson, Lauren, review of *Fireman Small, Booklist,* February 1, 1995, p. 1014.

Robinson, Lolly, review of *Big Black Bear, Horn Book,* March-April, 1994, p. 194.

Saccardi, Marianne, review of *Hamburger Heaven, School Library Journal,* May, 1999, p. 101.

Review of *Sergeant Hippo's Busy Week, Publishers Weekly,* March 23, 1998, p. 101.

Weisman, Kay, review of *The Officers' Ball, Booklist,* March 15, 1997, p. 1247.

Yee, Wong Herbert, *Big Black Bear,* Houghton Mifflin, 1993.

Yee, Wong Herbert, *Hamburger Heaven,* Houghton Mifflin, 1999.

For More Information See

BOOKS

Who's Who among Asian Americans, 1994-1995 edition, Gale, 1994.

PERIODICALS

American Bookseller, August, 1993; August, 1994.
Daily Tribune, May 14, 1999.
Detroit Free Press, February 24, 1993; September 20, 1995; November 15, 1999.
Detroit News, July 2, 1993.
Publishers Weekly, August 19, 1996, p. 69.
School Library Journal, July, 1996, p. 76; May, 1997, p. 117.

—*Sketch by J. Sydney Jones*

*   *   *

ZALLINGER, Jean (Day) 1918-

Personal

Born February 15, 1918, in Boston, MA; daughter of John Farquharson and Mabel (Souter) Day; married Rudolph Franz Zallinger (an artist and teacher), September 27, 1941; children: Peter Franz, Kristina, Lisa. *Education:* Massachusetts College of Art, diploma, 1939; Yale School of Fine Arts, B.F.A., 1942.

Jean Zallinger illustrated Helen Roney Sattler's detailed history of early man in the Western Hemisphere. (From The Earliest Americans.*)*

Addresses

Home and office—5060 Ridge Rd., North Haven, CT 06473. *Agent*— Dilys Evans, P.O. Box 400, Norfolk, CT 06058.

Career

Portrait painter, 1939—; Art & Architecture Library, Yale University, New Haven, CT, assistant, 1939-42; children's art instructor, New Haven, 1941-42; Yale University Press, New Haven, design assistant to Carl Rollins, 1941-43; freelance illustrator, 1942—; Applied Physics Laboratory, University of Washington, Seattle, technical illustrator and draftsman, 1951-53; Paier College of Art, Hamden, CT, professor of drawing and illustration, 1967-88. Women's Auxiliary, Yale, New Haven Hospital, vice president, 1963-68, 1969-70. *Exhibitions:* Yale University Gallery of Fine Arts, 1941-42; Paint and Clay Club Annual, 1942-43; Association of Graphic Arts Annual, 1969; John Slade Ely House, 1972; Master Eagle Gallery, 1984-88; Aetna Gallery, Hartford, CT, 1987; New Britain Youth Museum, 1987; Natural History Museum of Los Angeles County traveling show, 1987-91; Massachusetts College of Art, 1992; Paul Mellon Art Center, 1993; Lyme, CT, Academy Art Gallery, 1994. *Member:* Society of Children's Book Writers and Illustrators, Audubon Society, John Slade Ely House (committee on selection for shows), Yale Club of New Haven, O.C. Marsh Fellows (Peabody Museum of Natural History), English Speaking Union (New Haven Branch), New Haven Paint and Clay Club, Arts Council of Greater New Haven, North End Club, Fortnightly, Art Gallery Associates of Yale University.

Awards, Honors

Purchase Prize, New Haven Paint and Clay Club, 1948; Junior Library Guild Award, 1965, for *They Turned to Stone,* and 1993, for *The Earliest Americans;* International Board on Books for Young People Honor List, 1968, for *Valley of the Smallest: The Life Story of a Shrew;* outstanding science trade book designations, National Association of Science Teachers/Children's Book Council, 1976, for *Biography of an Armadillo,* 1977, for *Biography of a Fish Hawk* and *I Watch Flies,* 1979, for *Your Skin,* 1980, for *Nature's Champions,* 1982, for *Dinosaurs, Asteroids, and Superstars,* and 1990, for *The Book of Eagles;* notable book designation, Children's Literary Center, Library of Congress, for *The Book of Eagles;* Distinguished Alumnus Award, Massachusetts College of Art, 1992.

Illustrator

Cornelius Osgood, *Winter,* Norton, 1953.
Robert Lemmon, *All about Strange Beasts of the Past,* Random House, 1957.
Lemmon, *All about Monkeys,* Random House, 1958.
Little Golden Stamp Book of Insects, Golden Press, 1958.
Roy Chapman Andrews, *In the Days of Dinosaurs,* Random House, 1959.
Herbert Zim, *Fish,* Golden Press, 1959.

D. Joslyn, *I Like Birds,* Whitman, 1960.
Katherine Hitte, *Hurricanes, Tornadoes, and Blizzards,* Random House, 1960.
Alex Crosby, *Junior Science Book of Beavers,* Garrard, 1960.
George Fichter, *Flying Animals,* Golden Press, 1961.
Butterfly Puzzle, Springbook, 1962.
Lemmon, *Junior Science Book of Big Cats,* Garrard, 1962.
Crosby, *Junior Science Book of Pond Life,* Garrard, 1964.
Julian May, *They Turned to Stone,* Holiday House, 1965.
Aileen Fisher, *Valley of the Smallest: The Life Story of a Shrew,* Crowell, 1966.
Jean George, *The Moon of the Owls,* Crowell, 1967.
May, *They Lived in the Ice Age,* Holiday House, 1967.
J. J. McCoy, *House Sparrows, Ragamuffins of the City,* Seabury, 1968.
George, *The Moon of the Deer,* Crowell, 1969.
Lee Ford, *Water Boatman's Journey,* Seabury, 1969.
Seymour Simon, *Discovering What Earthworms Do,* McGraw, 1969.
George Mendoza, *Digger Wasp,* Dial, 1969.
Simon, *Discovering What Frogs Do,* McGraw, 1969.
Helen Hoke, *First Book of Arctic Mammals,* Watts, 1969.
Simon, *Discovering What Goldfish Do,* McGraw, 1970.
George H. Kimble, *Hunters & Collectors,* McGraw, 1970.

Zallinger provided the artwork for this easy-to-read version of the Charles Dickens classic. (From Oliver Twist, *adapted by Les Martin.)*

Taylor Alexander, *Botany* (field guide), Western Publishing, 1970.

Ross E. Hutchins, *The Mayfly,* Addison-Wesley, 1970.

Joanna Cole, *Cockroaches,* Morrow, 1970.

Frances Behnke, *What We Find When We Look under Rocks,* McGraw, 1971.

Simon, *Discovering What Gerbils Do,* McGraw, 1971.

Lewis W. Walker, *Survival under the Sun,* Doubleday, 1971.

Burke Davis, *Biography of a Leaf,* Putnam, 1972.

Alexander Martin, *Weeds,* Western Publishing, 1972.

May, *Plankton: Drifting Life of the Waters,* Holiday, 1972.

Gladys Conklin, *Insects Build Their Homes,* Holiday, 1972.

Francine Jacobs, *Sea Turtles,* Morrow, 1972.

Lisbeth Zappler, *The Natural History of the Tail,* Doubleday, 1972.

Mary Adrian, *Secret Neighbors: Wildlife in a City Lot,* Hastings, 1972.

Simon, *Discovering What Crickets Do,* McGraw, 1973.

Alan M. Fletcher, *Fishes That Hide,* Addison-Wesley, 1973.

Alice Hopf, *Biography of an Ant,* Putnam, 1974.

Simon, *Birds on Your Street,* Holiday, 1974.

Adrian, *Wildlife on the Watch: A Story of the Desert,* Hastings, 1974.

Zappler, *The Natural History of the Nose,* Doubleday, 1974.

Conklin, *I Like Beetles,* Holiday, 1975.

Jacobs, *The Sargasso Sea: An Ocean Desert,* Morrow, 1975.

Hopf, *Biography of an Armadillo,* Putnam, 1975.

Wong and Wessel, *My Snail,* Addison-Wesley, 1976.

Conklin, *I Watch Flies,* Holiday, 1976.

Jacobs, *A Secret Language of Animals: Communication by Pheromones,* Morrow, 1976.

Morton, *Herbs and Spices,* Western Publishing, 1976.

Davis, *Biography of a Fish Hawk,* Putnam, 1977.

Jacobs, *Sounds in the Sea,* Morrow, 1977.

Hershell H. Nixon and Joan Lowery Nixon, *Oil and Gas: From Fossils to Fuels,* Harcourt, 1977.

Zim, *Little Cats,* Morrow, 1978.

Zim, *Alligators and Crocodiles,* Morrow, 1978.

Zim, *Your Skin,* Morrow, 1979.

Alvin and Virginia Silverstein, *Nature's Champions: The Biggest, the Fastest, the Best,* Random House, 1980.

Arnold, *Sex Hormones: Why Males and Females Are Different,* Morrow, 1981.

Hopf, *Biography of a Komodo Dragon,* Putnam, 1981.

Myers, *Sea Creatures Do Amazing Things,* Random House, 1981.

Branley, *Dinosaurs, Asteroids, and Superstars: Why the Dinosaurs Disappeared,* Lippincott, 1982.

Rae Paige, *Sesame Street Question and Answer Book about Animals,* Western Publishing, 1983, expanded as *The Whole Wide World: A Question and Answer Book,* 1990.

Helen Roney Sattler, *Baby Dinosaurs,* Lothrop, 1984.

Sattler, *Sharks: The Super Fish,* Lothrop, 1986.

Daniel Cohen, *Dinosaurs,* Doubleday, 1986.

Sattler, *Whales: The Nomads of the Sea,* Lothrop, 1987.

(With others) Liza Alexander and others, *Animals, Animals: Featuring Jim Henson's Sesame Street Muppets,* Western Publishing, 1989.

Sattler, *The Book of Eagles,* Lothrop, 1989.

Rita Golden Gelman, *Monsters of the Sea,* Little, Brown, 1990.

Les Martin, adaptor, *Oliver Twist,* Random House, 1990.

Myra Cohn Livingston, editor, *Poems for Brothers, Poems for Sisters,* Holiday House, 1991.

Cathy East Dubowski, adaptor, *Peter Pan,* Random House, 1991.

Charles Dickens, *Oliver Twist,* Random House, 1992.

Sattler, *The Earliest Americans,* Clarion, 1993.

Sattler, *The Book of North American Owls,* Clarion, 1995.

Fay Robinson, *Great Snakes!,* Scholastic, Inc., 1996.

Robinson, *Mighty Spiders!,* Scholastic, Inc., 1996.

Robinson, *Amazing Lizards!,* Scholastic, Inc., 1999.

Has also illustrated National Wildlife Butterfly stamps, 1963-90. Contributed illustrations to such publications as *World Book Encyclopedia, Life Magazine, Time Life Books* (Australia, 1964), and *Colliers Encyclopedia.*

Work represented in permanent collections, including New Haven Paint and Clay Club; Kerlan Collection, University of Minnesota; DeGrummond Collection, University of Southern Mississippi; The Northeastern Children's Literature Collection, Homer Babbidge Library, University of Connecticut; and Jane Voorhees Zimmerli Art Museum, Rutgers University.

Sidelights

Jean Zallinger is an illustrator who worked for an academic press for many years while developing her skills as an illustrator of children's books. With over seventy-five titles to her credit, Zallinger has gained particular renown for her penciled renderings of animals, and has exhibited her work at galleries throughout the United States. Writing of her contribution to *Monsters of the Sea,* a nonfiction work by author Rita Golden Gelman, *School Library Journal* contributor Frances E. Millhouser noted that "Zallinger's exciting, full-color double-page illustrations ... make this [book] a delight for browsers."

Born in Boston, Massachusetts, in 1918, Zallinger received her early art training at the Massachusetts College of Art, graduating in 1939. Married two years later to fellow artist Rudolph Franz Zallinger, she attended Yale School of Fine Arts in New Haven, Connecticut, and earned her bachelor's degree there in 1942. The Zallingers made their permanent home in the New Haven area, and raised a son and a daughter.

After her graduation from the Massachusetts College of Art, Zallinger gained experience as a portrait painter before becoming involved in technical design and teaching. In 1942 she began working as a freelance illustrator, contributing her talents to works by Yale professors. Three years later she received her first opportunity to illustrate a children's book, when the publishing company Norton offered her a contract to illustrate *Winter,* a nonfiction work for children by Cornelius Osgood. It was the first of many nonfiction works that Zallinger has illustrated.

Written by Helen Roney Sattler and illustrated by Zallinger, **The Book of North American Owls** *gives readers information about the behavior and physical characteristics of twenty-one different types of owl species.*

Zallinger's early work incorporated colored or black lead pencils on Mylar, exemplified by titles such as *In the Days of Dinosaurs, Discovering What Earthworms Do,* and her award winning collaboration with author Aileen Fisher, *Valley of the Smallest: The Life Story of a Shrew.* Since the 1970s and 1980s, however, she has added watercolor to her pencil work, augmenting it with black and white pencil duotone.

Among Zallinger's most successful works have been her collaborations with author Helen Roney Sattler, with whom she has produced *Baby Dinosaurs, Sharks: The Super Fish, The Earliest Americans,* and *The Book of North American Owls. Sharks* is a detailed dictionary of the many varieties of these often feared fish. In a favorable review in *Horn Book,* Mary M. Burns commented on Zallinger's "copious shaded drawings" filled with detail, as well as her "pleasant full-page scenes." *The Earliest Americans* is a study of archeological and other evidence of the first human settlement on the North American continent. Praising Sattler's text for its scholarly approach and objectivity, *School Library Journal* reviewer Patricia Manning said, "Zallinger's strong, meticulous, sepia-toned artwork is informative as well as decorative." "Zallinger's ... intricate pencil drawings ... are invaluable extenders of the text," agreed Ilene Cooper in her *Booklist* assessment of *The Earliest Americans.*

In *Whales: The Nomads of the Sea,* another Zallinger-Sattler collaboration, *School Library Journal* contributor Frances E. Millhouser praised the illustrator's "subtle gray line drawings ... [which] illustrate beautifully ... the movements of an animal perfectly adapted to its environment." Reviewing the same work, a *Publishers Weekly* critic called Zallinger's illustrations "powerful pictures [that] convey just how mighty these creatures are," while in *School Library Journal* Patricia Manning praised the book's "glorious illustrations in soft grays," deeming them "accurate and non-sensational." Of *The Book of North American Owls,* which the two women completed in 1995, *Horn Book* reviewer Margaret A. Bush wrote, "The tall, handsome volume follows the pattern of earlier Sattler-Zallinger collaborations with carefully detailed color drawings intertwined with a well-crafted text on every page."

Since Sattler's death in 1992, Zallinger has continued to illustrate children's nonfiction. Among her more recent efforts are realistic drawings for *Great Snakes!* and *Mighty Spiders!* by Fay Robinson, and illustrations for a new edition of *Oliver Twist* by nineteenth-century British author Charles Dickens.

Works Cited

Burns, Mary M., review of *Sharks: The Super Fish, Horn Book,* July-August, 1986, p. 469.

Bush, Margaret A., review of *The Book of North American Owls, Horn Book,* May-June, 1995, p. 345.

Cooper, Ilene, review of *The Earliest Americans, Booklist,* May 1, 1993, pp. 1586-87.

Manning, Patricia, review of *The Earliest Americans, School Library Journal,* June, 1993, pp. 122-23.

Manning, review of *Whales: The Nomads of the Sea, School Library Journal,* December, 1987, p. 91.

Millhouser, Frances E., review of *Monsters of the Sea, School Library Journal,* May, 1990, p. 116.

Millhouser, review of *Whales: The Nomads of the Sea, School Library Journal,* December, 1987, p. 91.

Review of *Whales: The Nomads of the Sea, Publishers Weekly,* December 25, 1987, p. 76.

For More Information See

BOOKS

Illustrators of Children's Books: 1957-1966, Horn Book, 1968.

PERIODICALS

Horn Book, January-February, 1988, p. 88.

Publishers Weekly, October 19, 1984, p. 48; May 30, 1986, p. 66; May 10, 1991, p. 74; April 6, 1998, p. 79.

School Library Journal, August, 1986, pp. 96-97; May, 1995, p. 115; July, 1998, p. 103.*

*   *   *

ZUROMSKIS, Diane
See STANLEY, Diane

ZUROMSKIS, Diane Stanley
  See **STANLEY, Diane**

Cumulative Indexes

Illustrations Index

(In the following index, the number of the *volume* in which an illustrator's work appears is given *before* the colon, and the *page number* on which it appears is given *after* the colon. For example, a drawing by Adams, Adrienne appears in Volume 2 on page 6, another drawing by her appears in Volume 3 on page 80, another drawing in Volume 8 on page 1, and so on and so on . . . .)

YABC

Index references to *YABC* refer to listings appearing in the two-volume *Yesterday's Authors of Books for Children,* also published by The Gale Group. *YABC* covers prominent authors and illustrators who died prior to 1960.

P

Author Index

The following index gives the number of the volume in which an author's biographical sketch, Autobiography Feature, Brief Entry, or Obituary appears.

This index includes references to all entries in the following series, which are also published by The Gale Group.

YABC—*Yesterday's Authors of Books for Children: Facts and Pictures about Authors and Illustrators of Books for Young People from Early Times to 1960*

CLR—*Children's Literature Review: Excerpts from Reviews, Criticism, and Commentary on Books for Children*

SAAS—*Something about the Author Autobiography Series*